A FIRST COURSE IN MODULA-2

A FIRST COURSE IN MODULA-2

LOWELL A. CARMONY
Lake Forest College

ROBERT L. HOLLIDAY
Lake Forest College

COMPUTER SCIENCE PRESS
An Imprint of W. H. Freeman and Company • New York

Library of Congress Cataloging-in-Publication Data

Carmony, Lowell A., 1943-
  Modula II/Lowell Carmony, Robert L. Holliday.
    p.   cm.
  ISBN (invalid) 0-7176-8229-4
  1. Modula-2 (Computer program language) I. Holliday, Robert.
II. Title. III. Title: Modula two. IV. Title: Modula 2.
QA76.73.M63C37   1990
005.13′3–dc20   89-22261
                                            CIP

Printed in the United States of America

Computer Science Press

An imprint of W. H. Freeman and Company
41 Madison Avenue, New York, NY 10010
20 Beaumont Street, Oxford OX1 2NQ, England

1 2 3 4 5 6 7 8 9 0   RRD   9 9 8 7 6 5 4 3 2 1 0

Contents

6 More Control Structures   91

7 Procedures and Functions   117

PREFACE

This Modula-2 text uses a rich set of examples and a gentle, but sound, pedagogical style to introduce the reader to all the concepts normally presented in CS 1, the first course in the ACM curriculum. The text, because of its wide variety of topics, can also be used as a Modula-2 language manual in a course in programming language design. The emphasis of the text is on problem solving and top-down, structured design of algorithms, rather than the narrow syntax of the Modula-2 language. All significant algorithms are developed in pseudo-code before they are presented in Modula-2.

This text presents a focused discussion of disciplined programming techniques. A complete chapter (Chapter 8) is devoted to this topic. This chapter discusses structured programming, the top-down design process, algorithmic design, the advantages of pseudo-code, commenting conventions, and the debugging process. Specific examples of the design and debugging processes are given. This chapter comes immediately after the chapter introducing procedures and functions since these are the real tools of disciplined programming. Any discussion of disciplined programming before procedures and functions is necessarily abstract.

Assertions and loop invariants are becoming a popular and valuable method of commenting. Informal preconditions and postconditions for procedures and functions are used consistently throughout the book. Assertions and loop invariants are introduced and discussed, but, in a first course, we prefer an informal style of commenting rather than a strictly formal style of assertions.

Chapters on external modules, sets, procedure types, and nested modules provide advanced material for the student, and make it possible for the text to be used as a language reference in a programming language design course.

A key feature of this text is its interesting, fresh examples. Examples, such as the duel of Hamilton and Burr (Chapter 8) and the game of Bagels (Chapter 7) are challenging as well as truly interesting to the student. A large number of stimulating and interesting exercises are also included, as we firmly believe that the student will not learn Modula-2, let alone problem solving, without extensive practice.

REMARKS TO THE INSTRUCTOR

Chapters 1 to 4 provide introductory material. In an advanced course, or with students who already know a block-structured language, such as Pascal, these chapters can be covered quickly. Chapters 5 to 11 contain the core material on Modula-2 where control structures, procedures and functions, arrays, records, and user-defined types are introduced. In addition, Chapter 8 provides a detailed discussion of the problem-solving process. Chapters 12 to 17 compose the advanced topics and, with minor exceptions, these topics can be covered in any order, providing the instructor with the flexibility to design the course as needed.

Chapter 1 provides an introduction to Modula-2, the programming process, and our real objective: problem solving. Chapter 2 introduces a first Modula-2 program with read, write, and assignment statements and concludes with an extensive discussion on the need for attention to program clarity. The next brief chapter, Chapter 3, picks up on this topic and seeks to explain what structured programming is and why it is important. We also examine what Modula-2 has to offer us in regard to writing good programs. Chapter 4 formally introduces the elementary numeric and character data types and discusses conversions among the numeric types.

Chapters 5 and 6 introduce the BOOLEAN type and Modula-2's control structures: the IF, the LOOP, the REPEAT/UNTIL, the WHILE, the FOR, and the CASE statements. Chapter 7 introduces procedures and functions and gives special attention to local and global variables, as well as value and variable parameters. Informal preconditions and postconditions are used in all procedures and functions. Chapter 8 is devoted to the topics of program design, implementation, and debugging. The problem-solving process is detailed in 8 steps and a simulation of Alexander Hamilton's famous duel with Aaron Burr is used to illustrate the process. Debugging skills are also discussed and illustrated.

Chapter 9 introduces user-defined types and discusses the CHAR type in more detail. Chapter 10 introduces arrays and discusses linear and binary search as well as insertion, bubble, and selection sort. Chapter 11 introduces the important topic of records, including variant records.

Chapter 12 introduces pointers and linked lists and Chapter 13 introduces recursion for the instructor who wants to preview these topics for students going on to a second course. Quick sort is included as an example of a recursive sort.

Chapter 14 provides an introduction to separately compiled modules. The two examples that are worked out are MyInOut, which provides a library of special I/O routines and Monte, which provides a library of Monte Carlo (random-number generation) techniques.

Chapter 15 introduces sets, discusses their restrictions in Modula-2, and provides several examples where sets are the data structure of choice, allowing elementary solutions to otherwise complex problems. The chapter also shows how we can use our programming skills to overcome some of Modula-2's restrictions on sets.

Chapter 16 introduces procedure types and, as an example, illustrates a module that can graph any real function passed to it.

Chapter 17 introduces nested modules and discusses the scope rules of such modules, including static variables.

Lowell A. Carmony
Robert L. Holliday
Lake Forest
January 8, 1990

Chapter 1

INTRODUCTION

The digital electronic computer is an omnipresent force in today's society. Computers are there when we pay our bills, get money from the bank (to pay our bills), set our VCRs, and ride our exercise bicycles.

Doctors use computers to aid in complex diagnoses. Reactions to this phenomenon usually range from: "Aren't computers amazing?" to "I don't want a computer practicing medicine on me!" Such diverse opinions indicate that, despite the fact that computers are everywhere, their role is still misunderstood by many people.

What is a computer? A dictionary definition might be: an electronic device capable of carrying out logical and arithmetic instructions, to include the storage and retrieval of data, without human intervention. In everyday terms, a computer is simply a tool to aid in the solution of problems. With this definition, there should be no reason to view the computer in a negative light. We should think of the computer as being more like a hammer than like an evil being intent on taking over the world, stripping us of our privacy on the way. If an unstable individual causes some destruction with a hammer, most people would probably not lobby for the removal of hammers from society. Yet, when an individual receives a phone bill in excess of a million dollars, it is the computer that is perceived as the culprit. So whatever a computer is, its role in today's society is often misunderstood.

It is probably safe to say that the computer is the most remarkable tool ever invented. Why is that? Well, let's compare its abilities to those of a hammer. A hammer is pretty much a hammer. While it can serve other purposes—for example, perform as a paperweight—a hammer is usually called upon to do hammer-like jobs. In particular, a hammer would probably make a pretty ineffective saw.

A computer, on the other hand, can be a very general-purpose device. For example, a manufacturing business can use a computer to figure the payroll, handling all the deductions required by law, as well as special deductions requested by individual employees. It can then print the checks. That same computer can also handle inventory

1

control, triggering orders to purchase new parts when the quantity on hand drops below a predetermined level. The computer can do thousands of calculations to help a forecaster determine the appropriate level of manufacturing. It can help manage the daily schedule of the company president, beeping when it is time for a meeting or even dialing a telephone at the appropriate time. Uses in education, recreation, and home life are just as prevalent.

Computers are amazing because they are fast (working at the speed of light) and accurate. But they are useful because they are general-purpose machines—they are **programmable**. A **computer program** is simply a sequence of instructions that we want the computer to execute. The program is also called an **algorithm**, a step-by-step recipe for solving a problem.

This book will introduce the reader to the science (others would say art) of programming. We want to be able to write programs so that we can make a computer do what we want it to. To do this, we really need to accomplish two goals. Since computers don't really understand English (unfortunately), we first need to learn to communicate with the computer in a language that it can understand. There are many languages we could choose—in the next section, we explain our decision to use the Modula-2 programming language.

The second, and more important goal, is to develop an ability to formulate algorithmic solutions to problems. At its most fundamental level, the programming process involves taking an algorithmic solution to a problem and translating it into a sequence of statements (the program) written in a programming language that is understandable by the computer. If we are unable to come up with the solution to begin with, all our mastery of programming language will do us no good. To emphasize the importance of this goal, we state the following basic principle: **The computer cannot solve any problem that the programmer cannot, at least in theory, solve**. The last section of this chapter addresses problem solving

In our modern society, while most people do learn to drive cars, most people don't learn how to repair them or build better ones. Similarly, while almost everyone could benefit by learning how to use computers, not everyone needs to learn to program them. Programming is a difficult activity. In fact, *good* programming may be beyond the capability of many working programmers today. The vast majority of people with the ability to write an income-tax program would probably use a commercially available program rather than write their own. Still, there is a large need for good programmers in business, science, and industry. And, like chess—which some people find difficult or boring, while others devote their lives to it for the sake of sheer enjoyment— programming is fun for many people. In fact, there are many good programmers who find it hard to believe that they get paid for doing something they enjoy so much. And even for readers of this book who do not plan to become professional programmers, there is much value in learning how to harness the power of the computer to make it do what we want it to.

WHY MODULA-2?

In this section, we present the reasons why Modula-2 is the vehicle we have chosen for this introductory computer-science course. But first we want to introduce some terminology and present a little of the history of computer science.

Modern computers are referred to as **digital** machines. Essentially, this means that computers operate based on the presence or absence of an electronic signal. The presence of a signal is denoted symbolically as a 1, while the absence of a signal is denoted by a 0. Since these are the only two quantities a computer understands, a computer is referred to as a **binary** machine, and the symbols 0 and 1 make up the binary number system (just as the 10 different symbols 0, 1, 2, 3, 4, 5, 6, 7, 8, 9 constitute the digits of the decimal number system). The symbols 0 and 1 are referred to as **binary digits**, shortened to **bits**. A group of eight bits is referred to as a **byte**. The byte is a common unit of measurement for computer storage because that is how much space is used to store a single alphabetic character of information. Still, at the most basic level, to enter information into a computer, one needs to be able to enter the correct sequence of bits. To extract information from a computer, one needs to be able to interpret a sequence of bits. This kind of communication is called programming in **machine language**. The very earliest programmers on the very earliest computers programmed this way. Such programming was a very difficult and tedious task since, among other obstacles, the programmer had to communicate in long, difficult-to-read strings of 0s and 1s.

In the late 1950s, **high-level languages** appeared—the two most important being COBOL (COmmon Business Oriented Language) and FORTRAN (FORmula TRANslator). These languages look very much like English. The job of a high-level language is to make communication with the computer easier. By removing the large obstacle of machine-language programming from the programming process, high-level languages allow the programmer more freedom to concentrate on solving the problem at hand. High-level languages make programming much less specialized, technical, and tedious, thus opening up programming to the masses.

How do these high-level languages work? The computer is still essentially a binary device, understanding only 0s and 1s. The developers of high-level languages must provide a mechanism by which English-like computer programs written by people are translated into an equivalent binary program (a string of 0s and 1s) that the computer understands and carries out. This translation is performed by a **compiler**. A compiler, contrary to what many people unfamiliar with computer terminology think, is not a piece of machinery. It is a computer program! In fact, compilers are very complex computer programs that usually take teams of programmers several years to perfect (many people doubt that a real-world compiler is ever perfect). So, a FORTRAN compiler is a program that translates FORTRAN computer programs into machine-language programs. Later, you will use a Modula-2 compiler to translate your Modula-2 programs into a form that your computer can execute.

In the past 30 years, there have been several hundred high-level languages. Many of these have been special-purpose languages that have not attracted wide audiences. A few have become very popular. Debates among proponents of various programming languages tend to be as emotional as any kind of debate that occurs in the computer-science industry. People tend to have more arguments over which language is better than over which computer is better.

The important languages of the 1950s were FORTRAN and COBOL (still among the most widely used languages in the world). From the 1960s, PL/I, Algol, and BASIC deserve mention. PL/I, with the support of IBM, was designed to combine the numeric capabilities of FORTRAN with the data-processing (business) capabilities of CO-

BOL. For several reasons, PL/I never lived up to its potential. One criticism is that the language was too large and, thus, too complex and unreliable (really meaning that PL/I compilers are too complex and unreliable). Algol, designed by an international committee, was embraced by the academic world, but never gained acceptance in the business world (a trend that continues today). Although developed in the 1960s, BASIC had its greatest influence in the mid-to late 1970s as the "language of the small microcomputer." It was high-level languages, along with affordable personal computers, that really opened up programming to the masses.

Four more recent languages—Pascal, C, Ada, and Modula-2—are commonly used for teaching introductory computer science at the college level.

Pascal, introduced in 1972 by Niklaus Wirth of Switzerland (who was also involved in the design of Algol), became the language of the academic world in the late 1970s. Although its use in the business world is becoming more widespread, it was intended to be a small language designed for the teaching of structured programming techniques. **Structured programming** has been one of the most important buzzwords in programming since the mid-1970s. Simply stated, as computers have become more sophisticated and the processes controlled by computers have become more complex, programs themselves have become more difficult to manage. One thing that languages can contribute is a capability of writing complex programs that are well-structured—i.e., easy to read, easy to change, and easy to understand. Early versions of FORTRAN, COBOL, and BASIC are usually not considered structured languages, while Pascal and the others mentioned above are. Pascal does have serious weaknesses, some of which will be pointed out in later chapters of this book. Nonetheless, many professionals, particularly educators, feel that the Pascal philosophy provides the best way to develop competent, modern-day programmers.

C, developed by Dennis Ritchie of Bell Labs in 1971, has many features desired of a programming language, and C users tend to be a very dedicated group. Although we consider it an excellent all-around language, we feel that C is not the best choice for a beginning language. Without going into detail, we feel that C programs tend to be less readable than others and that some of the low-level features of C can be abused by beginning programmers. C is easy to learn *after* you learn the basic concepts of programming. But we believe that the basic concepts are easier for the beginner to learn in a language like Modula-2.

Ada, touted by many people as the language of the future, was developed at the request of the United States Department of Defense (DOD) to replace (and update) COBOL. Because of its DOD backing, detractors of Ada say that it is doomed to success. The main criticism of Ada is the same as the criticism of PL/I—it's too big and tries to be all things to all people. Since Ada is the language that is to control all embedded weapons systems on DOD equipment, can we afford to have a language that is difficult to implement? After all, Star Wars systems have to work on the *first* try. Later, you can judge for yourself how difficult it is (in a small language) to get a simple program to run on the first try. Whether these criticisms of Ada are valid, Ada may well be too big and cumbersome, certainly as a first language for beginning programmers. So, although Ada contains almost every interesting feature that can be found in a programming language, its size and the fact that good, fast, inexpensive microcomputer Ada compilers are unavailable keep it from becoming our choice for a first language.

Thus, we come to Modula-2. Also developed by Wirth (in 1978), Modula-2 may well become the language of the 1990s, at least in the academic world. It is certainly a logical transition from Pascal, and it incorporates some important improvements over Pascal. It is difficult in this introductory chapter to explain in detail the significant improvements of Modula-2 and why they are important. We will simply state here that Modula-2 provides an effective way to break a large program up into separate **modules**. These modules play an important role in such areas as **separate compilation** (the ability to translate into machine language a part of a large program, without necessarily having access to the entire program) and **concurrent processing** (for example, simultaneously carrying out two or more separate parts of a single program using more than one computer). While these concepts are important to a beginning programmer, the power of a module comes from its capability of **information hiding** or **data abstraction**. These terms will be explained later in the book. Suffice it to say that these data-handling capabilities of Modula-2 are critical to enable a programmer to construct well-structured solutions to difficult programming problems.

Modula-2 is based on Pascal. An important observation is that Pascal is also the parent of Ada—the designers of Ada used Pascal as a starting point. Thus, if Ada does become the language of the future, an important by-product of learning Modula-2, with its data-abstraction and concurrent-processing capabilities, is that learning Ada becomes much easier.

What do all these computer languages have in common that makes them useful to thousands of people? Why don't we just use English? Well, programming languages have a small vocabulary with exact, picky syntax. We must say exactly what we mean and mean exactly what we say. Programming languages are not for writing poetry. They are for expressing algorithms—instructions to a machine. The strict syntax is needed so that the machine (compiler) can translate a program into its low-level machine language. We can't expect the computer to figure out what we are saying. We must be very precise. There is a famous story of a Venus Viking probe that was lost due to a missing comma in a FORTRAN program. High-level programming languages are a compromise between low-level machine languages and English.

So, why not English? Well, imagine a person and a machine reading the following four sentences. Somehow, we expect the person to be able to figure out what it refers to in each sentence, while it seems pretty difficult to imagine how a machine could make the same determination:

1. I've never been skiing, but I took a plane to Colorado and gave *it* a try.
2. I've never been adventuresome, but I took a hang glider to the park and gave *it* a try.
3. I've never been adventuresome, but I took a bus to the roller coaster and gave *it* a try.
4. I've never been given legal advice, but I took an architect to the Zoning Review Board and gave *it* a try.

We conclude this section on a somewhat technical note. A modern high-level programming language consists of more than just the rules that a programmer must follow to write legal programs. In addition to those rules, referred to as **syntax rules**, a programming language needs an **implementation environment**; that is, a compiler and all the accompanying **software** (computer programs) necessary for a particular computer to be able to understand and execute the high-level-language programs. In particular, this accompanying software, usually called **systems programs**, includes such programs as an **editor** (a word-processing program that allows the computer user to create and modify a computer program) and a **linker** (a program that puts all the necessary pieces of a user program together, after they have been translated by the compiler, so that they can be executed).

A Modula-2 environment also includes standard **library** modules. For readers of this book, the most important library routines are those for managing input and output, abbreviated **I/O**. I/O—that is, how information is placed into and retrieved from a computer—is what varies most among the various models and manufacturers of computers. By including these standard library modules as part of the Modula-2 environment, Modula-2 isolates the most system-dependent parts of the compiler, making programs less I/O dependent and, hence, more standardized.

LEARNING/TEACHING PROBLEM SOLVING

As mentioned previously, the most important part of a computer scientist's job is to solve the problem at hand. Of secondary importance is the ability to translate this solution into a computer program. There will always be people around with the ability to do this second task. There are standard teaching techniques for developing this kind of skill. In fact, this book hopes to teach the reader how to program in Modula-2.

What we wish we had was a sure-fire method to teach people how to solve problems. Unfortunately, no one really knows how to do this. Much problem solving is based on experience, so practicing is certainly a key component. But there are many frustrated Algebra I students who have practiced word problems over and over, able to work every single problem in a textbook, but unable to work the problem asked of them on an examination because it is slightly new and different from anything they have seen before. Somehow, all that practice has to be combined with some kind of insight. We believe that insight can be developed if you work at it. We'll state some simple guidelines for problem solving and illustrate each of these with a problem.

Don't give up too soon!

At least, don't give up before trying all the obvious approaches. Some teachers like to say, "Work up to the point of frustration—then work a little more." It has been our experience that giving up too soon is the most common reason that students fail to solve problems. Consider the following problem:

A boy is sent to a stream with a 5-quart jug and a 3-quart jug and is asked to bring back 4 quarts of water. How can he do it?

We have posed this problem to beginning programming students and most of them, after just a few minutes (seconds?) of thought, say "I don't know. I don't see how the boy can get anything other than 3 quarts or 5 quarts." This seems to be a case of giving up too soon. There just aren't that many things the boy can do—he can fill jugs from the stream, and he can pour water from the jugs back into the stream. He can also pour water from one jug to another. For example, it should be pretty easy to see how to get 2 quarts—fill the 5-quart jug and use it to fill the 3-quart jug. Then 2 quarts remain in the bigger jug. Once we see how to get 2 quarts, maybe we should see if we can get 1 quart. Certainly, if we can isolate 1 quart and if we have a 3-quart jug, we should be able to get 4 quarts. Before long, we should arrive at the following solution:

Fill up the 3-quart jug and pour it into the 5-quart jug. Fill up the 3-quart jug again, and pour as much possible into the 5-quart jug. Now empty the 5-quart jug back into the stream and pour the remaining 1 quart from the 3-quart jug into the 5-quart jug. Now fill the 3-quart jug and pour it into the 5-quart jug. Presto! There are 4 quarts in the 5-quart jug.

Simplify the problem wherever possible

The value of this principle is obvious. An illustration follows:

A man is looking at the portrait of a man. He recites the following poem:

"Brothers and sisters have I none.
This man's father is my father's son."

Whose portrait is the man looking at? The most common response to this question is the incorrect "He is looking at a portrait of himself." The second most popular incorrect answer seems to be "his father." To get the correct answer, let us make a simple substitution. If a male has no brothers or sisters, then he is his father's son. So the poem is rewritten as:

"Brothers and sisters have I none.
This man's father is me."

Correcting for bad grammar, we could say:

"Brothers and sisters have I none.
I am this man's father."

Now it is clear that the man is looking at a portrait of his son.

Try specific examples

When a general solution to a problem is not obvious, look at a specific case. In particular, try to look at a *simple* specific case. Consider the following problem:

You go to a restaurant where you are promised a 10 percent discount on your check. Sales tax is 5 percent. Would you prefer the restaurant to apply the discount before adding the sales tax, or after?

It turns out that it doesn't matter. To see this, let's take a specific example where the check comes to $100. If we apply the discount, the new subtotal is $90 and so the final total is $94.50. If we add the tax before discounting, the total comes to $105. A $10.50 discount again leaves $94.50. The first method involved multiplying the check amount by 0.9 and then multiplying by 1.05. The second method multiplies by 1.05 and then by 0.9. Since we know that the order of multiplications is immaterial, both methods are equivalent.

Break problems up into manageable pieces

This is sometimes referred to as a **divide-and-conquer** strategy or a strategy of **stepwise refinement**. While this is a valuable strategy in all areas of problem solving, it is of particular importance in computer programming, and we will have much more to say about it throughout the remainder of this book. Most real-world programming applications are too complex to be tackled as one large problem. This is essentially what structured programming is all about. The usefulness of a programming language is often judged by its ability to let the programmer do exactly this—break a problem up into pieces. For example, the separate modules of a Modula-2 program may attack separate parts of a problem.

Consider the following problem:

The only persons who live in a certain apartment house are young couples and their children.

1. There are more children than adults.
2. There are more adults than boys.
3. There are more boys than girls.
4. There are more girls than families.
5. Each family has at least one child.
6. No two families have the same number of children.
7. Every girl has at least one brother.
8. Every girl has at most one sister.
9. One family has more children than all the other families put together.

How many families are there, and how many boys and girls are there in each?

This is not a particularly easy problem to solve. We should attempt to proceed a little at a time to a solution. We begin the solution here and ask the reader to finish it in the exercises at the end of this chapter.

Step 1. We first will find the number of families, without worrying about the number of boys or girls in the various families. We will show that there are three families by eliminating all other possibilities.

One family: The number of adults is two and the number of families is one. But there must be fewer boys than adults, but more boys than girls, and more girls than families. This is clearly impossible with one family and two adults.

Two families: Since there are four adults, we must have fewer than four boys. But since there are two families, there must be at least three girls. Now we have a contradiction, because there must be more boys than girls.

Four families: Not possible. See the exercises.

Five families: Not possible. See the exercises.

Six or more families: Not possible. See the exercises.

Step 2. Now that we know that there must be three families, we show that there must be four girls.

Since there are three families, there are six adults and there must be at least four girls. If there were more than four girls, there would have to be more than five boys. But since there are only six adults, there can't be more than five boys. So there are exactly four girls.

Step 3. Next we determine that there are five boys.

This is easy. There are four girls and six adults, so there must be exactly five boys.

Step 4. We now determine the breakdown of girls in each family. See the exercises.

Step 5. We finally determine the breakdown of boys in each family. See the exercises.

THE PROGRAMMING PROCESS

Since programming is a specific kind of problem solving—namely, finding an algorithmic solution to a problem—we'll make a few remarks particularly appropriate to programming:

1. Be sure that the problem is completely understood. In computer jargon, know the exact **specifications** of the problem. What is the program supposed to accomplish? If there are data to be examined, in exactly what form will the data appear? If a report is to be printed, what is the desired format of the report?
2. Carefully design the overall structure of your solution.
3. Write your solution in **pseudo-code** first. We will have more to say about this in later chapters. For now, just think of this as "Say what you are going to do in English before you write it out in a programming language."
4. Test programs with various data. Although you may have arrived at a solution by using simple, specific cases, when your program is complete, try it on some general data or particularly difficult data.
5. Be prepared to make numerous modifications to your first design. The more well thought out your program design, the more likely it is that you will complete the program.

IDENTIFIERS AND VARIABLES

We are often asked what sort of person makes a good programmer. In particular, people asking this question usually want to know, "Do I need to be good at math to be a good programmer?" There are certainly some common characteristics, since both kinds of activities center around problem solving. Both a mathematician and a programmer need to be very logical and organized and have the ability to proceed step by step to a solution. But programming is not mathematics and, with the exception of specialized scientific programmers, many programmers can do their jobs without any knowledge of advanced mathematics such as calculus and differential equations. This is not to say that programmers shouldn't take such courses—certainly the kinds of problem-solving skills that can be developed in a calculus course may prove very useful to a programmer.

However, there is one notion from mathematics—in fact, from high-school algebra—that is important for beginning computer programmers: the idea of a **variable** (or unknown). In solving word problems about the ages of Dick, Jane, and Sally, it is common for students to say, "Let X represent Dick's age, let Y represent Jane's age, and let Z represent Sally's age." If we are told that Dick is as old as the combined ages of Jane and Sally, we would agree that "$X = Y + Z$" represents this fact. Moreover, if we know that $Y = 7$, $Z = 4$, and $X = Y + Z$, then we could conclude that $X = 11$.

Variables are also very important in programming. They are sometimes called **identifiers**. Just as in algebra, they are used to name quantities that we want to work with. But in addition to naming quantities, they also name, or correspond to, memory locations in the computer where we store and retrieve information. This connection between an identifier in a program and a memory location in the computer that contains information about that identifier is the most crucial early concept to understand for beginning programmers. The reader will see examples of this in the next few chapters.

EXERCISES

1.1 Find a second way for the boy at the stream to bring home 4 quarts of water.

1.2 If a chicken-and-a-half lays an egg-and-a-half in a day-and-a-half, how long does it take a chicken to lay a dozen eggs?

1.3 Glass A contains a liter of wine and Glass B contains a liter of water. A teaspoon of wine is taken from Glass A and placed into Glass B. The resulting mixture in Glass B is well stirred and then a teaspoon of the mixture in taken from Glass B and placed into Glass A. Is there more water in the wine or more wine in the water?

The next three exercises refer to the problem posed in the chapter.

1.4 Show that there cannot be four or more families by arguing that each case will result in too many boys.

1.5 Show that the breakdown of girls in the three families is: no girl, two girls, and two girls.

1.6 Show that the breakdown of boys in the three families is: one boy (only child), one boy (with a two-girl family), and three boys (with a two-girl family).

1.7 At a party with five couples, the host goes around to each person and asks how many people he or she shook hands with. (No one shakes hands with himself or herself or his or her spouse.) No two answers given to the host are the same. How many hands did the hostess shake?

Chapter 2

A FIRST MODULA-2 PROGRAM

It is time to consider some simple Modula-2 syntax. Listing 2.1 shows our first program, FirstExample. The line numbers are simply for the discussion given below and are *not* part of the program. Figure 2.1 shows sample output from the same program. The program is simple and not very useful, but its purpose is not to dazzle you, but rather to illustrate the structure of a simple Modula-2 program. At this point, some of the details of the program will be mysterious to the reader, but it would be very instructive to examine carefully Listing 2.1 and Figure 2.1 to see if you can determine how the output is generated by the program.

```
 1      MODULE FirstExample;
 2
 3      (* This first example squares and cubes the integer of your
 4      choice. Do not, however, be too greedy, as cubing 32 already
 5      causes integer overflow in many systems. *)
 6
 7      FROM InOut IMPORT ReadInt, WriteInt, WriteString, WriteLn;
 8
 9      VAR Number, Square, Cube : INTEGER;
10
11      BEGIN
12        WriteLn;
13        WriteString('Please enter an integer: --> ');
14        ReadInt(Number);
15        Square := Number * Number;
16        Cube := Square * Number;
17        WriteLn;
18        WriteString('The square of ');
```

```
19      WriteInt(Number, 0);
20      WriteString(' is ');
21      WriteInt(Square, 0);
22      WriteString(' and its cube is ');
23      WriteInt(Cube, 0);
24      WriteLn
25      END FirstExample.
```

Listing 2.1

```
Please enter an integer: --> 17
The square of 17 is 289 and its cube is 4913
```

Figure 2.1

THE MODULE HEADING

We now examine the program of Listing 2.1 line by line. Every Modula-2 program begins with a **module heading**. This heading contains the keyword MODULE, followed by an identifier of the user's choice. Keywords are words that the language recognizes as having particular fixed meanings. There are seven keywords (MODULE, FROM, IMPORT, VAR, INTEGER, BEGIN, and END) in FirstExample. They are easy to spot, since in Modula-2 keywords are always capitalized. Modula-2, unlike most computer languages, is case sensitive, which means that you must type MODULE, not Module or module. The purpose of the module heading is to mark the beginning of the program and to give a name to the program.

IDENTIFIERS

The word following MODULE is chosen by the user to identify the program. The user also chooses names for variables, such as Number, Square, and Cube on line 9 of the program. All these names for things are called **identifiers**. We will also commonly call them **variables**. In Modula-2, identifiers must begin with a letter (A to Z, or a to z) and then can contain only letters and digits (0 to 9). In particular, an identifier may not contain any blanks. Thus, the following are legal identifiers:

X	NumKids	Election88
p2t3z	NumAdults	Election90

and the following are illegal Modula-2 identifiers (why?):

Hungry?	Hot-dog	Cold Turkey
2ForTea	%Total	Paid$

Niklaus Wirth's definition of Modula-2 says that identifiers can be any length. However, some compilers limit the length of identifiers. You should check your manuals to see if your compiler has any such limitations. For example, if the compiler should happen to look only at the first eight characters, then `Election88` and `Election90` would be the same identifier to that compiler. Most compilers normally consider at least the first 30 characters, so this is usually no problem.

In this text, we will use the convention of capitalizing the first letter of our identifiers. We do this for readability. Since blanks are not allowed, when we want to run words together, we will also capitalize the first letter of each distinct word. For example, `NumKids` and `NumAdults` are two good identifiers that are easy to read. Consider the identifiers `Popelement` and `PopElement`, which are the same except for the case of the fourth letter. The first begs to be read as "Pope lament," while the second can be read only as "Pop Element," which makes a lot more sense if we are using this identifier to store the element that we have "popped off" from something.

This brings us to our final, but most important, point about Modula-2 identifiers. Modula-2 doesn't care whether you use identifiers like `X` and `p2t3z` or identifiers like `NumKids` and `NumAdults`. They are all legally formed Modula-2 identifiers. But, as discussed above, the latter two are easy to read—*and easy to understand*. It is clear that `NumKids` and `NumAdults` are being used to count the number of children or adults, respectively, in some setting. No one will ever guess what `X` or `p2t3z` mean. Because a program is a form of communication, you should strive to make that communication as clear as possible. One simple way to do that is to use well-chosen, meaningful identifiers.

Beginners often think that they are writing programs to communicate solely with the computer, so `X` is as good as `MaxScore` when dealing with a moron. Students would be wise to consider that they are really writing programs to be read by another person, called a grader. This grader, being human, will be much more kindly disposed to your program if it is clear. The quickest way to make an otherwise good program unclear is to use poor identifiers. And don't forget that there is often another person who reads your programs—you! It's pretty embarrassing when you have trouble reading the program you wrote a month ago because you did such a poor job.

Our insistence on clarity is not just academic. On the contrary, clarity in programs is even more important in the real world than in academia. First, real-world problems tend to be a lot larger than the standard assignments given to students. A program with 5000 identifiers obviously has even more need for well-chosen identifiers than does a short program with 5 identifiers. Second, real-world programs are often worked on by teams of programmers. In such a situation, it is essential that you be able to read the programs of others and that they be able to read your programs. We summarize this discussion as a programming principle:

To make your programs readable, always choose meaningful identifiers. Capitalize first letters to make your identifiers readable. Avoid `X` like the plague.

BLANK LINES

The second, sixth, eighth, and tenth lines of the program `FirstExample` are blank. These blank lines are included to increase the readability of the program. They divide the program into its major sections and help to make this separation apparent to the human eye. Judicious use of white space makes your programs more readable.

COMMENTS

Lines 3, 4, and 5 form a comment. The syntax of a comment in Modula-2 is as follows:

```
(* Blah, blah, blah—for as many lines
   as you like—blah, blah, blah        *)
```

A comment begins with the two-character sequence (* and ends with the sequence *). Between these delimiters, you can put anything (with one exception) you wish. Note that comments can run over several lines. The only thing not permitted inside a comment is *), since this sequence ends the comment.

Comments are completely ignored by the compiler. Comments are provided to supply information to humans who read your program. The judicious use of comments can greatly improve the readability of your program. Every MODULE should begin with a comment explaining the purpose of that module. Comments should also be used to explain any tricky points in the program. Most beginners fail to use enough comments, but it is possible to use too many or to use inappropriate comments. For example, a comment on every line makes a program less readable, rather than more readable. Avoid comments like:

```
Square := Number * Number;              (* Square the Number and
                                           put it in Square. *)
```

which comments the obvious. Trust the reader to have the intelligence to be able to read the statement without the comment. This leads to our second programming principle:

Use comments to explain the major sections of your program. Begin each module with such a comment. Comment any tricky or nonobvious statements, but avoid trivial comments.

IMPORTATION FROM THE LIBRARY INOUT

Modula-2 contains no built-in input and output statements. Instead, these kinds of procedures are available in separate, external libraries. The rationale for doing this is that it keeps the core language small; it isolates the input and output routines, which are the most system-dependent routines of the whole compiler; and it means that a program need import only those routines that it is actually going to use, which keeps the program small, too. Unfortunately, the use of external libraries means that the beginner must learn a little about the process of importation, and it also means that the language is not completely standard and portable, since different compiler developers will supply slightly different libraries with their software. In this chapter, however, we will be using only one such library, InOut, which *should* be standard across all Modula-2s. The library InOut, as described here, is as described in Wirth's definition of Modula-2 in his book, *Programming in Modula–2*, third edition. We will describe Wirth's suggested standard libraries, but the reader must be aware that not all Modula-2s adhere strictly to Wirth's standards. However, all should have the standard library, InOut. The most important of Wirth's standard libraries are listed in Appendix A.

Line 7 of FirstExample simply asserts our intention to IMPORT several I/O (input and output) procedures FROM the library InOut. Notice carefully how the identifier InOut is spelled. Modula-2 is case sensitive and will not understand you if you type Inout, INOUT, inout, or anything except exactly the sequence of uppercase and lowercase letters: InOut. The procedures that we import (note their spelling, too) are ReadInt and WriteInt, which read and write integers, respectively. The procedures WriteString and WriteLn write strings and lines, respectively. The use of these procedures is illustrated in the module and is discussed in more detail below.

If you know any other computer language, you are probably surprised to see that Modula-2 has so many write statements. This is because Modula-2 has no generic *write*; indeed, it has no *write* at all. Instead, it has libraries that supply many different kinds of output statements. This means that if your program has no need for decimal numbers, then you do not need to burden your program with routines for reading or writing such numbers. For now, we need only understand that line 7 is necessary to get the I/O procedures needed for our present module.

VARIABLE DECLARATIONS AND INTEGER TYPES

Modula-2 requires that you declare every variable, or identifier, that you use. This declaration process, shown in line 9 of FirstExample, names the variables that will be used in your module and lists the types of these variables. The type of a variable indicates the possible range of values that the variable can assume and indicates what the legal operations are for that variable. FirstExample, to keep things simple, has only INTEGER variables. An integer is a whole number, positive, zero, or negative. The range of an integer can be compiler dependent, but is often from -32768 to 32767. As we shall see, the operations of addition, subtraction, multiplication, and division, as well as some others, can be applied to integers. More details concerning integers are given following the discussion of our first module, FirstExample.

The reason that Modula-2 requires every identifier to be declared is so that it can protect you from yourself. For example, what should the computer do if you declare the identifier Square at line 9, but accidentally type Squire later in the program? The computer is not smart enough to know what you intended! Indeed, in a large dungeons-and-dragons program, you might really want the two distinct identifiers Square and Squire. The best that the system can do is to recognize that Squire was not declared; it does this by issuing you an undeclared-identifier error message when you try to compile your program. There are two ways to make the error message go away. If you accidentally typed Squire for Square, then correct your typing mistake and replace the i with an a. If, on the other hand, you really intended to use the variable Squire, you must add it to the list of declarations. It is very important to realize that the action you take to make an error message go away depends on what *your* intention was.

THE EXECUTABLE BODY OF THE PROGRAM

The body of a Modula-2 program is caught between the keywords BEGIN and END. It is here that the executable statements are found. The executable statements are those that cause actions to be performed. Our simple program, FirstExample, has only three such types of statements: *write* statements, *read* statements, and *assignment* statements. We now discuss each in turn.

WRITE STATEMENTS

The `WriteLn`s—read w*rite lines*—at lines 12, 17, and 24 cause a carriage return to be executed. That is, this statement returns the cursor to the left-hand side of the next line. The `WriteLn` at line 17 is especially critical, because it ends the first line of output and begins the second. Notice the spelling of `WriteLn` with its uppercase `L`.

The `WriteString`s at lines 13, 18, 20, and 22 cause the exact message that is given within single quotes to be displayed. Such a quoted sequence of characters is called a **string**. We use strings in this simple example to give the user instructions and to label results. Note the extra space before and after the word *is* in the string on line 20. The string `' is '` is four characters long and consists of a blank, an `i`, an `s`, and another blank. In contrast, the string `'is'` is only two characters long. If we were not careful about extra spaces within the quotes, we would get poorly formatted output such as:

```
The square of17is289and its cube is4913
```

The `WriteInt`s at lines 19, 21, and 23 cause the value of the given integer identifier to be displayed. For example, `WriteInt(Number, 0)` causes the current value of `Number` to be written to the screen. `WriteInt` also expects a second value, which is zero in each of our examples. This value, when positive, gives the number of columns that you want the value to be printed in. Zero simply means "take whatever space you need," so 17 prints in two columns, 289 in three, and 4913 in four.

Note that each of the write statements, except `WriteLn`, uses parentheses. Also notice the comma in the `WriteInt` statement.

READ STATEMENTS

The only read statement used in our simple example is the `ReadInt` at line 14. This causes execution of the program to halt and to wait until the user types an integer at the keyboard and hits the return key. The `ReadInt` will not tell the user that it is expecting an integer. How is the user to know whether to type an integer or his or her name? The answer is that the programmer must prompt the user for the appropriate response. This is the purpose of the `WriteString` at the previous line, line 13. Always remember to prompt the user with a `WriteString` that gives instructions before a read statement. The arrow (-->) of that prompt is simply two minus signs, -, followed by a greater than sign, >.

ASSIGNMENT STATEMENTS

Lines 15 and 16 are our two assignment statements. They cause expressions to be evaluated and values to be assigned to identifiers. The symbol * denotes multiplication. For example, the statement

```
Square := Number * Number;
```

causes the current value of Number to be multiplied by itself and the result to be stored in Square. Likewise, the line

```
Cube := Square * Number;
```

results in the cube of the Number being stored in Cube. The longer statement

```
Cube := Number * Number * Number;
```

would accomplish the same result, but it is slower, since it involves two multiplications by the computer instead of one.

It is important to realize that the assignment operator is not symmetric. That is,

```
Number * Number := Square;              (* ILLEGAL Assignment. *)
```

is not a legal statement. Only a single variable may appear on the left-hand side of the assignment statement, and this variable receives the value of the expression from the right-hand side of the statement.

It is also important to note that the assignment operator is denoted by :=. You must type the colon and the equal sign with no space between them. The reason for this is that together they denote the assignment operator, while separately they denote other things. We have seen the colon used in variable declarations, and later we will see the equal sign used as a test for equality.

You should now understand what each statement in the body does and see how this simple program prompts the user to enter a number, how it squares and cubes that input, and how it outputs its results.

THE END

Reasonably enough, the end of a Modula-2 program is marked with an END that also includes the name of the module. Also, note very carefully that there is a period following the name. A common beginner's error is to forget that period. You must have it, or the compiler will complain bitterly.

SEMICOLONS

Note that most of the lines in our program FirstExample have semicolons at the end of them. The semicolon is used in Modula-2 to separate statements, not to terminate them. This means that it is used more like the comma in English than the period. A period (or an exclamation point or question mark) terminates the end of each sentence in English. The comma, however, separates a group of items, and there is no comma at the end of a list. For example, consider a list of programming languages:

FORTRAN, Algol, Pascal, Modula-2

Here we use three commas to separate four items. There is no comma after the last item.

Note that there is no semicolon after line 24 in `FirstExample`. This is because there is no Modula-2 statement following it (`END` is a keyword, not a statement). There are also no semicolons after lines 3, 4, and 5, because these lines form a comment and are ignored by the compiler. There is also no semicolon after line 11, since `BEGIN` is also a keyword. All the other lines in `FirstExample` do have semicolons after them, and they all are required.

Actually, Modula-2 is quite forgiving about extra semicolons, so your program will compile if you put in semicolons at the end of lines where they are not needed. In this text, however, we will try to exhibit programs without any superfluous semicolons.

EDITING, COMPILING, LINKING, AND RUNNING PROGRAMS

Now that you have seen a complete Modula-2 program, you probably want to see if you can get it to work on your system. It is a good idea to use a simple and syntactically correct module if this will be your first attempt at steering a Modula-2 program through your computer. That way, you can focus your efforts on learning the details of your system. Later, you will get many chances to write your own modules.

Unfortunately, it is impossible for us to know the details of your system, so you will have to get some local help on the particulars of the steps below. Sources for this information include your instructor if you are in a Modula-2 class; the computer center at your installation; friends who have used Modula-2 on your system; and, as a last resort, reading the manuals that came with your Modula-2 compiler.

The four steps involved in running a program are:

1. Creating/editing the source program.

You must create a file such as `FIRST.MOD` that contains the Modula-2 source code (the program) shown in Listing 2.1. An editor is really just a specialized word-processing program that lets you type in your program and then modify it as needed. Indeed, if you already know a word processor, you may be able to use it as your Modula-2 editor. Be sure to save your program before you exit the editor!

2. Compiling the program.

Each Modula-2 compiler has its own special commands. You will need to learn how to invoke the compiler at your installation. The compiler, if it finds no errors, will translate your Modula-2 source code into a specialized machine code called **object code**. However, if errors are found, they will be listed and you will have to return to the editor to correct them. Only when you get a clean compile can you proceed to step 3.

3. Linking the program.

Your object code is not a complete program. It must be linked or joined with other modules before your program can run. For example, it is the linker's job to find `WriteString`, etc., in the `InOut` library module and make it available to your module. Again, you will need to learn the local command that links your program.

4. Running the program.

If your program linked without errors, then you are ready to run it. This is usually very simple, but, again, how this is done will vary from installation to installation.

This seems like a lot of effort to run a program, but hopefully steps 2, 3, and 4 are one-line or even one-keystroke commands that you quickly learn to use without even thinking about them. For example, some Modula–2 compilers for the IBM-PC can be set up so that single function keys save, compile, link, and run your program.

SOME REMARKS ABOUT OPERATIONS ON INTEGERS

So far, the only operation on integers that we have discussed is multiplication. Of course, the computer can also add (+), subtract (-) and divide (DIV). No explanation is needed for + and -, but DIV deserves some discussion. The DIV operator is extremely simple if you can remember back to when you were in the third grade and did problems like:

$$\begin{array}{r} 3 \\ 5 \overline{)\,19} \end{array}$$

Do you remember that you said something like, "Five goes into nineteen three times," or "Nineteen divided by five is three," and you didn't worry about the remainder? That is exactly what DIV does. It is the integer division operator, and it keeps, without rounding, the result of an integer division. Here are some more examples:

```
37   DIV 8   has the value  4
11   DIV 2   has the value  5
3    DIV 5   has the value  0
21   DIV 7   has the value  3
-5   DIV 3   has the value -1
```

You are probably surprised at this behavior of the DIV operator. Indeed, you may be a bit disappointed, since you expected 37 divided by 8 to be 4.625. In Chapter 4, we will learn that there are other numeric types and, in the *real* type, 37.0 divided by 8.0 does turn out as expected.

There is also an operator on integers that will recover the lost remainders from the previous examples. This is the MOD operator, and it is defined on positive integers by:

X MOD Y is the remainder when X is divided by Y.

For example:

```
37   MOD 8   has the value 5
11   MOD 2   has the value 1
3    MOD 5   has the value 3
```

21   MOD 7   has the value 0
-5   MOD 3   is not defined. Both operands to MOD must be positive.

Parentheses are needed in arithmetic expressions when you need to force some particular order of evaluation. For example, if you recall the famous formula for converting Fahrenheit temperatures to their Celsius equivalents:

$$C = (F - 32) * \frac{5}{9}$$

then in Modula-2 you might write:

```
Cels := (Fahr - 32) * 5 DIV 9;
```

On the other hand, to convert your height in feet and inches (5' 9") into inches (69"), you do not need parentheses:

```
Height := Feet * 12 + Inches;
```

The reason that this last statement needs no parentheses is that the system knows that, when given the choice, it should multiply before adding. These conventions are called the **precedence rules**, and, fortunately, they follow normal algebraic conventions. Much more will be said about precedence in Chapter 4. For now, suffice it to say that the multiplicative operators (*, DIV, and MOD) have precedence over the additive operators (+ and -). And within one type of operator (additive or multiplicative), operations are carried out from the left to the right. This last sentence means that the expression

```
 8 - 4 - 2
```

evaluates from the left as (8 - 4) - 2 instead of 8 - (4 - 2), giving the value 2 instead of 6.
  Be aware that the expression

```
Cels := 5 DIV 9 * (Fahr - 32);
```

is incorrect, because 5 DIV 9 is zero and, thus, the entire expression always evaluates to zero no matter the value of Fahr. Remember this example and be careful of integer divisions.
  Using our conventions of evaluating multiplications and divisions first, and from the left, we see that the rather complex expression

```
A * B - C DIV D * E + F * G
```

is equivalent (up to integer arithmetic) to the algebraic expression

$$ab - \frac{c}{d}e + fg$$

Likewise, the expression

```
(A*B + C) DIV (D - E)
```

is equivalent (up to integer arithmetic) to:

$$\frac{\cdot ab + c}{d - e}$$

Learn to use parentheses to add clarity to your expressions. In this regard, the first expression is also equivalent to

```
(A * B) - ((C DIV D) * E) + (F * G)
```

and this latter is preferred because it is clearer. On the other hand, too many parentheses can make expressions unreadable. Our expression is also equivalent to the ugly mess:

```
(((A * B) - ((C DIV D) * E)) + (F * G))
```

The moral of this example is that you should use parentheses with the goal of making your expressions clear. Do not strive to use the minimum number of parentheses, and do not use superfluous parentheses.

SYNTAX DIAGRAMS

Modula-2 constructs can be defined pictorially. For example, Figure 2.2 defines the concept of an identifier. By following the arrows, you can go around the loop as many times as you want before finally exiting, thereby producing any legal identifier. This picture, called a **syntax diagram**, is clearly equivalent to our previous definition of an identifier as any string of one or more letters and digits that begins with a letter.

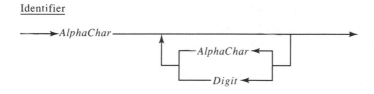

Figure 2.2

We will continue to use verbal definitions for the introduction of new concepts, because we believe that the reader should be able to express the ideas in words. However, syntax diagrams do provide a powerful method for summarizing Modula-2 syntax, and so we provide a complete set of syntax diagrams in Appendix B. As the reader learns more about Modula-2, Appendix B will become an ever more valuable quick-reference guide to the exact syntax of Modula-2.

SOME REMARKS ON PROGRAMMING STYLE

Much will be said in the chapters to follow about style in programming. It is at least as important as style in composition in natural languages. Your objective is not just to get a program that runs and produces correct output, but also to produce a form of communication. As such, the program will need to follow certain rules of style to be acceptable to other users. We have only begun, but already we can make the following points about well-written programs:

Use white space properly

A well-composed program is pleasing to the eye. One way to accomplish this is by judicious use of blank spaces and blank lines (called **white space**). Put blank lines between major sections of your program to help the human eye to see these subdivisions. Use blanks in statements to make them easy to read. For example, the assignment statement

```
Cost:=Price*Qty+Tax;
```

is not as easy to read as any of the following:

```
Cost := Price * Qty + Tax;
```

```
Cost := Price*Qty + Tax;
```

```
Cost := (Price * Qty) + Tax;
```

Please note that anywhere a blank is permitted, more than one blank is allowed. You can use blanks except within keywords of the language. Thus, you can't write BEG IN or E N D, of course. Please recall that blanks are not allowed in identifiers, so if you want an identifier to count employees, use an identifier such as NumWorkers, and not Num Workers. Also, remember that := is the assignment operator and that : =, with a space in it, will be rejected by the compiler.

Use meaningful identifiers

This has already been stated as a programming principle, but it is so important that we repeat it here. Compare the assignment statement

```
x := p * y * y;
```

with the equivalent statement

```
Area := Pi * Radius * Radius;
```

Anyone knows what the second statement means, but to understand the first, you have to know a lot about the program. Using well-chosen identifiers is one of the most effective things that a programmer can do to provide clarity in programs, since the use of meaningful identifiers makes the program almost self-documenting. Get in the habit from the beginning of using good identifiers, even in short programs.

Use indentation in programs

Another great aid to the human eye is indentation of program lines. Module FirstExample is very simple, but it already shows some use of indentation. As we develop program structures, we will have much more to say about indentation. Basically, its purpose is to display immediately to the human eye the extent of certain portions of the program. If you don't use indentation, your programs will quickly become unreadable, because the reader can't easily determine where major blocks of your program begin or end.

Use comments

Comments are provided for the human readers of your program. Good commenting of programs is a very valuable skill. We will have much to say about documenting programs in the pages to follow. Most people err on the side of too few comments, but it is possible to clutter up a program with too many. Comments should be written to aid an intelligent reader of your program. In the trivial program FirstExample, we have used only one comment which explains the purpose of the program. Minimally, please always include such a comment in every module that you write. Another good idea is to include your name as a part of a comment, particularly if you are learning Modula-2 in a classroom situation. Again, as we develop more complex programs in Modula-2, we will discuss the need for more extensive documentation of programs. For now, it is a good idea to get in the habit of commenting all your programs.

Because we are honest, we will point out that white space, comments, indentation, and meaningful variables are not required by the computer. The compiler will accept your programs even if they do not contain these elements. However, especially if you are in an institution (educational, we hope), your programs may not be accepted by your teacher unless they contain all of the above elements. It may help you to accept and use these conventions if you know that they are generally accepted in computer science and are not imposed just because your instructor is mean. In the next chapter, we will attempt to describe where we are going and why this fuss about style is really important.

COMMON ERRORS IN PROGRAMMING

This section tries to warn the reader about common errors that we have seen students make over the years. We wish we could protect you from making these errors in the first place, but, realistically, you will probably go ahead and make them anyway. Actually, you should not be afraid to make errors. Everyone does make them, especially in learning a new language, and there is much that can be learned from your errors.

You should also learn to be confident that you can find and fix your own errors, for you cannot really call yourself a programmer unless you can debug your own programs. Do not sit for hours without getting help on an error message, but also do not be so insecure that you seek help before the error beep has completely sounded! Remember that the computer is almost certainly not broken, but rather that you have violated the syntax of Modula-2. Look again carefully at our examples and discussion. Keep foremost in mind what you are trying to do: You are trying to solve a problem, not make an error message go away. Therefore, trying things at random is very unlikely to help. You should seek to understand why the system is giving you an error message, so that you can fix it properly and avoid it in the future.

Even though we are only getting started in Modula-2, there are already many possible ways to make errors. Here are some of our favorites:

Improper use of case. Remember that Modula-2 is case sensitive. Keywords must be in uppercase (BEGIN, not Begin), imported items must be spelled correctly (WriteLn, not Writeln), and even your own identifiers must be written consistently. If you declare the identifier NumKids, then Numkids will be flagged as undeclared.

Illegal assignment operator. Programmers with experience in other languages may tend to write = for the assignment operator. This is not tolerated by the Modula-2 compiler, and you must type := with no space between the colon and the equal sign.

Undeclared identifiers. Every identifier *that you intend to use* must be declared in the VAR statement. Typographical errors often cause you to get the undeclared-identifier error message. Realize that the system is only saying that the indicated identifier is not declared; it is not ordering you to declare it! Check to see if you really forgot to declare the identifier, or (more likely), due to some typo, the system is failing to recognize the identifier you *intended.*

Illegal identifiers. Recall that identifiers cannot include blanks or spaces. Nor can they contain special characters like $ or %.

Improper use of semicolons. Don't forget that a semicolon must be used between each two Modula-2 statements to separate them. Learn to look at the line *above* the error message to see if a semicolon has caused the problem.

Missing period at end. Don't forget that Modula-2 requires a period at the end of the module name on the END statement.

Continued comment error. This is the most puzzling of the simple errors discussed here. Suppose you have (you think) two comments in your program as follows:

```
(* This is comment one. This module ...

VAR  A : INTEGER;
...
```

```
(* This is comment two. Now we ...   *)
BEGIN
  A := 0;
  ...
```

When this runs, you will get an undeclared-identifier error for A at the assignment statement just after the BEGIN. But anybody can see that A has been properly declared!

The problem is that you forgot to end your first comment with the *) symbols. Therefore, the compiler treats everything from the first (* to the next *), several lines below, as a comment. This means that your declaration, as well as the second (*, is treated as part of the comment and, hence, is ignored by the compiler. Therefore, the identifier A really is undeclared!

This is an example of a situation in which the error message issued by the machine is not very helpful. Remember this example, and its symptoms. If the compiler is ignoring a section of your code, check for an open comment around that section of code.

EXERCISES

2.1 Classify each of the following identifiers as legal or illegal. For the illegal ones, indicate why they are invalid.

a) %Wrong   b) Wow!

c) WhyNot?   d) iLLeGal

e) Maybe   f) 5Stars

g) Not Sure   h) Couldn'tBe

i) A2ndChance   j) Xqb3z

Which of the legal ones are poor choices for identifiers in real programs? Why?

2.2 Write each of the following algebraic expressions as a correct Modula-2 assignment statement. Use the integer division operator, DIV, for the divisions. Where the formula has obvious meaning, use proper Modula-2 identifiers. For example,

$a = l * h$

becomes

```
Area := Length * Height;
```

a) $a = \dfrac{bh}{2}$ b) $F = \dfrac{9}{5}C + 32$

c) in = 12(ft + 3•yd)   d) $x = \dfrac{ab - cd}{e + f - g}$

2.3 Write a module to solve the following problem. Fred's wife, Wilma, has made Fred clean up his messy garage where he has thrown his beer bottles over the last 43 years. If Fred has 15,273 bottles in the garage and can get a $1 deposit back for each case of 24 bottles, how much will Fred get back, and how many extra bottles will he still have?

2.4 Write a module to solve the following problem. Ferty Lizer runs a garden shop and continually has to stop and figure out how many bags of fertilizer a customer needs for his or her particular lot. Write a progam that will automate this process for Ferty. The program should prompt the user to enter the length and width of the lot in feet (we assume that the lot is rectangular). The program should compute the area of the lot in square feet and then subtract 2500 square feet for the average house and driveway, where fertilizer is not to be applied. The program should then compute the number of whole bags needed if one bag of fertilizer covers 5000 square feet. Because of the nature of integer division, add one bag to the result obtained to ensure that the customer has enough fertilizer to finish the task (and that Ferty makes a nice profit).
For example, if Sally's lot is 100 feet by 125 feet, then the area of her lot is 12,500 square feet. Only 10,000 square feet of yard are to be fertilized. We see that Sally needs exactly two bags, but Ferty's algorithm will sell her three bags. Ferty prefers this, because if Sally applies the fertilizer a little more heavily than recommended, she will need the third bag, and she will be very upset if she cannot complete the job with the fertilizer sold to her on her first visit. And, of course, if Sally has an unopened bag left over, Ferty will cheerfully refund her money on her next visit to the store.
Be aware that integers are limited to 32767 in many Modula-2s. Therefore, do not run the program with anything but small, city lots. Note that a 200-foot by 200-foot acre already contains 40,000 square feet. In Chapter 4, we will learn about other types besides integers. The best thing you can do at this point to get around the problem is to divide the length and width by three, changing them to yards. Then find the area in square yards. But remember that one bag covers only 5000 DIV 9, or 555 square yards.

Chapter 3

STRUCTURED AND
MODULAR PROGRAMS

The first successful general-purpose electronic computers were built less than 50 years ago as part of the war effort during World War II. Hence, the science of programming—some would say the art of programming—is very young. Yet, much has happened in that short interval, and it is important that you understand a little of where we were, if you want to understand where we are going with a modern language like Modula-2.

Our first point is that programs written in the real world are often huge. Many programs are measured in tens of thousands of lines. Some number in the the hundreds of thousands or millions of lines. Today's production programs are orders of magnitude bigger than programs written in the 1940s and 1950s. It is obvious that big programs are inherently more complex to work with than are small ones. With a program of 50 lines, it is possible to remember the purpose of each line, even if it isn't self-evident. With a program of 50,000 lines, no human can recall what each line does, let alone what major sections of the program are supposed to do. The methods that have been developed to deal with the extra complexity due to the size of large programs are exactly the subject of this chapter.

Also, real programs are written not by single individuals, but by teams of people. But people come and go. Imagine how difficult it would be to inherit someone else's messy 50,000-line program! And programs have to be maintained to reflect the new social-security withholding rate or the new thrust of a rocket's engines. Programs have to be modified or extended to handle new cases. Too often, managers find that the only feasible way to modify a program is to throw it out and write it over, because huge programs are hard to debug, maintain, modify, or extend. Throwing out the original is very expensive and wasteful of the initial effort. There has to be a better way.

There are, of course, no 50,000-line programs included in this text. For one reason, such a listing would run about 1000 pages by itself! Nor will any of the exercises ask you to write such large programs. In education, we get to play mind games. Our example programs illustrate certain concepts and, hence, are quite brief. Your exercises are of the same nature. Yet, we will make a big deal of applying modern programming techniques to our examples, and we ask that you do the same in the exercises. The mind game that we are asking you to play is to pretend that every program, no matter how small or silly, is a real program that others will have to understand, maintain, modify, and extend. Hence, every program must be written to the standards developed below.

THE EVOLUTION OF STRUCTURED AND MODULAR PROGRAMMING

The first successful high-level language, FORTRAN, was released in April 1957. In the last 30 years, hundreds of languages have been developed to deal with the complexity of large programs. Over these 30 years, through popular languages like BASIC, Algol, PL/I, Pascal, C, and many others, an evolution has occurred. Modula-2 is at the current end of one of these evolutionary paths and contains many techniques for managing complexity. We'll now discuss six of these: structure, subprograms, modules, data sharing, data hiding, and local variables. Much more will be said of each of these in the chapters to follow. Indeed, these topics are the focus of the remainder of this text.

Structure

A language is said to be **structured** if it contains powerful constructs that allow the programmer to naturally express algorithms in that language. Examples of a structured and an unstructured language will make the point clear. Consider a very simple payroll program. The program will read an hourly wage and the number of hours worked that week and will determine the pay for the individual. The only complication is that we must pay double-time for any hours over 40. Thus, for regular pay, the formula will be

Pay is computed by wage * hours

while in the overtime case, we must use

Pay is computed by (wage * 40) + (2 * wage * hours over 40)

Also, we don't want to run the program a separate time for each employee, so we want the program to run once and loop through all the employees. When we get to the end, how will we indicate to the program that there are no more employees? The trick that we use is to have the user enter some ridiculous negative wage when she or he has completely entered all the real data. Since no one can earn a negative wage, the algorithm can use this absurd value as a signal to stop processing. Here, then, is our simple algorithm:

Continually loop through the following steps:

1. Enter an hourly wage

2. If the wage is negative then STOP, otherwise continue
3. Enter the hours worked for the given individual
4. If the hours worked are less than or equal to 40, then

    Pay is wage * hours

  Else

    Pay is (wage * 40) + (2 * wage * hours over 40)
5. Output the pay

You should trace the above algorithm supposing that the data entered are

   10 35
   12 50

   ...
   -1

to see how the first person gets paid $350 while the second gets $720, etc.

  Here is a segment of a Modula-2 program that expresses this algorithm (assuming integer values for the wages and hours):

```
LOOP
  WriteString('Please enter the next wage (less than zero
      to stop): ');
  ReadInt(Wage);
  IF Wage < 0 THEN EXIT END;          ( * Exit LOOP when done. *)
  WriteLn;
  WriteString('Please enter number of hours worked: ');
  ReadInt(Hours);
  IF Hours <= 40 THEN                             (* Regular Pay *)
    Pay := Wage * Hours
  ELSE                                           (* Overtime Pay *)
    Pay := (Wage * 40) + (2 * Wage * (Hours - 40))
  END;  (* IF *)
  WriteLn;
  WriteString('Your pay is $');
  WriteInt(Pay, 0)
END
```

  Contrast the above with an early BASIC program to solve the same problem:

```
10 PRINT "Please enter the next wage (less than zero to stop): "
15 INPUT W
20 IF W < 0 THEN GOTO 65
25 PRINT "Please enter number of hours worked."
30 INPUT H
35 IF H > 40 THEN GOTO 50
40 LET P = W * H
45 GOTO 55
```

```
50 LET P = (W * 40) + (2 * W * (H - 40))
55 PRINT "Your pay is $"; P
60 GOTO 10
65 STOP
70 END
```

You should be able to read and understand how both of the above program segments implement our algorithm, even if you don't understand all the details of the BASIC or Modula-2 solution. Even though the BASIC version is actually shorter, we contend that the Modula-2 version is clearer, because Modula-2 contains structures that make the expression of the algorithm more direct. BASIC, lacking these structures, is forced to use numerous GOTOs to implement the algorithm. We see that Modula-2 has a built-in LOOP statement as well as a powerful IF ... THEN ... ELSE to express the algorithm naturally. This is part of what we mean when we say that Modula-2 is a structured language. BASIC, on the other hand, is weak in control structures and uses four GOTOs in this short program. We will have much more to say about Modula-2's control structures in Chapters 5 and 6.

We realize, dear reader, that you may beg to differ with us. You may think that the BASIC program is just as easy to read as the Modula-2 segment. We will grant you that the above trivial program can easily be understood even in the nonstructured BASIC. But our point is not about that trivial example. Our objective was to explain, via an example, what is meant by structure within a language. Think how useful these structures will be in more complex situations. Again, in a short program, we can understand the GOTOs, but how can we remember what GOTO 3475, GOTO 4590, and GOTO 2355 mean in a 50,000-line program?

Subprograms

A feature that was first introduced in FORTRAN II early in 1958 and has been accepted ever since by programmers is the **subprogram**. This device allows a large program to be broken down into smaller, more manageable pieces. It is the programmer's way of applying the much revered problem-solving heuristic known as **divide and conquer**, which says that to solve a big problem, it is sufficient to break it into smaller problems and solve each of them in turn. From the programmer's point of view, it is not necessary to keep track of all the details involved in a large program; it is only necessary to understand the small piece you are now working on. If you understand how the problem was decomposed, then it is an easy task to build the solution to the original problem from the solutions to the smaller problems.

Suppose, for example, that your boss wants a program that outputs all the prime numbers between two values supplied by the user. For example, if the user enters 100 and 1000, then the program would print all the three-digit primes. (Recall that a prime is a whole number, like 17, that has no divisors other than 1 and itself.) Of course, this is not a very complex problem and can easily be solved without a divide-and-conquer technique, but play along with us and pretend that it is very complex. How do we approach this complex problem? Can we divide it into smaller pieces? Clearly, the first thing that needs to be done is to get the user to enter the range for our search for primes. Thus, we could write a subprogram **EnterData** that would obtain from the user these

Low and High values. Wouldn't it be nice if the computer already knew what a prime number was? Well, it doesn't, but we can still imagine a black box called **Prime** that will take a candidate number and tell us yea or nay, whether the candidate is prime or not. This black box is exactly the notion of a subprogram. Indeed, if we imagine that writing the subprogram **Prime** is too mathematical for us, we could hire a mathematician to do it for us, and then we could use that subprogram in our program. Here, then, is the structure of our *main* program that solves the original problem:

```
Call subprogram EnterData to get the Low and High range values
LOOP Candidate through all values from Low up to High
     Call Prime to see if Candidate is prime or not
     IF Candidate is prime THEN print it out
```

Several points are worthy of explicit mention. First, the main program for this complex problem is easy to understand, because it is short and makes clear, explicit calls to other "slave" subprograms. Second, each subprogram is short, because it does one clearly defined task. Therefore, each subprogram is easy to understand. Third, different subprograms can be written by different people, allowing groups of people a reasonable way to work on large programs. Finally, the main program is easy to debug, maintain, and extend. It is easy to debug, because each subprogram can be bench tested before being turned loose in the big program. Even if a bug appears in the final program, it is usually easy to determine which subprogram is in error, and once the error has been localized, it is usually easy to find and correct. The program is easy to maintain or extend, since only certain subprograms need to be changed, and it is clear from the decomposition which these are. The result is a large program that does not have to be thrown out, but can be modified.

Subprograms in Modula-2 are called procedures and functions. They are explained in detail in Chapter 7.

Modules

Often, modular programming means using subprograms as we have discussed above to divide a program into modules. Modula-2 uses the term **module** in a stronger sense to mean a super subprogram. Consider an example. Suppose you have a 72,343-line "employee benefit package" and you find that the federal government has just changed the social-security witholding rate from 7.15 percent to 7.35 percent. If your program is well written, only one line, where you define this important value, needs to be changed. But then all 72,343 lines need to be recompiled before your program can be run again. Even on a fast system, this will require several minutes. It seems silly, since only one line has changed, that all need to be recompiled, even those subprograms that have nothing to do with this particular number. That is exactly the point of the module in Modula-2. A module is a piece of your program that can be compiled separately. A module may consist of one or several related subprograms, or it may consist of just constant declarations of the type we are talking about. The point is that if our huge program is broken into 10 modules, then only the module that changes will have to be recompiled. Modules, then, provide another way to make the debugging, maintainence, and extension of large programs more manageable. We discuss modules in detail in Chapters 14 and 17.

Data Sharing

Once a program is broken into subprograms, the subprograms need some way to communicate with each other and with the main program. Consider our simple example of the subprogram Prime. Prime needs to be given a Candidate number to consider. After Prime makes its decision, it needs to return via some means a yea or nay to the main program. The subprogram EnterData needs no input from the main program, but it does have to pass back the two values, Low and High, for the main program to use. Hence, we see that some means of **data sharing** between subprograms is necessary, and that this data sharing can go in either direction. Chapter 7 discusses several ways in which data can be shared between subprograms. Chapters 14 and 17 discuss data sharing between modules.

Data Hiding

The opposite side of data sharing is, of course, **data hiding**. Each subprogram or module may have private details that are nobody else's business. The integrity of the program will be better preserved if these details are not available for other subprograms to accidentally or maliciously interfere with. For example, if you hired a mathematician to write the Prime subprogram for you, she or he might supply you with a separately compiled module from which you could get the Prime subprogram, without being able to see the details of how the mathemagician did her or his magic. Data hiding is also called **data abstraction** and is discussed in Chapters 14 and 17.

Local Variables

Another important consequence of data sharing/hiding is that different people should be able to write subprograms or modules without worrying about the variables they elect to use in the internal details of their subprograms or modules. There should be a way for these details to be local to a subprogram and, therefore, not accessible outside of the subprogram or module. This means that two different subprograms should be able to have **local variables** with the same names without the system confusing them. If you wonder why two subprograms would both want to use the same identifier for different purposes, consider this: You are writing a new subprogram for an existing 50,000-line program. How can you be sure that the identifiers you need locally have not been used elsewhere? Wouldn't it be nice if you could use the identifier Count if it seemed appropriate without worrying about whether anyone had ever used it before? In a language that supports local variables, this can be done, and the identifier Count can be used locally in as many different subprograms as you want without confusing the system. Without this feature, the power of the divide-and-conquer strategy would be greatly compromised. Divide and conquer gives us a way to focus our attention on one subprogram without worrying about the details of the whole problem. If we didn't have local variables, we wouldn't be able to write a subprogram without knowing all the details of the entire program. Local variables and their declaration and use are discussed in detail in Chapter 7 on procedures and functions (Modula-2's subprograms).

WHY MODULA-2?

No computer language is perfect, and the introduction in the last three decades of hundreds of computer languages only serves to underscore this point. FORTRAN II, introduced in 1958, was a surprisingly powerful language for its day and was the standard language of American universities in the 1960s and early 1970s. FORTRAN supported subprograms, separate compilation units (modules), and local variables and had decent data-sharing mechanisms, but was particularly weak in control structures and data hiding. In the mid-1970s Pascal began to replace FORTRAN as the standard language taught in most American universities. The main reason for this was that Pascal was very strong in control structures, while still providing subprograms with local variables and good data-sharing techniques. Pascal, however, was designed as a small language for education, did not support separate compilation (modules), and did not have good data-hiding capabilities. As a result, Niklaus Wirth, Pascal's creator, introduced Modula-2 to correct some of these oversights in Pascal. Modula-2's strengths are that it supports all the concepts discussed above, while remaining a small and manageable language. Since the mid-1980s a trend can be seen in American universities away from Pascal toward Modula-2. Thus, while Modula-2 will not be accepted by everyone, there is general agreement that Modula-2 is a state-of-the-art language that incorporates modern features that facilitate the development of reliable software.

DOCUMENTATION

Another feature of well-written software, no matter what language is used, is documentation, or comments. In a large project, this documentation will take two forms, external and internal. **External documentation** takes the form of a manual or guide to the software being developed. Good external documentation can ease the task of maintenance immensely. Keeping external documentation current can be difficult, but it is, of course, important to maintain the documentation as well as the software. Incorrect documentation is probably worse than none at all!

Internal documentation is documentation within the module itself, and this is the kind of documentation that we will stress in this text. Again, the importance of documentation grows with the size of the program, but documentation should be used in all programs, large and small. The only reason to use documentation is to provide clarity to your programs, so the only firm rule is "Use comments when they will help an intelligent human reader of your program"! However, since the above rule is found by most beginners to be too vague to be helpful, we will provide, in the chapters to come, many discussions about commenting. Because commenting programs is such an individualistic process, your instructor or boss may set additional guidelines for your computer center, but the guidelines that we will develop are widely accepted software-engineering procedures.

CONCLUSION

This brief chapter has tried to provide you with a rationale for the topics to come and the reason for our fussiness with the style of programs that you will be writing. The purpose was simply to provide you with the big picture, so that you will appreciate the details that are about to unfold. Too many beginners approach a language with their total attention on the syntax of that language. Their obsession is to get a program that runs, and, with that narrow focus on detail, they can't understand where they are going or why. While you must use the language correctly to get programs to run, we implore you to keep one eye on the concepts being developed. Our objectives are to develop broad problem-solving tools and to learn to write clear, easily maintained programs. These are the valuable skills that the reader can take from this text. Modula-2 is simply our vehicle for this trip.

EXERCISES

3.1 If you know another computer language, write the payroll segment in that language. Is your language structured or unstructured? Explain.

3.2 A large program written in an unstructured language is sometimes referred to as "a plate of spaghetti." Explain this analogy with respect to the task of maintaining a large program.

3.3 What happens to the BASIC program of the text if we forget the GOTO at line 45? What does this say about the task of debugging unstructured programs?

3.4 Use divide and conquer to explain what is meant by the divide-and-conquer problem-solving technique.

3.5 A positive integer is called **perfect** if it is the sum of its proper divisors. For example, six is perfect, since $6 = 1 + 2 + 3$, and 1, 2, and 3 are the only divisors of six (other than 6 itself). Twelve, on the other hand is not perfect since $12 \neq 1 + 2 + 3 + 4 + 6$.

a) Verify by hand calculations that 28 is perfect.

b) Suppose that a mathematician has written a **SumDivs** procedure for you that will sum the proper divisors of whatever positive integer you give it. Write an outline in English using a LOOP and an IF construct, and using SumDivs, for an algorithm to find all perfect numbers between 6 and 500. Do not attempt to execute your algorithm by hand! We will return to this problem in Chapter 7.

3.6 Describe the operation of subprograms such as GiveRules, CheckWin, CheckLegalPlay, etc. for a game of tic-tac-toe. Using your subprograms, write an English main program that plays a game of tic-tac-toe with a human against the computer. Assume appropriately named subprograms that allow the human to enter a play and allow the computer to choose a play intelligently. You do not have to describe how the subprograms actually work. Rather, your task is to write the global documentation that describes black boxes that you could use to get the computer to play tic-tac-toe.

Chapter 4

NUMERIC AND CHARACTER DATA TYPES

Modula-2 is said to be a **strongly typed** language. This means that identifiers in Modula-2 are declared to be of some specific **type** that cannot change during the program. The type indicates the kind of values that the identifier can take on, as well as the operations that can be applied to the identifier. In this chapter, we'll consider the numeric and character data types of Modula-2. The numeric types are for quantities like test scores (87) and grade point averages (2.375); among the operations that we can perform on such types are the normal arithmetic operations of addition, subtraction, multiplication, and division. The character types are for quantities like grades ("B") or names ("Modula-2"), and while the operations that can be applied to such quantities are not well known, they are, as you will see, very elementary.

Football can be considered to be a strongly typed game. Some players are offensive, some defensive. Some are quarterbacks, some are tight ends, some are tackles, etc. The legal operations that each player can perform, such as using his hands to block or throw the ball, depend upon his type. For example, it is an error at run time if the quarterback throws the ball to the offensive tackle instead of the tight end. Such a type mismatch will be flagged by the officials. Likewise, Modula-2, at *compile time*, will check your program and flag any type-mismatch errors that you have committed. For example, if Num and Ch are numeric and character identifiers with the values 87 and 'B', respectively, then each of the following involves a type mismatch that will be flagged by the compiler (why?):

```
Num := 451 - "a";          (* Illegal Type Mismatch *)
Ch := Ch + 2;              (* Illegal Type Mismatch *)
Num := Ch;                 (* Illegal Type Mismatch *)
```

NUMERIC DATA TYPES

There are three different numeric data types in Modula-2. Each type is used in a slightly different application. We quickly introduce the three types, INTEGER, CARDINAL, and REAL, so that you can contrast them. Full details of each type then follow the introductory remarks.

The INTEGER type, introduced in Chapter 2, is for *signed* whole numbers, such as -17, 0, and 2381. The INTEGER type would be appropriate, for example, for recording the temperature (Celsius or Fahrenheit) in International Falls, Minnesota, since it can be positive, negative, or zero there on any given day.

The CARDINAL type is for *nonnegative* whole numbers such as 0, 2381, and 50000. Since the sales of this book can't be negative (we hope), the CARDINAL type would be appropriate for recording the quantity of this book sold in International Falls, Minnesota. Obviously, CARDINALs and INTEGERs are very similar, and the differences between them are discussed below.

The third numeric type is the REAL type, which is used to represent numbers with a *decimal point* such as -210.98, 0.0, and 3.14159. REALs are clearly appropriate whenever nonwhole valued data are present. For example, the REAL type is appropriate when the average weight of politicians' brains is measured (0.000003418 gram). The alert reader should be asking, "Why isn't the REAL type all that we need?" After all, -17.0, 0.0, 2381.0, and 50000.0 are REALs for each of the INTEGER and CARDINAL examples given above. This is a good question—and it is answered after the details of each type are given.

THE INTEGER TYPE

The INTEGERs, again, are signed whole numbers that can be positive, negative, or zero. They never contain a decimal point or a comma. Thus, -312, 0, and 24567 are legal INTEGERs, but 3.0 and 25,000 are not legal INTEGERs. The range of INTEGER values is dependent on your computer system, but most 16-bit micros allow INTEGER values between -32768 and 32767, while bigger 32-bit machines allow values between -2147483648 and 2147483647. These strange values arise from the way that INTEGERs are stored in the computer, 32767 being $2^{15} - 1$ and 2147483647 being $2^{31} - 1$. Thus, using 16-bit INTEGERs, 25000 + 25000 already causes **overflow**, since the sum is too large to be represented as an INTEGER. Overflow should be caught by Modula–2 and reported as a run-time error. This provides you with a way to experimentally determine the size of the INTEGERs on your system: Write a module that reads two INTEGERs and writes out their sum. By entering larger and larger values, you can determine when overflow occurs on your system. An alternative and more exact method is to use the built-in functions MIN and MAX that should be standard with your compiler. MAX and MIN, given types, respond with the largest and smallest values, respectively, of that type. Thus:

```
WriteInt(MAX(INTEGER), 12);
WriteInt(MIN(INTEGER), 12);
```

is the heart of a module that will write out the limits of the INTEGER type on your system. We leave the details of such a module to the reader with the following remarks: The 12 in the WriteInt simply tells the system to write its result in 12 columns. You should be aware that Wirth has added MAX and MIN in the third edition of his definition of Modula-2 and, hence, they may not be found in all current Modula–2 compilers. If they are not present in your Modula-2, it is no great loss. Although they are handy for the purpose at hand, they are certainly not critical to the development that follows.

Operations on INTEGERs

The operations on INTEGERs include addition, subtraction, multiplication, and division. The first three of these are denoted, respectively, by +, -, and *, and behave completely as expected. That is:

23	+	18	is	41	-34	+	7	is	27
23	-	18	is	5	-34	-	7	is	-41
23	*	18	is	414	-34	*	7	is	-238

INTEGER division is denoted by DIV, and, as mentioned in Chapter 2, gives whole results. That is, 7 DIV 3 is 2, 17 DIV 5 is 3, -17 DIV 5 is -3, and 2 DIV 7 is 3. INTEGER division may seem peculiar, and it is important to note that there is also a REAL division, discussed below, that gives fractional results. However, there are instances where INTEGER division is exactly what is needed. For example, see Exercises 2.3, 2.4, and 6.8 to 6.12.

Obviously, something is lost in an INTEGER division such as

```
Quot := 7 DIV 3;
```

What is lost is traditionally called the **remainder**. The remainder can be recovered with the INTEGER operator, MOD, as follows:

```
Rem := 7 MOD 3;
```

The expression

```
X MOD Y
```

represents the remainder when X is divided by Y. In Modula-2, both X and Y must be positive for X MOD Y to be defined. For example, 7 MOD 3 is 1, 8 MOD 3 is 2, and 9 MOD 3 is 0. The MOD operator gets its name from the term **modulus**, which is a synonym for remainder.

Assignment is another operation that can be applied to INTEGERs. Recall that := is the assignment operator and that an assignment has the form

```
variable := expression
```

For example, assuming that all the variables are INTEGER identifiers, the following are all valid assignments:

```
Count := 0;
Excess := Total - Loss;
FullCases := NumBottles DIV 24;
TotalHt := 12*Feet + Inches;
```

For these assignments to make sense, we must also assume that all the variables on the right-hand sides already have values. That is, it is ridiculous to express Excess as the difference of Total and Loss, unless Total and Loss themselves have meaningful values. These variables could have received values through previous assignments or via ReadInt discussed below.

It is also important to realize that Excess does not need a value before the assignment discussed above. The reason is that Excess *receives* a value from the assignment, but does not *participate* in the evaluation of the expression. All variables on the right-hand side of an assignment participate in the evaluation of the expression and, hence, must have values before the assignment.

Consider the following assignment:

```
Count := Count + 1;
```

Here, Count appears on both sides of the assignment operator. This is legal and very useful. The effect is to take the current value of Count, increment it by 1, and store the new value back in Count. If Count is 17 before execution of the statement, then Count is 18 after execution. Note that since Count appears on the right-hand side, it participates in the evaluation of the expression and must have a value before the assignment. Also, as the variable on the left-hand side of the assignment, Count receives the value of the expression. The moral of this example is that := should *not* be read as "equals," because "Count equals Count plus one" is nonsense. Rather, := should be read as "is assigned" or "becomes," so that the statement is read as "Count is assigned (the value) Count plus one" or "Count becomes Count plus one."

Parentheses can be used in expressions to provide clarity and to force the evaluation that you intend. For example:

```
TotalHtIns := 12 * (Feet + Inches);
```

and

```
TotalHtIns := (12 * Feet) + Inches;
```

are clearly different. Indeed, assuming that Feet has the value 5 and Inches has the value 9, these expressions assign the values 168 and 69, respectively, to TotalHtIns. Apparently, from the identifiers used, the second expression is the correct one in this case.

There are conventions that apply in the absence of parentheses to govern the order of evaluation of expressions. Fortunately, these conventions are the same as the conven-

tions of elementary mathematics and are known as **precedence rules**:
 In the absence of parentheses:

1. Multiplicative operators (multiplication, division, and remaindering) are done
   before additive operators (addition and subtraction).
2. Within any type of operator (multiplicative or additive), evaluation is done from the
   left to the right.

Thus, for example, in

```
TotalHtIns := 12 * Feet + Inches;
```

the multiplication is done first. Hence, this is equivalent to the second assignment
above. As a more complex example, we see that in

```
a := b + c - d * e DIV f;
```

we first do the multiplicative operators from the left. We multiply d by e and then divide
this result by f. Then we do the additive operators from the left. We add b and c and
then subtract from that sum the result of our earlier division. Thus, the above is
equivalent to the expression

```
a := ((b + c) - ((d * e) DIV f));
```

While equivalent, neither of the previous two statements is very clear or readable. The
first is difficult to understand because it has no parentheses, and the second is cluttered
with them. We suggest that the preferable form of the statement is

```
a := (b + c) - (d * e DIV f);
```

The reader should remember that parentheses can be used to provide clarity to
expressions and should not strive to omit every possible parenthesis. Nor should the
reader overuse parentheses. As in all things, moderation is best.

Input and Output with INTEGERs

As mentioned in Chapter 2, there is a standard library, InOut, that contains ReadInt
and WriteInt. Recall that to import these functions into your module, you add the line

```
FROM InOut IMPORT WriteInt, ReadInt;
```

just after the MODULE heading.
 ReadInt expects only one argument; namely, the identifier that you want to receive
a value in the read. For example:

```
ReadInt(Temp);
```

will halt the execution of your program and allow you to enter an INTEGER from the keyboard. When you type the return key, the system will assign the value you entered to the variable named in the `ReadInt` and resume execution. Remember that each such read should be preceded by a `WriteString` (discussed below) to provide the user with a prompt for the input.

`WriteInt` expects two arguments: the variable whose value you want written and the number of columns that you want that value written in. For example:

```
WriteInt(Temp, 3);
WriteInt(Temp, 10);
```

tell the system to write the value of `Temp` in 3 and 10 columns, respectively. If the value of `Temp` is 73, then these statements will advance the cursor 3 and 10 positions on the screen while printing " 73" and "   73", respectively. If more columns are given than are needed, the value will be right-justified in the columns. A useful variant of the field width is to use zero:

```
WriteInt(Temp, 0);
```

This does not mean "write the value of Temp in zero columns," but rather "write the value of `Temp` in the minimum number of columns necessary." Thus, if Temp is 73 as indicated, two columns will be used to display "73". On the other hand, if `Temp` is 5043, four columns will be used to display the value of `Temp`. It is important to note that you must supply some field width with every `WriteInt`. That is:

```
WriteInt(Temp);        (* ERROR. Field Width must be supplied. *)
```

is invalid and will be flagged by the compiler.

The CARDINAL Type

The CARDINALs are whole numbers that are positive or zero, but never negative. Thus, 0, 4375, and 40000 are legal CARDINALs. Like INTEGERs, CARDINALs never contain decimal points or commas, so 3.0 and 25,000 are not legal CARDINALs. In many situations, such as counting, negative numbers cannot arise, so CARDINALs are the appropriate type to use. The advantage of CARDINALs over INTEGERs is that since no sign needs to be stored with CARDINALs, their range is about twice that of positive INTEGERs. For example, the normal limits of CARDINALs are 0 to 65535 (instead of 32767) on 16-bit machines and 0 to 4294967295 (instead of 2147483647) on 32-bit machines. Again, the function `MAX` can be used to report the largest CARDINAL on your system. The statement

```
WriteCard(MAX(CARDINAL), 12);
```

will accomplish this. Note that `MAX`, when applied to CARDINAL, returns the largest CARDINAL value and is written with `WriteCard`, not `WriteInt`.

Operations on CARDINALs

The operations on CARDINALs are basically the same as those for INTEGERs. The operators +, -, *, `DIV`, and `MOD`, as discussed above, can all also be applied to CARDINALs. However, some care must be exercised with subtraction, since the expression

```
X - Y
```

is not a CARDINAL if `Y` is larger than `X`. CARDINALs should be used only where negative values cannot occur. INTEGERs should be used if negative results are possible.

Assignment is, of course, permitted with CARDINAL variables and takes the same form as before:

```
variable := expression;
```

The only difference is that the expression must return a CARDINAL value. For example, if `NumStudents` is a CARDINAL variable, then the following are valid assignments (unless overflow occurs on the second one):

```
NumStudents := 0;
NumStudents := NumStudents + 1;
```

Note that the constants 0 and 1 (and 17 and 2345) can be used as either INTEGER or CARDINAL constants. That is, if `Count` is an INTEGER and `NumStudents` is a CARDINAL, then both

```
NumStudents := NumStudents + 1;
Count := Count +1;
```

are valid assignments. However:

```
Total := Count + NumStudents;          (* ERROR. Type Mixing. *)
```

is invalid whatever the type of `Total`, since `Count` and `NumStudents` are of different types. As we shall see below, there is a way to force a type conversion so that the above sum can be computed. But the reader must keep in mind that the simple expression given above will not work.

Input and Output with CARDINALs

As you would guess, the library module `InOut` also contains the two functions `WriteCard` and `ReadCard`. They can be imported to your module and used just like `WriteInt` and `ReadInt`. The details are therefore omitted.

The REAL type

REAL numbers contain a decimal point. In Modula-2, REALs must have a digit to the left of the decimal point and never contain a comma. Thus:

```
3        -- All INVALID as REALs --
.5
25,000.0
```

are all examples of **invalid** REALs. The following are examples of valid REALs:

```
3.
3.0
0.5
25000.0
4894000000.0
0.000003418
```

As you recall (dimly?) from junior-high-school mathematics, large numbers like 4,894,000,000.0 or small numbers like 0.000003418 can be written more compactly in what is called **scientific notation**. For example, the above values can be written as

4.894×10^9

3.418×10^{-6}

or in any of the following equivalent forms:

4894.0×10^6

0.4894×10^{10}

$3418. \times 10^{-9}$

0.3418×10^{-5}

Most computer languages use a simplifed form of scientific notation for compact representation of REAL numbers. First, note that the base of the exponent is always 10. If we remember this, there is no reason to keep writing it down. That is, if we have the fractional part (say 0.3418) and the exponent (say -5), we can recover our number (0.3418 $\times$ 10⁻⁵). This leads to the following Modula-2 representations for our two REALs:

```
          0.3418 E -5
or        3.418 E -6
or        3418. E -9

          4.894 E 9
or        0.4894 E 10
or        4894.0 E 6
```

where the E separates the fractional part from the "E"xponent of 10.

The number of significant digits of precision for REALs is, of course, system dependent, and you will need to check the manuals for your installation or use MAX and MIN to determine the limitations of your REAL type.

Operations on REALs

The operations that can be applied to REALs include the normal arithmetic operations of addition, subtraction, multiplication, and division. These are denoted, respectively, by +, -, *, and /. The first three operate completely as expected and are not discussed further. REAL division is the *real* division operator that you expected all along:

13. / 5. is 2.6
-3. / 8. is -0.375
0.0 / 3.14 is 0.0
21.0 / 7.0 is 3.0

As long as you remember to write any REAL constants with a decimal point, assignment works with REALs as expected. Thus, if Length is a REAL variable and you want to halve it, you can write

```
Length := Length / 2.0;        (* OK *)
```

or

```
Length := Length / 2.;         (* OK *)
```

Please note that

```
Length := Length / 2;          (* ERROR *)
```

or

```
Length := Length DIV 2;        (* ERROR *)
```

or

```
Length := Length DIV 2.0;      (* ERROR *)
```

will all be flagged as errors. In the first case, you are mixing the INTEGER constant 2 with the REAL division operator. In the second and third examples, the INTEGER DIV operator is being used with one or two REAL operands. No type mixing of this kind is allowed in Modula-2.

Precedence among the REAL operators is the same as discussed previously for INTEGER operators: The multiplicative operators * and / are done before the additive operators + and -, and within either level, evaluation is from the left to the right. Remember to use parentheses to provide clarity to your expressions. For example, the algebraic expressions

$$x = \frac{-b + \sqrt{b^2 - 4ac}}{2a} \qquad C = \frac{5}{9}(F\text{-}32)$$

can be expressed in Modula–2 (assuming all variables are REAL) as:

```
x := (-b + sqrt(b * b - 4.0 * a * c)) /( 2.0 * a);
```

and

```
Celsius := 5.0/9.0 * (Fahr - 32.0);
```

Here `sqrt`, pronounced "squirt," is the square-root function provided by Modula-2. This and other mathematical functions can be imported from the standard module `MathLib0`, which is discussed in detail in Chapter 7 and is summarized in Appendix A. Also note that Modula-2 has no built-in exponentiation (powering) operator, so we simply express b^2 as `b*b`. Many beginners are astonished to learn that such a simple (and useful) operator as exponentiation was omitted from Modula-2. It is, however, not a serious omission, since we can easily write our own exponentiation operation, and we shall learn how to do so in Chapter 7.

Input and Output with REALs

REAL I/O is done, as you would guess, with `ReadReal` and `WriteReal`, respectively. Notice that these functions must be imported from the library module `RealInOut`, rather than the module `InOut` where the INTEGER and CARDINAL I/O functions are found. For example, in a program that needed to do input and output on all the numeric types you could write

```
FROM InOut IMPORT WriteInt, ReadInt, WriteCard, ReadCard;
FROM RealInOut IMPORT WriteReal, ReadReal;
```

The order of these importations is not important. Either statement could be listed first, and the actual procedures to be imported can be listed in any order.

    `ReadReal` expects one argument, the REAL variable that you want a value to be assigned to. For example:

```
ReadReal(Area);
```

stops execution and allows you to enter a value into the REAL variable `Area`. As always, this read should be preceded by a prompt message so that the user of the program knows what type of value to enter.

    `WriteReal`, like the other writes, expects two arguments, the REAL variable whose value you want written and the number of columns that you want that value written in. For example:

```
WriteReal(Area, 20);
```

writes the value of Area in 20 columns, filling from the left with blanks if 20 columns are not needed. Area will be expressed in E notation, so 212.0 will be written (depending on the precision of your system) as

2.120000 E +002

In Chapter 7, we will learn how to force this value to print as 212.0.

The Need for INTEGERs, CARDINALs, and REALs

Earlier, we raised the question of why a language should have so many numeric types. After all, doesn't the REAL type include both INTEGERs and CARDINALs? Our answer—an unequivocal "Yes and No!"—deserves further explanation.

There are languages (BASIC is the best known example) where the only numeric type that most users are aware of is the REAL type. However, there are several disadvantages to using REALs exclusively. Some of these are:

1. REALs require more memory than do INTEGERs or CARDINALs.
2. REAL arithmetic is slower than INTEGER or CARDINAL arithmetic.
3. REAL arithmetic is not exact; INTEGER and CARDINAL arithmetic is.

It is common for the REAL 17.0 to occupy up to 8 bytes of storage, compared to the 2 to 4 bytes needed for 17 as a CARDINAL. Thus, the REAL 17.0 usually requires two to four times as much space as the CARDINAL 17. The REAL requires extra space because of the precision involved and the need to store REALs as a fractional part and an exponent. Thus, if you have 1000 test scores (whole numbers in the range 0 to 100) to store, the memory saved by using the type CARDINAL over the type REAL can be substantial.

Because of the complex way that REALs are stored, REAL arithmetic must be executed with completely different computer instructions than those used for INTEGER and CARDINAL arithmetic. That is:

X + Y

is evaluated differently if X and Y are REAL than if X and Y are, say, CARDINAL. Even on today's very-high-speed computers, REAL arithmetic is slower than the corresponding INTEGER or CARDINAL arithmetic.

However, the foremost reason for types other than the REAL type is that REAL arithmetic is inherently inexact, involving so-called **roundoff** errors. For example, using REALs to verify that the solution of a certain equation is 6.0, you should not be surprised if you get 5.99999999999, or even 6.00000000001. On the other hand, INTEGER and CARDINAL calculations, within their ranges, are always exact.

Put positively, INTEGERs and CARDINALs use less memory than REALs, are faster than REALs, and are exact (unless overflow occurs). Hopefully, this provides an adequate explanation of why Modula-2 has numeric types other than REALs. The alert reader may now ask, "Why do we need both INTEGERs and CARDINALs?" They are, after all, very similar. Indeed, languages like Pascal and FORTRAN have only the INTEGER and REAL numeric types, so clearly we could survive without the CARDINAL type. It is provided in Modula-2 to provide the user greater flexibility. In many applications, only nonnegative whole numbers are possible, and, as noted, with the CARDINAL type, one obtains twice the range of INTEGERs. Furthermore, with CARDINALs, should the result of a subtraction that is supposed to be nonnegative actually turn out to be negative, then a run-time error will result. While obtaining run-time errors is not our goal, it is better to get the error than to have the algorithm continue, as it would with the INTEGER type, and produce nonsensical results. Thus, the CARDINAL type provides an extra degree of protection in those cases where negative values are not supposed to arise.

For various reasons, the reader needs to take the time to understand the distinctions between the three numeric types in Modula-2. One reason, of course, is to be able to choose the appropriate type in a given application. Another reason is to be able to avoid illegal mixed-type expressions such as `Length/2` where `Length` is a REAL identifier. Finally, there are many built-in functions in Modula-2, and from a description of their actions, you should know the type of the result that the function computes for you. For example, we have already mentioned the `sqrt` function, which takes square roots. It should be obvious that `sqrt(Length)` returns a REAL value. There is a less well-known built-in function, `SIZE`, that returns the number of bytes used to store a particular variable. For example, if `Count` is an INTEGER variable, then `SIZE(Count)` will probably be 2 or 4 on your system. Since the size can never be negative or fractional, it should be obvious that `SIZE` returns a CARDINAL value. The user needs to be familiar with all three numeric types so that simple type mismatches involving functional expressions can be avoided.

Implementation of LONG Types Possible

There may actually be additional numeric types in your Modula-2 system. To provide extra precision, a Modula-2 compiler may also provide the so-called LONG types, LONGINT and LONGREAL. See the details of your system's documentation, or run an experimental module to determine whether or not they are present in your system. If present, they provide for extended precision when needed in calculations. They will, however, require extra memory for storage, and arithmetic operations will be some-what slower than for the regular types. We will not use the LONG types in this text.

CHARACTER DATA TYPES

The CHAR Type

The CHAR type is for single characters. Characters in Modula-2 are enclosed in single (') or double (") quotation marks. For example, the following are constants of type CHAR:

```
'A'
"A"
"a"
```

" "	a blank or space
' . '	the period
" $ "	the dollar sign
" ' "	the single quote
' " '	the double quote

A CHAR is a single character, so sequences of characters like "Mommy!" are *not* valid CHAR constants. Such sequences are strings and are discussed later.

Operations on CHARs

One of the operations that you can perform on CHARs is assignment. Thus, if Ch is an identifier of type CHAR, then the following is legal:

```
Ch := "Q";
```

Indeed, Modula-2 is always happy with an assignment when the type of the expression on the right matches the type of the identifier on the left. See if you agree with our assessment of the validity of the following three assignment statements:

```
Ch := Q;    (* ERROR unless Q is an identifier of type CHAR.  *)
Ch := '3';  (* OK, '3' is a fine character in Modula-2.        *)
Ch := 3;    (* ERROR! Type mismatch since 3 is an INTEGER.     *)
```

Another operation on CHARs is the CAP function, which makes a CHAR into uppercase. For example, if Ch has the value 'e', then the statement

```
Ch := CAP(Ch);
```

assigns the value 'E' to Ch. If Ch had already been uppercase, then the statement would have no effect on Ch.

There is no standard character set for use on computers. Fortunately, however, there is a standard set for use in Modula-2. It is the ASCII set, as defined by the American Standard Code for Information Interchange. This is a set of 128 characters including the letters A to Z, as well as a to z, the digits 0 to 9, and dozens of special symbols such as +, %, (,), and even characters that *ring the bell*. The characters are numbered from 0 to 127, as shown in Table 4.1. To find a character's ASCII code, add the row and column numbers determined by the character. For example, from the table we see that the ASCII code for A is 65 (64 + 1), while the ASCII code for Z is 90 (80 + 10).

Do not be concerned with the first 30 or so characters in Table 4.1. They are special control characters, many from the days of teletype transmissions, that we do not need to be concerned with in this book. Do note, however, that 32 is the ASCII code for the very useful blank character: ' '. Blank is a legitimate character, just like zero is a legitimate number.

ORD is the function that, when given a character, returns its ASCII code, a CARDI-NAL number. For example, ORD ('A') is 65 and ORD('a') is 97. ORD gets its name from the fact that it returns the ordinal (counting) position of the character in the ASCII

Table 4.1: The ASCII Character Set

	0	16	32	48	64	80	96	112
0	nul	dle		0	@	P	`	p
1	soh	dc1	!	1	A	Q	a	q
2	stx	dc2	"	2	B	R	b	r
3	etx	dc3	#	3	C	S	c	s
4	eot	dc4	$	4	D	T	d	t
5	enq	nak	%	5	E	U	e	u
6	ack	syn	&	6	F	V	f	v
7	bel	etb	'	7	G	W	g	w
8	bs	can	(	8	H	X	h	x
9	ht	em	)	9	I	Y	i	y
10	lf	sub	*	:	J	Z	j	z
11	vt	esc	+	;	K	[	k	{
12	ff	fs	,	<	L	\	l	|
13	cr	gs	-	=	M	]	m	}
14	so	rs	.	>	N	^	n	~
15	si	us	/	?	O	..	o	del

set. Note that, as is often the case with computers, ORD starts counting at zero instead of one. In Chapter 8, we will see that ORD is more general than we have indicated here. We will introduce user-defined types and learn that ORD can also be used with them.

CHR is an inverse of ORD. By this, we mean that CHR undoes what ORD does. That is, CHR takes a CARDINAL in the range 0 to 127 and returns the CHARacter that has that value as its ASCII code. For example, CHR(65) is 'A' and CHR(43) is '+'. Another way to say that ORD and CHR are inverses is to note that if Ch is a CHAR variable with any value, then

```
Ch := CHR(ORD(Ch));
```

reassigns Ch its old value. Likewise, if K is a CARDINAL in the range 0 to 127, then

```
K := ORD(CHR(K));
```

leaves the value of K unchanged.

To see an application of ORD and CHR, note that in Table 4.1 there is a constant difference of 32 between the ASCII values of any lowercase letter and its corresponding uppercase equivalent. That is, picking a letter such as m at random, we verify that ORD('m') - ORD('M') equals 109 - 77, or finally, 32. We can use this fact to convert a letter from uppercase to lowercase. Check that if Ch is an uppercase letter, then

```
Ch := CHR(ORD(Ch) + 32);
```

converts Ch to its lowercase equivalent. To make sure that you understand this last statement, we leave it to you to explain why the following is not equivalent:

```
Ch := CHR(ORD(Ch)) + 32;          (* This is an ERROR. Why? *)
```

Likewise, by subtracting 32 from an ASCII value, we can convert a lowercase letter to its uppercase equivalent. Recall that we can also use CAP as discussed above to do this latter conversion. There is, however, no built-in LOWER function, so we need our ORD and CHR trick for this operation.

One last remark about our operation for converting from uppercase to lowercase. The value 32 in the expression

```
Ch := CHR(ORD(Ch) + 32));
```

is what is called a **magic number**. In the statement, the value 32 appears with no justification, and if you were to forget our explanation, the statement would be most mysterious. That is one problem with the use of magic numbers. They can make programs very difficult to understand. Another problem is that they make a program difficult to modify or maintain. For example, suppose that the above line is in a big program that monitors the weather in major American cities. Since we commonly use the Fahrenheit system, the magic number 32 might also be used in another context within the same program. Imagine the nightmare that could ensue if the decision were made to change the program to the Celsius scale and, therefore, the programmer was ordered to change all 32s in the program to 0s. Suddenly, uppercase/lowercase conversion ceases to work, and it may be a long time before you discover that a confusion among magic numbers was the cause of the problem.

The moral of this lesson is that we should avoid the use of magic numbers whenever possible, and we have more to say about this in the section on CONSTants below. For now, we simply note that the use of a CARDINAL variable, DownShift, improves the readability and integrity of our program. Again, assume that Ch is currently an uppercase letter:

```
DownShift := ORD('a') - ORD('A'); (* Distance from upper to  *)
Ch := CHR(ORD(Ch) + DownShift);   (*lower case is fixed.     *)
```

Note that by using the expression ORD('a') - ORD('A'), we let the computer calculate the magic number for us. We don't even have to remember that particular value; we humans have enough other things to try to remember.

Input and Output with CHARs

Reading and writing single CHARs are done with Read and Write which must be imported from the module InOut. That is, if Ch is an identifier of type CHAR, then

```
Read(Ch);
```

stops execution until you enter a CHAR from the keyboard and then stores that CHARacter in Ch. Likewise:

```
Write(Ch);
```

writes the CHARacter value of `Ch`. Note that `Write` does not need, or accept, a second argument to tell it how many columns to use in writing a CHARacter, but rather always writes a single CHARacter in a single column.

There is also a special `WriteLn` procedure in `InOut` that is essentially the equivalent of the carriage-return key on an electric typewriter. That is:

```
WriteLn;
```

returns the cursor to the beginning of the next line. For example, can you determine the output of the following trivial module?

```
MODULE Trivial;
FROM InOut IMPORT Write, WriteLn;
VAR A, B, C : CHAR;
BEGIN
    A := 'a';
    B := 'b';
    C := 'c';
    Write(A);
    Write(B);
    WriteLn;
    Write(C);
    WriteLn;
    WriteLn;
    Write(C);
    Write(B);
    Write(A)
END Trivial.
```

We hope you agree that the output of `Trivial` will be

```
ab
c

cba
```

Note that multiple `WriteLn`s can be used to provide blank lines in the output. Use such techniques to make the output of your modules clear and readable. Also, we normally write one Modula-2 statement per line, but when they are short and associated with each other, it is permissible to write more than one statement per line. Indeed, the following body for our module would be quite acceptable Modula-2 style:

```
A := 'a'; B := 'b'; C := 'c';
Write(A); Write(B); WriteLn;
Write(C); WriteLn;
WriteLn;
Write(C); Write(B); Write(A)
```

The String Type

A **string** is simply a sequence of zero or more characters. Strings in Modula-2 are enclosed in single or double quotation marks:

```
"This is a string of STRANGE characters: $ % & * ! @ #"
'This is a string, too.'
```

The single and double quotation marks are called the string **delimiters**. If the string contains a single (double) quotation mark, then we must use the double (single) quotation mark as the delimiter:

```
"You can't delimit this string with single quotes."
'This "string" cannot be delimited with double quotes.'
```

   Unfortunately, strings are not first-class citizens in Modula-2. There is, in fact, no built-in string type, which explains why *string* has not been capitalized. There are, however, standard procedures in library modules that you can import and use for reading and writing strings. Since strings are so useful for names, addresses, etc., we indicate briefly at this point how to declare string identifiers and how to read, write, and assign such identifiers. In later chapters, we greatly extend our capabilities with strings.
   String is not a built-in type in Modula-2 because it is derivable from the CHARacter type. Recall that a string is simply a sequence of characters. To denote a sequence in Modula–2, we use the keyword ARRAY. Much more will be said about arrays in Chapter 10. For now, the reader should accept the following as a black-box declaration of the string variables Name and Address:

```
VAR  Name, Address : ARRAY[0..29] OF CHAR;        (* Strings! *)
```

The 0..29 indicates that Name and Address can contain up to 30 (again, counting starts at zero) characters. You can replace the 29 in this black box with whatever value is appropriate in your given application. For example, to declare a variable PhoneNum, we might write

```
VAR PhoneNum : ARRAY[0..11] OF CHAR;       (* Another String.  *)
```

since telephone numbers commonly consist of 12 characters (708-234-3100). Observe that even though we call it a number, a PhoneNum is a string, because it contains the character - as well as digits. Of course, we could store a telephone number as the (long) integer 7082343100, and how we store it should depend on what we want to do with it. If we just want to display it, the string 708-234-3100 is a lot more readable for humans. Also, it is difficult to think of any arithmetic operations to perform on telephone numbers. Indeed, when was the last time you averaged a list of telephone numbers?

Operations on Strings

The simplest operation on strings is assignment. If `Name` and `Address` are string variables, then we can assign them values with

```
Name := "Niklaus Wirth";
Address := '128 Bergstrasse';
```

The only word of warning in such assignments is that the literal string on the right-hand side must not exceed the maximum length of the string identifier. For example, if `Name` is declared, as above, as a string of at most 30 characters, then the following is in error:

```
Name := "Eunice McKinley Rumplestiltskin";
                                (* ERROR, too long. *)
```

Other operations on strings will be discussed in Chapter 14.

Input and Output with Strings

We have already seen the `WriteString` operation from the standard library module `InOut`. `WriteString` is frequently used with a literal string to provide a prompt for some kind of read. For example, if `Age` is a CARDINAL identifier, we might well prompt the user to enter his or her age with

```
WriteString("Please enter your true age: ");
ReadCard(Age);
WriteLn;
```

We would like the reader to consider some of the fussy details of the above segment. Note the blanks at the end of the literal string, but within the quotes. Why is at least one blank needed there? What is the `WriteLn` at the end of the segment for? Hint: What happens to the next prompting message if you forget the `WriteLn`? The point is that these fussy details are important, because omitting them makes the execution of your program look very unprofessional.

 `WriteString` can also be used with a variable. For example, if `Winner` is a string variable that has somehow been assigned a value—say `"Frank"`—then the segment

```
WriteString("Congratulations, ");
WriteString(Winner);
WriteString("! You are the winner.");
WriteLn;
```

prints the message:

```
Congratulations, Frank! You are the winner.
```

Again, please note how the comma, exclamation point, and spacing are achieved by careful attention to details.

There is, as you would guess, also a ReadString procedure in the Module InOut. Its behavior, however, is a little surprising, since ReadString reads only one word. That is, a blank or carriage return terminates the value read in. For example, if you have a string variable Name and you try to type "Niklaus Wirth" when the system pauses at

```
ReadString(Name);
```

then Name will have the value "Niklaus". Therefore, we shall have to be very careful with ReadString from InOut. For example, to enter a name we could use something like

```
WriteString('Please enter your name in the form "First Last".');
WriteLn;
WriteString("Do not enter any middle initial or middle name.");
WriteLn;
ReadString(First);
Read(Ch); Write(Ch);                    (* Read and echo the blank. *)
ReadString(Last);
WriteLn;
```

where First and Last are string variables of an appropriate length and Ch is a CHAR variable. ReadString echoes what you type: The characters you type at the keyboard are also printed to the screen. Read, on the other hand, does not echo the character typed; therefore, to see the blank, it is necessary to explicitly echo it to the screen with a Write. We cannot give you any good reason for these dissimilar behaviors—that's just the way it is. Actually, since the reads and writes are not part of the language, but are supplied in external libraries, the reader should be cautioned that the reads may not behave in exactly the same manner in all Modula-2s. This is unfortunate, and a bothersome detail, but not of great import to the development that follows.

Of course, the above segment is not bulletproof, because users do not always read or follow instructions. However, it will do for now. In the next chapter, we will learn how to handle a name, no matter what its form might be.

IDENTIFIER DECLARATIONS

Every identifier used in Modula-2 must be declared to be of some type. The reason for this is so that the system can help you find your typing errors and detect type mismatches for you. For now, all identifiers are declared in the VAR section of the program. They may be declared in any order. For example, to declare NumCredits, GPA (Grade Point Average), Salary, Name, Sex, and Age, we might write

```
VAR    NumCredits : CARDINAL;
       GPA, Salary : REAL;
       Name : ARRAY [0..29] OF CHAR;
       Sex : CHAR;
       Age : CARDINAL;
```

or equivalently

```
VAR    Salary, GPA : REAL;
       NumCredits, Age : CARDINAL;
       Sex : CHAR;
       Name : ARRAY [0..29] OF CHAR;
```

or equivalently

```
VAR    Name          : ARRAY [0..29] OF CHAR; (* String. *)
       Sex           : CHAR;
       Age           : CARDINAL;
       NumCredits    : CARDINAL;
       Salary        : REAL;
       GPA           : REAL;
```

Obviously, the last is the easiest to read, but the most tedious to enter. We believe that the extra effort is worth it and will attempt to present our variable-declaration lists in this form.

CONSTANTS

We have already seen enough examples to notice that special constant values such as

212	boiling point of water in the Fahrenheit scale
32	freezing point of water—or difference between lowercase and uppercase ASCII values of letters
3.14159	pi
2.54	number of centimeters in one inch

will appear frequently in programs. It is considered poor programming style to clutter your programs with these magic numbers. They are called magic numbers because if you don't happen to recall that there are 2.54 centimeters per inch, the use of 2.54 without comment can make for a very mysterious program.

One way to avoid magic numbers was discussed earlier: Declare an extra identifier, assign that identifier the approriate value at the beginning of the module, and then use the identifier instead of the magic value. For example, consider the following outline:

```
VAR    Pi         : REAL;
       Area       : REAL;
       Radius     : REAL;
BEGIN
  Pi := 3.14159;
  ...
  Area := Pi * Radius *Radius;    (* OK, assuming that Radius
                                     already has a value. *)
  ...
```

```
  Pi := 0.0;                       (* Legal, but DANGEROUS to further
                                       calculations with Pi. *)

  ...
END ...
```

Modula-2 provides a better way, known as CONSTants. Constants look like identifiers, but CONSTants are given initial values that may not change during the execution of the module. This means that you can be assured that your CONSTant does not accidentally get blown away. For example, the above segment using CONSTants would be

```
CONST  Pi = 3.14159;
VAR    Area   : REAL;
       Radius : REAL;
BEGIN
  ...
  Area := Pi * Radius *Radius;     (* OK, assuming that Radius
                                       already has a value.  *)

  ...
  Pi := 0.0;                       (* ERROR, a constant cannot
                                       be assigned a value. *)

  ...
  END ...
```

In particular, the assignment of a value to the CONSTant Pi will be flagged as an error by the compiler. Hence, CONSTants help to make your programs readable and secure. They also make programs easier to maintain. For example, if you decide that you need to use a better approximation of Pi, you need only change the CONSTant declaration to

```
CONST Pi = 3.141592653589793;
```

and recompile your module. If you had used the magic number 3.14159 throughout your program, you would have to find them all and change them all to the new value of Pi. It is easy to miss one or more occurrences of a magic number, leading to a very buggy program. Also, as discussed earlier, if you have two magic numbers both equal to 32, it can be difficult to change only the appropriate occurrences of one of them. But if we have two CONSTants:

```
CONST FreezePoint = 32;             (* Fahrenheit freezing point
                                         of water. *)

      DownShift   = 32;  (* Distance lowercase to uppercase. *)
```

then the program is easy to understand and modify if necessary.

Traditionally, CONSTant declarations come just before the VAR declarations, but these can come in any order. Also note the syntax whereby the identifier and the constant value are separated by an =, not a :=. This is because the CONSTant is truly equal to the given value.

PROBLEM SOLVING: AN EXAMPLE

If you were 5 feet 10 inches tall and lived in Europe (or almost anywhere else in the world, for that matter), you would be 178 centimeters tall. Let us write a module that will convert a height from the English system (feet and inches) to the metric system (centimeters). This is a very simple problem, but let us use it to illustrate an approach to problem solving that will prove very useful when more difficult problems arise. We need to determine

1. What will be input to the module
2. What should be output by the module
3. An algorithm to compute the output from the input

By deciding what the input will be, we do not mean to decide that the input will be the specific values 5 (feet) and 10 (inches). The actual values will, of course, be determined by the user of the program and cannot be known in advance. What is meant is to determine that the input will consist of two values representing the user's height in *feet* and *inches*. In other words, we see that we need two numeric identifiers, Feet and Inches. Are these REAL or CARDINAL? (why not INTEGER?) We will use the REAL type for illustration and to permit very precise people to enter their height as 5 feet 9.75 inches. But the type CARDINAL would also be reasonable in this case, since people do, in fact, usually round their height to the nearest whole inch.

To illustrate the string type, we will also include the user's name in the input to the module. This was not mentioned in the problem statement, but it will allow us to personalize the output.

The output in this simple case is clearly the height of the given individual in centimeters. Hence, we see that we need an identifier Cms. Since we chose REAL for the inputs, we will also choose REAL as the type for Cms.

More than the answer should be included in the output. For example, the output

```
1.7780E+002
```

is pretty meaningless. Minimal acceptable output would be

```
You are 1.7780E+002 centimeters tall.
```

Much better would be something like

```
John, at 5 feet 10 inches, you are 1.7780E+002 centimeters tall.
```

Often, it is a good idea to echo (repeat) all the input through the output. This makes the operation of the program much clearer. Also, recall that we have promised to show you how to print 1.7780E+002 in the more readable form 177.80 in Chapter 7.

In this case, an algorithm to convert from feet and inches to centimeters is quite simple. Let us consider one possible way to do it. Since we don't know how many centimeters there are in a foot, let's change the user's height completely into inches. Clearly, we can use

```
TotalInches := 12.0 * Feet + Inches;
```

but we see that we will need to declare a new identifier, TotalInches. Then to convert to centimeters, we simply use

```
Cms := CmsPerInch * TotalInches;
```

where CmsPerInch is the constant 2.54.

Many readers are now probably screaming that we don't need the extra identifier, TotalInches, because we can do the entire conversion all at once with

```
Cms := CmsPerInch * (12.0 * Feet + Inches);
```

Other readers may have noticed that we can determine the number of centimeters per foot and solve the problem with two constants:

```
CONST CmsPerInch   = 2.54;
      CmsPerFoot   = 12.0 * CmsPerInch;
...
Cms := CmsPerFoot * Feet + CmsPerInch * Inches;
```

Notice in this last case that we have a CONSTant defined via an expression and in terms of another CONSTant. This is permitted in Modula-2, as long as all the terms in the expression have already been defined.

Observe that even in this trivial case we have developed three ways to express the conversion algorithm. In more difficult problems, there will be dozens of ways to proceed. Your job is to find the simplest, clearest solution that you can. In this case, we like the middle solution best because it requires only one line and doesn't introduce any new identifiers or constants. Keep in mind, however, that trying to use as few identifiers as possible is not our objective. Our objective is clarity, and often auxiliary variables are needed to keep track of intermediate results. A more complex example at the end of this chapter will illustrate that extra identifiers can be very valuable.

The careful reader may have noticed that we have been using the magic number 12.0 throughout our examples. We plead guilty! However, we believe that in this context the number 12.0 is far less mysterious than the number 2.54. That is, nearly everyone knows what 12.0 means in this context, and we do not feel that the clarity of the program is increased by using another CONSTant, InchesPerFoot. On the other hand, 2.54 is not a well-known quantity, and the CONSTant CmsPerInch does add to the clarity of the program.

We should try to make our programs as user-friendly as possible. Without trying to define that overused term, we mention that clearly stating the purpose of the program to the user and providing clear and complete prompting messages are important ways to make the program easy to use and understand.

Finally, putting our discussion in order, we arrive at the following outline for our problem:

State the purpose of the program
Input the user's Name, and height in Feet and Inches
Compute the user's height in Cms using the relationship:

$$Cms \leftarrow 2.54 * (12.0 * Feet + Inches)$$

-- Make 2.54 a constant to avoid a magic number
Output the results with an echoing of the input

This outline is called **pseudo-code**. Pseudo-code is a mixture of English and Modula-2 constructs with which you outline the design of your module. To stress that our outline is not Modula-2, we have even used an arrow ($\leftarrow$) to indicate assignment. From the pseudo-code, it should be a piece of cake to write the actual Modula-2 statements that implement the design. The point is that given a hard problem, the interesting (and difficult) work is in the designing of the module in pseudo-code. The translation into Modula-2 should, with the pseudo-code, be very straightforward.

Murphy has a law related to this: "The sooner you begin actually programming, the longer the whole process will take!" Time spent in planning is time well spent. You should not sit down at the computer and begin composing your program. If the problem is at all complex, you will get lost in the detail and will probably produce, after many false starts, a program that is difficult to understand and therefore difficult to modify or debug. Rather, you should outline your solution in broad steps, providing as much detail as you can for each step. There are no rules for this pseudo-code language, so you can develop yours as you go along. To help you learn pseudo-coding, we will provide many examples in this text, and we urge you to look at them carefully.

Please note that our objective is *not* to learn Modula-2 syntax. After all, Modula-2 has only a few dozen keywords—anyone should be able to learn its syntax. Instead, our goal is problem solving with a computer. Hence, the most creative exercise is in the design of a solution and its expression in pseudo-code. We use Modula-2 to implement our design because of the many rich features of the language. Please do not forget this distinction between the design and implementation phases. With the proper design, the implementation is almost automatic. Without a proper design, no implementation can be successful. Do not try to skip the design phase—learn to pseudo-code as a step in designing your program.

We will never again spend this amount of time on the discussion of a simple problem. However, there are many points that we wanted to make to give the reader some guidance on methods to use when approaching the problems. Listing 4.1 finally displays the module HeightCm that will convert your height to centimeters.

```
MODULE HeightCm;

(* This module converts the user's height given in feet and inches
to the equivalent height in centimeters. To illustrate the REAL
type, we assume that the input will be REALs. To convert the height
to centimeters, we must know that

  one inch equals 2.54 centimeters.                              *)

FROM InOut IMPORT Write, WriteLn, WriteString, ReadString;
```

```
FROM RealInOut IMPORT WriteReal, ReadReal;

CONST CmsPerInch  = 2.54;
      Blank = ' ';

VAR   Name    : ARRAY[0..29] OF CHAR;        (* String. *)
      Feet    : REAL;
      Inches  : REAL;
      Cms     : REAL;

BEGIN    (* Obtain the input. *)
  WriteString("Please enter your first name: ");
  ReadString(Name);
  WriteLn; WriteLn;
  WriteString(Name);
  WriteStrin9 (",please enter your height in feet and inches.");
  WriteLn;
  WriteString("Enter your height in the form 5 10 or 5 10.5  ");
  ReadReal(Feet);
  Write(Blank);  (* Write a blank between the inputs. *)
  ReadReal(Inches);
  WriteLn; WriteLn;

  (* Convert to centimeters. *)
  Cms := CmsPerInch * (12.0 * Feet + Inches);

  (* Output the results in a readable manner. *)
  WriteString(Name);
  WriteString(", at ");
  WriteReal(Feet, 0);
  WriteString(" ft and ");
  WriteReal(Inches, 0);
  WriteString(" in you're ");
  WriteReal(Cms, 0);
  WriteString(" cms tall.")
END HeightCm.
```

Listing 4.1

Sample output from HeightCm would be of the form:

```
Alf, at 3.00E+000 ft & 4.50E+000 in you're 1.0287E+002 cms tall.
```

While the listing for HeightCm should be very easy to read and follow, an explanation for the line

```
Write(Blank);
```

is probably in order. This line is needed between the ReadReals so that a space will appear between the two inputs of the user. That is, if the code is just

```
ReadReal(Feet);
ReadReal(Inches);
```

and the user types the keys 5, space bar, 1, and 0, then 510 appears on the screen, since the space is not part of a legal REAL. With the Write(Blank), the input will appear as 5 10.

CONVERSIONS AMONG NUMERIC TYPES

Suppose we have three quiz scores and are asked to compute their average. It sounds simple enough to add up the scores and divide the sum by three. But suppose the quiz scores are CARDINALs and we want the average to be REAL. After all, for the student with scores of 86, 88, and 95, there is a big distinction between the REAL average 89.66667 and the CARDINAL average 89. But, as we have indicated several times, none of the following are legal if we assume that Quiz1, Quiz2, and Quiz3 are CARDINAL identifiers while Ave is a REAL identifier:

```
Ave := (Quiz1 + Quiz2 + Quiz3) / 3;      (*  Illegal Mismatch! *)
Ave := (Quiz1 + Quiz2 + Quiz3) / 3.0;    (*  Illegal Mismatch! *)
Ave := (Quiz1 + Quiz2 + Quiz3) DIV 3;    (*  Illegal Mismatch! *)
Ave :- (Quiz1 + Quiz2 + Quiz3) DIV 3.0;  (*  Illegal Mismatch! *)
```

The reader should pause to understand why each of the above assignments is illegal in Modula-2. The first two use the REAL divison operator /, but in neither case are both operands REAL. The third attempt computes a CARDINAL result, but then tries to assign it to a REAL identifier. The last attempt fails because it uses the CARDINAL division operator with a REAL operand.

The solution lies in the built-in conversion function FLOAT. FLOAT converts its CARDINAL input to its REAL equivalent. For example, if Count is a CARDINAL identifier with the value 231, then the statement

```
RealCount := FLOAT(Count);
```

assigns the REAL identifier RealCount the value 231.0.

Hence, in our problem with the average, we can write

```
Ave := FLOAT(Quiz1 + Quiz2 + Quiz3) / 3.0;
```

because both operands of the REAL division are now REAL. Note that it is not necessary to write

```
Ave := (FLOAT(Quiz1) + FLOAT(Quiz2) + FLOAT(Quiz3)) / 3.0;
```

which is more tedious to type and less efficient, since it involves three conversions instead of one and REAL additions instead of CARDINAL additions. You should try to keep the number of type conversions in any statement to a minimum.

The TRUNC function provides the conversion from REALs to CARDINALs. It does so by truncating the REAL to its whole part. Thus, TRUNC(17.945) is the CARDINAL 17. We leave it to the reader to argue that

```
WholeX := TRUNC(X + 0.5);
```

rounds X, a positive REAL, to WholeX, the nearest CARDINAL.

Be aware that in some Modula-2s, FLOAT and TRUNC convert REALs to and from INTEGERs instead of CARDINALs. You will need to check your manuals or try a module to see how TRUNC and FLOAT behave on your system.

Conversions between INTEGERs and REALs in Wirth's definition of Modula-2 are done by two functions in the module MathLib0. The function entier (French for *entire*) converts from REAL to INTEGER. The function entier is much like TRUNC; thus, entier(-12.6) is the INTEGER -12. The function real (note the lowercase this time) converts from INTEGER to REAL. Thus, real(-3) is -3.0.

Please remember that TRUNC and FLOAT are built-in (hence, uppercase) and can be used without importation in any program. On the other hand, entier and real must be imported from MathLib0 (zero, not the letter O) with a statement such as

```
FROM MathLib0 IMPORT real, entier;
```

Conversions between INTEGERs and CARDINALs can be accomplished by using specific type transfers. For example, if IntCount is an INTEGER with a nonnegative value and CardCount is a CARDINAL, then their sum can be placed in the CARDINAL variable Total with the statement:

```
Total := CardCount + CARDINAL(IntCount);
```

That is, the expression CARDINAL(IntCount) forces the conversion of its INTEGER input into an equivalent CARDINAL value. Of course, if Total is an INTEGER variable, we could write

```
Total := INTEGER(CardCount) + IntCount;
```

Time spent in planning a program can greatly reduce the need for conversions among numeric types. Using lots of conversions is a sign of a poorly designed program. However, the need for conversions, especially to and from the REAL type, will occasionally arise. Keep this section in mind and return to it when necessary.

EXAMPLE PROGRAM: SONNY TAN

As a conclusion to this chapter, let us consider the following problem:

Sonny Tan recently drove from the windy city of Chicago to the sunny beaches of Miami at a nearly law-abiding 67 mph. The distance driven was 1437 miles. While sitting on the beach, he began playing with his new digital wristwatch and observed that he blinked 7 times per minute and that each blink lasted for 12 hundredths of a second. Sonny realized that each time he had blinked while driving he had driven a short distance while "blind." How many miles did Sonny drive with his eyes closed on his trip from Chicago?

The input to the problem is clear. We are given the distance and speed Sonny drove and the frequency and duration of his blinking. We will make all of these constants (`Distance`, `Speed`, `Frequency`, and `Duration`) in our program to avoid any magic numbers. What are the types of these values? Obviously, the `Duration`, 0.12, is a REAL. The others (1437, 67, and 7) appear to be CARDINALs. Actually, each is an estimate or average and, hence, could easily be made REAL. However, to illustrate type conversions, we will use the CARDINAL type for the three constants `Distance`, `Speed`, and `Frequency`.

We are asked to determine the total number of miles that Sonny drove with his eyes closed. It is possible to write down a one-line assignment statement for the necessary calculation, but it certainly seems more prudent to proceed in a logical, stepwise manner:

First, using the formula *distance equals speed times time,* we can turn this around to find the number of hours that Sonny's trip took:

Time in Hours ← Distance / Speed

where, to indicate that this is pseudo-code instead of Modula–2, we have again used ← to indicate assignment. Now, remembering that the frequency is given *per minute,* we can easily determine the number of blinks that Sonny made on his trip:

Number of Blinks ← Time in Hours * 60 * Frequency

Next, we can determine the amount of time (in seconds) that Sonny had his eyes closed by

Closed Seconds ← Number of Blinks * Duration

Since Sonny's speed is given in miles per hour, we need to convert the time Sonny's eyes were closed to minutes and then to hours:

Closed Hours ← Closed Seconds / 60 /60

Finally, again using *distance equals speed times time*, we can determine the distance that Sonny drove with his eyes closed:

Distance Blind ← Closed Hours * Speed

To make the output clear, we will echo the four constants and also provide some of the intermediate results. To create the need for even more conversions, we will make the number of blinks a CARDINAL, but use REAL for the other intermediate results. The output from our module Sonny, showing that Sonny drove more than 20 miles with his eyes closed, is

```
Sonny drove 1437 miles at 67 mph.
He blinked 7 times per min. Each blink lasted 1.20E-001 sec.
The trip took 2.14E+001 hours and Sonny blinked 9008 times.
He drove 1.08E+003 seconds with his eyes closed.
Sonny drove 2.01E+001 miles with his eyes closed.
```

The translation from our pseudo-code to Modula-2 should be straightforward. However, since we have intentionally mixed CARDINALs and REALs, we will need to use TRUNC and FLOAT to make explicit type conversions. Listing 4.2 shows our complete module Sonny.

```
MODULE Sonny;

(* This module determines the number of miles that Sonny Tan
   drove with his eyes closed on his trip from Chicago to Miami.

The given facts are as follows:

        Distance driven:                  1437 miles
        Speed:                            67 mph
        Number of blinks per minute:      7
        Duration of each blink:           0.12 seconds          *)

FROM InOut IMPORT WriteLn, WriteString, WriteCard;
FROM RealInOut IMPORT WriteReal;

CONST       Distance    = 1437;       (* miles              *)
            Speed       = 67;         (* mph                *)
            Frequency   = 7;          (* blinks per minute  *)
            Duration    = 0.12;       (* seconds            *)

VAR         TimeHrs           : REAL;
            ClosedSecs        : REAL;
            ClosedHrs         : REAL;
            DistanceBlind     : REAL;
            NumBlinks         : CARDINAL;
```

```
BEGIN
  TimeHrs := FLOAT(Distance) / FLOAT(Speed);
  NumBlinks := TRUNC(TimeHrs * FLOAT(60 * Frequency));
  ClosedSecs := FLOAT(NumBlinks) * Duration;
  ClosedHrs := ClosedSecs / 60.0 / 60.0;
  DistanceBlind := ClosedHrs * FLOAT(Speed);

  WriteString("Sonny drove ");
  WriteCard(Distance, 0);
  WriteString(" miles at ");
  WriteCard(Speed, 0);
  WriteString(" mph.");
  WriteLn;

  WriteString("He blinked ");
  WriteCard(Frequency, 0);
  WriteString(" times per min. Each blink lasted ");
  WriteReal(Duration, 0);
  WriteString(" sec.");
  WriteLn;

  WriteString("The trip took ");
  WriteReal(TimeHrs, 0);
  WriteString(" hours and Sonny blinked ");
  WriteCard(NumBlinks, 0);
  WriteString(" times.");
  WriteLn;

  WriteString("He drove ");
  WriteReal(ClosedSecs, 0);
  WriteString(" seconds with his eyes closed.");
  WriteLn;

  WriteString("Sonny drove ");
  WriteReal(DistanceBlind, 0);
  WriteString(" miles with his eyes closed.");
  WriteLn

END Sonny.
```

Listing 4.2

The careful reader of the module Sonny should make several observations. Again, we have used the magic number 60 (in the forms 60 and 60.0) several times in the program. We have done this because we believe that these 60s are not mysterious and do not need to be replaced by symbolic constants.

Earlier, we urged the reader to minimize the number of conversions that are applied in a statement. Yet, in the first assignment, we wrote

```
TimeHrs := FLOAT(Distance) / FLOAT(Speed);
```

instead of

```
TimeHrs := FLOAT(Distance DIV Speed);
```

Please be aware that these are *not* equivalent. For example, if Distance were 62 and Speed were 67, then the first assigns TimeHrs the proper value 0.92537. The second, however, assigns TimeHrs the value 0.0 (why?). This illustrates that some care is needed when converting from CARDINALs to REALs without losing accuracy. As a general rule, DIV should be avoided if the result is to be converted to REAL. However, to use / note that it is necessary to FLOAT both operands to REAL.

   The second assignment statement is even more complicated, since it uses both TRUNC and FLOAT:

```
NumBlinks := TRUNC(TimeHrs * FLOAT(60 * Frequency));
```

We leave it to the reader to argue that the above is more accurate than the following:

```
NumBlinks := TRUNC(TimeHrs) * 60 * Frequency;
```

   We have intentionally gotten ourselves into the need for these TRUNCs and FLOATs to illustrate their use and the pitfalls that await the unwary. One cannot always avoid the use of TRUNC and FLOAT, so it is best to know how to use them well. In Sonny's case, however, we could have declared all identifiers to be REAL and avoided the need for conversions.

CONCLUSION

In many ways, this chapter ends the introductory material on Modula-2. In these first four chapters, we have learned a little about where Modula-2 came from and a little about where we are going in our study of structured programming with Modula-2. We have seen our first simple, complete modules, and we have learned details of importation, types, constants, variable declarations, input/output, assignments, and conversions. We've also learned about operator precedence.

   While we hope that you enjoyed the Sonny Tan example, we freely admit that it would have been more appropriate to solve the problem with a calculator than with a computer. The same is true of the exercises that follow, but we hope that you will write modules for them anyway, even if you use a calculator to check the computer. The point is that at this early stage, we do not know enough to tackle more interesting and difficult problems. All that is about to change, as the next half dozen chapters introduce the fundamental control and data structures that allow us to solve more interesting problems. Yet, it is important that you understand the introductory material well before you continue the voyage into more complex material. We urge you to solve several of the following problems on the computer before proceeding. Reading a text provides only a passive knowledge of programming. To obtain an active knowledge, it is necessary to write your own programs. To learn to swim, it is necessary to get wet!

EXERCISES

4.1 Write and run a module that experimentally finds INTEGER overflow on your system. This not only will determine the range of INTEGERs for your system, but will acquaint you with run-time errors. Your module should prompt for two INTEGER inputs and then output their sum. See the section on INTEGERs for suggested limits on INTEGER values.

4.2 Write and run a module that uses MAX and MIN to find the limits of INTEGERs, CARDINALs, and REALs on your system. If available, also find the limitations of the LONGINTs and LONGREALs.

4.3 Write and run a module that uses the built-in function SIZE to determine the storage size of INTEGERs, CARDINALs, REALs, and CHARs on your system. If available, also find the size of LONGINTs and LONGREALs.

4.4 Assume that I, J, and K are CARDINAL identifiers and that X, Y, and Z are REAL identifiers. Which of the following are valid/invalid assignment statements? For those that are invalid, write a correct version.

a) X := I + J - K;

b) Y := FLOAT(I/J);

c) K := TRUNC(X + 2);

d) J := TRUNC(FLOAT(K) / Z) + 1.0;

e) Z :- (X - (FLOAT(J) DIV FLOAT(K)) / Y;

4.5 Modify the module Sonny of the text so that the user is prompted to enter the speed that Sonny drove on his trip to Miami. If everything else stays the same, what do you think will happen to the distance Sonny drives with his eyes closed if he drives 75 mph? What if his grandmother drives at 35 mph? Make your guesses and then check them by running your modified program. Can you explain what you observe?

4.6 The amount of beer brewed in the United States is 4,894,000,000 gallons annually. At a recent Eta Pizza Pie fraternity convention, the brothers wondered how far the stack would reach if all this beer was put into 12-ounce cans stacked end to end. In particular, how many times would the stack reach to the moon? To solve this problem you need to know:

One 12-ounce can is 4.75 inches tall.
There are 128 ounces in a U.S. gallon.
There are 5280 feet per mile, and, of course, 12 inches per foot.
The distance to the moon is 239,000 miles.

Warning: Because of the size of the quantities involved, make all identifiers REAL. That is, although 4894000000 looks like a CARDINAL, it is obviously an estimated value (and too big for the CARDINAL type in most Modula–2s) and, therefore, the real constant 4894000000.0 should be used instead.

4.7 Write an interactive program for Pepi Roni's Pizza Parlor that will help Pepi keep track of orders. The program should obtain the customer's first and last names and phone number. In addition, the program should prompt for and obtain the number of small, medium, and large pizzas ordered. Small pizzas are $6.95, medium ones are $8.95, and large ones are $10.95. Don't forget to add 6 percent sales tax. The output of the module should be a clearly written summary of the order showing the name and phone number of the customer; an itemized listing of the number and the cost for small, medium, and large pizzas ordered; the sales tax; and the grand total.

Chapter 5

FUNDAMENTAL
CONTROL STRUCTURES

It is in this chapter that the real power of computers is demonstrated. Until now, we have used the computer primarily as a calculator. And most people are very comfortable with the idea of machines performing numeric calculations. What makes computers powerful and useful is that we can program them to do several calculations, one after the other. Some of the exercises in the previous chapter required programs of this type. The flow of control of these programs is very simple—statements are executed in the order in which they occur in the program.

In this chapter, we are going to learn how to alter the flow of execution in a program. There are two basic methods of doing this: **conditional** execution—executing certain parts (or skipping certain parts) of the program at certain times—and **repetition**—repeating certain parts of the program as many times as we need.

It is the conditional execution ability of computers that probably makes them seem almost human, or intelligent, to many users. People can have simple conversations with computers; computers can proofread documents and find misspelled words; computers can play chess against humans and take advantage of their blunders. In all these applications, the computer has the power to make decisions, and it is this power in a machine that disturbs some people. However, these same people are not disturbed by a parking meter that can decide when we have parked in a space too long. Nor are they concerned about a toaster that knows when the bread has been toasted long enough. Why, those toasters are so amazing that even the old-fashioned ones were able to know whether someone wanted toast that was light, medium, or dark! How did they know? Of course, a person told the toaster before putting it in action by setting a selector switch. If the switch is on light, toast for one minute, on medium for a minute and a half, on dark for two minutes. Computers work the same way. The programmer tells the computer, ahead of time, that if certain things are true, then certain other things are supposed to be accomplished. It's just that with computers, we can tell them lots of these instructions and then they can carry out very complex tasks. So the first thing we need is a mechanism by which the computer can determine if a certain thing is true or not. These things are called **conditions**, and Modula-2 has a special data type for dealing with conditions called the **BOOLEAN** type.

THE BOOLEAN DATA TYPE

This type is named after George Boole (1815-1864), the English mathematician who studied and characterized many of the laws of formal logic. A variable of type BOOLEAN can take on only two possible values: TRUE and FALSE. For example, if we declare a BOOLEAN variable Maybe with

VAR Maybe : BOOLEAN;

then the following assignment statement is legal:

Maybe := TRUE;

Of course:

Maybe := 2 + 2;   (* ILLEGAL *)

is illegal because we have a type conflict. The left-hand side of the statement is of type BOOLEAN, while the right-hand side is of type INTEGER.

To give you an idea of the purpose of the BOOLEAN type, we can make the above statement legal by typing a few more characters:

Maybe := (2 + 2 = 4);

Now the right-hand side is also of type BOOLEAN because it consists of a simple condition. A condition consists of the comparison of two expressions by a **relational operator**. The relational operators of Modula-2 and their meanings for the simple types are given below:

Symbol	Meaning
=	Equal
<>	Not equal
#	Not equal
<	Less than
<=	Less than or equal to
>	Greater than
>=	Greater than or equal to

So, it should be easy to see that the two statements Maybe := TRUE and Maybe :=

(2 + 2 = 4) have the same effect—each causes the variable Maybe to take on the value TRUE. Note that the statement Maybe := (2 + 2 = 5) is syntactically legal. But since 2 + 2 is not equal to 5, the condition on the right-hand side evaluates to FALSE, and this value is then assigned to Maybe.

There are special operations that can be performed on BOOLEAN types, but the numeric operations cannot be performed on these types. It doesn't make sense to try to add or multiply two BOOLEAN values. Addition and multiplication are operations that are defined for numeric types. For the BOOLEAN type, there are three logical operators: AND, OR, and NOT. These operators do *exactly* what their names suggest they do. For example, if Maybe and Possibly are two BOOLEAN variables, then the expression

Maybe AND Possibly

is of type BOOLEAN also. Its value is TRUE if *both* Maybe *and* Possibly are TRUE. If either of them is FALSE, then the **compound** condition is FALSE. Likewise, the compound condition

Maybe OR Possibly

is TRUE if *either* Maybe *or* Possibly is TRUE. The compound OR-condition is FALSE only if Maybe and Possibly are both FALSE.

The NOT operator is different from AND and OR in that it is a **unary** operator: It operates on a single BOOLEAN expression. The effect of the NOT operator is to reverse the value of the BOOLEAN expression. So,

NOT Maybe

is TRUE if Maybe is FALSE, and it's FALSE if Maybe is TRUE.

Just as the numeric operations can be described with tables (e.g., the multiplication table for the numbers 0,1,2,...,9), we can describe the logical operators with tables as well:

AND	TRUE	FALSE
TRUE	TRUE	FALSE
FALSE	FALSE	FALSE

OR	TRUE	FALSE
TRUE	TRUE	TRUE
FALSE	TRUE	FALSE

NOT	TRUE	FALSE
	FALSE	TRUE

Note how small the tables are. That is because there are only two possible BOOLEAN values. Also note that the tables are easier to memorize than is the multiplication table. That's because the values are what they should be; i.e., the values correspond to the

meanings of the English words *and*, *or*, and *not*.
  Consider the following statement:

  I will marry a girl if she is nice and beautiful or rich.

It is not quite clear what is meant here. Must the girl be nice, and then either beautiful
or rich? Or maybe nice and beautiful is one acceptable combination, while being just
rich is also good enough. What is needed is either some parentheses:

  I will marry a girl if she is (nice and beautiful) or rich.
  I will marry a girl if she is nice and (beautiful or rich).

or a rule that tells us what order to use in evaluating ANDs and ORs. Modula-2
precedence rules state that NOT has the highest precedence, followed by AND, and then
by OR. Even though we have these rules, it is still a good idea to use parentheses to help
make groupings clear. Moreover, because the logical operators (NOT, AND, OR) have
precedence over the relational operators (=, <, etc.), there are many occasions where
parentheses are required to enclose the simple conditions of a compound logical clause.
For example, suppose that A, B, C, and D are all INTEGER variables. Then the
following is a correct compound condition:

```
(A < B) OR (C >= D) AND (B = D)
```

We can add a pair of parentheses to make the expression clearer:

```
(A < B) OR ( (C >= D) AND (B = D) )
```

to indicate that the AND operation is performed before the OR. But we cannot remove
any parentheses from the original. That is:

```
(A < B)  OR C >= D AND (B = D)
```

generates a type-mismatch error. That is because OR has a higher precedence than >=,
so the compiler will attempt to evalute

```
(A < B) OR C
```

But (A < B) is of type **BOOLEAN**, while C is of type **INTEGER**. The moral here is
to enclose conditions formed from relational operators in parentheses. Parentheses to
distinguish between logical operators should be used when they add clarity.

CONDITIONAL STATEMENTS

Now it is time to investigate the statements of Modula-2 that put all of this logic
business to work. The statement that we now consider is the IF statement. There are
several forms of the IF statement. We start with the simplest, the IF...THEN. The

syntax of this statement is

```
IF condition THEN sequence-of-statements END
```

The condition is any BOOLEAN-valued expression. Any sequence of legal Modula-2 statements may appear between the keywords THEN and END. The intended meaning of this statement is clear: If the condition evaluates to TRUE, then the statement sequence is executed; if the condition is FALSE, the statement sequence is omitted. In either case, the program continues by executing the statement following the IF...THEN. For readability, we paragraph an IF...THEN like this:

```
IF condition THEN
   Statement1;
   Statement2;
   Statement3
END; (* IF *)
```

Notice the use of the semicolons after Statement1 and Statement2, but not after Statement3. Recall that a semicolon separates statements. So place a semicolon after a statement if there is another statement following it. Statement3 does not have a statement following it. Statement3 is simply followed by the keyword END. We place a semicolon after END with the assumption that there is another statement following the IF...THEN. Because END is a keyword that is used in conjunction with many different keywords, we include a comment to indicate that it is marking the end of an IF-statement.

To see an example of the simple IF...THEN, suppose we are considering a program that handles the checkout at a grocery store using an optical scanner. Suppose there are REAL variables ItemPrice, TotalPrice, and Tax, and a BOOLEAN variable Taxable. Further, suppose that whenever an item is scanned, the computer reads its price into the variable ItemPrice and also determines whether the item is taxable by giving the appropriate value to Taxable. Suppose the tax rate is 6.5 percent. Then the statements that process the item after it is scanned might look like this:

```
(* Item has just been scanned. *)
TotalPrice := TotalPrice + ItemPrice; (* Add in current item.*)
IF Taxable THEN
Tax := Tax + 0.065 * ItemPrice       (* Add Tax, if necessary.*)
END; (* IF *)
(* Next Statement Here *)
```

The logic of the above example should be very clear. The use of the simple IF...THEN is called for because in the case of nontaxable items, we need do nothing extra. It is only in the case of the taxable items that we need to figure the tax.

A few comments are in order. First, many beginners tend to write

```
IF Taxable = TRUE THEN
```

While this is perfectly legal, it is unnecessary. Since Taxable is of type BOOLEAN, we don't need to compare it to TRUE to see if it is TRUE. In most cases, the condition will be more readable without the comparison.

Second, to avoid the use of a magic number like 0.065, it would be better to have a CONSTant TaxRate. The program is then easier to change when the tax rate inevitably goes up. Instead of searching for all the 0.065s in the program, we simply change the one constant assignment.

Third, it is very important that the statement before the IF...THEN is completely understood. The assumption is that we are accumulating the total price of a customer's bill. We do this by adding in the price of each new item as we scan it. Recall that the assignment statement is executed by evaluating the expression on the right-hand side (in this case by adding the price of the new item to the total price) and placing the result back into the left-hand side. The reader should see that if TotalPrice is 10.75 and ItemPrice is 0.53 before execution of the statement, then TotalPrice receives the new value of 11.28 after execution of the statement. This kind of statement occurs over and over in computer programs. In fact, note that the statement in the THEN clause is also of this same type.

THE IF...THEN...ELSE STATEMENT

The first variation of the conditional statement that we look at is used when we have some action to take if a condition is true, and some other action to take if it is false. Recall in the previous example that we didn't need to do anything in the false situation.

The syntax, shown in our paragraphing style, is

```
IF condition THEN
   Statement Sequence 1
ELSE
   Statement Sequence 2
END; (* IF *)
...next statement....
```

As before, it is easy to guess how this statement works. If the condition is TRUE, we execute Statement Sequence 1, skip Statement Sequence 2, and continue with the next statement. If the condition is FALSE, we skip Statement Sequence 1, execute Statement Sequence 2, and continue with the next statement. So, an IF...THEN...ELSE is used in an either/or situation.

For example, suppose we took a telephone poll for a political candidate. In compiling our results, we might want to know how many male and female respondents there were. Suppose Sex is of type CHAR, and MaleCount and FemaleCount are of type CARDINAL. Then, the following segment might process the counting:

```
WriteString('Enter the sex of the respondent(M or F): ');
Read(Sex);
WriteLn;
IF Sex = 'M' THEN
```

```
   MaleCount := MaleCount + 1
ELSE
   FemaleCount := FemaleCount + 1
END; (* IF *)
```

Notice again that there is no semicolon after either counting statement, although placing a semicolon after either of them would not produce an error.

A counting statement like `MaleCount := MaleCount + 1` is very common in programming. In fact, it is so common that Modula-2 provides a special incrementing operator (later we call it a procedure), `INC`. In its simplest form, the operator `INC` takes an INTEGER or CARDINAL variable and adds 1 to its value. Thus, we could write the statment equivalently as `INC(MaleCount)`. Not surprisingly, Modula-2 also has a decrementing operation, for subtracting 1 from an INTEGER or CARDINAL variable. This operator is written `DEC`.

To see the full generality of the `IF...THEN...ELSE`, let us point out that either clause may be compound, i.e., may consist of more than one statement. In fact, each clause may be as lengthy as we wish. Moreover, the statements in the `THEN` or `ELSE` clauses need not be assignment statements. Let us suppose that we ask two questions in our telephone poll—the sex of the respondent and whether the respondent supports our candidate. Suppose the second answer is stored in a CHAR variable `Answer` and that we have CARDINAL variables `MaleSupport` and `FemaleSupport`. To count the number of supporters we have of each sex, the segment could be written like this:

```
WriteString('Enter the sex of the respondent (M/F): ');
Read(Sex);
WriteLn;
WriteString('Does respondent support Sen Bullthrower (Y/N)? ');
Read(Answer);
IF Sex = 'M' THEN
   INC(MaleCount);
   IF Answer = 'Y' THEN
      INC(MaleSupport)
   END (* Inner IF *)
ELSE
   INC(FemaleCount);
   IF Answer - 'Y' THEN
     INC(FemaleSupport)
   END (* Inner IF *)
END; (* IF *)
```

Conditionals with More Than Two Alternatives

Obviously, the next enhancement we need is the ability to deal with more general situations than either/or situations. For example, suppose our telephone poll is broken down by age, instead of sex, into the following groups: 18 to 30, 31 to 55, 56 to 70, over 70. To handle this situation, we can employ the `IF... THEN... ELSIF... THEN... ELSIF... THEN......... END` statement.

The extra dots before the END indicate that we can have as many ELSIF...THEN pairs as we want. Notice the spelling of ELSIF. The IF part of the ELSIF indicates that we need to make another Boolean test. This makes sense, since we have more than two alternatives. In the case of only two alternatives, as in the last example of Male and Female, if the first alternative fails, we know that the second alternative holds. In the poll by age groups, if the tested age does not fall into the first group that we test for, we must test further to find which age group it does belong in. The following segment counts respondents by age group, but it is *intentionally inefficient*. We discuss improvements to this segment shortly.

```
WriteString('Enter the age of the respondent: ');
ReadCard(Age);
WriteLn;
IF Age > 70 THEN                            (* Inefficient Version *)
   INC(ReaganPeer)
ELSIF (Age > 55) AND (Age <= 70) THEN
   INC(Senior)
ELSIF (Age > 30) AND (Age <= 55) THEN
   INC(Worker)
ELSIF (Age > 17) AND (Age <= 30) THEN
   INC(Yuppie)
END; (* IF *)
```

First we assume that all variables are of type CARDINAL. The execution of the above segment should be clear. If a condition is TRUE, the clause for that condition is executed, all remaining tests and clauses are skipped, and control passes to the statement following the END. If a condition is FALSE, its clause is skipped and the next condition is evaluated. The conditions are tested in the order in which they appear, so the first condition that is satisfied has its clause executed. We mention this because it is possible for conditions to overlap (although in this case there is no overlap). Suppose a respondent who is 12 years old participates in the poll. In this case, that individual is not counted in any age group. The point is that it is possible that none of the clauses is executed.

The inefficiency involves all the compound conditions. Before we address the inefficiency, we would like to point out that the compound conditions at least are phrased correctly from a syntactic point of view. That is, if we want to test the value of Age and see if it is between 55 (exclusive) and 70 (inclusive), the proper way to do it is as shown in the segment above. We repeat it here:

```
IF (Age > 55) AND (Age <= 70) THEN
```

Recall that compound conditions are formed by using the BOOLEAN operators AND and OR. Beginning programmers, probably due to experience with mathematical notation, often try to express compound conditions as

```
IF 55 < Age <= 70 THEN
```

This will generate a syntax error, because the compiler will compare Age and 55, obtaining either TRUE or FALSE for an intermediate result, and then it will attempt to compare this BOOLEAN result with the CARDINAL value 70. Of course, it makes no sense to compare a BOOLEAN value with a CARDINAL value, so you get an error message. Remember, compound conditions are built with AND or OR.

So, the conditions in the above segment are correct. But they are inefficient, because we don't need compound conditions at all in this case. Consider the second alternative: (Age > 55) AND (Age <=70). How do we ever arrive at this alternative in the first place? Well, the first alternative must be FALSE. If the first alternative is TRUE, we would execute its clause, updating the ReaganPeer count, and then skip everything else. But if the first alternative is FALSE and we arrive at the second alternative, we already know that Age must be less than or equal to 70. So there is no need to test this condition again. The reader should see that, in a similar manner, all subsequent conditions can be simplified and the segment should read as follows:

```
WriteString('Enter the age of the respondent: ');
ReadCard(Age);
WriteLn;
IF Age > 70 THEN
  INC(ReaganPeer)
ELSIF (Age > 55) THEN
  INC(Senior)
ELSIF (Age > 30) THEN
  INC(Worker)
ELSIF (Age > 17) THEN
  INC(Yuppie)
END; (* IF *)
```

Beginners very often test for unnecessary conditions, and we caution against that. The most blatant abuse of this is the following:

```
IF Sex = 'M' THEN
  INC(MaleCount)
END; (* IF *)
IF Sex = 'F' THEN
  INC(FemaleCount)
END; (* IF *)
```

Although this may not look much longer than the IF...THEN...ELSE version we saw earlier, it is much less efficient. This version always performs two tests when only one is necessary. We caution the reader again—even if a Boolean test fails, there is still information obtained. Use that information, if possible, to make subsequent testing more efficient.

THE IF...THEN...ELSIF...THEN...ELSIF...THEN.......ELSE...END

Now we put all our options together. The ELSE clause is, as always, optional. Without it, we have the example of the previous section. If the ELSE clause is present, it must be the very last alternative. Its presence gives us an escape option in case none of the preceding conditions is true. For example, suppose we wanted to count the number of respondents to our poll, even if they are under 18 years of age. We could add a final ELSIF...THEN pair to our age example as follows:

```
....
ELSIF (17 < Age) AND (Age <=30) THEN
  INC(Yuppie)
ELSIF (Age <= 17) THEN
  INC(WorthlessNonVoter)
END; (* IF *)
```

This would work, but the careful reader who paid attention to all our remarks about efficiency should see that this last test is unnecessary. If we ever get to the last test, Age must certainly have a value less than or equal to 17. Why test for it? If, by the process of elimination, we know that the last possible alternative is true, we should place its action in an ELSE clause. So, the new segment, to include the youngest respondents, is

```
WriteString('Enter the age of the respondent: ');
ReadCard(Age);
WriteLn;
IF Age > 70 THEN
  INC(ReaganPeer)
ELSIF (Age > 55) THEN
  INC(Senior)
ELSIF (Age > 30) THEN
  INC(Worker)
ELSIF (Age > 17) THEN
  INC(Yuppie)
ELSE
  INC(WorthlessNonVoter)
END; (* IF *)
```

We again point out that the various clauses—the THEN clause, ELSE clause, and ELSIF clauses—may be as complex as we want them to be. They can include as many statements as we want, and each of these statements can be any legal Modula-2 statement. So the THEN clause of an IF.. THEN.. ELSE may contain several IF... THEN... ELSIF... THEN... ELSIF... THEN... ELSE statements. This ability to nest such constructs is demonstrated many times in subsequent portions of this book. In Modula-2, this nesting is easy to follow if we remember that each IF has exactly one corresponding END. Then we can always determine which clauses belong to which IF statement. We also use indentation to show which clause a statement belongs to.

We conclude this section on conditional statements with one more word about efficiency. Suppose, in our example, we also wanted to update a variable that simply counts the total number of individuals called in our poll. Many beginners write this:

```
WriteString('Enter the age of the respondent: ');
ReadCard(Age);
WriteLn;
IF Age > 70 THEN
  INC(ReaganPeer);
  INC(Total)
ELSIF (Age > 55) THEN
  INC(Senior);
  INC(Total)
ELSIF (Age > 30) THEN
  INC(Worker);
  INC(Total)
ELSIF (Age > 17) THEN
  INC(Yuppie);
  INC(Total)
ELSE
  INC(WorthlessNonVoter);
  INC(Total)
END; (* IF *)
```

While the above segment is correct, its only value is to show another example with compound clauses and a correct use of semicolons. Where is the inefficiency? Obviously, the same statement, INC(Total), is repeated five times. If there is a statement common to all clauses of a conditional statement, factor it out. That is, place it either before or after everything. Unnecessary repetition is as inefficient as unnecessary testing of Boolean conditions. The segment should read

```
WriteString('Enter the age of the respondent: ');
ReadCard(Age),
WriteLn;
IF Age > 70 THEN
  INC(ReaganPeer)
ELSIF (Age > 55) THEN
  INC(Senior)
ELSIF (Age > 30) THEN
    INC(Worker)
ELSIF (Age > 17) THEN
  INC(Yuppie)
ELSE
  INC(WorthlessNonVoter)
END; (* IF *)
INC(Total);
```

REPETITION VIA THE LOOP STATEMENT

The previous example segments in this chapter have demonstrated how useful the ability to test conditions is in programming. However, if each of the previous segments were executed only one time in a computer program, they would be pretty worthless. The telephone poll could be used to call only one person. The grocery checkout segment could run only on the super express line—One Item/Cash Only. What we need to expand our capabilities is a construct that allows us to repeat our actions many times. In this chapter, we look at the most basic repetitive construct. In the next chapter, we'll look at some very useful alternatives.

The process of repeatedly executing a segment of a computer program is called **looping**. One way to establish a **loop** in Modula-2 is with the LOOP statement. Its syntax is

```
LOOP
   Sequence of statements
END;
```

As with the conditional statements, the intended meaning of this construct should be easy to guess. We simply execute the statement sequence, then we do it again, then again, then again, etc. In fact, the basic construct here might be called an **infinite loop**. A reader who has any familiarity with programming might realize that this sounds like a bad thing. Programs with unintentional infinite loops have a serious error in logic and waste computer assets. Programs with infinite loops simply keep doing the same task, over and over again, forever.

Before we continue, we should at least point out why a language would even allow a construct like an infinite loop. Consider a computer that has only one purpose—to measure the temperature in a nuclear reactor and sound an alarm if the temperature reaches a certain danger level. The program that oversees this monitoring essentially needs to be in an infinite loop. In English, it might look something like this:

```
Loop
   Read the temperature
   If the temperature > danger level then
       sound the alarm
End
```

We would want this program to run from the time that the nuclear reactor becomes active until it is deactivated.

A more common example of a program in an infinte loop is the **operating system** of a computer. The operating system is the software that controls the overall operation of a computer. For example, when a microcomputer is turned on, there is usually some sort of blinking cursor placed on the screen. That cursor is placed there by the operating system. The operating system allows the user to type, allows the user to execute various programs, even allows the user to play computer games. All the time that the computer is on, the operating system program is executing. And it keeps running until someone turns the computer off.

LOOP with Conditional EXIT

In this book, we will not have any use for writing programs with infinite loops. So if we want to use the LOOP statement, there must be a way of terminating the loop. Modula-2 uses a very simple method of doing this—the EXIT statement. The EXIT statement has the simplest syntax of all Modula-2 statements—it consists simply of the keyword EXIT. Execution of an EXIT statement inside a LOOP causes flow of control to pass to the statement following the keyword END that corresponds to the keyword LOOP. Consider for a moment the silly example below:

```
LOOP
    Statement 1;
    Statement 2;
    Statement 3;
    EXIT;
    Statement 4;
    Statement 5
END; (* LOOP *)
Statement 6;
```

With this construct, statements 1, 2, 3, and 6 would be executed. We call this example silly because it would never make sense to write a LOOP with an unconditional EXIT statement in it. Such an exit would be executed the first time—there would never be any occasion where the LOOP would actually perform as a LOOP. Instead, the EXIT statement needs to occur in some conditional clause. Then we can control how many times the loop executes. Observe that *the condition that governs the EXIT must eventually become TRUE*, or we are still stuck in an infinite loop. So a more realistic LOOP looks like this:

```
LOOP
    Statement 1;
    Statement 2;
    Statement 3;
    IF TimeToQuit THEN
      EXIT
    END; (* IF *)
    Statement 4;
    Statement 5
END; (* LOOP *)
Statement 6;
```

In the LOOP construct above, we repeatedly execute statements 1, 2, and 3, then test to see if we should quit. If not, we execute statements 4 and 5, return to the top of the loop, and execute the first three statements again. This process continues (possibly forever) until the Boolean test for TimeToQuit becomes TRUE. Then we would exit the loop and continue with statement 6.

It is time for an example of a complete program that uses both a conditional statement and a loop construct.

ULAM'S CONJECTURE—A COMPLETE MODULE

The example that we'll consider is a numeric one. In fact, it is a very famous problem—still unsolved to this day—that has drawn the attention of many mathematicians over recent years. The problem itself is extremely easy to understand. In fact, the problem can be described to a third-grade arithmetic class.

Let's consider three rules:

1. If a number is even, divide it by 2.
2. If a number is odd, triple it and then add 1.
3. Stop if you ever get to 1.

Now let's pick any positive CARDINAL, say 7, and apply the appropriate rule to it. Since 7 is odd, we apply rule 2 and we get 22. Let's apply the appropriate rule again, obtaining 11. Let's keep going for awhile:

7 22 11 34 17 52 26 13 40 20 10 5 16 8 4 2 1

If we try another number, say 12, we generate the following sequence:

12 6 3 10 5 16 8 4 2 1

It has been conjectured that no matter what positive CARDINAL number we begin with, the pattern will always reach 1. This has been tested on thousands of numbers, and it always works. But no one has been able to prove that it works for all numbers.
We are not going to attempt to prove Ulam's conjecture here. Instead, we'll simply write a program that allows us to input any number from the keyboard and then print out the sequence of numbers generated by the above rules. We'll also count how long it takes us to get to 1. The program is shown in Listing 5.1.

```
MODULE Ulam;

(* This program prints out the sequence generated by Ulam's
Conjecture, also called the "3n + 1 Problem." We use an
IF...THEN...ELSE to determine what action to take and a LOOP with
conditional EXIT to print the sequence until a 1 is (hopefully)
reached.                                                        *)

FROM InOut IMPORT ReadCard, WriteCard, WriteString, WriteLn;

VAR Count  : CARDINAL;          (* Count how long it takes
                                           to get 1. *)

    Number : CARDINAL;          (* Number for generating
                                        the sequence. *)
```

```
BEGIN
  WriteLn;
  WriteString('Enter a positive integer greater than 1: ');
  ReadCard(Number);
  WriteLn;
  WriteLn;
  WriteString("The sequence generated is ");
  WriteLn;
  WriteCard(Number, 4);
  Count := 0;
  LOOP
    IF Number MOD 2 = 0 THEN              (* Number is even. *)
      Number := Number DIV 2
    ELSE                                  (* Number is odd.  *)
      Number := 3 * Number + 1
    END; (* IF *)
    WriteCard(Number, 6);
    INC(Count);
    IF Number = 1 THEN
      EXIT
    END (* IF *)
  END; (* LOOP *)
  WriteLn;
  WriteString('It took ');
  WriteCard(Count, 0);
  WriteString(' steps to reach 1')
END Ulam.
```

Listing 5.1

We hope that the idea behind the program is simple enough that the logic of the program is easy to follow. We simply read in a number from the keyboard, print it, set a counter equal to 0, and then successively generate and print the sequence, counting as we go. Since we want to read only one number and since we want only a single final count, the statements pertinent to these actions appear outside the LOOP. Don't put statements inside loops that are to be executed only once.

What if Ulam's conjecture isn't true? What if we happen to enter a positive integer that doesn't work? Then we would have an infinite loop, because the condition that controls the exit, namely Number = 1, would never become true. Realize that this infinite loop isn't really a mistake. If our job is to print out the sequence generated by the two rules of halving or tripling and adding 1, such a sequence would be infinite, and our infinite loop would be doing what it is supposed to. However, we expect the loop to terminate (because Ulam's conjecture seems to be true); we just don't know when. So, in this case, the LOOP with conditional EXIT is the perfect programming construct to handle this situation.

We should point out that this program could lead to CARDINAL overflow. We might start with a large odd number, and when we triple it and add 1, we could end up with a number that is larger than MAXCARDINAL. For example, 50001 is a legal CARDINAL on all systems, but 150004 is not legal on many systems. But even if we start with a small number, we really have no idea what numbers we might generate before reaching 1 (assuming we do reach 1). There are actions we could take to prevent overflow, like examining the number before we triple it. We leave this to the reader. Finally, the formatting width of 6 was chosen arbitrarily. If the numbers stay small, this will give a nice columnar output. Once the numbers get large, the output might begin to run together. In this case, it would be a good idea to insert a `Write(' ')` after each `WriteCard(Number, 6)` to ensure that we have spaces between each number in the output sequence.

The next program, in Listing 5.2, demonstrates some string capabilites of Modula-2. We write a program that plays a word-guessing game. Player 1 enters a secret word at the keyboard and then Player 2 tries to guess the word. After each guess, the computer provides a hint to Player 2 by stating whether the guess comes before or after the secret word in the dictionary. The computer is able to do this because the alphabetical ordering of the letters is built into the computer just as the numeric ordering is. That is, the computer knows that 'A' < 'B' (A comes before B) just as it knows that 3 < 5. To avoid confusion with uppercase and lowercase, we assume that all typing during the playing of the game is in uppercase. In a later chapter, we will see how to program around this potential difficulty.

This example also illustrates an alternative way of importing. Instead of using

```
FROM InOut IMPORT ReadString, WriteString, WriteLn, WriteCard;
```

as we have in all our previous examples, we do an **unqualified** IMPORT:

```
IMPORT InOut;
```

This type of importation makes available to us all the routines in the InOut package. The advantage of this is that it is not necessary for us to list each individual routine that we intend to use in our program. However, there is a disadvantage to this method. When we reference the various routines in the module, we must *qualify* them. That is, we must let the system know, for example, that WriteString belongs to the InOut package. Thus, we end up with statements like:

```
InOut.WriteString('Player 1—Enter a secret word: ');
```

Because of this inconvenience, we prefer the method of specifically listing the imported routines using FROM and usually use that method throughout the book.

```
MODULE WordGuess;

(* This module plays a 2-person word-guessing game. If the word is
not guessed in 20 guesses, the game is terminated.             *)

IMPORT InOut;
```

```
VAR   SecretWord  : ARRAY[0..9] OF CHAR
      GuessedWord : ARRAY[0..9] OF CHAR;         (* Strings. *)
      Guesses     : CARDINAL;

BEGIN
  InOut.WriteLn;
  InOut.WriteString('Player 1—Enter a secret word: ');
  InOut.ReadString(SecretWord);
  ClearScreen;                          (* See remarks in text. *)
  Guesses := 0;
  LOOP
    INC(Guesses);
    IF Guesses = 21 THEN                       (* Terminate game. *)
      EXIT
    END;  (* IF *)
    InOut.WriteLn;
    InOut.WriteString('This is Guess # ');
    InOut.WriteCard(Guesses);
    InOut.WriteLn;
    InOut.WriteString('Player 2—Guess the secret word: ');
    InOut.ReadString(GuessedWord);
    InOut.WriteLn;
    IF GuessedWord = SecretWord THEN
      EXIT
    ELSIF GuessedWord < SecretWord THEN
      InOut.WriteString('The word comes after your guess.')
    ELSE
      InOut.WriteString('The word comes before your guess.')
      END (* IF...THEN...ELSIF *)
  END; (* LOOP *)
  InOut.WriteLn;
  IF Guesses = 21 THEN
      InOut.WriteString('Game is over. Secret Word was ');
      InOut.WriteString(SecretWord)
  ELSE
    InOut.WriteString('You guessed the correct word in ');
    InOut.WriteCard(Guesses, 0);
    InOut.WriteString(' guesses.'')
    END (* IF..THEN...ELSE *)
END WordGuess.
```

Listing 5.2

It is very important for the reader to understand exactly how the WordGuess program works. Beginners who try to write this program are often unable to see how the program can be a general one, working for any secret word that Player 1 wants to enter, when the program must be written without Player 1 ever being around. This is precisely the power of variables. Player 1's secret word will be read by the computer into the memory location named `SecretWord`. Since we don't know what that word will be, we always use the variable name `SecretWord` in the program. During any particular play of the game, the contents of the memory location `SecretWord` will contain the secret word for that game.

We assume that `ClearScreen` clears the screen so that Player 2 cannot see the secret word. Most systems have such a command, but it probably won't be exactly of this format. The reader should find the proper screen-clearing command for his or her system. If all else fails, a sequence of about 24 `WriteLn` statements will manage to clear the screen, as ungraceful as this might be. Of course, we could put a single `WriteLn` statement in a loop that executes 24 times. In Chapter 7, we learn to write such a procedure gracefully!

As for comments on the logic of the program, note that we count the guess first, and don't even allow the player to make a 21st guess. Also observe that we don't need to test for `GuessedWord > SecretWord`. If we get beyond the tests for `GuessedWord = SecretWord` and `GuessedWord < SecretWord`, we know that `GuessedWord > SecretWord`. That is why we use an `ELSE` instead of a second `ELSIF`.

Again, we remark that the comments following each keyword `END` are a good idea as programs become more complex. `END` is a keyword used with several different keywords, and such comments can help the reader keep the proper pairs of keywords matched up.

One-Entry/One-Exit Control Structures and Loop Invariants

In the preceding example, notice that there are two possible exits from the loop—Player 2 either guesses the word or uses up all 20 guesses. Many computer scientists feel strongly that a loop should never have more than one exit. Because programming constructs that alter the flow of execution can make it difficult to follow complex algorithms, these constructs should be kept as simple as possible. One way to keep them simple is to insist that all control structures have exactly one entry point and exactly one exit point. We agree in principle with this philosophy, and most of the examples in this text adhere to this belief. Still, we think there are circumstances where multiple exits from a loop can simplify the programming logic involved. In the previous example, multiple exits are the natural way to program that loop. In such cases, the `EXIT` statement provides a graceful, yet controlled, way to formulate the algorithm. Still, we caution the reader that most loops are best programmed with a single exit and state that the one-in/one-out philosophy is a sound one.

As computer programs become more and more complex, there is concern about how one might ever really know that programs are in fact correct—that is, that they do what they are supposed to do. The notion of a **loop invariant** is gaining favor in the computer-science world as a method for proving the correctness of programs. While this topic is appropriately discussed at a more advanced level, the idea is important enough to hear about in a first course. Essentially, a loop invariant is an assertion about the state of the program environment each time the flow of control reaches the beginning of the loop. In fact, as its name implies, the invariant assertion should remain true during the execution of the body of the loop on each iteration and should still be true upon loop termination. In the word-guessing example, an invariant involving the variable `Guesses` is

```
(Guesses = 21) OR
(Guesses = the actual number of guesses made by Player 2)
```

Note that this is clearly true before the loop, since `Guesses` is 0 and Player 2 has yet to make a guess. In the body of the loop, `Guesses` is incremented. If it is incremented to 21, we exit the loop and the assertion is still true. If `Guesses` is not equal to 21, Player 2 gets to make another guess, so `Guesses` in fact remains equal to the number of guesses made by Player 2. If the guess by Player 2 is correct, we exit the loop without any further incrementing of `Guesses`, so the assertion is still true. The fact that the assertion is true prior to the loop, remains true throughout execution of the loop body, and is true upon exit from the loop proves that the module does, in fact, count the guesses of Player 2 correctly. The real value of assertions and loop invariants is seen in proving the correctness of complex algorithms, but we hope the reader can see how assertions and loop invariants can be useful even in simple programs. We encourgage you to attempt to formulate loop invariants as you practice your programming skills in the exercises.

PSEUDO-CODE

For our final example of this chapter, we return to a numeric example. Again, we ask the reader not to be intimidated. This example, like Ulam's conjecture, requires only knowledge of simple arithmetic. We are going to write a program that determines if a given positive integer is a prime number. Recall that a prime number is a positive integer greater than 1 with no divisors other than itself and 1. For example, 17 is prime since the only numbers dividing evenly into 17 are 1 and 17. The number 15 is not prime, since 3 and 5 divide evenly into it.

While we work through this example, we are going to demonstrate a **stepwise-refinement** process using **pseudo-code**. Pseudo-code means stating in English (at least, not in a programming language) what we intend to do. Stepwise refinement, also called **top-down** design or **divide and conquer**, simply means that we keep breaking the problem down into smaller and smaller pieces. The idea behind this strategy is that if we can get the pieces small enough, solving the problem (i.e., translating our pseudo-code into a Modula-2 program) will be easy.

At the highest level, our problem involves

1. Reading a number from the keyboard
2. Determining if the number is prime
3. Printing the results of our determination

That is a pseudo-code solution (or at least an outline for a solution). Our task is eventually to translate this outline into a program. Already it is easy to translate steps 1 and 3—we just use some reads and writes. What we need to do is refine step 2:

2. Determine if a number has any divisors (other than itself and 1):
   a. If a number is even and not 2, it is not prime (2 is a divisor)
   b. If a number is odd, test the odd numbers smaller than it to see if any of them divide evenly—if we find a divisor, the number isn't prime

Now let's get detailed about step 2b. We can tell if a number divides evenly into another number by using the MOD operator. A number is prime if it doesn't have any divisors (other than 1 and itself). How long do we need to keep looking for divisors? It turns out that we need look only up to the square root of the number. That is because divisors occur in pairs. For example 3, divides evenly into 24, since 24 = 3 * 8. The numbers 3 and 8 are called **cofactors** of 24. Clearly, both cofactors of a number can't be larger than the square root of the number, because the product of those cofactors would then be larger than the original number. Thus, here is our pseudo-code plan for step 2b:

Start trial Divisor at 3, the first possible odd divisor
LOOP
    If Divisor is larger than the square root of the Candidate then
        Candidate is prime
    Quit with a prime
    Else if Divisor divides evenly into Candidate, then
        Candidate is not prime
        Quit without a prime
    Else
        Add 2 to the trial Divisor to obtain next odd trial Divisor
END

Now that we have refined our solution, translation of steps 1, 2a, 2b, and 3 into a Modula-2 program is straightforward. The program is given in Listing 5.3.

```
MODULE PrimeTester;

(* This program reads an integer larger than 1 from the keyboard
and determines whether it is prime.                            *)

FROM InOut IMPORT ReadCard, WriteString, WriteLn;
FROM MathLib0 IMPORT sqrt;

VAR   Prime        : BOOLEAN;
      Candidate    : CARDINAL;
      Divisor      : CARDINAL;

BEGIN
  WriteString('Enter an integer larger than 1 for "Testing": ');
  ReadCard(Candidate);
  WriteLn;                       (*Step 1 of Pseudo-code complete. *)
```

```
IF Candidate = 2 THEN          (* Handle 2 as a special case. *)
   Prime := TRUE               (* It's the only even prime. *)
ELSIF Candidate MOD 2 = 0 THEN
   Prime := FALSE                 (* Step 2a of Pseudo-code. *)
ELSE
   Divisor := 3;              (* Begin Step 2b of Pseudo-code. *)
   LOOP
     IF Divisor > TRUNC(sqrt(Candidate)) THEN
                                      (* Both operands *)
       Prime := TRUE;                 (* of type CARDINAL. *)
       EXIT                     (* Get out with a "Yes." *)
     ELSIF Candidate MOD Divisor = 0 THEN
       Prime := FALSE;                 (* Divisor found. *)
       EXIT                     (* Get out with a "No." *)
     ELSE
       Divisor := Divisor + 2        (* Try next divisor. *)
     END (* Inner IF *)
   END (* LOOP *)
END; (* Outer IF *)

WriteLn;                          (* Step 3 of Pseudo-code. *)
IF Prime THEN
   WriteString('Your number is prime.')
ELSE
   WriteString('Your number is not prime.')
END (* IF *)
END PrimeTester.
```

Listing 5.3

While there are many ways to program a test for primality, we like this version because it demonstrates all the important concepts of the chapter. We used a BOOLEAN variable, and we have a conditional statement with a loop nested inside it and another conditional nested inside the loop.

We urge the reader to trace carefully the execution of this program with candidates like 24, 29, and 35. We also urge the reader to develop a personal pseudo-code strategy for solving problems. Such a strategy is invaluable as the problems that we try to solve become more complicated. There will be several illustrations of pseudo-code in later chapters.

EXERCISES

5.1 There is an inefficiency in the PrimeTester program. The built-in square-root function is a time-consuming operation, yet it may be required several times. Introduce a new variable so that we only have to compute the square root of the candidate number once.

5.2 Write a program that helps Goldilocks test porridge. In particular, write a program that reads positive integers from the keyboard. These represent the temperatures of bowls of porridge. After reading each number, print the message "Too Hot" if the temperature exceeds 140 degrees, "Too Cold" if the temperature is below 90 degrees, and "Just Right" if the temperature is between 90 and 140 degrees. Terminate input with a 0, and then print a summary of the number of bowls of each kind that there were.

5.3 It is a fact that the **harmonic series**

$1 + 1/2 + 1/3 + 1/4 + 1/5 + ...$

becomes as large as we like if we simply add enough terms. For example, we can add enough of the fractions to make the sum larger than a million. This, however, would take many terms. Write a program that determines how many terms are necessary to make the sum exceed 5.

5.4 Write a program that reads in a sequence of positive integers followed with a 0 and computes the average of the positive integers. The 0 value is not part of the data— it is called a **trailer** value. It signifies that the end of the data has been reached.

Chapter 6

MORE CONTROL STRUCTURES

In this chapter, we'll add some convenience to our looping capability—we'll see some new kinds of statements that execute loops. We also introduce the notion of a **text file**. Text files add convenience to our ability to work with data. There are many cases where we don't want to enter data interactively from the keyboard while a program is running. With text files, we don't have to.

The reader should understand that the new loops introduced here don't give us any new computational power. Any program that we can write with the statements introduced in this chapter could also be written using just the LOOP statement from Chapter 5. But there is indeed convenience to be gained from the variety of loops— certain situations are most cleanly handled with a particular kind of loop. Many programmers develop an affection for a specific loop and use that kind almost exclusively. There is nothing wrong with this approach. But a good programmer should be comfortable with all the loops and be able to recognize situations when one kind might be better than another.

Later in the chapter, we'll point out the differences in the loops. For now, let us discuss the similarities among loops. All loops (except an infinite loop) have four essential features. There is the **loop body**—the statements that we want executed repeatedly. Loops are controlled by a Boolean condition, and all loops contain a **test of the controlling condition** to determine whether or not to execute the loop body. In fact, the location of this test is the primary difference among the looping constructs. Somewhere in the body of the loop there must be a **modification of the controlling condition**, so that the loop eventually terminates. Finally, prior to the loop body is an **initialization section,** where variables that are referenced within the loop body (either on the right-hand side of assignment statements or in conditional expressions) receive initial values. In particular, the controlling Boolean condition is often initialized here.

If we look back at the WordGuess program of the previous chapter, we see that the loop body consists of the statements that process a guess. There are actually two conditions for termination—`Guesses` = 21 or `GuessedWord` = `SecretWord`. Notice that we initialize `Guesses` to 0 immediately prior to the loop body, we modify `Guesses` in the first statement of the loop body, and we test the condition in the second statement. In all the examples that we do in this chapter, you should try to spot all four of these loop ingredients.

THE `REPEAT/UNTIL` LOOP

Like the `LOOP` statement, the `REPEAT...UNTIL` loop has a very simple syntax. It is

```
REPEAT
   Sequence of statements
UNTIL Condition
```

`Condition` represents a Boolean condition and, as you might guess, the loop body is repeatedly executed until the condition becomes true. Note that since the test of the Boolean condition comes after the loop body, the loop is executed at least once, even if the condition is true to begin with. `REPEAT/UNTIL` is equivalent to `LOOP/END` with a conditional `EXIT` at the end of the loop body.

Let us first consider a simple example. We'll write a segment that prints the positive integers from 1 to 20. Suppose that `Number` is of type CARDINAL. What do we need to do in the loop body? Print `Number` and increment `Number`. It turns out that it doesn't matter what order we do things in, as long as we are consistent (and careful!) about our initialization values and our termination test. We do it both ways for comparison:

```
(* Print before Increment *)      (* Increment before Print *)
Number := 1;                      Number := 0;
REPEAT                            REPEAT
   WriteCard(Number, 4);            INC(Number);
   INC(Number)                      WriteCard(Number, 4)
UNTIL Number = 21;                UNTIL Number = 20;
```

There should be no confusion about the selection of the initial and terminal values of `Number`. If there is, you should carefully hand trace the loop. A very common progamming mistake is to execute loops either one time too many or one time too few.

Let us write a complete program using a `REPEAT...UNTIL` loop. A 10-year-old boy, Marvin Boesky, invests $1000 and is guaranteed a 10 percent annual return on his money for as long as he wants. At what age will he become a millionaire? This situation is a good one for the `REPEAT...UNTIL` loop because we can keep track of the money *until* there is one million dollars. The key statement in the loop body of Listing 6.1 needs to update the amount each year. With a 10 percent earning, there will be `Amount + 0.10 * Amount` at the end of the year. It is more efficient to write this as `Amount * 1.10`, since we save an addition operation by doing this. We must also use a REAL variable for the amount.

```
MODULE BigBucks;

(* This program determines how old Marvin Boesky will be when he
becomes a millionaire, if he invests $1000 and earns 10% each year.
                                                                    *)

FROM InOut IMPORT WriteString, WriteLn;
FROM RealInOut IMPORT WriteReal;

CONST PerCent = 0.10;

VAR    Amount  : REAL;
       Age     : CARDINAL;

BEGIN
  Amount := 1000.0;                    (* Initialization Phase. *)
  Age := 10;                               (* Marvin's age now. *)
  REPEAT
    Amount := Amount * 1.10;
    INC(Age)                             (* Alter Condition. *)
  UNTIL Amount >= 1000000.0;             (* Test Condition. *)
  WriteLn;
  WriteString('Marvin Boesky will be ');
  WriteCard(Age, 0);
  WriteString(' years old when he becomes a millionaire.');
  WriteLn;
  WriteString('At that time he will have ');
  WriteReal(Amount);
  WriteString(' bucks.')
END BigBucks.
```

Listing 6.1

THE WHILE LOOP

The next construct that we'll consider is the WHILE loop. As its name implies, the body of a WHILE loop executes while a certain condition remains true. The format is

```
WHILE condition DO
    Sequence of Statements
END;
```

So a WHILE/DO is equivalent to a LOOP/END with a conditional EXIT at the top of the loop body. We do the same simple example of printing the positive integers from 1 to 20:

```
(* Print before Increment *)     (* Increment before Print *)
Number := 1;                     Number := 0;
WHILE Number <= 20 DO            WHILE Number <= 19 DO
  WriteCard(Number, 4);           INC(Number);
  INC(Number)                     WriteCard(Number, 4)
END; (* WHILE *)                 END; (* WHILE *)
```

The WHILE loop might be appropriately considered the opposite of the REPEAT/UNTIL loop. First, the test for executing the loop occurs at the top of the loop in the WHILE, as opposed to the bottom of the loop in the REPEAT/UNTIL. Moreover, the conditions that perform equivalent tasks, one using a WHILE loop and the other a REPEAT/UNTIL loop, are exact opposites. For example, in the segment where we print Number before we increment, the WHILE condition is Number <= 20, whereas the REPEAT/UNTIL condition is Number > 20 (although we wrote it as Number = 21).

There is one major distinction between the two loops. Although the REPEAT/UNTIL loop body is always executed at least once (since the test is at the end), it is possible that a WHILE loop may not execute at all. The reader may wonder why we would need a WHILE loop that doesn't ever execute. It turns out that such instances are rather common in programming. For example, suppose we have a program that processes sales figures for a small business by having a secretary enter, at the end of each business day, the amount of each of the sales. Such a loop might be processed using either a REPEAT/UNTIL or a WHILE. We demonstrate both loops (warning the reader that one of them has a bug):

```
REPEAT                           WHILE Answer = 'Y' DO
  WriteLn;                         WriteLn;
  WriteString('Enter amount: ');   WriteString('Enter amount: ');
  ReadReal(Amount);                ReadReal (Amount);
  Total := Total + Amount;         Total := Total + Amount;
  WriteString('More (Y/N)? ');     WriteString('More (Y/N)? ');
  Read(Answer);                    Read(Answer);
  Write(Answer);                   Write(Answer);
  WriteLn                          WriteLn
UNTIL Answer = 'N';              END; (* WHILE *)
```

Which segment is better? Which has the bug? Assuming that these are all the statements concerned with this portion of the program, then the WHILE loop has a bug. Why? Because the first thing the WHILE does is to check the controlling condition— is Answer equal to 'Y'? But Answer hasn't been given a value yet. Answer should have a value before it is used in an expression. How do we fix this? Typically, with WHILE loops, since the condition is tested first, we must be sure that we initialize the condition before we enter the body of the loop. Thus, we should add the following before the WHILE statement:

```
WriteString('Is there an intital amount? (Y/N)? ');
Read(Answer);
Write(Answer);
WriteLn;
WHILE ....same as before
```

Since we still need the modification phase of the loop, similar statements still need to remain at the bottom of the loop. Now it appears that the WHILE loop is more complicated than the REPEAT/UNTIL loop. Nonetheless, in this circumstance, we feel that the WHILE loop is preferable. What about those very slow days when there are no sales? Here, the REPEAT/UNTIL version would still execute one time, which makes no sense. It might be argued that it wouldn't hurt to process a single sale of 0 and then answer that there are no further sales. But what if the processing loop also counted the total number of sales, or what if the loop had to attribute each sale to a salesperson? Then, a bogus sale of 0 might foul up several other records. The fact is that this loop simply shouldn't execute at all if there are no sales. Although a "band-aid" could be applied to the REPEAT/UNTIL to make it work properly in all cases, when the possibility of no executions of a loop exists, a WHILE loop is preferable to a REPEAT/ UNTIL.

As another example of the WHILE loop, what if Modula-2 didn't have an integer division operator (remember that, in fact, it does—DIV) and we wanted to write a segment that performs integer division for CARDINAL numbers. Recall that with integer division, 9 DIV 2 is 4. Well, one simple way to decide how many times 2 goes into 9 is to count how many times we can subtract 2 from 9 until we get a number that is smaller than 2. Listing 6.2 contains a program that performs integer division using repeated subtraction.

```
MODULE RepeatedSubtraction;

(* This program performs integer division via repeated subtraction
of the divisor from the dividend.                                *)

FROM InOut IMPORT WriteLn, WriteString, ReadCard, WriteCard;

VAR    Divisor       : CARDINAL;
       Dividend      : CARDINAL;
       Quotient      : CARDINAL;
       TempDividend  : CARDINAL;

BEGIN
  WriteLn;
  WriteString('Enter a nonnegative integer for the dividend: ');
  ReadCard(Dividend);
  REPEAT(* Use REPEAT/UNTIL loop to verify validity of input. *)
    WriteLn;
    WriteString('Enter a positive integer for the divisor: ');
    ReadCard(Divisor);
    WriteLn
  UNTIL Divisor > 0;                  (* Divisor can't be zero. *)

  Quotient := 0;
  TempDividend := Dividend;(* We want to save value of Dividend *)
```

```
    WHILE Divisor <= TempDividend DO(* for the output section. *)
      TempDividend := TempDividend - Divisor;
      INC(Quotient)
    END; (* WHILE *)

    WriteLn;
    WriteString('The quotient of ');
    WriteCard(Dividend, 0);(* This is why we used TempDividend. *)
    WriteString(' divided by ');
    WriteCard(Divisor, 0);
    Write String(' is ');
    WriteCard(Quotient, 0)
END RepeatedSubtraction.
```

Listing 6.2

This program contains both a REPEAT/UNTIL loop and a WHILE loop. The REPEAT/UNTIL loop is conveniently used to ensure that input data are valid. For example, the user of the progam may accidentally type in 0 for the divisor. This, if not caught, would lead to an infinite loop—which shouldn't be surprising, since division by 0 makes no sense. This use of the REPEAT/UNTIL is called a **filter** since it filters out bad input. The REPEAT/UNTIL loop is preferable here to a WHILE loop because it is simpler. To use a WHILE loop as a filter, it is necessary to ask for the first data value outside the loop (since the test is at the top of the loop), and then to repeat the request for input inside the loop. That is, the WHILE filter would look like this:

```
WriteLn;
WriteString('Enter a positive integer for the divisor: ');
ReadCard(Divisor);
WHILE Divisor = 0 DO
   WriteLn;
   WriteString('Enter a positive integer for the divisor: ');
   ReadCard(Divisor)
END;
```

The REPEAT loop is clearly simpler. And the fact that the loop must execute at least once is of no concern to us in this case. The loop, of course, must be executed once to get the first data item.

On the other hand, using the WHILE loop to calculate the quotient is preferable to using a REPEAT/UNTIL. That is because a simple REPEAT/UNTIL loop to figure the quotient would be incorrect! Suppose we attempted to divide 5 by 8. This is a legal operation that should produce 0 for the quotient. But a REPEAT/UNTIL loop would perform one subtraction and increment the quotient to 1 before comparing the divisor to the dividend. It would also try to assign the CARDINAL TempDividend a negative value, resulting in an error. This example shows that sometimes a WHILE loop is better, and sometimes a REPEAT/UNTIL loop is better. The Modula-2 programmer needs to be familiar with both the WHILE and the REPEAT/UNTIL to be able to choose the more appropriate loop in a given situation.

THE FOR LOOP

All the loops that we have used so far might be called **indefinite** loops: It isn't obvious, just from reading the loop body, how many times the loop will execute. There are many computer applications where we may know, in advance, exactly how many times we want to execute something. For example, if we had a program that processed some information for each state in the country, we might expect the processing loop to execute 50 times. Modula-2 provides a construct for executing such a **definite** loop, the FOR statement. In its simplest form, its syntax is

```
FOR variable := start TO finish DO
  sequence of statements
END;
```

Let us repeat one more time the example of printing out the positive integers from 1 to 20. This is precisely the kind of situation that the FOR loop was designed to handle.

```
FOR Number := 1 TO 20 DO
  WriteCard(Number, 4)
FND; (* FOR *)
```

Certainly, with this example, the FOR loop seems to be the simplest loop of all. It is. That is because all the loop essentials are handled automatically by the computer. The variable following the keyword FOR is called the **loop control variable**. As you might guess, a FOR loop works as follows: The control variable is initialized to the starting value; i.e., the expression before the keyword TO. The loop body is then executed. After each execution of the loop, the control variable is automatically incremented by 1. The loop continues to execute until the control variable takes on a value that is larger than the finishing value; i.e., the expression before the keyword DO. So we see that loop initialization, the test of the condition for executing the loop, and the alteration of the loop condition are all handled for us.

Actually, it may be possible that the body of a FOR loop will not be executed at all. While this may seem like an unusual case, if the initial value is already larger than the final value, the loop body is not executed.

For the time being, we assume that the loop control variable is of type INTEGER, CARDINAL, or CHAR. In a later chapter, we consider other possibilities. Similarly, start and finish must be expressions of the same type as the loop control variable. Although the most common use of the FOR loop employs an increment of 1 for the control variable, Modula-2 allows for some flexibility. An optional BY clause may follow the finish expression. This consists of the keyword BY followed by an INTEGER value, which then serves as the increment. So, if we wanted to print the even positive integers from 2 up to 20, we could write

```
FOR Number := 2 TO 20 BY 2 DO
  WriteCard(Number, 4)
END; (* FOR *)
```

If we wanted to go from 20 down to 1 (one at a time), we could write

```
FOR Number := 20 TO 1 BY -1 DO
  WriteCard(Number, 4)
END; (* FOR *)
```

If we wanted to print out the uppercase alphabet, we could write

```
FOR Letter := 'A' TO 'Z' DO
   Write(Letter)
END; (* FOR *)
```

To print the lowercase alphabet backward, we could write

```
FOR Letter := 'z' TO 'a' BY -1 DO
  Write(Letter)
END; (* FOR *)
```

In each of the examples so far, the control variable has played a major role in the loop body. However, the control variable need not serve any purpose but to count the number of times the loop executes. For example, if we wanted to print "Modula-2" 20 times, we could write

```
FOR Number := 1 TO 20 DO
  WriteString('Modula-2');
  WriteLn
END; (* FOR *)
```

Regardless of how the loop control variable is used, it must not be modified by any statement in the loop. The only change allowed to the control variable is the automatic modification performed by the system. Moreover, if the control variable is used (for another purpose) after the loop body, it should be reinitialized. That is, in the above examples, we shouldn't assume that Number has the value 20 or even 21 after the loop is complete.

Let us look at an example where the FOR loop is appropriate. We compute the sum of the first 100 positive integers, 1 + 2 + 3 + ... + 99 + 100. This is supposedly the problem that was posed to Carl Friedrich Gauss, the great German mathematician, by his first-grade teacher to keep him occupied in class. History has it that Gauss almost immediately arrived at the solution, 5050, by pairing 1 with 100, 2 with 99, 3 with 98, ..., 50 with 51 and multiplying 50 times 101. Our program is much less clever. We simply accumulate a running sum—we start with 0 and add 1, then 2, then 3, ... then 100. The solution is shown in Listing 6.3.

```
MODULE ConsecutiveIntegers;

FROM InOut IMPORT WriteString, WriteLn, WriteCard;
```

```
VAR    Sum    : CARDINAL;
       Number : CARDINAL;

BEGIN
  Sum := 0;
  FOR Number := 1 TO 100 DO
    Sum := Sum + Number
  END; (* FOR *)
  WriteLn;
  WriteString('The sum of the first 100 positive integers is ');
  WriteCard(Sum, 0)
END ConsecutiveIntegers.
```

Listing 6.3

The reader should understand the important step involved in accumulating the running sum: Sum := Sum + Number. Number is added to the old value of Sum (since Sum appears on the right-hand side of the assignment statement) and this becomes the new value of Sum.

An obvious way to make this program more flexible would be to add the capability of computing sums to any positive integer, not just 100. To do this, all we need to do is make the upper limit of the FOR loop a variable that we assign from the keyboard. So, we also import ReadCard, add the variable Upper of type CARDINAL, and insert the statements:

```
WriteString('Enter the upper limit for the sum: ');
ReadCard(Upper);
WriteLn;
```

change the loop heading to

```
FOR Number := 1 TO Upper DO
```

and change the output statements to

```
WriteString('The sum of the first ');
WriteCard(Upper,0);
WriteString(' positive integers is ');
```

Of course, FOR loops need not start with 1 and, in general, both the lower and upper limits of a FOR loop can be represented by any expression of the appropriate type.

TEXT FILES

We'll take a brief detour from our discussion of control structures to improve our capability to handle data for our programs. Our examples until now have required us to enter information from the keyboard. While this is convenient in many cases (e.g., purchasing airline tickets from a travel agent), there are many cases when interactive input is not convenient.

Why is it convenient when we purchase airplane tickets? Well, there is not a lot of information to be entered, and the actual information (i.e., our preferences, the prices, the flight schedules) is not known until we get around to making our flight arrangements. Thus, we need to have a dialogue with the computer in this situation.

However, in many cases, we might be dealing with a large amount of data that may be known in advance. In these cases, it may be preferable to place our data in a separate file (saved on disk like a program) and then let our programs know where to find the data. For example, suppose we needed to compute an average for 1000 positive integers. If we used interactive input (i.e., ReadCard), what would happen if we enter incorrectly the 800th data item? If we mistype this data item and don't realize it, we will likely get an incorrect result. If we realize what we have done, we can halt the program and begin again. Of course, this means that we must type in the first 799 data values again, even though we did those correctly the first time. In general, programs receiving data interactively from the keyboard might need to give the user a second chance to look at what has been typed so that it is clearly correct. However, these kinds of programs are subject to problems. The user gets into the routine of typing a number, then answering a question like "Correct?", then typing another number, etc. Not only have we complicated the data entry, but users often get careless and respond to requests for numbers with a "Y" (for yes, the input is correct). If this happens, the program may crash due to a type mismatch. What is needed is a way to manage the input—in this example, 1000 positive integers—that is separate from the program. This is what text files do for us.

Text files are created just as Modula-2 programs are. That is, you enter the editor just as if you were going to write a program. But all you do is type the data. You can correct typing mistakes as you go along, or you can return to the data file, just as you can a program file, and make any corrections, insertions, or deletions that are necessary. When the file is saved, name it appropriately, but give it an extension like .TXT or .DAT. This reminds the programmer that it is a text or data file instead of a program. When dealing with text files, Modula-2 systems assume that the extension is .TXT, if not otherwise specified (see the discussion on OpenInput below).

Now that we can store our data separately from our programs, we must learn how our programs can access the data. To do this, we need to import some additional library routines from the standard InOut library. In particular, we will need to import OpenInput, CloseInput, Done, EOL, and termCH. We demonstrate these routines in the examples that follow.

In computer programming, before a text file can be accessed by a program, it must be opened. In Modula-2, this happens when we invoke OpenInput. OpenInput performs an automatic prompt, asking us what file we want to open. Once we open a file, subsequent read instructions—for our purposes, we are concerned with Read (for reading CHAR) and ReadCard (for reading CARDINAL)—will expect their information to come from the data file in question, rather than from the keyboard. The format of a call to OpenInput is

OpenInput;

or

```
OpenInput('EXT');
```

Again, both of these calls to `OpenInput` cause the computer to prompt us for the name of the file. It is not necessary to type the full name of the file. With the first option above, the extention of `.TXT` is automatically added to the name that we type. With the second option, the user-supplied extension `.EXT` is automatically added. This option can be used if the extensions for data files are not always `.TXT`. For example, many programmers like to use the suffix `.DAT` for data files. In this case, we should use `OpenInput('DAT')`. When we are finished using files, we should close them. This helps protect the information on the disk. We close a file by simply writing

```
CloseInput;
```

FINDING THE AVERAGE, MAXIMUM, AND MINIMUM: A COMPARISON OF LOOPS

In this section, we'll look at three very common problems in programming and consider how they might be solved using the various kinds of loops. We'll examine a list of integers and then compute the average value of the list as well as the largest and smallest values in the list.

The previous example gives us a good start on figuring the average. All we need to do is compute a running sum of the integers and then divide by the number of integers involved. How might we go about determining the maximum and minimum values? Most beginners find this job difficult to translate into an algorithm, even though they can certainly scan a list of numbers themselves and report the biggest and smallest. How do they do it?

Let's just think about finding the maximum for now. All we really need to do, as we scan a list of numbers, is to remember the biggest number that we have seen to that point. Each time we look at a new number, we must determine if it is bigger than the one we are remembering. If it isn't, we just go on to the next one. If it is, that is the number that we remember. When we are finished looking at all the numbers, the one that we remember last is the biggest. A pseudo-code version of this algorithm follows:

Read first number
Remember first number   —The first number starts out being the biggest.
Repeat
  Read next number
  If next number is bigger, remember its value
Until we have examined all numbers

Notice how close the pseudo-code looks to the structure of a Modula-2 program; in particular, to a `REPEAT/UNTIL` loop.

We want to solve this problem with all the loop constructs. The first one that we'll try is the `FOR` loop. We dispense with that one first because it is fundamentally different from the rest. It requires that we know how large is the list of numbers that we are to examine. In fact, if this size is known, then we would agree that the FOR loop solution is probably simplest. Unfortunately, in most general computer applications, this size is not known. Recall our earlier example of processing sales receipts at the end of the day. If a stack of those receipts is given to a secretary for entering into the computer, which of the following scenarios sounds more efficient?

1. Have the secretary first count all the receipts, enter this number into the computer, and then enter all the sales figures for processing.
2. Enter all the sales figures for processing, allowing the computer to count them as they are entered, and then enter a special value to indicate that the process is complete.

Obviously, the second method is better—computers count much more accurately and quickly than people do.

Information at the beginning of a set of data describing the data that follow (for example, the amount of data) is called **header** information. Information at the end to indicate that data processing is complete is called a **trailer**. Generally speaking, it is easier for the programmer to work with header information—it's nice to know what is coming. But, as the sales example above demonstrates, data are more likely to come with trailer information. To do the FOR loop solution to our problem, we suppose that the first piece of data appearing in the file NumHead.TXT is the size of the list. An example file might look like this:

```
5
20
12
8
17
6
```

The 5 is not the minimum of the data in the list. The purpose of the 5 is to tell you that exactly five legitimate data items follow.

Listing 6.4 shows the solution to our problem using a FOR loop.

```
MODULE AvgMaxMinViaFOR;

FROM InOut IMPORT WriteLn, WriteString, ReadCard, ReadInt,
                            WriteInt, OpenInput , CloseInput;

VAR     Max     : INTEGER;
        Min     : INTEGER;
        Sum     : INTEGER;
        Current : INTEGER;
        Size    : CARDINAL;
        Average : INTEGER ;
```

```
BEGIN
  OpenInput;              (* Respond with NumHead, our data file. *)
  ReadCard(Size);
  ReadInt(Current)           (* Read the first data value, which *)
                            (* starts out being the maximum, *)
  Max := Current;                 (* the minimum, and the sum. *)
  Min := Current;
  Sum := Current;
  FOR Entry := 2 TO Size DO
    ReadInt(Current);
    Sum := Sum + Current;          (* Add next number to sum. *)
    IF Current > Max THEN     (* New max? If so, remember it. *)
      Max := Current
    ELSIF Current < Min THEN (* New min? If so, remember it. *)
      Min := Current
    END (* IF *)
END; (* FOR *)

  Average := Sum DIV Size;    (* Compute an integer average. *)
  WriteString('The average of the list is ');
  WriteInt(Average, 0);
  WriteLn;
  WriteString('The maximum value in the list is ');
  WriteInt(Max, 0);
  WriteLn;
  WriteString('The minimum value in the list is ');
  WriteInt(Min, 0);
  CloseInput
END AvgMaxMinViaFOR.
```

Listing 6.4

A few remarks are in order about the module of Listing 6.4. First, observe how the use of a text file makes the program simpler —there is no need for prompts to enter the size of the list or the next value to be tested. Of course, using text files requires that the programmer know the structure of the text file. The programmer must know that the number of data items to follow is the first item in the file. This program assumes that there is at least one number in the list and, in fact, this number is treated separately from the rest of the list (as hinted at in the pseudo-code). If Size is 1, the program still works correctly, since the FOR loop does not execute at all (its lower value already exceeds its upper value). We also point out that many beginners, in testing for the maximum and the minimum, use two separate IF statements:

```
IF Current > Max THEN
  Max := Current;
IF Current < Min THEN
  Min := Current;
```

This is less efficient than the IF...THEN...ELSIF structure above, because it always makes two conditional tests. Observe that if Current is in fact larger than Max, then it certainly won't be smaller than Min, so it is wasteful to make that test.

Now we'll consider this problem using the indefinite loops. Here we use a trailer value in our data—that is, a bogus data value whose purpose is simply to mark the end of the data. We must be careful that our trailer value cannot also be a valid data value. For example, if we knew that all the entries in the list were positive, we could use 0 as a trailer. But what if the list is allowed to contain 0s and negative entries? In our examples, we use 32767 (MAX(INTEGER) on many systems) as a trailer. So a typical file, NumTail.Txt, might look like this:

```
3
17
12
8
32767
```

This file contains four legitimate data items. The 32767 is not the maximum value, nor does it participate in the computation of the average.

The other major change that we must keep in mind for the indefinite loops is that we must now count the number of entries (to determine the average). Listing 6.5 shows the LOOP version, which is very similar to the FOR version.

```
MODULE AvgMaxMinViaLOOP;

FROM InOut IMPORT WriteLn, WriteString, ReadCard, ReadInt,
                                WriteInt, OpenInput, CloseInput;
CONST  Trailer = 32767;

VAR    Max      : INTEGER;
       Min      : INTEGER;
       Sum      : INTEGER;
       Current  : INTEGER;
       Size     : CARDINAL;
       Average  : INTEGER;

BEGIN
  OpenInput;            (* Respond with NumTail, our data file. *)
  ReadInt(Current);              (* Read the first number, which *)
                          (* starts out being the maximum, *)
  Max := Current;                  (* the minimum, and the sum. *)
  Min := Current;
  Sum := Current;
  Size := 1;
  LOOP
    ReadInt(Current);
    IF Current = Trailer THEN
      EXIT      (* Exit Loop because Trailer has been found. *)
```

```
    END; (* IF *)
    INC(Size);                    (* Count the number of entries. *)
    Sum := Sum + Current;          (* Add next number to sum. *)
    IF Current > Max THEN     (* New max? If so, remember it. *)
      Max := Current
    ELSIF Current < Min THEN  (* New min? If so, remember it. *)
      Min := Current
    END (* IF *)
  END; (* LOOP *)

  Average := Sum DIV Size;     (* Compute an integer average. *)
  WriteString('The average of the list is ');
  WriteInt(Average, 0);
  WriteLn;
  WriteString('The maximum value in the list is ');
  WriteInt(Max, 0);
  WriteLn;
  WriteString('The minimum value in the list is ');
  WriteInt(Min, 0);
  CloseInput
END AvgMaxMinViaLOOP.
```

Listing 6.5

Next, we look at the REPEAT. . .UNTIL version. One of the issues with REPEAT loops is: Where in the loop does the reading of the value occur? It is usually most convenient if we can read at the bottom of the loop, right before the loop test. Then, if we get the trailer value, we exit the loop. Otherwise, we repeat the body again. But if we read at the bottom, this implies that we process at the top of the loop and that we have our first value as we enter the loop. This is the case here. The reader should note that the first value gets processed inside the loop just like all the subsequent values. In particular, we compare the first value to the Max and Min, even though we already know that the first value was used to initialize Max and Min. While this may seem slightly inefficient, we prefer it to the following alternative.

We could completely process the first element outside the loop. This means that as soon as we get into the REPEAT loop, we must read the next value. Of course, we don't process that value if it is the trailer. Thus, we have two possible strategies shown side-by-side below. We prefer the version on the left and use it in the sample program.

```
Read first value          Read first value
REPEAT                    Process first value
  Process value           REPEAT
  Read next value           Read next value
Until Value = Trailer       IF Value <> Trailer THEN
                              Process next value
                            END
                          UNTIL Value = Trailer
```

Listing 6.6 shows the solution with a REPEAT/UNTIL, again assuming a text file such as NumTail.Txt with a trailer value to mark the end of the data.

```
MODULE AvgMaxMinViaREPEAT;

FROM InOut IMPORT WriteLn, WriteString, ReadCard, ReadInt,
                                WriteInt, OpenInput, CloseInput;
CONST Trailer = 32767;

VAR    Max      : INTEGER;
       Min      : INTEGER;
       Sum      : INTEGER;
       Current  : INTEGER;
       Size     : CARDINAL;
       Average  : INTEGER;

BEGIN
  OpenInput;            (* Respond with NumTail, our data file. *)
  ReadInt(Current);              (* Read the first number, *)
                                 (* which starts out being the *)
  Max := Current;                (* maximum and the minimum. *)
  Min := Current;
  Sum := 0;
  Size := 0;
  REPEAT
    Sum := Sum + Current;
    INC(Size);
    IF Current > Max THEN    (* New max? If so, remember it. *)
      Max := Current
    ELSIF Current < Min THEN (* New min? If so, remember it. *)
      Min := Current
    END; (* IF *)
    ReadInt(Current)
  UNITL Current = Trailer;

  Average := Sum DIV Size;    (* Compute an integer average. *)
  WriteString('The average of the list is ');
  WriteInt(Average, 0);
  WriteLn;
  WriteString('The maximum value in the list is ');
  WriteInt(Max, 0);
  WriteLn;
  WriteString('The minimum value in the list is ');
  WriteInt(Min, 0);
  CloseInput
END AvgMaxMinViaREPEAT.
```

Listing 6.6

Finally, we'll solve the same problem using a WHILE loop. The solution is shown in Listing 6.7. Again, we assume a text file such as NumTail.Txt with 32767 as a trailer value marking the end of the data.

```
MODULE AvgMaxMinViaWHILE;

FROM InOut IMPORT WriteLn, WriteString, ReadCard, ReadInt,
                          WriteInt, OpenInput, CloseInput;

CONST Trailer = 32767;

VAR     Max      : INTEGER;
        Min      : INTEGER;
        Sum      : INTEGER;
        Current  : INTEGER;
        Size     : CARDINAL;
        Average  : INTEGER;

BEGIN
  OpenInput;     (* Again respond with NumTail, our data file. *)
  ReadInt(Current);(* Read the first number, which starts out *)
  Max := Current;        (* being the maximum and the minimum. *)
  Min := Current;
  Sum := 0;
  Size := 0;
  WHILE Current <> Trailer DO
    Sum := Sum + Current;
    INC(Size);
    IF Current > Max THEN      (* New max? If so, remember it. *)
      Max := Current
    ELSIF Current < Min THEN (* New min? If so, remember it. *)
      Min := Current
    END; (* IF *)
    ReadInt(Current)
  END; (* WHILE *)

  Average := Sum DIV Size;     (* Compute an integer average. *)
  WriteString('The average of the list is ');
  WriteInt(Average, 0);
  WriteLn;
  WriteString('The maximum value in the list is ');
  WriteInt(Max, 0);
  WriteLn;
  WriteString('The minimum value in the list is ');
  WriteInt(Min, 0);
  CloseInput
END AvgMaxMinViaWHILE.
```

Listing 6.7

This version is almost exactly like the REPEAT/UNTIL version. Notice that in a WHILE loop, it is also preferable to have the subsequent read statement at the bottom of the loop (just before the test on the next go-around). If it is at the top, this would lead to a more complicated structure, just as in the previous case:

Read first number
Process first number
WHILE Number <> Trailer DO
    Read subsequent Number
    IF Number <> Trailer THEN
        Process
END

We'll make some concluding comments about the various loop structures. The FOR loop is probably the simplest and the favorite of beginning programmers. It is also the least general. We must know in advance the number of times the loop should execute, and we must control the loop based on an integer value (or slightly more general values, as we see in later chapters). Many loops in computer programming are controlled by a noninteger condition—e.g., when a certain name is reached or when a certain answer is given.

Of the indefinite loops, the LOOP is the most flexible, since the programmer can choose where to put the test for termination. If a situation calls for a termination test in the middle of a loop body, this is most naturally achieved using the LOOP. However, there are certainly many cases where the naturalness of the syntax of the WHILE or the REPEAT/UNTIL makes one of these the best choice. For example, compounding interest *until* $1,000,000.00 is accumulated begs for a REPEAT/UNTIL, and paying bills *while* you still have money begs for a WHILE.

NESTED LOOPS

Just as Modula-2 allows conditional statements nested inside other conditionals, it also allows us to nest loops inside each other. For a simple example, we'll consider a grading program for computing quiz averages. Suppose a teacher gives 10 quizzes during the semester, and students are required to take five quizzes, with the option of taking as many more as they like. Now, the teacher doesn't mind counting how many students are in the class, so this value is entered first into a text file. However, the teacher doesn't want to count how many quizzes each student has taken. So for each student, the teacher carefully enters a single data line consisting of the student's name (in the form First Last) followed by the quiz scores (separated by blanks). We present a program that prints out the quiz average for each student. To do this, we need to be able to work our way through the data file.

Obviously, we determine the class size by reading the first data item in the file. On the next line, we expect to find a name. When reading a string from a text file, Modula-2 uses the blank space as a delimiter. That is, a blank will terminate the reading of a string. So, if we have a data line that looks like:

```
Lowell Carmony 70 80 90 80 80 90
```

and we attempt to read a string, Modula-2 reads up to the first blank. We must do two reads to get both the first and the last names. Once we have read the name, we can get the quiz scores. One nice feature of text files is that we can mix numeric and character data, as long as we process the data with the appropriate kind of read statement. How do we know how many quiz scores to read for Lowell Carmony? Modula-2 organizes text files into lines. It also provides a system flag for keeping track of when we are at the end of a line in a text file. This flag is called EOL, and it is assigned to the system variable termCH (note the strange capitalization) when we have read the last data item on a line. In general, termCH is the character that terminated the reading operation. So we can use the condition

```
termCH = EOL
```

to help us determine if we have reached the end of the file. That way, the teacher needs neither to count the quizzes nor to place a trailer value at the end of each student's list of quiz scores. Our program is given in Listing 6.8.

```
MODULE QuizAverage;

(* This program computes quiz averages for a class of students.
There are a maximum of 10 quizzes. Each student must take at least
5 quizzes.                                                        *)

FROM InOut IMPORT WriteLn, ReadString, WriteString, ReadCard,
                  WriteCard, OpenInput, CloseInput, termCH, EOL;

TYPE   Name = ARRAY[0..19] OF CHAR;

VAR    ClassSize     : CARDINAL;
       NumQuizzes    : CARDINAL;
       Student       : CARDINAL;
       CurrentScore  : CARDINAL;
       Total         : CARDINAL;
       Average       : CARDINAL;
       First         : Name;
       Last          : Name;

BEGIN
  OpenInput;
  ReadCard(ClassSize);(* Read value to determine class size. *)
  FOR Student := 1 TO ClassSize DO
    ReadString(First);                          (* Read names. *)
    ReadString(Last);
    Total := 0;
    NumQuizzes := 0;
```

```
    REPEAT            (* Loop reading quizzes for this student. *)
      ReadCard(CurrentScore);
      Total := Total + CurrentScore;
      INC(NumQuizzes)
    UNTIL termCH = EOL;

    Average := Total DIV NumQuizzes;
    WriteLn;
    WriteString('The average for ');
    WriteString(First);
    Write(' ');
    WriteString(Last);
    WriteString(' is ');
    WriteCard(Average, 0)
  END; (* FOR *)
  CloseInput
END QuizAverage.
```

Listing 6.8

Although the logic of the above program should be pretty clear, there is an important point to emphasize here. The most common error of beginning programmers is to omit or misplace the initialization statements for `Total` and `NumQuizzes`. The reader should recognize the potential disaster that this error can cause. If the statements appear before the `FOR` loop, then they are executed only once. That is, the variable `Total`, which is supposed to compute a quiz total for a particular student, computes the quiz total for the entire class. Likewise, `NumQuizzes` computes the total number of quizzes taken by the class. So the teacher ends up computing a class average instead of class members' averages. Clearly, we need to reset `Total` and `NumQuizzes` to 0 before we begin processing a student's average. Since we need to do this once for each student, those statements belong inside the `FOR`. Figuring out how many times a statement is executed determines where it belongs: outside all loops, inside all loops, or inside one loop but outside another. It is probably safe to say that misplaced initializations are one of the major causes of faulty programs when nested loops are involved.

We'll also make a few remarks related to text files. First, observe that we don't initialize `termCH`. `termCH` is maintained by the system. It is initialized through the call to `OpenInput` and is modified each time we read a new piece of data from the file. This is true in general of these special file variables. We can use their values to control our programs, but we don't have to worry about how these quantities are given values. The system takes care of everything for us. Also, although we were able to handle the names easily enough in this example, the fact that Modula-2 uses the space to delimit strings can cause problems. For example, suppose we had a file to process that contained on each line the name of a city and the high temperature in that city for the month of August. Then, a simple sequence like

```
ReadString(City);
ReadCard(Temp);
```

won't work on a file that contains

```
Chicago 95
Boston 98
San Francisco 72
New York 93
Miami 101
...
```

because ReadString(City), the third time through, will take 'San' for the value of City and attempt to read 'Francisco' for the value of Temp.

We'll close this section with one more text file example, one that demonstrates the system-maintained variable Done. Done works best with files that are processed character by character. When we read data out of text files, the system automatically keeps track of whether there are any data left that haven't been processed. When we open a file, Done is set to TRUE (if there is any information in the file). As long as we are successful in reading information from the file, Done remains TRUE (that is, we were successful in doing something; i.e., our job was Done). When we are unable to read from a file, because we have exhausted our input, Done is set to FALSE. So, if we have a text file called Typing.Txt that looks like this:

```
Now is the time
for all good
men to come to the
aid of their country.
```

then the following segment would print this information to the screen, assuming that we imported Done from InOut and answered the prompt generated by OpenInput by naming the text file Typing

```
OpenInput;
WHILE Done DO
   Read(Ch);
   Write(Ch)
END; (* WHILE *)
```

Again, we don't have to do anything to Done—it's all handled by the system. But we can let Done monitor when there is nothing left in the file. Because of the way Modula-2 modifies Done (specifically, it doesn't set Done to FALSE as the last data item is read), we don't use Done with numeric data, but only, as illustrated, with CHAR data.

THE CASE STATEMENT

We'll finish this chapter by turning our attention back to conditional constructs. In addition to the various forms of the IF...THEN statement, Modula-2 provides an alternative conditional construct that can be used in certain cases. This construct is the

CASE statement, and its syntax is best described by looking at a simple example. Suppose our computer-happy teacher from before gives a 5-point quiz and then wants to send out the results via electronic mail to all the students. The teacher, however, wants to attach a label to the scores. One way to do this employs nested IFs:

```
IF Score = 5 THEN
  Mark := 'Exceptionally Good'
ELSIF Score = 4 THEN
  Mark := 'Very Good'
ELSIF Score = 3 THEN
  Mark := 'OK'
ELSIF Score = 2 THEN
  Mark := 'Shaky'
ELSIF Score = 1 THEN
  Mark := 'Lousy'
ELSE
  Mark := 'Exceptionally Lousy'
END; (* IF *)
```

A CASE statement that performs the same task is

```
CASE Score OF
  5 : Mark := 'Exceptionally Good' | (* Vertical Bar separates *)
  4 : Mark := 'Very Good'          | (* CASE options.          *)
  3 : Mark := 'OK'                 |
  2 : Mark := 'Shaky'              |
  1 : Mark := 'Lousy'              |
  0 : Mark := 'Exceptionally Lousy'
END; (* CASE *)
```

Now that we have seen an example, let's discuss this construct in detail and describe the options available. The keyword CASE must be followed by an expresson that (for now) is of type INTEGER, CARDINAL, or CHAR. This expression is called the CASE selector. The integer values 5, 4, 3, 2, 1, and 0 are called the CASE labels. CASE labels must be constant values—that is, they are not allowed to be variables or expressions. As one might guess, the CASE statement works by matching the value of the selector with one of the labels and then executing the statement (or sequence of statements) that corresponds to that label. In the example above, there must be a match. If there isn't— that is, if the above case statement were executed with a selector value of 6—Modula-2 would give an error during execution. There is a way to avoid such an error. Modula-2 allows a CASE statement to have an optional ELSE clause. This clause must follow all the label options. Thus, we could modify the above to

```
CASE Score OF
  5 : Mark := 'Exceptionally Good'  | (* Vertical Bar separates *)
  4 : Mark := 'Very Good'           | (* CASE options.          *)
  3 : Mark := 'OK'                  |
  2 : Mark := 'Shaky'               |
  1 : Mark := 'Lousy'               |
  0 : Mark := 'Exceptionally Lousy'
  ELSE
     WriteString('Invalid grade—See me!')
END; (* CASE *)
```

Notice that the CASE statement is fundamentally different from an IF...THEN statement in the following respect. Both constructs may have an optional ELSE clause to catch all the suspicious cases. But if an ELSE clause is not included and a value falls through the net, the CASE statement generates an error, while the IF statement simply causes no action.

The CASE statement is syntactically simpler and more readable than the IF...THEN. One of the options that makes it even simpler is multiple labels on a single option. Suppose the quiz of the previous example had been a 10-point quiz, but the teacher still wanted to send the same basic messages. The following CASE statement accomplishes this:

```
CASE Score OF
  10  : Mark := 'Exceptionally Good'    |
  8,9 : Mark := 'Very Good'             |
  6,7 : Mark := 'OK'                    |
  4,5 : Mark := 'Shaky'                 |
  2,3 : Mark := 'Lousy'                 |
  0,1 : Mark := 'Exceptionally Lousy'
  ELSE
     WriteString('Invalid grade—See me!')
END; (* CASE *)
```

This certainly seems preferable to

```
IF Score = 10 THEN
  Mark := 'Exceptionally Good'
ELSIF (Score = 8) OR (Score = 9) THEN
  Mark := 'Very Good'
ELSIF ......
```

A syntactic restriction of the CASE statement is that a label may not appear on more than one option. That is, there must not be more than one match of the CASE selector with a label.

Finally, the labels in a CASE statement can be represented by a **subrange**. A subrange is useful when there are several *consecutive* labels for a single option. Suppose our teacher wanted to group all those scoring less than 7 together.

```
CASE Score OF
   10   : Mark := 'Exceptionally Good'        |
   8,9  : Mark := 'Very Good'                 |
   7    : Mark := 'OK'                        |
   0..6 : Mark := 'In Trouble'                |
   ELSE
     WriteString('Invalid grade—See me!')
END;
```

The subrange 0..6 is equivalent to 0,1,2,3,4,5,6.

Finally, we point out that any of the case options can be compound. That is, if we were keeping counts of the various kinds of scores, we could write

```
CASE Score OF
   10   : Mark := 'Exceptionally Good'; INC(NumExGood)   |
   8,9  : Mark := 'Very Good'; INC(NumVGood)             |
   etc.
```

In the exercises that follow, we suggest that you try a variety of constructs. Don't just stick with the REPEAT/UNTIL statement. Try all the loops. Try a CASE statement instead of an IF...THEN. It might also be worthwhile to solve a single exercise in more than one way, allowing more opportunity to compare the different constructs.

EXERCISES

6.1 Write a program that prints out a table of squares and cubes for the first 25 positive integers.

6.2 A piece of paper is 0.005 of an inch thick. How thick would the paper be if we folded it in half 40 times? Note that each time we fold the paper over on itself, it becomes twice as thick.

6.3 Write a program that creates a table of Celsius-to-Fahrenheit temperature conversions. Allow the user to enter the starting point and ending point of the table. The conversion formula is

$$F = 9/5 * C + 32$$

6.4 Write a program that reads a list of integers from the keyboard and prints out the maximum. Suppose that the list can contain any integer, positive, negative, or 0. Unlike the example in the chapter, it will be necessary to determine the end of the list by asking the user if there are more numbers to enter and using the answer to this question as the trailer.

6.5 Create a text file that contains the names of U.S. cities, each followed by an integer representing a temperature. Then write a program to print out the lowest temperature in the file, as well as the city that recorded this temperature. (Note: Make sure that each city has a one-word name.)

6.6 Repeat exercise 6.5, but allow for the possibility that at most three cities tie for the coldest temperature. Run your program with test files where there is no tie, a two-way tie, and a three-way tie.

6.7 The population of the town of Mudville was 650 in 1980. Since the joy went out of Mudville back when Mighty Casey struck out, the town has experienced a population decline of 8 percent per year. What is the last year that the Mudville Nine will be able to take the field? Solve the problem using a CARDINAL for the population of Mudville, then solve it using a REAL.

6.8 (Armstrong Numbers) The number 153 has the interesting property that $1^3 + 5^3 + 3^3 = 1 + 125 + 27 = 153$. That is, 153 is equal to the sum of the cubes of its own digits. Are there other three-digit numbers that have this property? Write a program that tests all three-digit numbers and prints out those that have the above property. You should find four of them (including 153). These numbers are called Armstrong Numbers.
Hint: Use DIV and MOD and divisors like 10 and 100 to break a number into its digits.

6.9 (Perfect Numbers) A number is said to be perfect if it is the sum of its own divisors (excluding itself). For example, 6 is perfect since $6 = 1 + 2 + 3$ and 1, 2, and 3 are all the divisors of 6. Verify by hand that 28 is also perfect. Write a program that finds the first perfect number after 28.

6.10 (Abundant Numbers) A number is abundant if it is less than the sum of its divisors (excluding itself). For example, 12 is abundant, since $12 < 1 + 2 + 3 + 4 + 6$. Write a program that finds all abundant numbers less than 500. Since 1 is a special case, begin your search at 2. Do you notice anything about all the numbers on your list?

6.11 (Odd Abundant Numbers) Despite the impression given by Exercise 6.10, there do exist odd abundant numbers. Write a program to find the smallest one. Use the results of Exercise 6.10 to start your search at 500. Even with this headstart, your program may take a while to execute.

6.12 Modify the program of the previous chapter that tests a number for primality and print out a table of all primes less than 500. Remove the test of even numbers and test only odd ones. Handle 2 and 3 as special cases, and begin testing candidates with 5, using a starting trial divisor of 3.

6.13 Consider a progressive tax based on the following six tax brackets:

Income Range	Tax Rate
Up to $4999.99	3%
Up to $9999.99	8%
Up to $14999.99	15%
Up to $19999.99	24%
Up to $24999.99	35%
Over $24999.99	50%

Write a program that reads in an income value from the keyboard and computes the tax on this value. Read the value as a whole dollar amount, and use DIV to convert the value into one of six tax brackets. Then use a CASE statement to determine the tax.

Chapter 7

PROCEDURES AND FUNCTIONS

The development of procedures and functions is needed so that we can truly implement our divide-and-conquer problem-solving strategy. Recall that the divide-and-conquer paradigm requires that we decompose a large problem into smaller units and repeat this process until we have small, manageable, understandable units. These units can then be implemented as small, separate subprograms. Procedures and functions play the role of subprograms in Modula-2. For now, think of procedures and functions as black boxes that do small, distinct tasks for us. At this point, we do not want to cloud the issue by distinguishing between procedures and functions. Think of them both as slave subprograms that will do tasks at our bidding. The main module then calls or invokes these procedures and functions to do its work. We will give many examples in the pages to follow, but for now consider a simple generic example without worrying about actual Modula-2 syntax. Many simple problems can be solved with the following three subunits:

1. Obtain the input data from the user.
2. Calculate some simple results.
3. Output the results in an understandable form.

A module using this design with a black box for each subunit would be structured as shown in Figure 7.1. Note that the body of the Main module is short and, therefore, easy to read and understand. If the reader needs further details about the operation of any of the black boxes, that information can be obtained from looking at their definitions. But these specifics are separated from the main module—which, therefore, is not crowded with all the details of the entire program.

MODULE Main;

Importations and constant and variable declarations for Main

Definition of black box 1: Obtain the input data

Definition of black box 2: Calculate results

Definition of black box 3: Output the results

BEGIN (* Body of Main Module in pseudo-code, not Modula-2 *)
    Call the "Obtain the Input Data" subprogram
    Call the "Calculate Results" subprogram
    Call the "Output the Results" subprogram
END Main.

Figure 7.1

In a specific problem, one can choose appropriate names for the procedures and functions, as well as the identifiers. This makes the module nearly self-documenting. For example, we leave it to the reader to guess what the following Modula–2 segment is designed to do:

```
BEGIN
   AskUser(Name, HtFeet, HtInches, Weight, Sex);
   FindPerfectWt(HtFeet, HtInches, Weight, Sex, IdealWeight);
   Display(Name, HtFeet, HtInches, Weight, Sex, IdealWeight)
END ObesityTester.
```

Note that our black boxes can have **inputs** to them and **outputs** from them. Hopefully, it is obvious that AskUser's job is to prompt the user for various personal information and output the data back to the main module for further use. Likewise, from the context, it is hopefully clear that FindPerfectWt takes as input the data about the user's height, weight, and sex and outputs an IdealWeight for that user. Notice that FindPerfectWt does not care whether the user's name is Dave or Sue, since this is clearly not relevant to its task. Display takes as input all the data and prints it to the screen in a readable format. As such, Display is very simple, but, as we know, all the WriteLns, WriteStrings, WriteCards, etc., for Display can be very lengthy and tedious. The advantage of using Display is that the statements that tend to clutter the main module are removed and kept in the definition for Display, where they can be inspected or modified if necessary.

Procedures and functions make Modula-2 an **extensible** language. By this we mean that it is possible to extend the language by using procedures and functions. Imagine how simple it would be to determine an individual's ideal weight if Modula-2 had a built-in black box named `FindPerfectWt` that did all the work for you! Of course, Modula-2 doesn't contain such a built-in black box, but it is easy to define your own `FindPerfectWt` black box and then use it to solve the given problem. This is the great problem-solving tool that procedures and functions provide: When presented with a problem, we should ask ourselves not "What Modula-2 construct can I use to model this problem?" but "What black boxes do I need to design that will enable me to divide and conquer this problem?" This strategy, also called **top-down design**, further subdivides those black boxes, if necessary, until manageable units are obtained. The implementation of these units as Modula-2 procedures and functions should then be straightforward. Note, once again, that our discussion has been primarily concerned with *design,* not *coding,* in Modula-2. If you are spending too much time debugging code or are not getting programs to run (as is often the case with beginners), that is a sure sign that you are not spending enough time in the design phase before going to the implementation phase. It should be clear that you won't have much success implementing a design that you don't really understand.

THE DISTINCTION BETWEEN PROCEDURES AND FUNCTIONS

It is time to discuss what procedures and functions are and to indicate the small, but important, ways in which they differ from one another. Let us begin with functions. **A function is a black box that returns, through its name, exactly one value back to the calling environment**. You have already used functions in Modula-2. For example, `FLOAT` is an example of a built-in function that converts CARDINALs into REALs. For example, if K is the CARDINAL 7, then `FLOAT(K)` is the REAL value 7.0. Note that

```
FLOAT(K);                        (* ERROR, Incomplete Statement *)
```

is not a complete statement in Modula-2, since it names just a value, not a complete action. To make it into a complete statement, some action needs to be done with the value. For example, each of the following is valid:

```
WriteReal(FLOAT(K), 0);
IF FLOAT(K) = X THEN
  WriteString('K and X are "equivalent".')
END; (* IF *)
```

In contrast to functions, **procedures are black boxes that name complete actions**. They return no value through their names, but, as we shall see, they can return results. In this respect, procedures are a generalization of functions. A very simple example of a built-in procedure is `HALT`, which simply halts program execution. `HALT` is an example of a procedure that returns no result. Since procedures, in contrast to functions, name complete actions, they stand alone as a single statement. The following are examples of valid procedure invocations:

```
ExplainPurposeOfModule;
AskUser(Name, HtFeet, HtInches, Weight, Sex);
HALT;
```

ExplainPurposeOfModule is a procedure, like HALT, with no inputs and no outputs. Apparently, it is composed of a long string of WriteStrings that explain to the user what the present module is all about. AskUser is a module with five outputs or results, as its job appears to be to obtain values for the five arguments listed with it.

The single most troublesome distinction for beginners is that functions never stand alone as complete statements, while procedures always do. This is because the function is simply holding a value, while the procedure is naming a complete act. This difference will also explain the subtle ways in which function definitions differ from procedure definitions. However, let us first look at some of the standard functions and procedures supplied with Modula-2.

SOME USEFUL STANDARD FUNCTIONS AND PROCEDURES

The most commonly used procedures and functions, such as taking square roots or absolute values, are provided in the language, so that the user does not need to recreate them. In Modula-2, some of these are built into the language (always present) and others, less commonly used, are provided in a module MathLib0, which is short for "Mathematical Library Zero." Tables 7.1 and 7.2 list the most common procedures and functions. A complete listing of the built-in standard procedures is provided in Appendix C, and the most useful libraries are listed in Appendix A, but check your own Modula-2 documentation, as it may well provide additional ones. Each of the functions and procedures listed in Tables 7.1 and 7.2 is discussed briefly in a paragraph following the table. In Table 7.1, we use the abbreviations "Func" and "Proc" to denote functions and procedures, respectively. All the objects in Table 7.2 are functions. For now, the phrase **ordinal type** means INTEGER, CARDINAL, or CHAR, but in the next chapter it will also include all user-defined types.

The ABS *function* returns the absolute value of its input. ABS will accept INTEGER or REAL inputs and returns the same type as the input. Thus, ABS(-14) is the INTEGER 14, while ABS(-7.5) is the REAL 7.5. Why is there no ABS for CARDI-NALs?

The CAP *function* returns the uppercase equivalent of its input, which should have a letter value. If the input is already uppercase, CAP just returns that value.

The CHR *function* returns the CHARacter whose ASCII value is represented in its CARDINAL input. For example, CHR(65) is the CHARacter "A". See Table 4.1 for more details.

DEC is the decrement *procedure*. DEC(x) reduces its input by 1. For example, if Ch is a character identifier with the value "Q", then

```
DEC(Ch);
```

reassigns Ch the value "P". If Index is a CARDINAL (or INTEGER) identifier with the value 7, then

Table 7.1: Some Built-in Functions and Procedures of Modula-2

Name	Type of Input	Type of Result	Func/Proc
ABS(x)	x of any numeric type	same as input type	Func
CAP(ch)	ch of type CHAR	CHAR	Func
CHR(k)	k of type CARDINAL in the range 0 to 127	CHAR	Func
DEC(x)	x any ordinal type	same as input type	Proc
FLOAT(k)	k of type CARDINAL	REAL	Func
HALT	none	none	Proc
INC(x)	x any ordinal type	same as input type	Proc
MAX(T)	T any type name	same as input type	Func
MIN(T)	T any type name	same as input type	Func
ORD(x)	x any ordinal type	CARDINAL	Func
SIZE(x)	x of any type	CARDINAL	Func
TRUNC(x)	x of type REAL	CARDINAL	Func
TSIZE(T)	T any type name	CARDINAL	Func

```
DEC(Index);
```

reduces Index to 6. As such, it is shorthand for the longer statement:

```
Index := Index - 1;
```

DEC will not work with the REAL type, but only with types like CARDINAL, INTEGER, and CHAR, where each value, except the first, has a logical previous value. Previous values in the CHAR type are defined by the ASCII ordering of the characters as given in Table 4.1.

The procedure DEC also has a second form for decrementing by more than 1. For example, if we again assume that Ch has the value "Q" and Index the value 7, then

```
DEC(Ch, 3);
DEC(Index, 2)
```

reduces Ch three letters to "N" and Index by two to 5.

FLOAT is the *function* that converts CARDINALs to REALs. FLOAT was discussed extensively in Chapter 4.

HALT, as previously mentioned, is a *procedure* that simply halts the execution of a program.

INC is the increment *procedure*. If Ch and Index are CHARacter and CARDINAL identifiers with the values "Q" and 7, respectively, then

```
INC(Ch);
INC(Index);
```

makes them "R" and 8, respectively. INC will not work with the REAL type.

The procedure INC also has a second form. For example, if Ch and Index are again "Q" and 7, then

```
INC(Ch, 5);
INC(Index, 2);
```

makes them "V" and 9, respectively.

MAX and MIN are *functions* that return the largest and smallest values of the given type. For example, on many machines, MAX(INTEGER) and MIN(INTEGER) will be 32767 and -32768, respectively. MAX and MIN were added by Niklaus Wirth in the third edition of his definition of Modula-2 and, hence, may not be found in all Modula-2 compilers.

ORD is the ordinal or counting *function* that returns the position of its argument in the sequence that defines that type. ORD is not defined for the REAL type, but only for types where each element (except the first) has a previous element and each element (except the last) has a next element. For now, ORD is most useful with the CHAR type, where it provides an inverse to the CHR function. For example, ORD("A") is the value 65. ORD will also be very useful with user-defined types, as discussed in Chapter 9.

SIZE and TSIZE are *functions* that return the amount of memory a particular system uses to store an object. SIZE wants an identifier as its input, and TSIZE wants a type name. For example, if K is a CARDINAL, then SIZE(K) and TSIZE(CARDINAL) will both return 2 on many systems, since CARDINALs often require 2 bytes of storage in microcomputer implementations of Modula-2.

TRUNC is the *function* that truncates REALs to CARDINALs by chopping off the fractional part. For example, TRUNC(8.957) is 8, without a decimal point. See Chapter 4 for more discussion of TRUNC.

All the objects in Table 7.2 are functions. Remember that they are not built in, but must be imported from MathLib0.

The arctan, cos, and sin are the standard trigonometric functions. We expect that the reader who has need for them knows what they are for and knows that they expect arguments measured in radians.

Likewise, exp and ln are the natural exponential and logarithmic functions with base e. For exponents, such as X^5, we have to write our own function, which we will do shortly.

The function sqrt is the standard square-root operator. The functions entier and real perform conversions from REAL to INTEGER types and vice versa. For

Table 7.2: Mathematical Functions from MathLib0

Name	Type of Input	Type of Result
arctan(x)	x of type REAL	REAL
cos(x)	x of type REAL	REAL
entier(x)	x of type REAL	INTEGER
exp(x)	x of type REAL	REAL
ln(x)	x of type REAL	REAL
real(i)	i of type INTEGER	REAL
sin(x)	x of type REAL	REAL
sqrt(x)	x of type REAL	REAL

example, `entier(-35.84)` is -35 and `real(-47)` is -47.0.

Note that all the functions in `MathLib0` are in lowercase. For some reason, this seems particularly difficult to remember in `real`'s case.

USER-DEFINED FUNCTIONS

As our first example, let us write the missing power function so that we can easily compute expressions such as X^5. For this simple example, we will assume that the base (X) is REAL while the exponent is a CARDINAL. Let us agree to call our function `Power` and note that we expect `Power(X, K)` to return us a REAL value. For example, `Power(1.5, 3)` should be the REAL value $(1.5)^3 = 3.375$.

Every function definition begins with a header that tells

1. The name of the function
2. The name and type of each input to the function
3. The type of the output of the function

For `Power` this header will be

```
PROCEDURE Power(X : REAL; K : CARDINAL) : REAL;
```

From this, it is obvious that the name of the object being defined is `Power` and that `Power` expects two inputs—the first must be REAL, and the second must be

CARDINAL. It is the final REAL on the end that indicates that Power is a function and that it is returning a REAL value through its name. To conserve on keywords, Modula uses the keyword PROCEDURE to introduce both function and procedure definitions. As we shall see, the only difference in procedure headings is that they fail to have a final value stated (because the procedure carries no value back through its name). In this book, we will follow the practice of including with each function a comment that reminds the reader that it is a function, not a procedure, being defined.

With two other exceptions, the body of the definition of a function looks exactly like the body of any module definition. The first exception is that a function definition must contain a RETURN statement that tells the system what value to return through the function name. Finally, END Power at the end of the definition is followed by a semicolon rather than a period. With these distinctions carefully in mind, study Listing 7.1, which contains the complete definition of function Power.

```
PROCEDURE Power(X : REAL; K : CARDINAL) : REAL;

(* This function raises X to the power K by performing successive
multiplications. Note that if K is zero, Power returns the value
1.0.                                                              *)

VAR   LoopIndex  : CARDINAL;
      Product    : REAL;

BEGIN
   Product := 1.0;
   FOR LoopIndex := 1 TO K DO
     Product := Product * X
   END;  (* FOR *)
   RETURN(Product)
END Power;
```

Listing 7.1

Listing 7.1 shows why **subprograms** is a good name for functions. Except for very minor differences, the function Power looks like a small program. We see that functions can have their own VARiable declarations. They can also have CONSTant declarations and can use FORs, IFs, and WHILEs. They can use any construct that we have introduced for modules, except for importation, which must be done at the main module level. As long as you can remember the syntax for the function heading, can remember to include a RETURN statement, and can remember not to use a period at the end of the function definition, functions are easy to write.

The RETURN statement does not need to be the last statement in the body of the function, but it often is. Also, there can be several conditional RETURNs. An example of these possibilities is given by the following fragment of a function body that determines a percentage to be applied to the full fare to determine the fare to be charged for a given individual depending on that individual's age:

```
IF (Age < 13) OR (Age > 64) THEN
  RETURN (0.50)            (* Kids and Senior Citizens at 50%. *)
ELSE
  RETURN (1.00)              (* Adults pay full fare of 100%. *)
END  (* IF *)
```

Notice that every identifier used in the body of the function Power in Listing 7.1 is listed in one of two places. It is either in the function heading or in the VAR list inside the function. For now, we make the rule that **every identifier used in any function should be found in one of these two places.** Later, after more examples and after we introduce procedures, we will have much more to say about this subject, and we will see that our rule (while still a good one) can be relaxed a little.

The identifiers listed in the VAR section within the function are called the **local** variables of the function. They are created when the function is invoked and are destroyed when the function has completed its task. Thus, they cannot be accessed from outside the function—and that is why they are called local to the function. They can be thought of as scratch or work variables that the function needs to complete its task. For example, our algorithm to compute X^5 needs a LoopIndex to count from 1 to 5. This LoopIndex is neither input to nor output from the function, but is needed simply for the function to do its work properly. These local variables can even have the same names as variables in the outer module, and the system will keep them separate. That is because memory isn't allocated for the local variables LoopIndex and Product until Power is invoked. If such variables exist in the outer environment, then these new ones mask the old ones and Power will be able to see only the local LoopIndex and Product. When Power has completed its execution, memory storage for the local variables is reclaimed and the other LoopIndex and/or Product are again unmasked. We will have much more to say about this subject, the scope of an identifier, later in this chapter.

The identifiers listed in the function heading within the parentheses are called the **dummy** or **formal parameters** to the function. We shall simply call them the parameters for the function. For the function Power, these parameters serve to provide it with the necessary inputs. After all, how can Power raise X to the Kth power if it doesn't know what the values of X and K are?

However, it is important to realize that we can invoke Power with any pair of REAL and CARDINAL values. That is, if we have a module in which Principal, Rate, and BalanceDue are REAL and Term is a CARDINAL, then the total amount due at the end of the loan with compound interest is

$$BalanceDue \leftarrow Principal * (1.0 + Rate)^{Term}$$

and it is legal to write this in Modula-2, assuming that Principal, Rate, and Term already have values, as

```
BalanceDue := Principal * Power(1.0 + Rate, Term);
```

The identifiers or expressions that we actually use when we invoke a function are called the **arguments** or **actual parameters.** We shall simply call them arguments in contrast to the parameters used to define the function. The actual arguments do not have to be the same as the dummy parameters, but they can be. This means that we do not have to remember what the dummy parameters were. We can use new arguments, or we can accidentally use the same names—either way, no harm will come to us!

PRECONDITIONS AND POSTCONDITIONS

In this text, we will use a system of commenting procedures and functions known as **preconditions** and **postconditions**. The preconditions state the conditions that must be true *before* the procedure or function is called, and the postconditions state the conditions that the procedure or function promises will hold *after* the procedure or function has completed its invocation. As such, preconditions and postconditions are like a contract for a job to be done. For example, suppose you are having the interior of your house painted. The preconditions are the things that you promise to do, such as move the furniture and take down the pictures, before the painters come. The postconditions are the things that the painters promise will be true, when they finish, such as two coats of paint on all the walls. Preconditions and postconditions can help determine liability when something goes wrong. For example, if you forgot to take down your $48,000,000.00 Rembrandt and the painters put two coats of green paint over it, who is at fault?

In programming, preconditions and postconditions can help in debugging. If a module is producing garbage, then the preconditions and postconditions can help find the guilty procedure or function (determine liability). For if the precondition holds, but a procedure or function fails to live up to its promise, then there is clearly a problem in that procedure or function. On the other hand, if the preconditions do not hold, then the procedure or function is exonerated, since the contract is null and void if the preconditions are not satisfied at the time the procedure or function is invoked.

For these reasons, and others to be discussed below, we will use preconditions and postconditions with our procedures and functions. We urge you to do so, too. Since this is a first course, we do not formalize these notions. Rather, we leave our preconditions and postconditions in an informal (readable) style. The reader should be aware that more advanced courses in computer science may make a formal study of these kinds of **assertions** and use them to prove program correctness.

For Power, the preconditions are simply that the arguments used in the call must have REAL and CARDINAL values that do not cause REAL overflow when the powering operation is performed. Normally, when we write the procedure or function, we do not know what the arguments will be, so we will express the preconditions and postconditions in terms of the parameters. We will abbreviate preconditions to "Pre:" and, thus, for Power we would write something like:

```
(*Pre: X and K already have values such that X to the Kth power does
not cause overflow.                                                    *)
```

The postcondition for Power is simply that it does correctly compute X^K. We will abbreviate postconditions to "Post:" and for Power we might write

```
(*Post: The function Power returns X to the Kth power.                 *)
```

A TABLE OF SMALL POWERS

It is time to see how our function `Power` fits into a complete module that uses it to do something practical. For this purpose, consider the module `Table` of Listing 7.2, which produces a table of the squares, cubes, and fourth powers of the first 15 whole numbers. For this module, the type of the input to `Power` has been changed to CARDINAL, and its output type is therefore also changed to CARDINAL. To make this clear, the function has been renamed `CardPower`. Notice that the definition of the function comes after the `VAR` section of the main module and before the `BEGIN` of the main module. It is important to realize that the system reads and accepts the function definition, but does not execute the function until it is invoked in the main module. As always (so far), execution begins with the first statement after the `BEGIN` of the main module.

```
MODULE Table;

(* This module illustrates a user-defined function, CardPower, to
calculate a table of some numbers and their small powers.     *)

FROM InOut IMPORT WriteCard, WriteString, WriteLn;

VAR    Index  : CARDINAL;
       Expon  : CARDINAL;

PROCEDURE CardPower(J, K : CARDINAL) : CARDINAL;

(* Pre: X and K already have values such that X to the Kth power
does not cause overflow.
Post:   The function Power returns X to the Kth power.         *)

VAR    LoopIndex  : CARDINAL;
       Product    : CARDINAL;

BEGIN
  Product := 1;
  FOR LoopIndex := 1 TO K DO
    Product := Product * J
  END;  (* FOR *)
  RETURN(Product)
END CardPower;              (* End definition of function Power. *)

BEGIN                           (* Body of main module Table. *)
  WriteString("A small table of squares, cubes,
            and fourth powers:");
  WriteLn; WriteLn;
  WriteString("  Number     Square     Cube    Fourth Power");
  WriteLn;
```

```
  FOR Index := 1 TO 15 DO
    FOR Expon := 1 TO 4 DO
      WriteCard(CardPower(Index, Expon), 10)
    END;  (* Inner FOR *)
    WriteLn
  END  (* Outer FOR *)
END Table.
```

Listing 7.2

The output from module `Table` is of the following form:

```
A small table of squares, cubes, and fourth powers:

Number Square Cube   Fourth Power
1      1      1      1
2      4      8      16
3      9      27     81
4      16     64     256
...    ...    ...    ...
15     225    3375   50625
```

The reason that the table stops at 15 is that 16^4 already causes **CARDINAL** overflow on many systems.

Note that in the heading for `CardPower`, we have written

```
PROCEDURE CardPower (J, K : CARDINAL) : CARDINAL;
```

This is shorthand for

```
PROCEDURE CardPower (J : CARDINAL; K : CARDINAL) : CARDINAL
```

That is, when several consecutive parameters have the same type, they may be listed together (separated by commas) to conserve on space and typing. Notice that there is a semicolon separating parameter declarations. For example, to declare an INTEGER function, `Weird`, with two REAL, one CHAR, and two BOOLEAN parameters, we could write

```
PROCEDURE Weird(X1, X2 : REAL;  Ch : CHAR;  S1, S2 : BOOLEAN) :
                                                         INTEGER;
```

which also points out that if a function declaration is too long to fit on one line, we can break the heading at any reasonable point and simply continue it indented on the next line. At any reasonable point means at any place where a blank could appear. You cannot break a line in the middle of an identifier or type name.

Notice in Listing 7.2 that we have indented the declarations and body of function `CardPower`. This is so that the reader's eye can quickly see that these are not the declarations and main body of the module. The main body begins, as always, at the leftmost BEGIN in the entire listing. We will soon see that procedures and functions can have other procedures and functions nested within them. At that point, proper use of indentation becomes very important to preserve the readability of programs.

A FUNCTION EXAMPLE: THE SEARCH FOR PERFECT NUMBERS

Let us consider a more interesting problem from arithmetic where we can illustrate the divide-and-conquer strategy. Pythagoras, the famous mathematician of ancient Greece, was reportedly fascinated with perfect numbers. A whole number is perfect if it is exactly the sum of its own proper divisors. By divisors, we simply mean numbers that divide another number evenly. For example, 1, 2, 3, 4, 6, and 12 are the divisors of 12. By proper, we exclude the number itself, so the proper divisors of 12 are 1, 2, 3, 4, and 6. Therefore, 12 is not perfect, since

$$12 \neq 1 + 2 + 3 + 4 + 6 = 16$$

The smallest perfect number is 6, since

$$6 = 1 + 2 + 3$$

The next perfect number is 28, since

$$28 = 1 + 2 + 4 + 7 + 14$$

The next perfect number is much larger, and you are not likely to find it by playing around. Hence, let's write a module to find the next perfect number.

To approach this problem with a top-down design, we should ask ourselves what black box(es) we would wish for to make the problem easy to solve. Obviously, if Modula-2 had a built-in SumDivs(Num) function that returned the sum of the proper divisors of Num, then we would be in the clear, since a number is perfect only if it satisfies the equality test: Num equals SumDivs(Num). That is, if we had SumDivs, then we could start at 29 and just keep trying whole numbers until we found the next perfect one.

We know that there is a next perfect number, but you don't—and anyway, our module might miss perfect numbers, due to a bug, and keep on and on in its search. This would not be an infinite loop, since CARDINAL overflow would eventually occur. However, it is a good idea always to put a limit to such a search. If we are wrong about there being a next perfect number, or if the program is buggy and keeps searching on and on, then we will eventually be told that we have reached the limit of our search. Of course, if we find a perfect number, then we should stop the search and not continue on to the limit. To help us decide when to stop, we can use a BOOLEAN variable, Found. We can summarize our ideas in the following pseudo-code:

Initialize the Limit of the Search to some arbitrary value, say 5000
Set Found to False to indicate we haven't found a perfect number yet

Set Candidate to 28 to begin the search
Repeat
    Increment the Candidate
    If Candidate = SumDivs(Candidate) then
    Set Found to True--Perfect number has been found
Until Found or Candidate > Limit of the Search
If Found then
    Write out Candidate as the next perfect number
Else
    Write out a message that the search failed up to the given limit

This pseudo-code certainly isn't Modula-2, but it won't be difficult to implement it in Modula-2, assuming the existence of the function SumDivs. Before we write SumDivs, notice that Candidate was initialized to 28, not 29, since we incremented the Candidate before we tested it for perfecthood. If anything about the above pseudo-code is not clear, you should initialize Candidate to 6 and trace the outline step by step to see how it finds 28.

Our divide-and-conquer process has left us with a function, SumDivs, to design. If this were a difficult function to write, we could continue to break it down into more manageable pieces. As it turns out, however, SumDivs is very easy to write if we make the following observation: All the possible proper divisors of a given number are between 1 and half of the number. To decide if one number divides another evenly, we simply use MOD, since MOD gives us the remainder. That is:

TrialDivisor divides Num evenly

if and only if

The remainder upon division of Num by TrialDivisor is zero

Expressed in Modula-2, this can be written as the assertion (not statement):

```
(Num MOD TrialDivisor) = 0
```

Finally, of course, we need to keep a running summation of those TrialDivisors that do evenly divide the given number. Hence, we have the following pseudo-code outline for the function SumDivs:

Function SumDivs(Num) finds the sum of the proper divisors of Num:
    Initialize local variable Sum to zero
    For TrialDivisor ← 1 to half of Num --local var TrialDivisor
      If Num MOD TrialDivisor is zero then
        Sum ← Sum + TrialDivisor
    Return(Sum)

Again, the reader should trace this outline with a value of Num of 6 or 12 to see how SumDivs returns its result (6 or 16, respectively). Notice how every identifier used in

SumDivs is either a dummy parameter (Num) or a local variable (Sum, TrialDivisor) of the function SumDivs.

Listing 7.3 shows the complete module Perfect with the function SumDivs. Observe how closely the structure of the module follows the outline given by the pseudo-code. This indicates that our design was complete and that the implementation phase proceeded without trauma!

```modula2
MODULE Perfect;

(* This module searches for the next perfect number after 6 and 28.
A number is perfect if it is the sum of its own proper divisors.
For example,

6 = 1 + 2 + 3

and

28 = 1 + 2 + 4 + 7 + 14

To find perfect numbers, the main module calls the user-defined
function SumDivs(Num), which simply returns the sum of the proper
divisors of its input. The module reports failure if it finds no
perfect number before a predetermined limit for the search.  *)

FROM InOut IMPORT WriteLn, WriteCard, WriteString;

CONST   LimitOfSearch = 5000;

VAR   Candidate  : CARDINAL;
      Found      : BOOLEAN;

PROCEDURE SumDivs(Num : CARDINAL) : CARDINAL;

(* Pre: Num has a CARDINAL value.
Post:   The function SumDivs returns the sum of the divisors
of Num unless overflow occurs.                                *)

VAR   TrialDivisor : CARDINAL;
      Sum          : CARDINAL;

BEGIN
  Sum := 0;
  FOR TrialDivisor := 1 TO (Num DIV 2) DO
    IF (Num MOD TrialDivisor) = 0 THEN     (* Divide evenly? *)
      Sum := Sum + TrialDivisor
    END  (* IF *)
  END;  (* FOR *)
```

```
   RETURN(Sum)
END SumDivs;

BEGIN                                          (* Body of main module Perfect. *)
   Found := FALSE;   (* We haven't found a perfect number yet. *)
   Candidate := 28;(* Begin the search at the perfect number 28. *)
   REPEAT
      INC(Candidate);
      IF Candidate = SumDivs(Candidate) THEN
          Found := TRUE                 (* EUREKA! We have found it. *)
      END  (* IF *)
   UNTIL Found OR (Candidate > LimitOfSearch);
   IF Found THEN
      WriteCard(Candidate, 0);
      WriteString(" is the next perfect number.")
   ELSE
      WriteString("No additional perfect number was found. ");
      WriteCard(LimitOfSearch, 0)
   END  (* IF *)
END Perfect.
```

Listing 7.3

Module `Perfect` does find another perfect number, and its output is

```
496 is the next perfect number.
```

We leave it to the reader to verify that this is correct.

PARAMETERLESS FUNCTIONS: A QUIRK

Occasionally, we have need for a function with no input parameters. For example, suppose you are writing the next successful computer game and you want to give the user the option at the end of the game of playing again. In pseudo-code, we could write

```
Repeat
   Play the game
Until the user wants to quit
```

The unit "the user wants to quit" can be implemented as a BOOLEAN function that prompts the user and returns a Boolean indicating whether play should continue or not. As such, it has no input from the main module and, hence, no parameters. A quirk of Modula-2 syntax requires that every function have parentheses, even if it has no parameters. Thus, our pseudo-code would appear in Modula-2 as

```
REPEAT
  PlayGame(NumDragonsDestroyed, NumDamselsSaved)
UNTIL UserQuits();
```

where `PlayGame` is the procedure that actually plays the game and `UserQuits` is our simple **BOOLEAN** function. Listing 7.4 shows the full definition of the function `UserQuits()`. Note that it ends with a semicolon, not a period, since this is just a procedure, not a complete module.

```
PROCEDURE UserQuits() : BOOLEAN;

(* Pre: None.
Post:   This function returns TRUE if the user indicates she or
he wants to quit by typing "y" or "Y"; otherwise, it returns FALSE.
                                                                  *)


VAR Answer : CHAR;     (* Local variable for user's response. *)

BEGIN
  WriteString("Would you like to quit? (Y/N):  ");
  Read(Answer); Write(Answer);(* Echo the input to the screen. *)
  WriteLn;
  Answer := CAP(Answer);        (* Make sure we have uppercase. *)
  IF Answer = "Y" THEN
    RETURN(TRUE)                       (* Player is a quitter. *)
  ELSE
    RETURN(FALSE)            (* Player does not want to quit. *)
  END  (* IF *)
END UserQuits;
```

Listing 7.4

Notice that we have used the built-in `CAP` function to make sure that the response of the user is in uppercase. We do this because many people do not follow instructions well and will enter "y" instead of "Y" in response to our prompt. We could eliminate the `CAP` function and write the `IF` as

```
IF (Answer = "Y") OR (Answer = "y") THEN ...
```

but this is clearly not as simple as our `IF`.

Note in Listing 7.4 that we have also used `Write(Answer)` immediately after the `Read(Answer)` to make sure that the character pressed by the user appears on the screen. This is not necessary to the execution of the function, but it is usually disconcerting to the user when a key is pressed and nothing appears on the screen.

SIMPLE USER-DEFINED PROCEDURES

Let us now turn to the subject of procedures. As we know, a procedure does not return a value through its name. Therefore, a procedure heading looks like a function heading except that there is no final type given. Also, because it returns no value through its name, a procedure has no RETURN statement within it. These are the two minor differences between the syntaxes of procedure and function definitions.

Let's consider two simple procedure examples. Suppose you are writing a program that produces a large report. To impress the boss, you decide you will put strings of * across the page at various points

```
****************************************************************************
```

to help divide the report into sections. Of course, it isn't difficult to write such code, but it's tedious to keep repeating it. If we define a procedure Stars to do this task for us, then we can invoke Stars with the simple and clear statement

```
Stars;
```

as many times as we wish in our program. Listing 7.5 shows the listing that defines Stars. Note that Stars has no parameters and no type and, of course, no RETURN statement. Stars is a very simple procedure with only one local variable to Count the 80 columns of the screen. Also note that, in contrast to the parameterless function UserQuits() just discussed, a parameterless procedure does *not* have parentheses. This is another minor difference between procedures and functions in Modula-2.

```
PROCEDURE Stars;

(* Pre: None.
Post:   A line of 80 "*"s is printed.                              *)

VAR Count : CARDINAL;

BEGIN
  WriteLn;
  FOR Count := 1 TO 80 DO
    Write("*")
  END;  (* FOR *)
  WriteLn; WriteLn
END Stars;
```

Listing 7.5

The procedure Stars is not very flexible. It prints 80 stars whether that is what you want or not. Let's define a new procedure Break(Symbol, Length) that will print whatever symbol you want and as many of that symbol as you want. For example:

```
Break("$", 40);
```

will print 40 dollar signs, while

```
Break("+", 60);
```

will print 60 plus signs. Listing 7.6 shows the definition of the procedure Break(Symbol, Length). Notice how the extra flexibility over the simple procedure Stars is obtained from the two input parameters Symbol and Length. Observe how these replace the constants from the listing of Stars.

```
PROCEDURE Break(Symbol : CHAR; Length : CARDINAL);

(* Pre: Symbol has some CHAR value and Length some CARDINAL value.
   Post:   A line of Symbols of the given Length is printed.      *)

VAR Count : CARDINAL;

BEGIN
  WriteLn;
  FOR Count := 1 TO Length DO
    Write(Symbol)
  END;  (* FOR *)
  WriteLn; WriteLn
END Break;
```

•   Listing 7.6

Again, note that all the identifiers used in procedure Break are listed in one of two places. They are either parameters listed in the procedure heading or local variables declared in the procedure. Again, it is our temporary rule that every identifier used in a procedure or function must be found in one of those two places.

VALUE AND VARIABLE PARAMETERS

For simplicity, we have concealed one relevant fact about parameters. There are two kinds of parameters in Modula-2: value and variable parameters. **Value** parameters are the kind that we have illustrated in our examples so far. **Variable** parameters, as we will see below, are indicated by the keyword VAR.

With a value parameter, it is the value of the actual argument that is passed to the procedure or function. If the parameter is a value parameter, then the procedure or function makes a *copy* of the actual argument. This means that the procedure or function *cannot* change the value of an argument passed by value, since it is only the copy, not the original, that can be modified by the procedure or function.

How, then, can a procedure, which has no RETURN statement, pass any results back to the calling environment? The answer is provided by the other kind of parameter:

A variable parameter is an *alias* for the actual argument, and, hence, any changes to a variable parameter are immediately reflected in the actual argument.

Let us consider a specific example that was mentioned before. The procedure FindPerfectWt takes the height of the user in Feet and Inches and his or her Sex and determines the IdealWeight for that user. Feet, Inches, and Sex should be value parameters in FindPerfectWt, since the procedure must have these values, but it should not change them. (It shouldn't do a Sex change operation, for example.) On the other hand, FindPerfectWt computes (by some unspecified means) a new value for IdealWeight. Thus, IdealWeight must be a variable parameter. This means that the heading for FindPerfectWt is

```
PROCEDURE FindPerfectWt(Feet, Inches : CARDINAL; Sex : CHAR;
                                    VAR IdealWeight : REAL);
```

You indicate value parameters by not doing anything special. That is, a value parameter is what you get if you don't specify a variable parameter by using VAR.
The value and variable parameters can come in any order, so

```
PROCEDURE FindPerfectWt(VAR IdealWeight : REAL; Feet, Inches :
                                    CARDINAL; Sex : CHAR);
```

is also an acceptable heading for the procedure. While both headings for FindPerfectWt are acceptable, we shall have to remember the order of the parameters in the heading we use, because in any invocation of the procedure, the actual arguments have to be in the same order.
If the procedure Strange has two REAL variable parameters and two CHAR value parameters, then the heading for Strange can be written

```
PROCEDURE Strange(VAR X, Y : REAL;  A, B : CHAR);
```

Note, in particular, that the VAR applies only to X and Y. The effect of the VAR ends at the semicolon following REAL.

RIGHT AND WRONG: THE NEED FOR VARIABLE PARAMETERS

Experience in teaching many hundreds of students over many years has shown us that a very common programming error that beginners make is to forget the VAR in a parameter that needs to be a variable parameter. So that you will understand the severity of this error, we will write incorrect and correct versions of a very simple, but useful, procedure. Our procedure is Swap(J, K), and its objective is to swap or exchange the values of J and K, which we assume are CARDINAL identifiers. The first thing to realize is that

```
J := K;        (* Incorrect first attempt at the body of Swap. *)
K := J;
```

does *not* properly swap the values of J and K. To see this, suppose that J is 3 and K is 7 before the above statements. After the first assignment, we see that both J and K have the value 7. Hence, the second assignment has no effect and surely does not assign K the value 3. The easiest way to rectify this problem is to add a temporary variable, Temp, where the value 3 can be placed before it is lost. Please trace the following segment to see that it does correctly exchange the values of J and K:

```
Temp := J;                    (* Store the old value of J in Temp. *)
J := K;                         (* Put K's old value into J. *)
K := Temp;                      (* Put J's old value into K. *)
```

Listing 7.7 shows a module Wrong that uses this segment in a procedure Swap.

```
MODULE Wrong;

(* This module illustrates a common beginner's error involving the
failure to use VAR parameters.                              *)

FROM InOut IMPORT WriteString, WriteLn, WriteCard;

VAR    J  : CARDINAL;
       K  : CARDINAL;

PROCEDURE Swap(J, K : CARDINAL);
(* Pre: J and K have CARDINAL values.
Post:   The values of J and K are interchanged (supposedly). *)

   VAR Temp : CARDINAL;              (* A temporary for the swap. *)

   BEGIN
     Temp := J;
     J := K;
     K := Temp
   END Swap;

BEGIN                           (* Body of main module Wrong. *)
   J := 38;
   K := 695;
   WriteString("Before the swap the values of J and K are ");
   WriteCard(J, 0);
   WriteString(" and ");
   WriteCard(K, 0);
   WriteLn;

   Swap(J, K);

   WriteString("After the swap the values of J and K are ");
```

```
    WriteCard(J, 0);
    WriteString(" and ");
    WriteCard(K, 0);
    WriteLn
END Wrong.
```

Listing 7.7

Here is the output of Wrong:

```
Before the swap the values of J and K are 38 and 695
After the swap the values of J and K are 38 and 695
```

Wait a minute! Something is wrong with Wrong. The values of J and K were not exchanged. The problem, as we have already indicated, is that both of Swap's parameters must be variable parameters if the actual arguments, J and K, of the module are to be changed by the procedure Swap, even though it uses the same dummy parameters J and K. It is important to see why Wrong does not work. When Wrong is invoked, the values of the module's J and K (38 and 695) are passed to Swap, which stores these values in its own *copies* of J and K. Swap then exchanges the values of the copies, but no change is made to the originals! This is demonstrated in Figure 7.2, which shows a snapshot of memory just before the END of the execution of procedure Swap.

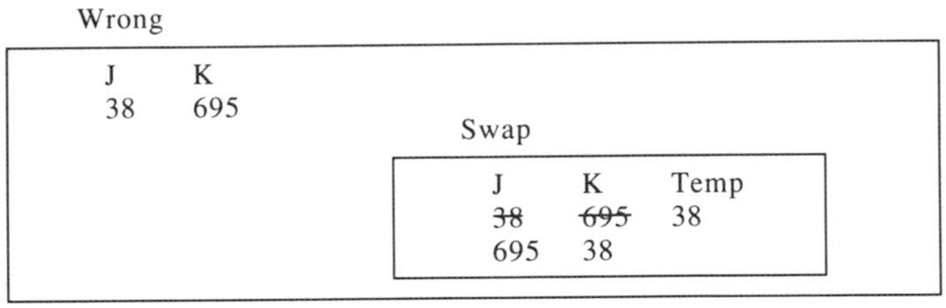

Figure 7.2

When Swap is finished executing, the memory for Swap's copies of J and K and Swap's local variable Temp is reclaimed by the system. Hence, Swap fails to exchange the values of the original J and K. It is worth noting that if we put a sequence of writes (try it!) inside of Swap just before its END, then we would see that Swap has swapped the values of its J and K.

What is needed is something like Figure 7.3 where the J and K of Swap are really the original J and K. This is exactly what variable parameters do for us.

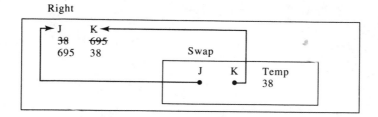

Figure 7.3

Listing 7.8 shows the module R i ght, which is exactly like module Wrong except for its name, the comment, and the critical fact that the parameters to Swap are variable.

```modula-2
MODULE Right;

(* This module illustrates correct usage of VAR parameters.   *)

FROM InOut IMPORT WriteString, WriteLn, WriteCard;

VAR    J : CARDINAL;
       K : CARDINAL;

PROCEDURE Swap( VAR J, K : CARDINAL);       (* Note the VAR !! *)
(* Pre: J and K have CARDINAL values.
Post:   The values of J and K are interchanged.              *)

VAR Temp : CARDINAL;               (* A temporary for the swap. *)

  BEGIN
    Temp := J;
    J := K;
    K := Temp
  END Swap;

BEGIN                              (* Body of main module Right. *)
  J := 38;
  K := 695;
  WriteString("Before the swap the values of J and K are ");
  WriteCard(J, 0);
  WriteString(" and ");
  WriteCard(K, 0);
  WriteLn;

  Swap(J, K);
```

```
    WriteString("After the swap the values of J and K are ");
    WriteCard(J, 0);
    WriteString(" and ");
    WriteCard(K, 0);
    WriteLn
END Right.
```

Listing 7.8

Finally, the output of Right is right:

```
Before the swap the values of J and K are 38 and 695
After the swap the values of J and K are 695 and 38
```

ANOTHER EXAMPLE FROM ARITHMETIC

Somebody once noticed that the number 3025 has the odd property that

$$3025 = (30 + 25)^2$$

Let us write a module to find all four-digit numbers with the property that they are equal to the square of the sum of their left and right parts. This would be easy if Modula-2 had a built-in Parts(Num, Left, Right) procedure that would separate Num into its two 2-digit parts. If Modula-2 also had a SqrSum(J, K) function that would return the square of the sum of its inputs, then we could solve the problem with the following outline:

> For Num from 1000 to 9999   --Try all four digit numbers
>   Call Parts to separate Num into Left and Right
>   If Num = the square of the sum of Left and Right then
>   Write out Num as one of the numbers we seek

We have solved the problem with a main module that will use the two subunits Parts and SqrSum. Parts(Num, Left, Right) will be a procedure because it computes two results, Left and Right, and a function should return only one value through its name. Thus, we see that Left and Right will be VAR parameters to Parts. After all, it is Parts' job to assign values to these parameters. Num, on the other hand, can be a value parameter to Parts. It is easy to separate Num by using DIV and MOD tricks. Here is the pseudo-code for Parts:

> Procedure Parts(Num, VAR Left, VAR Right)   --This separates Num into its
>   Left and Right halves. Since it is easy to forget, we have shown Left and Right
>   as VAR parameters.
>   Left ← Num DIV 100
>   Right ← Num MOD 100

Since SqrSum returns a single value, it can be written as a function. Here is its pseudo-code:

Function SqrSum(J, K)
   Return($(J+K)^2$)   --the square of the sum of J and K

Listing 7.9 shows the entire module OddProp, which finds all four-digit numbers with the given odd property. Note how the function SqrSum is invoked from within the condition of the IF statement, while the procedure Parts, as a complete statement, stands on a line by itself. Also notice that the dummy parameters used to define Parts are the same as the actual arguments in the module, but that the dummy parameters to SqrSum are different from the actual parameters. Both ways are valid and, in our final example of the chapter, we'll offer some advice about our preferences for the dummy parameter names.

Notice the important preconditions to procedure Parts. If Parts is not given a four-digit number, it is not responsible for the results. The preconditions and postconditions make it clear that Num is a value parameter to Parts, while Left and Right must be variable parameters. Thus, another advantage of using preconditions and postconditions is that they help the beginner answer the all-important question of when to use a value or variable parameter. For this reason alone, we urge you to use preconditions and postconditions with all procedures and functions that you write.

```
MODULE OddProp;

(* This module finds all four-digit numbers like 3025 that have the
odd property that they are equal to the square of the sum of their
left and right halves:

   3025 = (30 + 25) * (30 + 25)                                    *)

FROM InOut IMPORT WriteLn, WriteString, WriteCard;

VAR    Num   : CARDINAL;
       Left  : CARDINAL;
       Right : CARDINAL;

PROCEDURE Parts(Num : CARDINAL; VAR Left, Right : CARDINAL);
(* Pre: Num is a four-digit CARDINAL.
Post:   Left is assigned the left two digits of Num and Right
        is assigned the right two digits of Num.            *)

  BEGIN
    Left  := Num DIV 100;
    Right := Num MOD 100
  END Parts;
```

```
PROCEDURE SqrSum(J, K : CARDINAL) : CARDINAL;
(* Pre: J and K have CARDINAL values.
Post:   The function SqrSum returns the square of the sum of
        J and K, unless overflow occurs.                        *)

  BEGIN
    RETURN((J + K) * (J + K))
  END SqrSum;

BEGIN                              (* Body of main module OddProp. *)
  WriteString("Here are the 4-digit numbers equal to the");
  WriteLn;
  WriteString("square of the sum of their halves:");
  WriteLn;
  FOR Num := 1000 TO 9999 DO        (* Try all 4-digit numbers. *)
    Parts(Num, Left, Right);
    IF Num = SqrSum(Left, Right) THEN
      WriteCard(Num, 0); WriteLn
    END  (* IF *)
  END  (* FOR *)
END OddProp.
```

Listing 7.9

The output from OddProp finds the three numbers 2025, 3025, and 9801 that have the given property. We invite the reader to check by calculator that these do have the stated property.

PROCEDURES AND FUNCTIONS: WHY DOES MODULA-2 HAVE BOTH?

Since procedures and functions are so similar, students often ask why the language bothers to have both concepts. Couldn't we just have one or the other? Sometimes, beginners even get frustrated enough to ask why the language bothers to have functions or procedures at all. Couldn't we just put the code "in line" and do away with the need for procedures and functions (and therefore parameters) altogether? We now proceed to try to answer these reasonable questions, starting with the latter question first.

Theoretically, it is true that any program written with procedures and functions can also be written equivalently without any procedures or functions. As suggested above, one simply replaces the function or procedure call with specific code that does the same task. Therefore, procedures and functions do not add any new power to the language. Rather, we use procedures and functions because they provide clarity to our programs, support a structured approach to problem solving, and help us avoid repetitive code. We now discuss these three important points in more detail:

1. Procedures and functions add clarity to our programs

Without procedures and functions, a module quickly becomes too long for the human mind to grasp quickly and understand. If we don't use procedures and functions to hide some of the details, all the specifics of the module must be handled at once. In even moderately complex situations, this can be overwhelming. A good rule of thumb is that no subunit of the whole program should be more than one page long. Each subunit should do one clearly specified task that is reflected in its name. Thus, the main module becomes a short sequence of statements involving calls to various subprograms. As such, the main module is easy to read and very closely resembles its pseudo-code outline.

2. Procedures and functions support a structured approach to problem solving

Procedures and functions make the language extensible and allow us to think with a top-down or divide-and-conquer approach to problem solving. Rather than solve the whole problem at once, we decompose the problem into smaller subproblems. Each of these in turn is subdivided, if necessary, into smaller pieces. When we have decomposed the problem into manageable pieces, we need some way to reassemble the pieces to provide the solution to the original problem. Procedures and functions, and the easy way that we can invoke them from one another, allow us to implement our design in a straightforward manner. Of course, as the problem becomes more complex, this reason for using procedures and functions becomes even more valid. Our examples have been fairly simple, since we have just begun to study these concepts. We invite the reader to consider the final example of this chapter—a program listing of approximately five pages—and how complex and difficult it would be to understand if it were written without procedures and functions.

3. Procedures and functions help us avoid repetitive code

Suppose you are writing a game (or Lotto simulation) where you have to compare a user's three-digit number, `UserNum`, digit by digit against another three-digit number, `DailyWinNum`—because the payoff, if any, depends on the number of digits the user has correct. It might be convenient to have a procedure `Split(Num, Huns, Tens, Ones)` that would split a three-digit number into its digits. That is, `Split` would separate 384 into the 3, the 8, and the 4. The point is that we need `Split` twice, once to split the `UserNum` into its digits, and once to split the `DailyWinNum` into its three digits. If we didn't use a procedure, we would have to write very similar code twice. With a procedure, we can define the procedure `Split(Num, Huns, Tens, Ones)` *once* and invoke it *twice*:

```
Split(UserNum, UserHuns, UserTens, UserOnes);
...
Split(DailyWinNum, WinHuns, WinTens, WinOnes);
```

Since `Split` can split any three-digit number into its parts, the same `Split` can be applied to both the `UserNum` and the `DailyWinNum`. It is not necessary, as beginners often do, to write two separate `Split` procedures. `Split` is completely general and can be invoked in many different ways. Observe the flexibility that is permitted by being able to use arguments that are distinct from the dummy parameters. This is the power of procedures and functions. Learn to use it well.

Now, hopefully having convinced you that procedures and functions are useful, we turn to the question of why we have both in the language. After all, it is fairly easy to see that any function can be rewritten as a procedure. We leave this as an exercise with the remark that you will need to change the number of parameters.

To see that we could also eliminate procedures and replace them with functions, we consider a specific example. Note that `Split(Num, Huns, Tens, Ones)` as a procedure returns three results through the variable parameters `Huns`, `Tens`, and `Ones`. Hence, we could replace `Split(Num, Huns, Tens, Ones)` with three functions `SplitHuns(Num)`, `SplitTens(Num)` and `SplitOnes(Num)`, each of which would return one result. While possible, three functions are less convenient and less clear than one procedure. They are also probably less efficient, because the three functions may each have to repeat some of the computations that the procedure does once.

We also point out that we could write a function that would be equivalent to a parameterless procedure—such as `PurposeOfModule`—that uses `WriteString` to print many lines of description, but computes no result. We could replace this procedure with the function `ModulePurpose()`, which `WriteStrings` the descriptions and then returns some value such as zero, which is then not used by the calling unit.

Also notice that the invocations will differ because we are using functions instead of procedures. Thus, in our first example, we could replace

```
Split(UserNum, UserHuns, UserTens, UserOnes);
```

with

```
UserHuns := SplitHuns(UserNum);
UserTens := SplitTens(UserNum);
UserOnes := SplitOnes(UserNum);
```

and in the second case, we could replace

```
PurposeOfModule;
```

with

```
DiscardValue := ModulePurpose();
```

where `DiscardValue` is a new and otherwise unused CARDINAL identifier.

This long argument, which has shown that it is possible to replace procedure calls with function calls, has hopefully also shown why we don't want to do so in practice: It is not convenient! It is awkward to write three functions for the one procedure `Split` or to use the dodge of returning a garbage value. Although we have shown the concepts to be equivalent, it is the convenience of a procedure that can return zero or more results that makes it a concept worth keeping.

In the exercises, we have asked you to show how functions can be rewritten as procedures. This is simpler and less awkward to do than rewriting procedures and functions; still, the reasons that we keep functions in the language are convenience and custom. We are familiar with many functions like ROUND and sqrt from previous studies. It would be awkward if we couldn't use these functions in the natural way. Furthermore, functions, since they return a value and do not name a complete statement, can be nested within one another and used within other Modula-2 statements. For example, the fragment

```
IF ROUND (sqrt(X) - sqrt(Y)) < Cube(Z) THEN ...
```

would be many lines longer with the need for several additional identifiers if we had to replace the functions ROUND, sqrt, and Cube (assumed to be user-defined) with procedures. We leave the details to the reader in the exercises.

In summary, we have both procedures and functions in the language for the convenience of the programmer. There are many instances where functions are the natural construct to use. There are also many instances where we need a black box that returns zero, or two or more, results. In such an instance, a procedure is the natural construct to use.

The reader should be able to identify easily when to use a procedure and when to use a function. Programming practice says that functions are appropriate in those situations with zero or more inputs and *exactly one output*. This output, of course, is carried back through the name of the function via a RETURN statement in the body of the function.

While legal in Modula–2, it is considered poor programming style to use VAR parameters with functions. The reason for this is that we expect a function to take a number of inputs, make no changes to their values, but somehow compute and return a *single* result through the function's name. VAR parameters allow functions to return other results by modifying the parameters. This leads to unexpected *side effects* and confusing code. For example, it is possible, but not good style, to replace the procedure Split(Num, Huns, Tens, Ones) with one function HunsSplit(Num, Tens, Ones) that returns the value of the hundreds digit through its name and the values of the tens and ones digits through the VAR parameters Tens and Ones. This means that we replace

```
Split(Num, Huns, Tens, Ones);
```

with

```
Huns := HunsSplit(Num, Tens, Ones);
```

It seems to be the asymmetry of the situation that makes this a poor programming style. It is obvious that the statement is changing the value of Huns. At the same time, the obvious nature of this assignment conceals the fact that Tens and Ones are also receiving values. We believe that clarity is enhanced by insisting that functions *not* be allowed to have such side effects. Hence, in this text, functions will always have (with one exception discussed in Chapter 10) value, not VARiable, parameters, and functions will return exactly one result. We urge you to adopt this convention in your programming also and to reserve the use of VAR parameters to procedures, which must, of necessity, use them to return their results.

THE PRETTY PRINTING OF REAL NUMBERS

It is time to complete a promise made earlier for a procedure `WriteRealPretty` that will print REAL numbers such as 2.12000000E+002 in the more readable form 212.0. `WriteRealPretty(RealNum, Left, Right)` will print `RealNum` with `Left` digits to the left of the decimal point and `Right` digits to the right of the decimal point. Our procedure will be a basic one that won't be fancy. We leave it to the exercises to make several improvements on our procedure. For example, our `WriteRealPretty` doesn't suppress leading zeroes, so if you ask for the above number to be printed with five digits to the left of the decimal point (and one to the right) it will print

```
00212.0
```

In addition, our `WriteRealPretty` prints only positive numbers; we leave it to you to add code to print a minus sign, if appropriate. Furthermore, our version does not round the last digit, so if you ask for 3.07 to be printed with one decimal place you will get

```
3.0
```

instead of

```
3.1
```

as you should. Worse, if you do not supply enough places to the left of the decimal point, our `WriteRealPretty` will not work properly. For example, 212.0 prints as

```
E2.0
```

when we ask for only two places to the left of the decimal. Again, we leave it to the reader to improve upon our version of `WriteRealPretty`.

   Let us explain the strategy of `WriteRealPretty` with an example. Suppose our call to `WriteRealPretty` is

```
RealNum := 57.123;
WriteRealPretty(RealNum, 3, 2);
```

which should, of course, produce output of 057.12. The first thing `WriteRealPretty` does is divide `RealNum` by 10 three (`Left`) times, making `RealNum` have the value 0.057123. Now `WriteRealPretty` calls a procedure `PullOffDigit` that "pulls off" the tenths digit of `RealNum` and prints it. That is, the procedure `PullOffDigit` prints the 0 and makes `RealNum` 0.57123. The next call to `PullOffDigit` prints the 5 and returns the value 0.7123. Thus, all `WriteRealPretty` has to do is call `PullOffDigit` `Left` number of times, print the decimal point, and then call `PullOffDigit` `Right` more times. The reader should pause to see how this produces, character by character, the output 057.12. Furthermore, since `RealNum` is a value parameter to `WriteReal-Pretty`, it is a copy of `RealNum`, not the original, that is modified by `WriteReal-Pretty`.

The procedure PullOffDigit is short but tricky, using several conversions and ORD and CHR tricks. Let us trace how the 5 is printed and 0.7123 is returned by PullOffDigit if RealNum is 0.57123. First, RealNum is multiplied by 10.0 to give us 5.7123. Using TRUNC, we can clearly obtain the CARDINAL Digit 5 from this value. This Digit must then be converted to ASCII for printing, using ORD and CHR techniques that have been discussed earlier. Finally, the Digit is again FLOATed and subtracted from RealNum to give a new value to RealNum:

5.7123 - 5.0 = 0.7123

All these details are given in Listing 7.10 for a module Pretty that shows the procedure WriteRealPretty and its subprocedure PullOffDigit. The reader should study this listing with care.

```
MODULE Pretty;
(* This module pretty-prints real numbers by putting them in
ordinary decimal notation. You supply the number to be printed and
the number of places desired to the LEFT and to the RIGHT of the
decimal point.

The procedure does not suppress leading zeroes, does not handle
negative numbers, does not round the last digit, and does NOT handle
errors very well. All these improvements are left to the reader as
exercises!                                                        *)

FROM RealInOut IMPORT WriteReal, ReadReal;
FROM InOut IMPORT Write, WriteString, ReadCard, WriteLn;

VAR    RealNum : REAL;
       Left    : CARDINAL;
       Right   : CARDINAL;

PROCEDURE WriteRealPretty(RealNum : REAL; Left, Right : CARDINAL);

(* Pre:  RealNum, Left, and Right all have values.
Post:    Left digits of RealNum left of the decimal point, a decimal
point, and the Right digits to the right of the decimal point are
printed.
Remark: WriteRealPretty does not work properly if RealNum has more
than Left digits to the left of the decimal point. WriteRealPretty
prints leading zeros and does not round the last digit on the right.
These improvements are left as exercises.                          *)

VAR    Index : CARDINAL;
```

```
PROCEDURE PullOffDigit(VAR RealNum : REAL);

(* This nested procedure pulls off the next digit from RealNum and
prints it. That is, if passed 0.2681, it prints 2 and returns 0.681.
Pre:   RealNum has a REAL value between 0.0 and 1.0.
Post: The leftmost digit of RealNum is pulled off and printed. The
new value of RealNum is the fractional part of the old value
multiplied by 10.                                                *)

    VAR      Digit : CARDINAL;

    BEGIN
       RealNum := RealNum * 10.0                    (* Isolate the *)
       Digit := TRUNC(RealNum);               (* leftmost digit. *)
       Write(CHR(ORD('0' + Digit)));      (* Find ASCII & print. *)
       RealNum := RealNum - FLOAT(Digit);   (* Toss digit out .*)
    END PullOffDigit;

  BEGIN                      (* Body of procedure WriteRealPretty. *)
     FOR Index := 1 TO Left DO   (* Move decimal point to the *)
     RealNum := RealNum / 10.0                (* left in the copy *)
                                                 (* of RealNum. *)

     END; (* FOR *)

     FOR Index := 1 TO Left DO        (* Write the Left digits. *)
        PullOffDigit(RealNum)
     END; (* FOR *)

     Write('.');                       (* Write the decimal point. *)

     FOR Index := 1 TO Right DO     (* Write the Right digits. *)
        PullOffDigit(RealNum)
     END (* FOR *)
  END WriteRealPretty;

BEGIN                            (* Body of main module Pretty. *)
  WriteString("Please enter a real number: ");
  ReadReal(RealNum); WriteLn; WriteLn;
  WriteString("Please enter the number of places you want");
  WriteLn;
  WriteString("to the LEFT of the decimal point: ");
  ReadCard(Left); WriteLn;
  WriteString("Please enter the number of places you want");
  WriteLn;
  WriteString("to the RIGHT of the decimal point: ");
  ReadCard(Right); WriteLn;
```

```
    WriteReal(RealNum, 0);
    WriteString(' "pretty-printed" is: ');
    WriteRealPretty(RealNum, Left, Right); WriteLn
END Pretty.
```

Listing 7.10

If the user enters the number 212.04789 and asks for three digits on each side of the decimal, the output will be

```
2.1204789E+002 "pretty-printed" is: 212.047
```

as expected. However, round-off errors can sometimes give surprising results. For example if you enter 123.456 and ask for three digits on each side of the decimal, you will get

```
1.2345600E+002 "pretty-printed" is: 123.455
```

This happens because the computer is a binary, not a decimal, machine and can't represent our number exactly. This indicates yet another limitation of our Write RealPretty procedure, and of REAL numbers in general. Nonetheless, we think WriteRealPretty is better than trying to read those scientific expressions. Hence, we will freely use WriteRealPretty in the remainder of this book to express REALs in a readable form.

GLOBAL VARIABLES

Earlier, we stated the rule that every identifier that appears in a procedure or function should be listed as a parameter or declared as a local variable in that procedure or function. We indicated that this rule would be discussed, explained, and extended at a later date. To begin that discussion, let us consider the module GlobalSwap of Listing 7.11.

```
MODULE GlobalSwap;

(* This module illustrates the use of global variables. WARNING:
While legal, the use of global variables is not recommended as good
style.                                                            *)

    FROM InOut IMPORT WriteString, WriteLn, WriteCard;

    VAR J      : CARDINAL;
        K      : CARDINAL;
        Temp   : CARDINAL;
```

```
  PROCEDURE Swap;
(* Pre:  The global J and K have values.
Post:    The values of J and K are interchanged. The global Temp
also receives J's old value.                                    *)

  BEGIN
    Temp := J;
    J := K;
    K := Temp
  END Swap;

BEGIN                            (* Body of main module GlobalSwap. *)
  J := 38;
  K := 695;
  WriteString("Before the swap the values of J and K are ");
  WriteCard(J, 0);
  WriteString(" and ");
  WriteCard(K, 0);
  WriteLn;

  Swap;

  WriteString("After the swap the values of J and K are ");
  WriteCard(J, 0);
  WriteString(" and ");
  WriteCard(K, 0);
  WriteLn
END GlobalSwap.
```

Listing 7.11

Observe that none of the identifiers used in this version of Swap are declared as parameters or as local variables. Swap is using the variables of the outer module GlobalSwap and, hence, these variables are **global** to Swap. Modula-2 requires that each identifier used in the body of a procedure or function must be one of three kinds. Each such identifier must be a parameter (value or variable), a local variable, or global, by which we mean that the identifier is declared in some module, procedure, or function in which the current procedure or function is nested. Any identifier found by the compiler that is not of one of these three types will be flagged as an undeclared identifier.

We are going to argue that global identifiers, although legal and often popular with beginners, are generally to be avoided. What makes globals popular with the beginner? We believe that it is the perceived simplicity of globals and a lack of understanding of the correct use of parameters. After all, look at the invocation of Swap in Listing 7.11. It is simply

```
Swap;
```

with no parameters to worry about. Further, the definition of Swap in Listing 7.11 is simple because there are no local variables to worry about.

There are factors, however, that make the perceived simplicity of global variables shortsighted. These include the following:

1. The use of global variables hinders the clarity of programs

Imagine that our procedure Swap is part of a large program. Then, as we know, each time we invoke the global version of Swap, we simply write

```
Swap;
```

But how can we remember what gets swapped with what? On the other hand, with our version of Swap with parameters, we have to write

```
Swap(Profit, Loss);
```

from which it is immediately clear to any reader (and the IRS) what Swap is up to. We have given just one simple example, but the principle is clear. The use of globals will make the action of procedures and functions more difficult for the reader to fathom. In a simple program, the use of globals can perhaps be defended. But in complex programs, they will hinder program clarity.

2. The use of global variables hinders the flexibility of programs

The version of Swap using global variables always swaps the same two things (we can't remember what they are, though). Swap, written with parameters as in the module Right, is a fully general procedure that will swap any two variables (of the proper type). Thus, with such a general Swap(X, Y) procedure, we could invoke it at various times with

```
Swap(Profit, Loss);
...
Swap(MySalary, YourSalary);
...
Swap(This, That);
```

as long as all the arguments shown are identifiers of the same type as the dummy parameters X and Y. With global variables, we would need to write three separate although similar procedures—SwapProfitForLoss, SwapMySalaryForYourSalary, SwapThisForThat—to perform all the indicated swaps. A procedure with parameters is a *general* black box that will perform operations on the arguments that you supply. A procedure that uses global variables is a *specific* black box that does only one particular task. Avoid global variables to keep your procedures and functions general.

3.The use of global variables makes programs difficult to debug, maintain, and modify

The programmer who makes extensive use of global variables writes programs that are difficult to debug because identifiers are not restricted to certain sections of the program. For example, if the identifier X has a garbage value, then it can be that the main module, or any function or procedure that is accessing X globally, is causing the problem. This means that the programmer does not know where to look for the problem. With the proper use of parameters, the locus of the problem can be ascertained much more readily. Once we know where the error is, we can usually figure out what the problem is. The same remarks apply to maintaining and modifying programs. If the author used global variables, then your task of locating and changing a given set of identifiers in all the appropriate spots can be very difficult.

For example, suppose you had something valuable stored in the global identifier Temp. Then, after you invoke Swap, your information is lost and (mysteriously) Temp's value is now J's old value. This is because Swap uses the global Temp to do its interchange of J and K's values. Swap, properly written with two variable parameters and a local Temp, causes no such problems and protects any global Temp in the main module from harm.

In summary, we have many reasons to avoid the use of global variables. Do not fall into the trap of using them. They may seem simpler than learning to use parameters correctly, but this is only an illusion. In complex programs, the extensive use of globals is unacceptable.

Is there ever an instance when global variables should be allowed? On this point, authors and instructors differ. Many say categorically, "Never use globals!" We back away from a complete denial of global variables, but think their use should be very much restricted, for the reasons listed above.

Where would we permit the use of globals? Suppose that in a large program you have an Initialize procedure and a DisplayResults procedure. The Initialize procedure needs to initialize 17 various counters, flags, etc. It is rather tedious to define or invoke Initialize with all those arguments/parameters. Likewise, Display-Results, with parameters, needs to have 29 different things passed to it. We believe that, in such cases, it is permissible to use global variables with these procedures whose task is clear to everyone. Still, we think that globals, when used, should always be commented, so we would write

```
Initialize;       (* Initialize everything in sight, globally. *)
...
DisplayResults;                      (* Globals used to avoid long
                                        list of parameters. *)
```

In general, however, our advice to the beginner is to avoid the use of global variables. Hence, our original rule that every identifier used in a procedure or function must be a parameter or a local variable, while not strictly required by Modula-2, is still a good idea and is a generally accepted rule of good programming style.

SCOPE IN PROCEDURES AND FUNCTIONS

The **scope** of an identifier is that part of the module in which it is known and can be used. Recall that every identifier used in a procedure or function must be either a parameter, locally declared, or a global variable from some unit in which the current procedure or function is nested.

First, let us consider what happens if an identifier is declared more than once in the procedures and functions of a module. If an identifier is listed as a parameter and declared as a local variable, this will be flagged by the compiler as a **multiply declared identifier** error. That is, the parameters should not (indeed, cannot) be redeclared as local variables. The parameters represent those values that are carried in and out of the procedure or function, while the local identifiers represent the incidental scratch-work variables used by the procedure or function. No identifier can be both a parameter and a local variable at the same time. On the other hand, if a parameter or local identifier has the same name as an identifier from a nesting unit, then the parameter or local variable masks the global identifier, and the global identifier cannot be seen from the procedure or function. If there is no masking identifier, then the global identifier can be seen and referenced from within the function or procedure. As a simple example of some of these possibilities, consider Figure 7.4, which shows a main module, Global, and one procedure, Silly, with a snapshot of memory just before the execution of the writes in Silly. In Figure 7.4, a variable that has not been assigned a value is denoted by /. Because there is no context for this example, no preconditions and postconditions are shown for the procedure Silly.

```
MODULE Global;

FROM InOut IMPORT Write, WriteString, WriteCard, WriteLn;
FROM RealInOut IMPORT WriteReal;

VAR    X : CARDINAL;
       Y : CHAR;
       Z : REAL;
       W : CHAR;

    PROCEDURE SILLY(A : CHAR; X : REAL);

            VAR Z, B : CARDINAL;

            BEGIN
              Z := 100;
              B := 17;
SNAPSHOT ⟹   WriteReal(X, 10);
              Write(Y);
              WriteCard(Z, 10);
              WriteLn
            END Silly;
```

```
BEGIN
    X := 3;
    Y := "S";
    Z := 5.0;
    Silly(W, 0.8);
    WriteCard(X, 10);
    Write(Y);
    WriteReal(Z, 10);
    WriteLn
END Global.
```

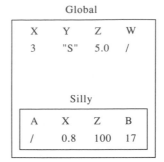

Figure 7.4

In particular, in Figure 7.4, note that the module Global has four identifiers of its own, X, Y, Z, and W. Silly has two parameters, A and X, and two local variables, Z and B. This means that the parameter X, which is of type REAL, masks the CARDINAL X of the module. Therefore, X within Silly is the REAL X, while X within the body of the module is a CARDINAL. Likewise, the local variable Z of Silly masks the global Z of the module. Y and W, however, are not masked and can be accessed globally by Silly. When Silly writes X, Y, and Z, it writes its own X and Z, but writes the Y of the main module. This produces the values 0.8, S, and 100. When we return from Silly to the main module, the memory allocated for Silly is reclaimed and all the identifiers of the module are unmasked. When the main module Global writes X, Y, and Z, the values produced are 3, "S", and 5.0.

The module Global doesn't do anything useful, so you might think that the example is silly as well. Since there is no context for the program, we have even used junk identifiers like X, Y, and Z in the module. However, the example is an important one because it shows us how, in a real example, we can use a parameter Cost or a local variable Index without worrying about whether we used that identifier somewhere else in the program. Even if we did, the system will keep all the instances separated for us. This is why we need to learn the scope rules of Modula-2.

Before we look at two more complex, pathological examples of scoping, we need to discuss in more detail how local variables and both value and variable parameters are handled by functions and procedures.

Each module, procedure, or function in Modula-2 has its own **environment** where the values of its identifiers are stored. These environments are nested within one another according to the way they were defined. For example, the box of Figure 7.4 shows the environment of procedure Silly nested within the main module Global. These environments, as previously mentioned, are dynamically created and destroyed. They are created upon procedure or function call and are destroyed upon exit from the procedure or function. The snapshot of Figure 7.4, therefore, shows a snapshot of the environments during the execution of procedure Silly. Before the call to Silly, or after the call to Silly, a snapshot would show only the main environment for Global.

Upon procedure or function call, a new environment is created, and the local variables and parameters are handled as follows:

1. Local variables are given memory space, but no value.
2. Value parameters are given memory space and are given the *value* of the corresponding argument at the time of the call.
3. Variable parameters are handled as pointers to the actual argument in the calling unit. Thus, the variable parameter is really an *alias* for the actual argument. That is, the variable parameter and the argument share the same memory location.

If an identifier is not found within the environment, then the system looks out into environments in which the current environment is nested until the identifier is found (or an undeclared identifier error is issued).

To illustrate these rules, consider the sample module Environments of Listing 7.12. Line numbers are supplied with the listing so that we can easily discuss the module.

```
1      MODULE Environments;

       (* This module illustrates the scope rules of Modula-2.
       Can you determine the output of this module?              *)

2      FROM InOut IMPORT WriteCard, WriteLn;

3      VAR  X, Y : CARDINAL;

4      PROCEDURE P1;

5        VAR  V : CARDINAL;

6        BEGIN
7          V := 1;
8          Y :=  2;
9          WriteCard(V, 10);
10         WriteCard(Y, 10);   WriteLn
11       END P1;

12     PROCEDURE P2;

13       VAR  X : CARDINAL;

14       PROCEDURE P3;

15       VAR Y : CARDINAL;

16       BEGIN
17         X := 5;
18         Y := 6;
19         V := 7              (* ERROR. P3 is nested inside P2,
                               which is nested in the main module.
                       None of these has a declaration of V. *)
20         END P3;
```

```
21     BEGIN                           (* Body of procedure P2. *)
22       X := 25;
23       Y := 35;
24       WriteCard(X, 10);
25       WriteCard(Y, 10); WriteLn;
26       P3;
27       WriteCard(X, 10);
28       WriteCard(Y, 10); WriteLn
29     END P2;

30     BEGIN              (* Body of main module Environments. *)
31       X := 100;
32       Y := 200;
33       WriteCard(X, 10);
34       WriteCard(Y, 10); WriteLn;
35       P1;
36       P2;
37       WriteCard(X, 10);
38       WriteCard(Y, 10); WriteLn
39     END Environments.
```

Listing 7.12

Observe in Listing 7.12 that procedure P3 at line 14 is defined within procedure P2. We have exaggerated the indentation to help the eye see the nesting of procedures in this module more readily. Indeed, this nesting is illustrated in Figure 7.5.

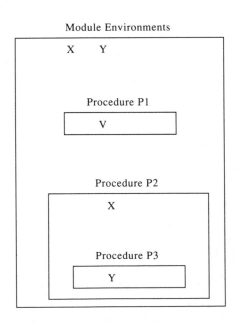

Figure 7.5

Figure 7.5 helps us see why the assignment at line 19 in procedure P3 is an undeclared-identifier error. P3 has no identifier V, so we look out into P2 because P3 was defined within P2 and is, therefore, nested within P2. P2 also has no identifier V, so we continue to look out, this time into the main module. Since V is also not found there, the use of V at line 19 is illegal. In this regard, the boxes of Figure 7.5 are often described as one-way glass, since you can look out, but you can never look into a box. The only V declared in this program is in P1. None of P3, P2, or even the main module can look into P1 and see this V. Only P1 can use V; it is *local* and therefore private to P1.

The notion of local/global is somewhat relative. P2 has a local X that masks—within P2—the global X of the module. This local X of P2 is global, however, to P3, since P3 is nested inside P2 and P3 has no X of its own. When an environment does not have an identifier, it is always the nearest *nesting* environment containing the identifier that supplies the identifier globally to that environment.

One important remark to make about the one-way glass analogy is that while P3 cannot use the V of P1, P3 can call P1 if it wishes. The point is that P3 can look out through its walls and through P2's walls and see P1. Therefore, it can invoke P1. (We'll present an example like this soon.) However, P3 cannot look into P1's walls and, therefore, cannot access P1's V. Likewise, P1, if it so desires, can invoke P2. But P1 cannot look into P2 and see P3. Likewise, the main module can invoke P1 and P2, but cannot invade P2's privacy and cannot see the P3 that is local to P2.

Let us trace the execution of module Environments and watch the environments dynamically grow and shrink as procedures are invoked and completed. Our trace will assume that line 19 has been deleted from the program.

It is important to realize that execution begins at line 31, the first executable statement in the main body of the module. Statements 31 to 34 are clear and produce our first line of output, the values 100 and 200. The situation after execution of line 34 is shown in the snapshot depicted in Figure 7.6a, since the main module is the only currently active unit.

Module environments

X	Y
100	200

Figure 7.6a

At line 35, procedure P1 is invoked. Hence, a new environment is created and P1's local variable V is given space. At line 7, that V is set to 1, and at line 8, the (global) Y of the main module is changed to 2. Thus, the writes at lines 9 and 10 produce the line containing the values 1 and 2. The environments, just before P1 ends at line 11, are as depicted in Figure 7.6b.

Module environments   Module environments

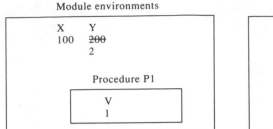

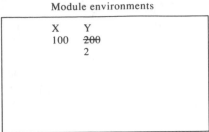

Figure 7.6b   **Figure 7.6c**

After execution of the call to P1, the memory used by P1's environment is reclaimed by the system. Thus, after execution of line 35, the snaphot is as depicted in Figure 7.6c. V is gone, but the change made to Y lingers on (showing one of the dangers of global variables).

When P2 is called at line 36, an environment for P2 is created, including space for a local X. Execution then continues in the body of P2, skipping the definition of P3. Hence, our trace continues at line 22, which sets the local X to 25. Notice that the global X is masked off from P2, and its value is not destroyed by P2. At line 23, it is the global Y that is changed to 35. Notice that it can't be P3's Y declared at line 15 that is referenced at line 23, since that Y doesn't even exist yet. The situation at the writes at lines 24 and 25 is reflected in the snapshot shown in Figure 7.6d. Of course, these produce a line of output containing the values 25 and 35.

Module environments

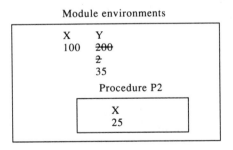

Figure 7.6d

At line 26, P2 calls P3. Since P3 was defined inside P2, the new environment for P3 is nested inside P2. This innermost environment has its own local Y and, at lines 17 and 18, the (global) X of P2 and P3's local Y are given the values 5 and 6, respectively. This is shown in the snapshot contained in Figure 7.6e. There are two Xs and two Ys in the snapshot of Figure 7.6e. But from P3's point of view, Y means its own Y and X means the closest surrounding X, which is P2's X. The X and Y of the main module are masked and, therefore, are not visible from P3.

Module environments

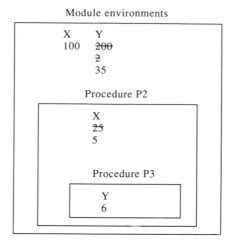

Figure 7.6e

When P3 ends, its environment is destroyed and execution returns to the caller, P2, which resumes execution at the output statements at lines 27 and 28. A snapshot of the program at this point is shown in Figure 7.6f. Clearly, the values output are 5 and 35.

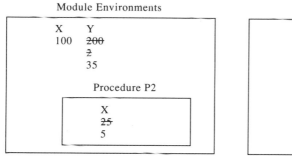

Module Environments

Figure 7.6f

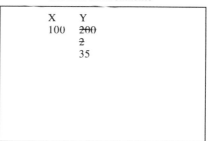

Module environments

Figure 7.6g

P2 is now finished and its environment is deleted. Execution of the program is returned to the main module, which originally called P2. Thus, the X and Y of the main module are printed at lines 37 and 38 and then execution of the entire module is complete. Just before the main module completes execution, we have the final snapshot shown in Figure 7.6g. To summarize, the output of the module is

```
100    200
1      2
25     35
5      35
100    35
```

ANOTHER SCOPING EXAMPLE

Our final, convoluted scope example is shown in Listing 7.13. The point is not that you will be writing such modules, but that if you understand how this perverse example works, then we believe that you really understand how scoping works in Modula-2 and will be able to use it to your advantage in writing large modules. Again, line numbers are supplied for ease in the discussion that follows. Observe that the output from module Scope is not obvious. It is not even easy to say how many lines of output are produced by Scope. We believe it is worth your time to study carefully and understand how the trace of Scope proceeds, but this lengthy example can be omitted on a first reading.

```
1       MODULE Scope;

        (* This module illustrates the scoping rules of Modula-2. Note
        that there are two procedures P1 in this example, showing that
        even procedures and functions have scope, and, in fact, scope
        for them is the same as scope for identifiers.

        Can you trace the execution of this module and determine its
        output?                                                     *)

2       FROM InOut IMPORT WriteCard, WriteLn;

3       VAR A, B, C : CARDINAL;

4       PROCEDURE P1(A : CARDINAL; VAR B : CARDINAL);
5         BEGIN
6           A := 5;
7           B := 6;
8           C := A + B;
9           WriteCard(A, 10); WriteCard(B, 10);
            WriteCard(C, 10); WriteLn
10        END P1;

11      PROCEDURE P2(VAR A :  CARDINAL; B : CARDINAL);
12        VAR  C : CARDINAL;
13        BEGIN
14          A := 10;
15          B := 20;
16          P1(50, C);
17          WriteCard(A, 10); WriteCard(B, 10);
            WriteCard(C, 10); WriteLn
18        END P2;
```

```
19      PROCEDURE P3;
20        VAR C : CARDINAL;

21        PROCEDURE P1(VAR X : CARDINAL);
22          BEGIN
23            X := 0
24          END P1;

25        BEGIN                            (* Body of P3. *)
26          C := 100;
27          P1(C);
28          WriteCard(A, 10); WriteCard(B, 10);
            WriteCard(C,10); WriteLn;
29          P2(B, A);
30          WriteCard(A, 10); WriteCard(B, 10);
            WriteCard(C, 10); WriteLn
31        END P3;

32      BEGIN                    (* Body of main module Scope. *)
33        A := 1000;
34        B := 2000;
35        C := 0;
36        WriteCard(A, 10); WriteCard(B, 10);
          WriteCard(C, 10); WriteLn;
37        P1(A, B);
38        P2(A, B);
39        P3
40      END Scope.
```

Listing 7.13

Figure 7.7 depicts the static nesting of the procedures as defined in the module Scope. When P3 calls P1, it will be its own local P1, since we always look locally before we look outside. In this case, inside P3, the local P1 masks the global P1 of the module. But if P2 or the main module calls P1, they have to call the P1 of the main module, since they cannot look through P3's walls to see its P1. As we will emphasize in the trace of this program, it is the *static* nesting of the procedure in Figure 7.7 that determines how the environments, as they are *dynamically* created, are nested inside one another.

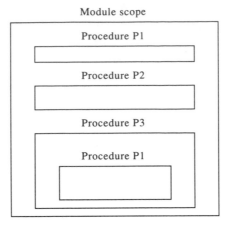

Figure 7.7

Execution of module Scope begins at line 33. Clearly, lines 33 to 36 produce a line of output containing the values 1000, 2000, and 0. At line 37, the procedure P1 is invoked with the arguments A and B. Procedure P1 has a value parameter A, which is passed the value 1000, and a variable parameter B. This means that P1 has its own copy, also called A, of the A of the module, while P1's B is really the B of the module. This is depicted, as P1 begins to execute, in the snapshot shown in Figure 7.8a.

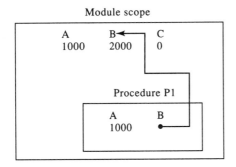

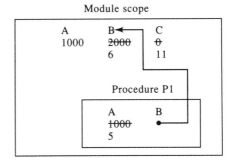

Figure 7.8a   **Figure 7.8b**

P1 executes three assignments at lines 6, 7, and 8. These change P1's copy of A; the real B through its alias B; and, globally, the C of the module. This is depicted in the snapshot shown in Figure 7.8b. The writes at line 9, therefore, produce the values 5, 6, and 11, as expected.

Upon completion of P1, its environment is discarded and execution returns to the calling program. P1 was called at line 37, so now P2 is called with the arguments A and B at line 38. In P2, the first parameter, A, is a variable parameter, and the second parameter, B, is a value parameter. P2 also has a local variable C. Thus, as P2 begins to execute, the snapshot is as shown in Figure 7.8c. We have denoted the value of C with a / to designate that space has been reserved for C, but no value has been assigned to it yet.

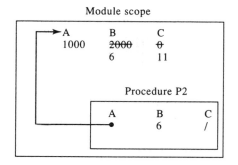

Figure 7.8c

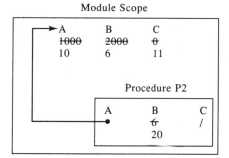

Figure 7.8d

Because A was a VAR parameter, the assignment at line 14 changes the actual argument A of the module. But since B was a value parameter, only the copy is modified at line 15. These changes are shown in Figure 7.8d.

At line 16, P1 is invoked with the arguments 50 and C. This means that a new environment for P1 must be created. The standard error is to draw this environment inside of P2, since P1 was called from within P2. Some languages do this, but not Modula-2. When a new environment is created, it is always created at the nesting level shown in Figure 7.7. In other words, environments are *dynamically* created and destroyed in Modula-2, but the nesting of these environments is *statically* determined by the nesting of the modules at the time of their definition. The situation, therefore, is correctly depicted in Figure 7.8e. Note that the value parameter A has the value 50 and that the variable parameter B of P1 is an alias for the C of P2, since P1 was called from within P2. It makes no difference whether P1's environment is drawn above (Figure 7.7), below (Figure 7.8e), or to the side of P2's. The point is that P1 and P2 are at the same level in the module, so neither environment is ever nested inside the other.

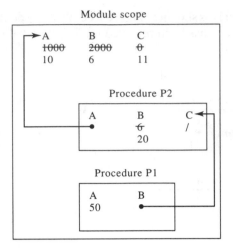

Figure 7.8e

P1 now executes its three assignments at lines 6, 7, and 8. Let us carefully trace these. The copy of A is changed to 5. C of P2, through its alias B, is changed to 6. C, which has to be the global C of the module, since P1 can't look inside P2, is reset to 11. Note that if P1's environment were erroneously nested within P2, then P1 would look out and see P2's C. This is why it is necessary to make such a big deal about the static nesting level of procedures in Modula-2. These changes are reflected in the snapshot shown in Figure 7.8f. Of course, the writes at line 9 of P1 access these same three variables and cause the values 5, 6, and 11 to be printed to the screen.

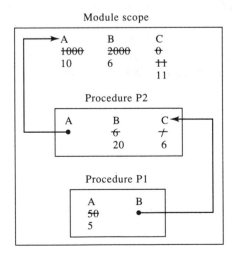

Figure 7.8f

When P1 finishes executing, its environment disappears and control is returned to the caller. Remember that P2 called P1 this time, so execution resumes at the writes of line 17. From P2's point of view, A, B, and C are the values 10, 20, and 6, and these are printed. P2 now completes its execution, its environment is reclaimed, and control passes back to the caller. P2 was called by the main module at line 38, so the last thing that the module does is call the parameterless procedure P3.

The call to P3 creates a new environment with one local variable, C. Execution of the body of P3 begins at line 26, with this C receiving the value 100. This is depicted in the snapshot shown in Figure 7.8g.

Module Scope

A	B	C
~~1000~~	~~2000~~	~~0~~
10	6	~~11~~
		11

Procedure P3

C
100

Figure 7.8g

At line 27, P3 calls P1. This is, of course, its own local P1. Hence, a new environment is created *and* it is nested within P3. The variable parameter X of P1 is an alias for the C of P3. P1's only action is to set this parameter to zero. This is depicted in the snapshot shown in Figure 7.8h.

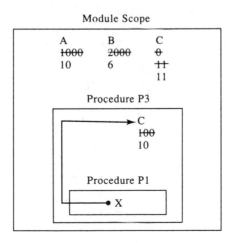

Module Scope

Procedure P3

Procedure P1

Figure 7.8h

P1, its short life completed, is destroyed, and control returns to the caller, P3, where, at line 28, P3 accesses A and B globally—and its own C—to print the values 10, 6, and 0.

P3, at line 29, now makes a perverse call to P2 with the actual arguments B and A that correspond to the dummy parameters A and B, respectively. That is, what P2 calls A is actually an alias for the global B, and what P2 calls B is passed the value (10) of A of the module. P2 also has a local variable C. This is shown, at the time P2 begins to execute, in Figure 7.8i. Note that P2's environment is not nested within P3's. Figure 7.7 explains why P1 was nested in P3, but P2 is not so nested.

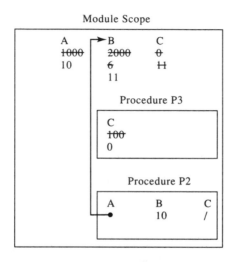

Figure 7.8i

As P2 begins to execute, it changes its variable parameter A to 10 (line 14), which results in the global B becoming 10. At line 15, the value parameter B is changed to 20. Next, P2 invokes P1 with the arguments 50 and C. This causes a new environment to be created, as shown in the snapshot contained in Figure 7.8j.

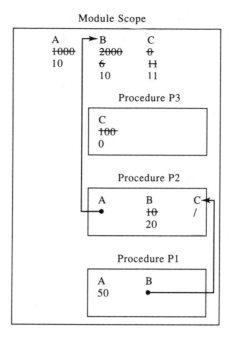

Figure 7.8j

P1 is now in control again. It assigns its own A, the C of P2 (through the alias B), and the global C the values 5, 6, and 11, respectively. It writes these values out, then goes away, leaving us with Figure 7.8k.

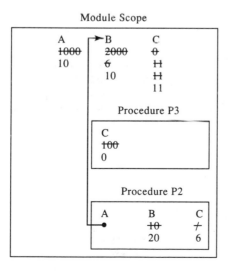

Figure 7.8k

Control is now returned to P2 at line 17, which writes out the values 10, 20, and 6. P2 now disappears and returns control to the writes at line 30, where the values 10, 10, and 0 are written. P3 disappears and returns control to the main module. Execution is complete, and the environment of the main module is also reclaimed.

We believe that if you take the time to understand this complicated example, you will reap large benefits. You will surely understand scoping in Modula-2 and should be able to trace and debug any program. You'll clearly understand the distinction between local and global variables, as well as the distinction between value and variable parameters. These are extremely important concepts, and that is why we have made such a fuss of these matters.

To summarize, the output of module Scope is

```
1000   2000   0
5      6      11
5      6      11
10     20     6
10     6      0
5      6      11
10     20     6
10     10     0
```

STRINGS AS PARAMETERS

Since the string is not a full-fledged type in Modula-2, a circumlocution is required to use a string as an argument/parameter in a procedure or function. The full details of the problem will not be discussed until Chapters 9 and 10, but suffice it to say that Modula-2 will not accept the heading

```
PROCEDURE AskUser(VAR Name : ARRAY[0..29] OF CHAR);
(* ERROR: Invalid type for the string parameter. *)
```

The problem is that Modula-2 does not accept the type specification as valid for a parameter. The way around the problem is to use the TYPE statement (there is much more on TYPEs in Chapter 9) to define a new string type. This is done by placing the following TYPE declaration in the main module just after the importation statement:

```
TYPE String30 = ARRAY[0..29] OF CHAR;
```

Then, the heading of the procedure can be written as

```
PROCEDURE AskUser(VAR Name : String30);
```

In other words, the TYPE statement allows us to give a short name to the complex type that we want to use. This short type name is then allowed in the procedure or function heading. That's all there is to using strings as parameters in procedures and functions. The use of strings as parameters is illustrated in our final example of the chapter. See the procedure GiveMessage below.

A FINAL EXTENDED EXAMPLE: THE GAME OF BAGELS

We conclude this chapter with another lengthy example, but this time of a real problem. This not only allows us to illustrate how procedures and functions can make a long program easy to understand, but also how our divide-and-conquer strategy applies in a more realistic situation.

We are going to write a module that will play the game of Bagels with the user. Assuming that most readers are not familiar with this game, we'll now explain how to play. First, the computer generates a secret three-digit number. To make it easier for the player, this secret number will be composed of three different digits, and the hundreds digit will not be zero. For example, the secret number might be 482. The player guesses three-digit numbers (with the same stipulations about distinct digits) until she or he guesses the secret number. The computer gives hints after each guess as follows:

1. The computer says "Fermi" for each digit in the guess that is in the same place in the secret number. For example, for a guess of 382, the computer will respond with "Fermi Fermi."
2. The computer says "Pico" for each digit in the guess that is in the secret number, but in another place. For example, the guess of 328 receives a "Pico Pico."
3. To give the user minimal information about the number, all "Fermi"s are printed before any "Pico"s. Thus, the guesses 284, 842, and 428 all generate the hint "Fermi Pico Pico."
4. Finally, to a guess with no correct digits at all, the computer responds with "Bagels"! When we play this game with students, they often groan when they get "Bagels," but you should realize that this gives a lot of information about the number.

The object of the game, of course, is to guess the computer's secret number in as few guesses as possible.

Students often ask why Bagels uses the terms Fermi, Pico, and Bagels. We respond that these are the international Bagels' conventions. Why does baseball use terms like "foul" ball? Why does football call a backward pass a "lateral"? Note that if a "lateral" is thrown laterally, then it isn't a lateral after all! There is no explaining terms in sports, and you will simply have to accept Bagels as it is.

Our explanation of the game can be summarized by the following pseudo code:

```
Give the user the instructions and some examples
Have the computer generate its secret number
Initialize a counter of the number of turns to zero
Repeat
    Obtain a guess from the user
    Increment the number of turns
    If the guess = the secret number then
        The game is over--congratulate the user
        Print the number of turns taken
    Else
        Analyze the digits of the guess and the secret number
            and give the user appropriate hints
Until the game is over
```

We may have no idea, for example, how to write a procedure that will generate a secret number, but that is the power of the divide-and-conquer approach. We separate the large problem into smaller pieces with which it would be easy to design a solution to the original problem. Later, of course, we will have to consider each subunit in turn. Let's imagine a black box that will generate a three-digit number. That black box might generate 333 or 747, a number with repeated digits, or 27, a number with the hundreds digit zero. Therefore, we should also have a procedure Split that will obtain the three separate digits for us, and a function Valid that will tell us whether the digits are distinct or not and whether the hundreds digit is nonzero. That way, we can have the computer keep repeating the generation of three-digit numbers until it finally gets it right! Furthermore, note that the user is supposed to enter a guess containing three different digits. We can use our procedure Split and our Valid function to test the user's guess and make the user repeat until she or he enters a valid guess. Here, then, is a slightly more detailed pseudo-code outline of our main module:

Give the user the instructions and some examples
Repeat
    Have the computer generate its secret number
    Split the secret number into its three digits
Until the three digits of the secret number are distinct (valid)
Initialize a counter of the number of turns to zero
Repeat
    Repeat
        Obtain a guess from the user
        Split the guess into its three digits
    Until the three digits of the guess are distinct (valid)
    Increment the number of turns
    If the guess = the secret number then
        The game is over--congratulate the user
        Print the number of turns taken
    Else
        Analyze the digits of the guess and the secret number
            and give the user appropriate hints
Until the game is over

Since the listing for the module Bagels is lengthy, we will show it to you in pieces, displaying each piece as we develop the pseudo-code for it. This again illustrates the power of the top-down approach. You can read and understand the main program without being concerned about all the details of the program. The body of the main module is shown in Listing 7.14a. Realize that this is the end of the listing, and there are many missing details yet to be supplied. But also note how readable the body of the module is and how closely it follows the outline of the pseudo-code developed above. Notice that we have tossed the pseudo-code into one more REPEAT loop that keeps playing the game UNTIL the user doesn't want to play again. We have also added a BOOLEAN GameOver to make it easy to recognize when the game is over. Little modifications are possible between the pseudo-code and the final version, but the pseudo-code should be designed to a sufficient level of detail that the implementation remains a straightforward task.

```
BEGIN                            (* Body of main module Bagels. *)
   Instructions;
   REPEAT                (* Loop until the player wants to quit. *)

      REPEAT(* Computer generates a SecretNum until it's valid. *)
         Generate(SecretNum);
         Split(SecretNum, SecretHuns, SecretTens, SecretOnes)
      UNTIL Valid(SecretHuns, SecretTens, SecretOnes);

      NumTurns := 0;(* User begin to guess the secret number. *)
      REPEAT         (* Loop until the user guesses correctly. *)
         REPEAT  (* Loop until the user enters a valid guess. *)
            Obtain(Guess);
            Split(Guess, GuessHuns, GuessTens, GuessOnes)
         UNTIL Valid(GuessHuns, GuessTens, GuessOnes);
         INC(NumTurns);                     (* Count the guess. *)
         GameOver := (SecretNum = Guess);      (* Lucky guess? *)
         IF GameOver THEN
            Summarize(NumTurns)
         ELSE
         Analyze(SecretHuns, SecretTens, SecretOnes, GuessHuns,
                                      GuessTens, GuessOnes)
      END  (* IF *)
      UNTIL GameOver

   UNTIL PlayerQuits()
END Bagels.
```

Listing 7.14a

We now consider each of our procedures and functions in turn, first to design them and then to implement them. Instructions, being a long list of WriteStrings, is so simple, however, that we do not display it in pseudo-code, but show it complete in Listing 7.14b. Notice that Instructions does ask if you want to see the rules, thus letting the user who knows how to play skip them.

```
PROCEDURE Instructions;

(* Pre:  None.
Post:   This procedure "WriteStrings" the rules if requested by
the user.                                                      *)

VAR     Ch : CHAR;       (* Local variable for user response. *)
```

```
BEGIN
  WriteString("Do you want the rules (Y/N)?  ");
  Read(Ch); Write(Ch); WriteLn;(* Read and echo the response. *)
  Ch := CAP(Ch);              (* Make sure response is uppercase. *)
  IF Ch = "Y" THEN
    WriteLn; WriteLn;
    WriteString("The computer generates a three-digit");
    WriteLn;
    WriteString("number with no digit repeated and the first");
    WriteLn;
    WriteString("digit nonzero. Guess the computer's");
    WriteLn;
    WriteString("number in as few guesses as possible. Your");
    WriteLn;
    WriteString("guess must also be a three-digit number with");
    WriteLn;
    WriteString("no digits repeated. You will be given hints:");
    WriteLn; WriteLn;
    WriteString('"Fermi" correct digit correctly placed.');
    WriteLn;
    WriteString('"Pico" correct digit, wrongly placed.');
    WriteLn;
    WriteString('"Bagels" if no digit is guessed correctly.');
    WriteLn; WriteLn;
    WriteString("For example, if the secret number is 482,");
    WriteLn;
    WriteString(' A guess of 127 a "Pico".');
    WriteLn;
    WriteString(' A guess of 842 a "Fermi Pico Pico".');
    WriteLn;
    WriteString('  A guess of 375 receives a "Bagels".')
  END;  (* IF *)
  WriteLn; WriteLn
END Instructions;
```

Listing 7.14b

Next, we tackle the Generate procedure that determines the SecretNum of the computer. Modula-2 as defined by Wirth does not include a random-number generator, so we will have to use some ad hoc method to generate the secret number. We will ask the user to enter three letters from the keyboard, and then we will perform some calculations on their ASCII values. If your version of Modula–2 has a random-number generator, then you could easily use it to generate the secret number. This shows another advantage of procedures, functions, and the modular approach to programming: We can replace one procedure or function with another, and, as long as the interface with the other procedures and functions is not changed, the entire module will function properly.

What sort of ad hoc methods shall we use to generate a number from the ASCII values of three letters? For simplicity, we will use CAP to make sure that the letters are uppercase; therefore, we know (see Table 4.1) that they have ASCII values between 65 and 90. If we simply add them, we won't get a very large number, and the hundreds digit would always be 1 or 2. Therefore, let's multiply them together. But wait: 90 * 90 * 90 is already 729000, well beyond CARDINAL overflow for many machines. By experimentation, we see that if we reduce each ASCII value by 50, then the values will be in the range 15 to 40 and, hence, the product will be between

$$15 * 15 * 15 = 3375$$

and

$$40 * 40 * 40 = 64000$$

or well within CARDINAL limits. But now we have more than a three-digit number, so we chop it down to three digits—say the middle three digits of the possible five. That is, if the number generated is 12345, we will keep the 234. Here, then, is the pseudo-code for a rather special-purpose Generate procedure:

Procedure Generate(VAR SecretNum)
   Repeat
      Obtain three letters Ch1, Ch2, Ch3 from the user
      Make sure Ch1, Ch2, and Ch3 are all uppercase
   Until Ch1, Ch2, and Ch3 are between "A" and "Z"
   SecretNum ¨ (ORD(Ch1) - 50) * (ORD(Ch2) - 50) * (ORD(Ch3) - 50)
   Reduce SecretNum by chopping off the left and right digits

The Modula-2 code for Generate is shown in Listing 7.14c.

```
PROCEDURE Generate(VAR SecretNum : CARDINAL);

(* This procedure generates the computer's SecretNum by asking the
user to enter three letters and doing some arithmetic on the
corresponding ASCII values.
Pre:  None.
Post: A CARDINAL value of at most three digits is assigned to
SecretNum.                                                      *)

VAR  Ch1, Ch2, Ch3 : CHAR;            (* Local variables
                                      for user input. *)
```

```
BEGIN
  REPEAT              (* Loop until the user follows directions. *)
    WriteString("Please enter 3 letters between A and Z:  ");
    Read(Ch1); Write(Ch1);  (* Read and echo the characters. *)
    Read(Ch2); Write(Ch2);
    Read(Ch3); Write(Ch3); WriteLn;
    Ch1 := CAP(Ch1);          (* Make sure they are uppercase. *)
    Ch2 := CAP(Ch2);  Ch3 := CAP(Ch3);
  UNTIL (Ch1 >= "A") AND (Ch1 <= "Z") AND (Ch2 >= "A") AND
            (Ch2 <= "Z") AND (Ch3 >= "A") AND (Ch3 <= "Z");

(* Now do ORD calculations with the ASCII values to get the
SecretNum. Multiplying the three ASCII values together could easily
cause CARDINAL overflow, so we subtract 50 from each value to keep
the product in range.                                           *)

  SecretNum := (ORD(Ch1) - 50) * (ORD(Ch2) - 50) * (ORD(Ch3) - 50);

(* SecretNum is supposed to be a three-digit number. It may now have
as many as five digits. We use DIV and MOD to keep only the middle
three.                                                          *)

  SecretNum := SecretNum DIV 10; (* Lop off the right digit. *)
  SecretNum := SecretNum MOD 1000;   (* Lop off fifth digit, *)
                                      (* if any. *)
END Generate;
```

Listing 7.14c

Our next procedure is Split, which separates its input Num into its three digits Huns, Tens, and Ones. As we know from several examples, we can use DIV and MOD tricks to do this. Hence, we omit the pseudo-code for Split and go directly to the Modula-2 version of Split in Listing 7.14d. Notice that we have defined Split using the generic parameters Num, Huns, Tens, and Ones—which are meaningful, but distinct from any of the actual identifiers of the module. We do this because we intend to invoke Split twice. After the computer generates its SecretNum, we will invoke Split with

```
Split(SecretNum, SecretHuns, SecretTens, SecretOnes);
```

to separate the computer's number into its digits. Later, when the user enters a Guess, we will again invoke Split in the form

```
Split(Guess, GuessHuns, GuessTens, GuessOnes);
```

to separate the user's Guess into its digits. We know that we can define Split with any three parameters, but since we intend to invoke Split in two distinct ways, it seems best to define Split with generic parameters. Also note that these two slightly different invocations of Split would not be possible if Split used global variables!

On the other hand, note that we defined Generate(SecretNum) with the dummy parameter SecretNum, which is the same as the actual identifier of the main module. We did this because we intend only one invocation of Generate:

```
Generate(SecretNum);
```

Hence, there is no confusion if the dummy SecretNum is bound to the actual SecretNum. Of course, it is legal to define Generate with some generic parameter such as Numb, but we see no advantage to doing so. In summary, here are our suggestions for selecting parameter names:

If the procedure or function is to be invoked exactly once, or always in exactly the same form, then it makes sense to choose the dummy parameters to be exactly the same identifiers as the actual arguments. If the procedure or function is to be invoked in more than one way, then it makes sense to select generic dummy parameters that are distinct from all of the actual arguments. Finally, realize that these are just suggestions to help programmers preserve their sanity; as the scoping examples have shown, Modula-2 doesn't care what you choose for dummy parameter names.

```
PROCEDURE Split(Num : CARDINAL; VAR Huns,Tens, Ones : CARDINAL);

(* Pre:  Num is at most a three-digit CARDINAL.
Post:    Huns, Tens, and Ones are assigned the hundreds, tens, and
ones digits of Num, respectively.                            *)

BEGIN
  Huns := Num DIV 100;
  Tens := (Num MOD 100) DIV 10;
  Ones := Num MOD 10
END Split;
```

Listing 7.14d

Note that Split has an important precondition that must hold before it promises to fulfill its contract. That is, if Num has the value 7483 when Split is called, Split is not responsible for the garbage values it returns.

The function Valid simply checks its three inputs, Huns, Tens, and Ones, to make sure they are all different and that Huns is not zero. If any of these tests fail, then Valid prompts the user to enter new data, whether this is in generating the SecretNum or in obtaining the Guess of the user. Valid is easy and is shown implemented in Listing 7.14e.

```
PROCEDURE Valid(Huns, Tens, Ones : CARDINAL) : BOOLEAN;

(* Pre:  Huns, Tens, and Ones are all single-digit CARDINALs.
Post:    The function Valid returns TRUE if its three arguments are
all different from one another, and the Huns digit is nonzero,
otherwise it returns FALSE.                                   *)
```

```
BEGIN
  IF (Huns = 0) OR (Huns = Tens) OR (Huns = Ones) OR (Tens = Ones)
                                                                 THEN
    WriteString("Number is invalid. Please try again.");
    WriteLn;       (* Prompt user to enter a different input. *)
    RETURN(FALSE)
  ELSE
    RETURN(TRUE)
  END  (* IF *)
END Valid;
```

Listing 7.14e

With the observation that a three-digit number must be between 100 and 999, procedure Obtain, which gets the user's Guess, is very simple to write. Note that Obtain does not have to check for distinct digits, since we can reuse Split and Valid to do that for us. Obtain is shown in Listing 7.14f.

```
PROCEDURE Obtain(VAR Guess : CARDINAL);

(* Pre:  None.
Post:    A three-digit CARDINAL is obtained from the user.    *)

BEGIN
  REPEAT
    WriteString("Please enter your three-digit guess: ");
    ReadCard(Guess); WriteLn
  UNTIL (Guess >= 100) AND (Guess <= 999)
END Obtain;
```

Listing 7.14f

Summarize is a very simple procedure that is shown in Listing 7.14g.

```
PROCEDURE Summarize(NumTurns : CARDINAL);

(* Pre:  NumTurns has a CARDINAL value representing the number of
guesses made by the user.
Post:    A congratulatory message and the number of guesses needed
to find the secret number are printed.                        *)

BEGIN
  WriteString("C O N G R A T U L A T I O N S  ! ! !"); WriteLn;
  WriteString("You guessed my secret number in only ");
  WriteCard(NumTurns, 0);
  WriteString(" turns."); WriteLn; WriteLn
END Summarize;
```

Listing 7.14g

Procedure `Analyze` takes the digits of the secret number and the digits of the guess, compares them, and gives appropriate hints. This is all rather straightforward, except for one detail. For example:

If SecretHuns equals GuessHuns then
    Give the user a "Fermi" message

and equivalent tests for the tens and ones digits will print the "Fermi"s, if any. Likewise:

If SecretHuns equals GuessTens or GuessOnes then
    Give the user a "Pico" message

along with two other similar `IF`s will print the "Pico"s, if any.

The difficulty is deciding when to print "Bagels." We could write a series of complex `IF`s, but it is easier to note that we say "Bagels" only if we didn't say "Fermi" or "Pico." We can record whether we gave any hints by using a BOOLEAN, `GaveHint`, which we initialize to `FALSE`, and change to `TRUE` whenever we give a "Fermi" or "Pico". If `GaveHint` is still `FALSE` after all the Fermi and Pico tests, then we know it's time to say "Bagels." This gives us the following outline to our pseudo-code for `Analyze`:

Procedure Analyze(SecretHuns, SecretTens, SecretOnes, GuessHuns, GuessTens,
                                                          GuessOnes)

    GaveHint ← FALSE

    If SecretHuns equals GuessHuns then
        Give the user a "Fermi" message
        GaveHint ¨ TRUE
    --Include two more such IFs to test for other Fermis

    If SecretHuns equals GuessTens or GuessOnes then
        Give the user a "Pico" message
        GaveHint ¨ TRUE
    --Include two more such IFs to test for other Picos

    If GaveHint is still FALSE then
        Give the user a "Bagels" message

Since we are continually giving messages and resetting `GaveHint`, we create a simple procedure `GiveMessage(Hint, GaveHint)` to do this for us. Note that we have nested `GiveMessage` within `Analyze`, since no other procedure or function has any need for `GiveMessage` and, thus, it can be local to `Analyze`. Also note that `GiveMessage` has a string parameter, so we will have to use a `TYPE` statement to declare a string type for this parameter. Since we want to print up to six characters in the string "Fermi " (don't forget to count the blank, too), we declare a new `String6` type. All these details are shown in Listing 7.14h, which includes `Analyze` and its sub-procedure, `GiveMessage`.

```
PROCEDURE Analyze(SecretHuns, SecretTens, SecretOnes,
                  GuessHuns, GuessTens, GuessOnes : CARDINAL);
```

```
(* Pre:  All six parameters have values between 0 and 9.
Post:    A 'Fermi' is printed for each Secret digit that is equal
to a corresponding Guess digit.

         A 'Pico' is printed for each Secret digit that is equal
to one of the other Guess digits.

         'Bagels' is printed if no other message has been
         printed.                                                   *)
```

```
TYPE   String6 = ARRAY[0..5] OF CHAR:
```

```
VAR    GaveHint : BOOLEAN;
```

```
PROCEDURE GiveMessage(Hint : String6; VAR GaveHint : BOOLEAN);
(* This nested procedure actually prints the Fermis and Picos, if
any.
Pre:   Hint has a value.
Post:  The value of Hint is printed and GaveHint is set
       to TRUE.                                                     *)

  BEGIN
    WriteString(Hint);
    GaveHint := TRUE
  END GiveMessage;

BEGIN                                (* Body of procedure Analyze. *)
  GaveHint := FALSE;         (* No hints have yet been given. *)

(* Check for a Fermi, which is a correct digit in the
   correct place.                                                   *)
  IF SecretHuns = GuessHuns THEN
    GiveMessage("Fermi ", GaveHint)  END;  (* IF *)
  IF SecretTens = GuessTens THEN
    GiveMessage("Fermi ", GaveHint)  END;  (* IF *)
  IF SecretOnes = GuessOnes THEN
    GiveMessage("Fermi ", GaveHint)  END;  (* IF *)

(* Check for a Pico, which is a correct digit, but
   in the wrong place.                                              *)
  IF (SecretHuns = GuessTens) OR (SecretHuns = GuessOnes) THEN
    GiveMessage("Pico ", GaveHint)  END;  (* IF *)
  IF (SecretTens = GuessHuns) OR (SecretTens = GuessOnes) THEN
    GiveMessage("Pico ", GaveHint)  END;  (* IF *)
```

```
    IF (SecretOnes = GuessHuns) OR (SecretOnes = GuessTens) THEN
      GiveMessage("Pico ", GaveHint)  END;  (* IF *)

(* Finally, if no hints have yet been given,
    supply a "Bagels."                                         *)
  IF NOT GaveHint THEN
    WriteString("Bagels")  END;  (* IF *)
  WriteLn; WriteLn
END Analyze;
```

Listing 7.14h

Next is the function PlayerQuits(), with no parameters, that returns TRUE if the user says she or he wants to quit, and FALSE otherwise. This simple function is shown in Listing 7.14i.

```
PROCEDURE PlayerQuits() : BOOLEAN;

(* Pre    None.
Post:    This function returns TRUE if the user wants to quit, and
FALSE otherwise.                                                *)

VAR Ch : CHAR;              (* Local variable for user response. *)

BEGIN
  WriteString("Would you like to quit? (Y/N)  ");
  Read(Ch); Write(Ch); WriteLn;
  Ch := CAP(Ch);
  IF Ch = "Y" THEN
    RETURN(TRUE);
    WriteString("Thanks for playing Bagels with me.")
  ELSE
    RETURN(FALSE)
  END  (* IF *)
END PlayAgain;
```

Listing 7.14i

Finally, Listing 7.14j shows the first portion of the module, the general comments, the importations, and the VAR declarations for identifiers used in the main module. Since the program is of some length, a procedure and function dictionary is also provided. Recall that the main body of the module Bagels was already displayed in Listing 7.14a.

```
MODULE Bagels;

(* This module plays the game of Bagels with the user. See the
Instructions procedure for the rules of the game. The module is an
example of procedures and functions and of the divide-and-conquer
problem-solving strategy.
```

The procedures used to solve the problem are:

Instructions
    A parameterless procedure that states the rules.

Generate(SecretNum)
    A procedure that returns the computer's SecretNum, a three-
    digit number.

Split(Num, Huns, Tens, Ones)
    A procedure that splits the three-digit number Num into its
    hundreds, tens, and ones digits.

Valid(Huns, Tens, Ones)
    A BOOLEAN function that indicates whether the digits are
    distinct and whether the first digit is nonzero.

Obtain(Guess)
    A procedure that obtains a guess from the user.

Analyze(SecretHuns, SecretTens, SecretOnes, GuessHuns, GuessTens,
        GuessOnes)
    A procedure that analyzes the digits of the secret number and
    the guess of the user and calls a nested procedure GiveMessage
    to give the appropriate hints.

Summarize(NumTurns)
    A procedure that congratulates the user when she or he finally
    guesses the secret number and tells the user the number of
    guesses needed.

PlayerQuits()
    A BOOLEAN function that asks if the user wants to quit the game.


```
    * * * * * * * * * * * * * * * * * *                    *)


FROM InOut IMPORT WriteLn, WriteString, WriteCard, Write, Read,
                                                      ReadCard;


VAR    SecretNum                            : CARDINAL;
       SecretHuns, SecretTens, SecretOnes   : CARDINAL;
       Guess                                : CARDINAL;
       GuessHuns, GuessTens, GuessOnes      : CARDINAL;
       NumTurns                             : CARDINAL;
       GameOver                             : BOOLEAN;
```

Listing 7.14j

CONCLUSION

We cannot overestimate the importance of this chapter in the development of problem-solving skills. Most real-world problems are too difficult to be attacked with a single program. The top-down, divide-and-conquer strategy, with its use of procedures and functions, provides an organized method for making difficult programs manageable. Often, very large programs of thousands of lines have a main program consisting of just a few dozen lines. These few lines are just procedure and function invocations.

The concepts of scope, local and global variables, arguments and parameters, value and variable parameters, and the dynamic handling of environments are all critical to understanding the programming processes and are relevant regardless of the language one is using.

EXERCISES

7.1 The text argues that any procedure could be replaced by an equivalent function. Give the converse of this argument and show how any function could be replaced by an equivalent procedure. As an example, include the procedure heading and the procedure invocation that would replace the function heading

```
PROCEDURE SomeFunc(X : INTEGER; Ch : CHAR) : INTEGER;
```

and the function invocation

```
WriteInt(SomeFunc(10, 'C'));
```

7.2 Add the following improvements to the `WriteRealPretty(Num, Left, Right)` procedure of the text:

a) Supress any leading zeros by replacing them with blanks, so that 212.0 prints, when `Left` is 4 and `Right` is 2, as " 212.00" instead of "0212.00".

b) Round the last digit printed on the right; so, for example, 3.587 prints as 3.59 instead of 3.58, when `Right` is 2.

c) Print a minus sign if `Num` is negative.

d) Print an error message when `Left` is too small to print all the digits of `Num` to the left of the decimal point.

7.3 Distinguish between the following pairs of concepts:

a) Local and global identifiers

b) Arguments and parameters

c) Value and variable parameters

7.4 What are the syntactical differences between a procedure definition and a function definition?

7.5 From the following descriptions, decide whether the object should be implemented as a procedure or as a function. Then write the heading for each procedure or function, including an indication of the value and variable parameters. Assume that each parameter is a CARDINAL.

a) `ExplainRules`, with no parameters, states the rules of the game.

b) `FtInToCms` converts a given height in feet and inches into an equivalent height in centimeters. For example, `FtInToCms` converts 5 feet and 10 inches into 178 centimeters.

c) `CmsToFtIn` converts a given height in centimeters into an equivalent height in feet and inches. For example, `CmsToFtIn` converts 178 centimeters into 5 feet and 10 inches.

d) `Squares` returns the squares of its two inputs. For example, given 4 and 12, `Squares` returns 16 and 144.

e) `SquareSum` returns the sum of the squares of its two inputs. For example, given 4 and 12, `SquareSum` returns 160.

7.6 Write guidelines for determining when a given subprogram should be written as a procedure and when it should be written as a function.

7.7 You are the Computer Science I instructor. You have just fought your way through a long program turned in by Ima Hacker that contains no procedures or functions. Write an essay explaining to Ima the need for procedures and functions.

7.8 You are still the Computer Science I instructor. You made Ima Hacker redo her work and now it contains procedures and functions, but without parameters, since Ima has used global variables extensively. Write an essay explaining to Ima the dangers and poor style caused by globals.

7.9 All functions are broken today! Instead of the functions `Abs(X)`, `Sqrt(X)`, and `Cube(X)` you will have to use the procedures `AbsProc(X,Y)`, `SqrtProc(X,Y)`, and `CubeProc(X,Y)` which set `Y` to the indicated function of `X`. Use the procedures to rewrite the following line of code:

```
IF Abs(Sqrt(X) - Sqrt(Y)) < Cube(Z) THEN WriteString('OK')
```

Hint: The one line will become at least five lines long and will need additional variables (which you may assume have been declared).

7.10 Write a program to simulate 50 rolls of two dice, a red die and a green die. The output should be a table consisting of three columns showing Red's value, Green's value, and the total value.

7.11 (Computer Roulette) Write a structured module that simulates the following perverse version of Russian Roulette. In a six-cylinder gun, place one silver bullet and two blanks. Three of the cylinders are left empty. Spin the cylinder and pull the trigger. If an empty chamber is beneath the firing pin, the gun goes "CLICK." If either a blank or the silver bullet is under the firing pin, the gun goes "BANG." After a brief pause, you find out whether you are still alive and still playing, or whether the game is over. Hint: Use a Read; to halt execution and allow the user to "pull the trigger" by typing the RETURN key. Simulate the pause after the BANG by giving the computer a big do-nothing loop such as:

```
For Index := 1 TO 20000 DO
  (*Nothing *)
END; (* FOR *)
```

This problem shows the value of simulations, which are often safer and less messy than the real event. Absolutely no extra credit will be given for anything other than a simulation of this event!

7.12 A dog, Cookie, has buried three bones randomly in her backyard, which is 50 feet by 50 feet. Naturally, she has forgotten where the bones are buried, so she randomly begins digging holes. Her nose is so good (and her holes so big!) that she will find a bone if she digs within 1 foot of it. That is, suppose a bone is buried at point (x,y). Cookie finds the bone if she digs at (x,y), (x-1,y), (x+1,y), (x,y-1), or (x,y+1). For simplicity, we assume x and y are integers. That is, Cookie only digs at points with integer coordinates.
Write a program to randomly bury three bones and then randomly dig holes until a bone is found. Have the program repeat the experiment 20 times so that Cookie gets a feeling for the average number of holes needed to find a bone. Make sure the program is structured by using functions and procedures. Also notice that Cookie is so dumb that she may dig the same hole more than once.

7.13 A man leaves a pub in a slightly tipsy state. His home is eight blocks west of the pub, while the jail is eight blocks east of the pub. The man is as likely to go east as west, and after each block he falls down. When he gets up, he goes east or west with equal probability. In his journey, if he passes the pub, he goes in for one last drink before continuing his journey. Write a structured program to simulate the man's walk, which ends when he reaches home or jail. The output should include the man's current position (three blocks east, etc.) and, at the end, the program should output the length (in blocks) the man walked and the total number of times he returned to the pub.

7.14 Write a procedure Time that converts a number N of seconds into hours, minutes, and seconds. For example, 3724 seconds is 1 hour, 2 minutes, and 4 seconds.

Chapter 8

PROGRAM DESIGN
AND IMPLEMENTATION

Now that we have seen a little of what programming in Modula-2 is like, it is time to pause and consider what we are really about: problem solving. As an introductory text in computer science, this book aims to teach you some of the concepts of fundamental importance in the application of computers to the solutions of problems. The language Modula-2 is the means we have chosen to implement our solutions, but Modula-2, with its fussy syntax, is not our main objective. If you take the time to learn the concepts discussed here, you will take something valuable and permanent away from this study.

By now, it is clear that a program will not run if you don't pay careful attention to semicolons and other syntax issues. It should also be clear that the placement of semicolons and the exact syntax of Modula-2's WHILE loop are hardly issues of such significance as to be studied at the college level. This chapter discusses and illustrates our real objective: a disciplined, structured approach to problem solving through stepwise refinement. This careful and reasoned approach to problem solving is the true benefit that you can take from this study. To see the importance of developing good problem-solving skills, as opposed to just a knowledge of Modula-2 syntax, consider the following two hypothetical students:

Student A knows Modula-2 forward and backward, but is weak in problem-solving skills. Student A likes to show off his (yes, these types are often male) knowledge by writing a 10-line program to illustrate any feature of Modula-2. But student A's problem-solving skills are so weak that he cannot use his knowledge to solve the simplest problem. Even though he is an expert in the language of the computer, he cannot form any meaningful utterances.

Student B is a good problem solver, but is weak in Modula-2 syntax. Student B writes good pseudo-code and then has to refer frequently to the Railroad Diagrams

(Syntax Diagrams) of Appendix C to translate the pseudo-code into Modula-2. However, other than being a bit slow, Student B is very successful.

Unfortunately, we have seen many students like student A. Student B is much rarer, since practice in programming does seem to teach Modula-2 syntax quickly. We hope that you, too, can learn to be a good problem solver who also recalls Modula-2 syntax— but the point of the example is that the syntax is easy to look up, while the problem-solving skills are not so easily obtained.

LEARNING PROBLEM-SOLVING SKILLS

How does one learn problem-solving skills? We believe that the only way to learn such skills is through disciplined practice. That is why this book has so many complete sample programs in the text and contains a large number of exercises. We urge you to read the book in an active mode—which means that you study, run, modify, and rerun the sample programs in the book as well as solve a significant number of the exercises. The passive learner who only attends lectures or just reads programs written by others will not learn problem solving on the computer.

One method of teaching swimming is to toss people into the deep end of the pool. Those who learn swim out, while the rest drown. Often, problem solving has been presented to students in much the same manner. Class discussions (often about Modula-2 syntax) take place in the wading pool, then the students find themselves in the deep end with no idea how to begin a solution to the assigned problem. Recognize that the responsibility for teaching and learning problem-solving skills is shared by the instructor, the text, and the student. The text and the instructor must present methods and examples. The student must study these materials carefully and practice the methods extensively. Unfortunately, there are no royal shortcuts to learning problem-solving skills.

In this chapter, we gather together in one place a discussion of problem-solving and disciplined programming strategies that have gained wide acceptance in computer science. Many of these topics have already been introduced, but in a somewhat abstract fashion. Now that we have discussed procedures and functions in the previous chapter, we can discuss these concepts much more concretely. In this chapter, we also provide a complete, annotated example of the problem-solving process. We urge you to study it carefully and to model your approaches after those given here. This is what we mean by the disciplined practice of problem-solving strategies. As this text continues to introduce new concepts and new Modula-2 syntax, we will continually return to the problem-solving methods discussed in this chapter. Study these examples carefully and return to this chapter as necessary when you find yourself in over your head with a particular problem.

THE PROGRAM DESIGN PROCESS

We'll now describe an eight-step process that outlines the typical development of software projects.

1. Problem Specification

In the real world, problems often come poorly specified. The person who wants the computer to do some task is often unaware of exactly what it is that she or he wants the computer to do. Often, several meetings are necessary between potential users and program design specialists before problem specifications can be written. It is important that both sides (user and programmer) agree on the specifications. The user must be satisfied that the specifications will properly solve the original problem, and the programmer must be satisfied that the specifications do fully and completely specify a problem that can be solved with the given resources in the given time.

In a text, we are constrained to *strive* to give you complete program specifications. Since you cannot easily query us about our intentions, we try to think of every possible question in advance. Your instructor, however, may wish to give you vague specifications for an assignment and let you define the problem in further discussion. In any case, it should be clear that proper specification of the problem is an important first step. Nothing is so frustrating (to the programmer) as users who keep changing their minds about what they want the computer to do.

2. Understanding the Problem

An essential step and, in our experience, one often shortchanged by students, is the simple task of taking the time to understand the given problem. This means several things. One is carefully reading (and rereading) the problem statement. One quick reading is almost certainly insufficient for understanding.

A second very important part of understanding the problem is to devise a small amount of data and work out by hand the output from the given data. In so doing, the emphasis should be on "*How* am I getting these results?" not just on "*What* are the results?" The data one prepares for these hand tracings need not be extensive, but should be diverse. That is, the data should be chosen to help you think about all the possible cases that could occur in real data.

We believe that this data-driven approach to understanding the given problem is probably the single most important component often omitted by students. We feel that these hand tracings should be written and should be kept by the student. They are extremely helpful for the next step, and many instructors demand to see such hand executions before they will give students help on a problem. In any case, it should be clear to the learner that failure to understand the problem will mean certain failure in the steps to follow. How can we expect to design, let alone implement, a plan to solve a problem that we don't even understand?

3. Designing an Algorithm

Now that we understand the problem, we can focus on designing a plan for its solution. This plan should be specified in a pseudo-code, so that our attention is on algorithm design rather than on the syntax of our programming language. In this stage, our hand executions from the previous step become very important in guiding our design. It is important to be able to step outside of ourselves and observe ourselves as we work. We need to do this because we are not interested in the actual results, but in the method used to obtain those results. This point of view is often foreign to beginners and requires some practice. Careful attention to the pseudo-code examples in the text and imitation of their styles is suggested. It is also at this stage that comments begin to take form as we outline the main points of the solution.

Of course, the design of the algorithm should proceed in a disciplined or structured manner. **Top-down** design is the suggested method. Top-down design has been discussed previously, but for completeness we'll describe the process again. Now that we have introduced procedures and functions, we have a concrete way to implement top-down design.

Top-down design simply means that we use the divide-and-conquer strategy to break our problem into manageable pieces. These pieces are then further subdivided as necessary to reduce the problem to modules that are easy to understand. This continued subdivision of parts of the program is called **stepwise refinement**. The point is that we continue to refine our descriptions until we are left with simple actions that will be relatively easy to implement.

Another important part of the design phase is to repeat the hand executions done above. This means to take the data developed and carefully trace the pseudo-code as if you were a literal-minded computer. The point of this step is to subject your algorithm to as many tests as you can. You may discover parts of your pseudo-code that are incomplete or incorrect. If so, you must modify your design to correct it. Again, this data-driven test of the algorithm is extremely important and a step that you should not omit, because it provides the best possible test of your design at this stage.

This third step in the problem-solving process is extremely important. You can't, of course, design an algorithm until you understand the problem, nor can additional steps proceed without a well-understood algorithm. Too often, we find students mired in the implementation phase without a real understanding of the design they are trying to implement. It should be clear that the implementation will not succeed unless you know what it is that you wish to implement! Remember Murphy's Law: *"The sooner you begin coding (implementing), the longer the whole process takes"* and spend time designing and testing your algorithm.

4. Implementation

This step should be a straightforward translation of the pseudo-code into Modula-2. If the pseudo-code has been refined sufficiently, this step proceeds quickly. Of course, it is via procedures and functions that a complex pseudo-code is implemented. In this manner, the main program greatly resembles the pseudo-code solution.

Documentation in the form of comments should be included as the translation occurs. Elsewhere in this chapter, we discuss commenting conventions that have helped programmers with their coding.

An important point (mentioned several times already) is that students too often try to start at the implementation phase. The danger in doing so is that you have to combine and juggle all the previous phases while considering the fussy syntax of a particular computer language. You may be worrying about the placement of semicolons when you should be worrying about *what* you are trying to express. Worse yet, if you do not really understand the problem, you are wasting your time deciding whether or not you need a semicolon. Even if you eventually succeed with the syntax, your program has no chance of running correctly. This is the road to ultimate frustration. If you find your efforts can be described like this, then you must go back to the understanding and design phases.

Another point worthy of mention is that the implementation phase is also not the end of the problem-solving process. Too often, students who do succeed at the implementation phase think that their work is complete. Just because a program runs without errors does not mean that it produces correct output. It only means that the program is free of syntax errors.

5. Testing and Debugging

Of course, if your implementation produces error messages, it needs to be debugged. The very minimum you need to do is to inspect the output and gauge the results for reasonableness. Is it reasonable that someone with quiz scores all between 60 and 90 has an average of 7482.39? Evidently not! Another use of your hand tracings is to check the computer's results on cases where you know the correct answers. The amount of data may be so extensive that you cannot check all the results, but you should spot-check your program by verifying some of its results. You can never be sure that your program is completely correct, and big commercial programs do occasionally blow up after many years in service. But you can at least check that your results are not garbage.

What do we do if we do have errors? This phase of finding and removing errors is called **debugging**. Debugging is another skill that is best learned with practice. You will probably generate several bugs of your own, but to ensure that you get plenty of practice, we have included intentionally buggy programs in the exercises at the end of this chapter. In another section of this chapter, we'll take up general methods of debugging.

6. Final Documentation and Proofreading

Your program is a form of communication. It is not just a communication with a computer, but also a communication with other humans. In a classroom situation, the other human is often a grader who will be more kindly disposed to your program if she or he can easily read and understand it. In the real world, your program will be read by colleagues and supervisors (or maybe you six months later). Thus, it is important that your program be as clear as you can make it.

Methods for providing program clarity have been discussed and illustrated throughout this book. Some of the most important are:

Comments. Well-chosen comments that help the intelligent reader should be included with the program. A suggested form for commenting is discussed in a separate section below. Large projects may even have external documentation in the form of user manuals.

White Space. The well-chosen use of blank lines helps to divide your programs into sections that make it easy to read and understand. Long programs should use white space to ensure that program listings are placed properly across page breaks.

Indentation. Make sure that you have observed standards of proper indentation for the bodies of procedures and functions as well as for WHILEs and IFs. Indentation is ignored by the compiler, but is one of the most important tools you have to make your program understandable.

Meaningful Identifiers. Check that your identifiers add to the clarity of your program. Avoid identifiers that are too short to convey meaning.

Procedures and Functions. Avoid long sections of code. Use the divide-and-conquer approach to make your solution readable in easily understood pieces.

Clear Output. Check that the output from your program is not only correct, but also will make sense and be clear to the user. For example, is the output labeled properly?

7. Production

Real-world programs enter a production phase where they are used in real situations. Often, at this point, the user decides that she or he wants some additional feature added, and the whole process begins again. In education, the production phase probably means simply running the program once or twice and turning in the results. If you are in charge of selecting the data, make sure that you select the data so as to show off your program. That is, make sure that the data let the program demonstrate that it handles all the different kinds of data that you can think of. You should have done this in the testing phase, because it's kind of embarrassing when the user (or grader) discovers an error in your program at this late stage.

8. Maintenance

This, again, is a critical concern in commercial programming. Constants such as the social-security withholding rate change, or new cases arise that must be accounted for. Therefore, it is necessary to modify the program. One test of how well the program was written is how easy (or difficult) it is to modify. In the past, managers often found it easier to throw a program out and start all over rather than to modify the program. That is why the structured and disciplined programming techniques that we have been emphasizing were developed. In education, we seldom have the time to let (make) students modify their own programs, but it would certainly make the need for a disciplined approach to programming very clear to everyone.

Other Problem-Solving Strategies

There are other problem-solving strategies that are often applicable to programming situations. One of the most famous is the suggestion to **solve a simpler problem first**. Your first effort does not need to be a program that solves the entire problem. If you plan your approach, you can often create for yourself a sequence of problems, each encompassing the others, that leads to the solution of the final problem. For example, suppose that you are to read a data file that contains many lines of the form:

```
M3.998Jacque Strappe
```

consisting of a character ('M' or 'F') representing sex, a real number representing a time in minutes to run a mile, and a name. Suppose that you are to print out the male and female winners of the race, as well as the average male and female times. You could, for example, successively solve the following sequence of problems:

1. Write a program to read and simply print out the data.
2. Modify the program so that it finds the male and female averages.
3. Modify the program so that it also finds the male and female winners.

This is an effective problem-solving strategy, and we recommend it highly when you have no idea how to begin. Begin with a simple problem and, later, add the complications one at a time.

   Another related problem-solving strategy is to **modify a solution to a previous problem**. This is essentially what we were doing in the above example, but this method can also be applied to programs that you have previously written or to sample programs from the book. Modeling your solution after a successful one is a very good way to get started. That is why it is very valuable to study all the sample programs with great care.

COMMENTING CONVENTIONS

Documentation is a very important, and very individualistic, part of the programming process. There is no magic rule that says every fourth line should be a comment. The trick is to comment programs well in the absence of such rigid rules. The basic rule is that comments should benefit the intelligent user. This means that you should not comment the obvious:

```
Count := 0;                          (*Initialize Count to zero*)
                                     (*EXAMPLE OF POOR COMMENT!*)
```

Nor should you comment every line. It is possible to overcomment just as it is possible to overindulge in any good thing. To give the beginner some aid to proper documentation, we suggest the following guidelines, which have been widely accepted as good principles of software design. Most of these principles have already been mentioned previously, but we gather them here for emphasis and easy reference. We divide comments into three broad kinds: local, procedural, and global.

1. Local Comments

Tricky or Difficult Statements. Any statement that will perhaps not be immediately clear to an intelligent reader should be commented. For example, when a "magimatical" formula is pulled out of the air, a comment should document this:

```
Distance := Length*Height*cos(Theta);        (*Theta in Radians*)
```

Another example is

```
...
WriteString('Do you want to play again? (Y/N) ');
Read(Resp);
Write(Resp);                         (* Echo response to the screen *)
    ...
```

Here, the purpose of the very simple `Write` statement has been made abundantly clear. Since this is easily forgotten, it is a good idea to document its need.

Section Documentation. A well-chosen comment before a major section of code can make the intent of that section instantly clear. For example:

```
(* Now find the maximum points scored and by whom. *)
...
```

makes the next section's intended purpose obvious. Combined with judicious use of white space (blank lines and indentation), these kinds of comments make a program a joy to read.

Assertions. A special form of a comment called an *assertion* is becoming a standard way to comment programs. An assertion is simply a comment that is true at the point where it is placed in the program. An example of assertions about a `WHILE` loop that is looking for a sentinel `'MickeyMouse'` might be

```
ReadString(Name);

Count := 0;
WHILE Name <> 'MickeyMouse' DO
   INC(Count);                    (* The value of Count is the number
                                      of names read so far.*)
   ...
   process the data for this person
   ...
   ReadString(Name)
END; (* WHILE *)
                (* Name is the sentinel value, 'MickeyMouse'. *)
...
```

The first assertion about the current value of `Count` states what is true every time we execute the body of the `WHILE` (and, therefore, this special assertion is called a **loop invariant**). The second assertion indicates what is true when we exit from the `WHILE`. Assertions are very important in an advanced subject known as program correctness, where we attempt to prove that a program is correct. Since this is a first course, we will continue to use informal assertions, but the reader should be aware that assertions and invariants do provide a way to comment programs.

END Documentation. The keyword `END` is overused in Modula-2. It is often very helpful, especially with `END`s that pile up together, to comment what each is actually the end of. For example:

```
   ...
   END (*IF*)
  END (*Inner WHILE*)
END (*Outer WHILE*)
...
```

Of course, the indentation also makes it possible to see what each END terminates, but the comment makes it obvious without the need to draw the eye up the page in a straight line.

2. Procedural Comments

By the generic term **procedural**, we mean both procedures and functions. These should always begin with a comment, so that the reader can quickly grasp what it is that the procedure or function does.

   Preconditions and **postconditions**, introduced in Chapter 7, are a special form of procedural comments that have gained wide acceptance. They state in contractual form what the procedure or function promises to do. The preconditions are conditions that must be true before you call the procedure or function. The postconditions are promises that the procedure or function says will hold afterward (if the preconditions were met). Preconditions and postconditions are helpful in many ways. First, they help us decide which parameters should be value and which should be variable. For example, any parameter mentioned in the postconditions as receiving a new value must be a variable parameter. Preconditions and postconditions also help in debugging a program by helping us locate the problem. If we have met the preconditions of a procedure, but it fails to uphold its postcondition, then we know that the procedure is not doing its stated job.

   To write preconditions and postconditions, we suggest that you first write an English description of what the procedure or function does, and then decide what must be true *before* the procedure acts and what will be true *after* the procedure acts. For example, suppose the procedure Split is to take a three-digit Number and return its Huns, Tens, and Ones digits. Pay attention to the little words like "takes" and "returns," because they tell us that for Split to do its work, Num must already have a three-digit value and that Huns, Tens, and Ones will be variable parameters receiving single-digit values. Thus, we can write:

```
PROCEDURE Split(Num : CARDINAL; VAR Huns, Tens, Ones : CARDINAL);
(*Pre: Num is a three-digit cardinal.
Post: Huns, Tens, and Ones are assigned the appropriate digits
      from Num.                                                 *)
```

Procedure and function bodies can, of course, have local documentation as discussed above, so the preconditions and postconditions are not the only comments in a procedure or function, but they are important comments and you should try to learn to write good preconditions and postconditions.

3. Global Comments

Global comments are comments for the entire program. This documentation should include, as a minimum, a comment at the beginning of the program telling what it is that the program does. In a class situation, it is a good idea to include your name and your instructor's name so that if your program gets lost, it can be returned to you. Global documentation for a larger program can also quickly indicate what procedures and functions will be employed in the solution of the problem and what the main variables are, as well as what they are for. The lengthy program `Bagels` at the end of Chapter 7 provides a good example of global documentation.

THE ART OF DEBUGGING

We think that there is much to be learned from debugging, and that is why we have included intentionally buggy programs in the exercises. Debugging is another skill that is best learned with practice. However, there are certain general guidelines to aid the beginner in developing this skill. These are gathered here for easy reference. Also, see the complete debugging example later in this chapter.

Debugging Strategies

1. Locate the problem
This simple suggestion is probably the most important aid to debugging. When you have a large program that produces garbage, you have no idea what the problem is. If you can locate the procedure, function, or section of code that is causing the problem, you are well on your way to finding the problem. In this regard, debugging is like lawn-mower repair. A lawn-mower repairperson must first decide whether the problem is in the electrical system or the fuel system. If the problem is electrical, then is it in the spark plug or the points? The repairperson continues in this manner until she or he has determined the exact location of the problem.

In a program, how does one locate the bug? Several suggestions that help locate a bug are now discussed.

2. Obtain additional output
Suppose that you have a program that reads the data and then produces nonsense. If you can identify several key intermediate steps and print out the values of these key variables, then you can help to identify the step at which the calculation went off the track. Additional output is obtained, of course, by inserting output statements like `Write, WriteCard, WriteString` into a program. These statements will then be deleted when the problem is found and fixed. We often use this technique as an aid in debugging student programs brought to us. We find it convenient to include a small identifying message. For example:

```
WriteString('Reading Data: ');
WriteString(Name); WriteLn;
WriteCard(Score); WriteLn;
```

placed in the main loop that (supposedly) reads the data will print the data as read. If all the data appears, then the program is working up to that point. If only some or none of the data is printed, then we have come a long way toward locating the problem.

3. Play computer
Playing computer means tracing the execution of the program step by step. At every

stage, you should compare your results with those produced by the program. When you add additional output to the program, you can get frequent checks on its work. When you find that your work agrees with the computer's up to a certain stage, then you have come close to isolating the problem.

Playing computer takes much patience and critical thinking. You must be careful to do exactly what you told the computer to do, not what you want the computer to do. Try to execute each instruction exactly as the computer would. In this manner, you can often catch a misstatement in your program.

4. Simplify the data

Sometimes, printing additional output results in a flood of output that is difficult to understand. Often, it is wise to reduce the amount of data given to the program until the bug is located. This may be as simple as creating a new, small test data file for the program. If a short data file exhibits the bug, then the human will be able to play computer and understand far more easily the modest amount of output produced by the smaller amount of data.

5. Bench-test procedures and functions

Suppose you have a procedure or function that you suspect is not doing its job. By bench-testing it, we mean to give it input and carefully monitor its output. In so doing, we isolate it from the other components and observe its behavior. Bench-testing is very simple to do. In this case, the preconditions and postconditions are very helpful. The preconditions tell us what we must do to be able to call the procedure or function. The postconditions tell us what is supposed to be true after the call. Thus, we simply create the preconditions, make the call, and test the postconditions. For example, to bench-test Split, whose heading and pre/post conditions are:

```
PROCEDURE Split(Num : CARDINAL; VAR Huns, Tens, Ones : CARDINAL);
(*Pre: Num is a three-digit integer.
Post: Huns, Tens, and Ones are assigned the appropriate digits
      from Num.                                                  *)
```

we merely place the following lines just inside our main BEGIN:

```
Num := 123;
Split(Num, Huns, Tens, Ones);
WriteString('Split Test');
WriteCard(Num, 5);
WriteCard(Huns, 5);
WriteCard(Tens, 5);
WriteCard(Ones, 5);
Halt;
```

The value 123 is arbitrary, but it is important that Num have some three-digit value when called. A good choice would be a data value for which the program has shown that it does not work properly. If the output from this segment is *not*

```
Split Test 123   1   2   3
```

then we know that there is a problem within `Split`. Unfortunately, if we get the correct output, we cannot completely exonerate `Split`, but if we make several such tests to `Split`, then we gain more and more confidence in `Split` and begin to look elsewhere for the problem. For example, before moving on, we might bench-test `Split` with a number that has repeated digits, like 122 or even 111.

Bench-testing is a powerful technique for gaining some confidence in your procedures and functions. It can and should be used as you write your procedures and functions to validate them as far as you possibly can.

A COMPLETE EXAMPLE: THE DUEL OF
ALEXANDER HAMILTON AND AARON BURR

The most famous duel in American history occurred in 1804, when Alexander Hamilton, the nation's first secretary of the treasury (of 10-dollar-bill fame), dueled with and was killed by Aaron Burr, vice president under Thomas Jefferson.

We are going to make some historically inaccurate, simplifying assumptions about the duel and then simulate the duel many times to decide whether it was fair or not. Even though Hamilton lost, we will assume that he was the better shot. In fact, we will arbitrarily say that Hamilton hits his target once in two tries, on the average, and that Burr only hits his target once in three tries, on the average. We will also assume that, 19th-century medical care being what it was, any hit means death. Knowing that he is the better shot, and being a gentleman (and also, apparently, a fool), Hamilton agrees to let Burr have the first shot. Hamilton will not shoot unless Burr misses, and then Burr will not get a second shot unless Hamilton misses, etc. Thus, the duel may go on for many shots with Burr getting the first (and every odd-numbered shot) and Hamilton getting the second (and every even-numbered shot) until death does them part.

Because dueling is no longer considered a gentlemanly sport, we wish to simulate the duel. Burr goes first, but Hamilton is the better shot. Therefore, it is not obvious who has the advantage. Which position would you choose? To determine who has the advantage, we will simulate a large number of duels and count how many times Burr wins and how many times Hamilton wins. Because it is of interest, let us also determine the average length (in shots) of a duel.

Let us now consider in detail how our eight-step problem-solving process could be applied to this problem.

1. The first step was getting the *problem specified completely*. Normally, in a text, we have to try to do this step for you. We didn't say how far apart Hamilton and Burr were standing, but that clearly isn't relevant since we know that at this distance, Hamilton hits 50 percent of the time and Burr hits 33-1/3 percent of the time. A relevant detail that has been intentionally omitted is the number of duels to simulate to get a feeling for who will be the winner. Let's now agree that we will simulate 100 duels. Otherwise, we hope we have included all relevant details in the problem description.

2. The next step, *understanding the problem*, is a major one. You should not proceed until you feel that you have assimilated the problem completely. Reread the problem description a couple of times and ask yourself questions about the situation. Be sure you realize that this duel is not like high noon in Tombstone where both players draw and shoot at the same time. Also realize that the phrase "Hamilton hits his target once in

two tries" does not mean that he always hits, then misses, then hits, then misses, etc., on every other shot. Rather, the phrase means that, like a fair coin that comes up heads, on the average, once in two flips, Hamilton hits Burr, on the average, once in two tries. It is possible, but not likely, for Hamilton to hit (or miss) Burr 10 straight times.

Another suggestion given for understanding a problem was to create a small amount of data and determine the output for those data. For this problem, unlike most, there are no input data, but we do strongly suggest that you use a die (singular of dice) to simulate a few duels by hand. We suggest a die because it is easy to get both the fractions 1/2 and 1/3 from a die. Explicitly, let us agree that if Hamilton rolls a 4, 5, or 6, then he hits Burr, while Burr hits Hamilton only if he rolls a 5 or a 6. Supposing the following 12 rolls of the die, verify that Hamilton wins 3 of the first 5 duels in an average of 2.4 shots:

4
3
6
2
5
1
1
4
6
5
2
4

3. The next step, *designing an algorithm*, is critical to what follows. We invite you, before reading further, to stop and design by stepwise refinement your own pseudo-code version of an algorithm for this problem. You will obviously not design exactly the algorithm that we do, but that is to be expected, since this step is the most creative and individualistic part of the whole process. That also explains why this step is so important in our whole problem-solving stratagem.

Our approach to this problem proceeds as follows: Wouldn't it be nice if there was a built-in Duel procedure that would simulate *one* duel for us and tell us who won and how many shots it took? Of course, there is no such built-in procedure, but that is the advantage of the divide-and-conquer strategy and the stepwise-refinement technique. For now, we can pretend that there is such a procedure and see how we would use it to solve the given problem. Later we shall have to focus our attention on Duel and see how it can be designed. We do see from our description of Duel that it needs two parameters, one to indicate who won and one to indicate how many shots were needed. Since we can indicate the winner with a 'B' or 'H', we can suppose that Duel's parameters are a CHARacter and a CARDINAL, respectively.

Given Duel, the main program becomes quite easy. It simply needs to invoke Duel 100 times and keep track of the number of wins by Hamilton and Burr as well as the total number of shots. Here is the pseudo-code:

Set a constant, NumDuels, to 100
Initialize HamWins and BurrWins both to zero

Initialize TotalShots to zero
Loop NumDuels times doing
    Duel(Winner, NumShots)   --Simulate one duel
    If Winner is 'H' then
        Increment HamWins
    Else
        Increment BurrWins
    Add NumShots to TotalShots
Output HamWins, BurrWins, and TotalShots/NumDuels (the average)

This, when implemented, will become our main program. It will be short and easy to understand. The loop will become a standard FOR but that is a detail that can be left to the implementation. Assuming that Duel(Winner, NumShots) does its job, you should trace the above pseudo-code to make sure that it performs as desired.

The cautious reader will point out that we still have a big procedure to write. In fact, it may seem that all we have done is to strip the trivial part away from the difficult part, leaving the difficult part yet unsolved. That may be, but let us now apply the same divide-and-conquer approach to procedure Duel. Realize that we now get to ignore the rest of the details and focus our efforts on simulating one complete duel. This procedure must let Burr shoot first and must continue while both are still living. Then, it must report the winner and the number of shots needed through its parameters. Hence, we already see that this procedure has no preconditions, but the following important postconditions:

Winner will be 'H' if Hamilton wins, and 'B" if Burr wins
NumShots will count the number of shots needed in the duel

The hard part of procedure Duel seems to be knowing how long the duel should continue. Sometimes it ends in one shot, sometimes two, sometimes more. It continues *while* they are both living. There it is! We can make the body of Duel a WHILE loop with a BOOLEAN BothLiving! Here is the broad pseudo-code outline as developed so far:

Initialize NumShots to zero
Initialize BothLiving to True   --Begin with both Hamilton and Burr healthy
While BothLiving
    Let them duel at one another

Now we further refine the statement "Let them duel at one another." This involves Burr taking the first shot (don't forget to count the shot). If he hits, he wins and BothLiving *is no longer* TRUE. If Burr misses, then Hamilton shoots (count it). If Hamilton hits, then he wins, and BothLiving *is no longer* TRUE. Otherwise, we keep looping. Putting this together with what we already had gives us the following outline:

Initialize NumShots to zero
Initialize BothLiving to True   --Begin with both Hamilton and Burr healthy
While BothLiving

```
   Increment NumShots                          --Count Burr's shot at Hamilton
   If Burr hit Hamilton then
      Set BothLiving to False
      Set Winner to 'B'                                               --Burr won
   Else  --Burr missed, so give Hamilton a chance
      Increment NumShots              --Count Hamilton's return shot at Burr
      If Hamilton hit Burr then
         Set BothLiving to False
         Set Winner to 'H'                                        --Hamilton won
```

Here, everything but the phrases "Burr hit Hamilton" and "Hamilton hit Burr" will be easy to implement. Assuming that these phrases operate as planned (they can be true or false), the reader should verify by hand that Burr could win in three shots, or Hamilton might win in two or six shots, for example.

Thus, all we are left with is designing some way to tell when one man shoots his opponent. Since the two opponents shoot in similar ways, we propose a BOOLEAN function, Shoots, with one input parameter. If this input parameter is 2, then one in two times, on the average, Shoots will return TRUE, but if the parameter is a 3, then only one in three times will Shoots return TRUE. Thus, the BOOLEAN condition "Burr hit Hamilton" can be replaced by the invocation Shoots(3), while the condition "Hamilton hit Burr" can be replaced by Shoots(2). Here, then, is our final pseudo-code for a duel:

```
Initialize NumShots to zero
Initialize BothLiving to True      --Begin with both Hamilton and Burr healthy
While BothLiving
   Increment NumShots                          --Count Burr's shot at Hamilton
   If Shoots(3) then                              --Did Burr hit Hamilton?
      Set BothLiving to False
      Set Winner to 'B'                                               --Burr won
   Else                              --Burr missed, so give Hamilton a chance
      Increment NumShots              --Count Hamilton's return shot at Burr
      If Shoots(2) then                           --Did Hamilton hit Burr?
         Set BothLiving to False
         Set Winner to 'H'                                        --Hamilton won
```

Finally, we need only to design Shoots(N), which will return TRUE once in N calls, on the average. The precondition for Shoots is that N has some positive value, and the postcondition is that Shoots will return TRUE about 1 of N times (on the average). Our strategy is to generate randomly a number between 1 and N and arbitrarily let 1 represent TRUE. To obtain the random number, we will use the random-number generator Generate discussed in the Bagels example of Chapter 7. The pseudo-code for Shoots(N) follows:

```
Let Randy be a random value returned by the Generate procedure
Let Randy be (Randy MOD N) + 1                    --A value between 1 and N
If Randy is 1 then
```

> Set Shoots to True
> Else
> Set Shoots to False

Using stepwise refinement, we have developed a main program that calls a procedure Duel. This procedure then invokes the function Shoots to actually simulate the duels. In this manner, we have broken a seemingly complex problem into several short modules. We have divided and conquered!

4. Now comes the easy part. Our final pseudo-code is so complete that the *implementation* shown in Listing 8.1 is a nearly direct translation of the pseudo-code.

```
MODULE HamBurr;
(*This module simulates the famous duel between Alexander Hamilton
and Aaron Burr to decide who had the best chance. It also determines
the average number of shots fired in each duel.            *)

FROM InOut IMPORT WriteCard, WriteString, WriteLn;
FROM RealInOut IMPORT WriteReal;

CONST NumDuels = 100;

VAR    HamWins     : CARDINAL;
       BurrWins    : CARDINAL;
       TotalShots  : CARDINAL;
       Count       : CARDINAL;
       Average     : REAL;

PROCEDURE Generate(VAR Num : CARDINAL);
(* See the Bagels module from the end of Chapter 7 for this procedure,
which generates a random number and assigns it to Num.        *)

PROCEDURE Shoots(N : CARDINAL) : BOOLEAN;
(*Pre: N has a positive value.
Post: The function Shoots, on the average, will be TRUE 1
      in N times.                                            *)

  VAR Randy : CARDINAL;    (*Local variable for random value. *)

  BEGIN
    Generate(Randy);                   (*Generate a random value *)
    Randy := Randy MOD N + 1;            (* between 1 and N. *)
    IF Randy = 1 THEN
      RETURN TRUE
    ELSE
      RETURN FALSE
    END (* IF *)
  END Shoots;                   (*Definition of function Shoots.*)
```

```
PROCEDURE Duel(VAR Winner : CHAR; VAR NumShots : CARDINAL);
(*This procedure simulates one duel between Hamilton and Burr.
Pre:   None.
Post:  Winner will be 'H' if Hamilton wins, and 'B' if Burr wins.
       NumShots will contain the count of the number of shots
       needed.                                                    *)

  VAR BothLiving : BOOLEAN;

  BEGIN
    NumShots := 0;
    BothLiving := TRUE;(*We begin with both contestants healthy.*)
    WHILE BothLiving DO
      INC(NumShots);              (*Count Burr's shot at Hamilton.*)
      IF Shoots(3) THEN                  (*Did Burr hit Hamilton?*)
        BothLiving := FALSE;
        Winner := 'B'                                (*Burr won!*)
      ELSE
        INC(NumShots);          (*Count Hamilton's shot at Burr.*)
        IF Shoots(2) THEN              (*Did Hamilton hit Burr?*)
          BothLiving := FALSE;
          Winner := 'H'
        END (* Inner IF *)
      END (* Outer IF *)
    END (* WHILE *)
  END Duel;                      (*Definition of procedure Duel.*)

BEGIN                        (*The main body of the module HamBurr.*)
  HamWins := 0;
  BurrWins := 0;
  TotalShots := 0;
  FOR Count := 1 TO NumDuels DO
    Duel(Winner, NumShots);                    (*Simulate one duel.*)
    IF Winner = 'H' THEN
      INC(HamWins)
    ELSE
      INC(BurrWins)
    END; (* IF *)
    TotalShots := TotalShots + NumShots
  END; (*FOR*)
  WriteString('After ');
  WriteCard(NumDuels, 0);
  WriteString(' duels the results are:'); WriteLn;
  WriteString('Hamilton won ');
  WriteCard(HamWins, 0);
  WriteString(' times.'); WriteLn;
  WriteString('Burr won ');
```

```
      WriteCard(BurrWins, 0);
      WriteString' times.'); WriteLn;
      WriteString('The average duel was ');
      Average := FLOAT(TotalShots)/FLOAT(NumDuels);
      WriteReal(Average);
      WriteString(' shots.'); WriteLn
   END HamBurr.
```

Listing 8.1

5. Now we need to *test* and, if necessary, *debug* our program. In this case, other than simple typing mistakes that led to easily located syntax errors, we had no bugs in the program. This is the perfect case of everything going as planned. If your pseudo-code is well designed, this will begin to happen to you, too! Later in this chapter, we'll discuss a buggy program so that we see what to do if the implementation does not proceed as planned.

This program is more difficult to verify, since we are not sure what kind of results to expect. We can bench-test Shoots to verify it by writing a main module as simple as

```
BEGIN(*Bench Test of Shoots(3) to verify its 1-in-3 accuracy.*)
   NumHits := 0;
   FOR Count :- 1 TO 300 DO
     IF Shoots(3) THEN
        INC(NumHits)
     END (* IF *)
   END; (* FOR *)
   WriteString('In target practice Burr hit the target ');
   WriteCard(NumHits, 0);
   WriteString(' out of 300 tries.'); WriteLn
END BenchTest.
```

In this case, we can also use our die to simulate 10 to 20 duels and verify that the computer's findings are in line with ours. In our run of HamBurr, we obtained the following output (where we have shown the REAL value as it would be written by WriteRealPretty:

```
After 100 duels the results are:
Hamilton won 52 times.
Burr won 48 times.
The average duel was 2.37 shots.
```

6. *Editing and documenting* of the program has been done throughout. Note how the comments began in the design phase and were preserved through to the final copy. Blank space and indentation have been used to make the presentation as pleasant as possible.

7. Now our program is ready for the *production* phase. In the real world, we deliver the program to the user (and pray that the user likes it). In education, we turn the program in (and pray that the instructor likes it).

8. *Maintenance* is our final step. In response to the user's comments, we may need to make some changes to the program. For example, based on our output above, the duel appears to be pretty fair. Maybe we should run the simulation 1000 or 10,000 times to see what the results are. Since our program is well designed, this is a trivial modification. A more serious modification would be to determine the length of the longest duel during the simulation, or to introduce the possibility of a wound without death in, say, two-fifths of all hits. However, we might also suppose that a hit reduces the wounded shooter's accuracy by half. We leave such modifications to the reader in the exercises.

A DEBUGGING EXAMPLE

We now present an example of buggy student work. It would be most instructive for the reader to attempt to debug the program before reading our explanation.

The following simple program attempts to read and average five quiz scores. Assume that there is a text file Quizzes.Txt with the following contents:

```
87
76
92
82
56
```

Our objective is to loop five times, reading and summing the scores. Then we simply divide by five to get the average. What could be simpler? Do you see anything wrong with BuggyAve, which purports to solve this problem?

```
MODULE BuggyAve;
(*This module tries to average the five scores in Quizzes.Txt.
                                                                    *)

FROM InOut IMPORT WriteString, WriteLn, ReadCard, WriteCard,
                                                    OpenInput;
FROM RealInOut IMPORT WriteReal;

VAR    Sum    : CARDINAL;
       Count  : CARDINAL;
       Score  : CARDINAL;
       Ave    : REAL;

BEGIN
   OpenInput;              (* Respond with Quizzes, our text file. *)
   Count := 1;
   Sum := 0;
   WHILE Count <= 5 DO
     ReadCard(Score);
```

```
    Sum := Sum + Score
  END; (* WHILE *)
  Ave := FLOAT(Sum) / 5.0;
  WriteString('The average of the five scores is ');
  WriteReal(Ave); WriteLn
END BuggyAve.
```

Listing 8.2

When BuggyAve runs, it does not produce any output. Depending on your compiler, you may get a mysterious error message such as "attempt to read past end of file," or your program may run and run. It shouldn't take the computer long to read, sum, and average five integers. Clearly, something has gone wrong even if we did not get an error message.

We do not understand why the program fails, but let's add an output statement to the loop to see what is going on. Suppose, therefore, that we add

```
WriteString('IN LOOP');
WriteCard( Score, 5);
WriteCard( Sum, 5);
WriteLn
```

to the end of the body of the WHILE loop. Note that this will also require that a semicolon be added to the previous line of the program. This time when we run the program, the output begins as follows:

```
IN LOOP      87      87
IN LOOP      76     163
IN LOOP      92     255
IN LOOP      82     337
IN LOOP      56     393
IN LOOP       0     393
IN LOOP       0     393
IN LOOP       0     393
...
```

and repeats that last line over and over, unless your system gives an error message after the fifth line of output. We can (and should) trace the first five lines of output to see that they are correct. It is apparent that the computer can't even count to five. The key to debugging this program is to investigate why the computer doesn't Count to five. So we should expand our writes to include the value of Count. With the statement

```
WriteCard(Count, 5);
```

before the `WriteLn` at the bottom of our `WHILE` loop, we obtain the output

```
IN LOOP     87     87     1
IN LOOP     76     163    1
IN LOOP     92     255    1
IN LOOP     82     337    1
IN LOOP     56     393    1
IN LOOP     0      393    1
IN LOOP     0      393    1
IN LOOP     0      393    1
...
```

from which it is clear that `Count` is stuck at 1. Oh my gosh, we forgot to increment `Count` in the body of the `WHILE`. No wonder `Count` never reaches five and no wonder the loop is infinite. That is, we are missing

```
INC(Count)
```

at the bottom of our `WHILE`, and as soon as we add it, the program runs correctly. The point is that the extra output finally made this omission clear. In the beginning, we had no idea what we were doing wrong. As soon as we printed the value of `Count`, our omission was obvious.

The previous example dealt with a very simple and short program to keep the discussion as brief and focused as possible. How do you debug a large program? In the same manner, but first analyze the behavior of the program to try to determine which section, procedure, or function is buggy. That is, by selective use of output statements, you determine where the program goes off the track. Then you apply all your Sherlock Holmes skills to that section of code. Take nothing for granted. Be suspicious of every statement, and follow the literal logic of the computer.

EXERCISES

8.1 What is an example of a Modula-2 syntax question? Why are we concerned with syntax at all?

8.2 What is our course objective, if not to learn Modula-2 syntax?

8.3 Describe in your own words the student's responsibility at each stage of the problem-solving process.

8.4 Why does executing data by hand help you to understand a problem and design an algorithm for it?

8.5 What are the advantages of using pseudo-code instead of just writing Modula-2 to begin with?

8.6 Describe the top-down design process. What are stepwise refinements?

8.7 Describe three debugging techniques.

8.8 Distinguish between local, global, and procedural comments. Give an example or two of each kind.

8.9 How do preconditions and postconditions aid in debugging procedures and functions?

8.10 Modify the program `HamBurr` of the text so that it:

a) Runs 1000 duels. (Does the duel seem to be fair to Hamilton and Burr?)

b) Assume that two-fifths of the time, on the average, when a person is hit he, is only slightly wounded and is able to continue, but only at 50 percent of his previous accuracy. Assume that on the second hit, the individual is killed. Simulate 100 duels with these new rules. Is the duel still fair? What happens to the average length of a duel?

c) Modify part b) to simulate 1000 duels and, in addition, print out how many times each was wounded but then went ahead to win the duel.

8.11 (This problem requires some mathematical knowledge)

a) In the original duel, find the probability that Burr wins after one and three shots, respectively. Find the probability that Hamilton wins in two and four shots, respectively. Argue that the duel is fair.

b) Argue that the expected length of a duel is given by the following (incomplete) summation:

$$1 * 1/3 + 2 * 1/3 + 3 * 1/9 + 4 *...$$

Add three or four more terms to this series and show that the expected length of a duel is 2.45 shots.

8.12 Each of the following five versions of the same program contains an error. The objective of the program is to read the following simple text file until it finds the trailer value `'BULLMOOSE'`, determining student averages on five quizzes as it goes. Play computer and debug each attempt.

Here are the contents of the text file `People.Txt`:

```
David Haines
98 65 74 58 88
Rachel Hertel
97 72 91 83 95
Tek Nology
88 45 87 46 62
BULLMOOSE
```

a.

```
MODULE BugQuizA;
(*This program tries to read People.Txt and print averages for each
student.                                                          *)

FROM InOut IMPORT WriteString, ReadString, ReadCard, WriteCard,
                                                         OpenInput;
FROM RealInOut IMPORT WriteReal;

VAR    Name    : ARRAY[0..29] OF CHAR;
       Quiz    : CARDINAL;
       Score   : CARDINAL;
       Total   : CARDINAL;
       Average : REAL;

BEGIN
  OpenInput;              (* Respond with People, our text file. *)
  ReadString(Name);
  WHILE Name <> 'BULLMOOSE' DO
    FOR Quiz := 1 TO 5 DO
      ReadCard(Score);
      Total := Total + Score
    END; (* FOR *)
    Average := FLOAT(Total)/5.0;
    WriteString(Name);
    WriteString(' your average is ');
    WriteReal(Average)
  END (* WHILE *)
END BugQuizA.
```

b.

```
MODULE BugQuizB;
(*This program tries to read People.Txt and print averages for each
student.                                                          *)

FROM InOut IMPORT WriteString, ReadString, ReadCard, WriteCard,
                                                         OpenInput;
FROM RealInOut IMPORT WriteReal;

VAR    Name    : ARRAY[0..29] OF CHAR;
       Quiz    : CARDINAL;
       Score   : CARDINAL;
       Total   : CARDINAL;
       Average : REAL;
```

```
BEGIN
  OpenInput; (* Respond with People, our text file. *)
  ReadString(Name);
  WHILE Name <> 'BULLMOOSE' DO
    FOR Quiz := 1 TO 5 DO
      ReadCard(Score);
      Total := Total + Score
    END; (* FOR *)
    Average := FLOAT(Total)/5.0;
    WriteString(Name);
    WriteString(' your average is ');
    WriteReal(Average);
    ReadString(Name)
  END (* WHILE *)
END BugQuizB.
```

c.
```
MODULE BugQuizC;
(*This program tries to read People.Txt and print averages for each
student.                                                          *)

FROM InOut IMPORT WriteString, ReadString, ReadCard, WriteCard,
                                                      OpenInput;
FROM RealInOut IMPORT WriteReal;

VAR    Name    : ARRAY[0..29] OF CHAR;
       Quiz    : CARDINAL;
       Score   : CARDINAL;
       Total   : CARDINAL;
       Average : REAL;

BEGIN
  OpenInput;              (* Respond with People, our text file. *)
  ReadString(Name);
  Total := 0;
  WHILE Name <> 'BULLMOOSE' DO
    FOR Quiz := 1 TO 5 DO
      ReadCard(Score);
      Total := Total + Score
    END; (* FOR *)
    Average := FLOAT(Total)/5.0;
    WriteString(Name);
    WriteString(' your average is ');
    WriteReal(Average);
    ReadString(Name)
  END (* WHILE *)
END BugQuizC.
```

d.
```
MODULE BugQuizD;
(*This program tries to read People.Txt and print averages for each
student.                                                        *)

FROM InOut IMPORT WriteString, ReadString, ReadCard, WriteCard,
                                                        OpenInput;
FROM RealInOut IMPORT WriteReal;

VAR    Name    : ARRAY[0..29] OF CHAR;
       Quiz    : CARDINAL;
       Score   : CARDINAL;
       Total   : CARDINAL;
       Average : REAL;

BEGIN
  OpenInput;              (* Respond with People, our text file. *)
  ReadString(Name);
  WHILE Name <> 'BULLMOOSE' DO(* Loop while name isn't trailer. *)
  Total := 0;      (* Reset Total to 0 each time in the loop. *)
    FOR Quiz := 1 TO 5 DO
      ReadCard(Score);
      Total := Total + Score
    END; (* FOR *)
    Average := FLOAT(Total)/5.0;
    WriteString(Name);
    WriteString(' your average is ');
    WriteReal(Average);
    ReadString(Name)
  END (* WHILE *)
END BugQuizD.
```

e.
```
MODULE BugQuizE;
(*This program tries to read People.Txt and print averages for each
student.                                                        *)

FROM InOut IMPORT WriteString, ReadString, ReadCard, WriteCard,
                                                        OpenInput;
FROM RealInOut IMPORT WriteReal;

VAR    Name    : ARRAY[0..29] OF CHAR;
       Quiz    : CARDINAL;
       Score   : CARDINAL;
       Total   : CARDINAL;
       Average : REAL;
```

```
BEGIN
  OpenInput;              (* Respond with People, our text file. *)
  ReadString(Name);
  WHILE Name <> 'Bullmoose' DO
    Total := 0;
    FOR Quiz := 1 TO 5 DO
      ReadCard(Score);
      Total := Total + Score
    END; (* FOR *)
    Average := FLOAT(Total)/5.0;
    WriteString(Name);
    WriteString(' your average is ');
    WriteReal(Average);
    ReadString(Name)
  END (* WHILE *)
END BugQuizE.
```

Chapter 9

USER-DEFINED TYPES

Early programming languages are often referred to as **action-oriented** languages. These languages were primarily used with scientific or numeric applications. The important parts of programs were concerned with the calculations involved and the anwers that were generated. These programs worked mainly on numbers.

In more modern applications, computers are called upon to simulate very complex activities: airplanes in flight, freeway traffic, cells in living organisms. In these kinds of applications, the object that is being manipulated is as important as the manipulations themselves. How the programmer decides to represent the objects has an impact on the algorithms dealing with these objects. Thus, modern languages have become more **object-oriented**.

A simple example of a difference between modern languages and older languages can be seen with the BOOLEAN type. Early languages, of course, used Boolean operations, but the results of these operations were usually represented as integers, 0 for FALSE and 1 for TRUE. These early languages did not use a BOOLEAN *type* with values TRUE and FALSE. This sometimes led to problems with compound conditions. We have seen that the correct way to test if a variable X has a value between 10 and 20 is to use a compound condition, two conditions separated by AND:

```
IF (10 < X) AND (X < 20) THEN . . .
```

Many beginners write, incorrectly, the following mathematical notation:

```
IF 10 < X < 20 THEN . . .
```

Of course, a Modula-2 compiler would recognize that this is an error due to a type incompatibility. The condition $10 < X$ would yield a BOOLEAN result, and then we are attempting to compare this BOOLEAN value with 20. In contrast, many versions of the BASIC programming language would allow this incorrect formulation, because the Boolean values are simply integers. So a beginner who writes incorrect code is not told that it is incorrect. What's worse, in these cases, the above incorrect version will always evaluate to TRUE, no matter what the value of X is! Why is that? Well, when we compare 10 to X, either 10 is less than X, in which case TRUE is represented by a 1, or 10 is greater than or equal to X, so that FALSE is represented by a 0. In either case, we end up comparing 0 or 1 to 20, so the second less-than comparison holds. Clearly, a BOOLEAN type that strictly models BOOLEAN operations is important. A language purist would say that BOOLEAN values are not integers—so don't treat them as if they were.

When Niklaus Wirth developed Pascal, he gave the programmer the ability to introduce new types of objects into the language. Such user-defined types have found their way into Ada, Modula-2, and other modern languages. The main advantage of these types is that the programmer is able to model more closely some real-world entity by using a type other than one of the standard, built-in types of a language; e.g., INTEGER, REAL, CHAR, CARDINAL, or BOOLEAN.

For a very simple example, suppose that a chemist is monitoring a reaction that may produce a solution that is one of four different colors, say brown, red, orange, or yellow. How might these colors best be represented? In older languages, a programmer would probably decide upon an encoding—that is, brown is 1, red is 2, orange is 3, and yellow is 4. While this can work, there are some drawbacks. First, it requires the programmer to document the encoding carefully so that another person reading the program knows what is going on. Even then, the program may be difficult to read—the reader may keep forgetting whether red is 2 or 3. Certainly, this might be likely if there were 10 different colors. A better method might be to have integer variables Brown, Red, Orange, and Yellow and initialize them to 1, 2, 3, and 4, respectively. Then the programmer could use the variable names instead of the numbers, writing statements like IF Color = Red THEN... instead of IF Color = 2 THEN.... In a language with constants, like Modula-2, it would be even better to use constants instead of variables. Then, it would be impossible to accidentally change the value of Red from 2 to 3. Still, Brown, Red, Orange, and Yellow would be integers and not colors. We could use them in any calculation that called for an integer value. Such use might not even make sense, like extracting the square root of Red, yet the computer would allow it because it doesn't distinguish between colors and integers. This may sound far-fetched, but in large, real-world programs, many different programmers have access to the same program, and not all of them are as careful as they should be. Wirth, and other language designers, felt that it would be nice if the programmer had the ability to invent a new type—a type for colors. Or a type for days of the week. Or anything else that might be needed.

USER-DEFINED TYPES

Let us look at an example to see how programmers can define their own types. Suppose we wanted a type to represent the months of the year. We could do this in Modula-2 as follows:

```
TYPE Months = (Jan, Feb, Mar, Apr, May, Jun, Jul, Aug, Sep, Oct,
                                                      Nov, Dec);
```

The above is a TYPE definition. That is, Months is the name of a type, just as INTEGER and BOOLEAN are type names. Type definitions occur before the statement section of a program, up with the constant definitions and variable declarations. These kinds of declarations can occur in any order, and there can be more than one of a given section. For example, a program could contain a variable-declaration section followed by a type section, followed by a constant section, followed by another type section, and so on.

A type like Months is called an **enumerated** type. We have enumerated, or listed, the possible values that we can assign to a variable of type Months. Another way to say this is that Jan, Feb, ..., Dec are the **constant** values of this type. Of the simple built-in types, INTEGER, CARDINAL, CHAR, and BOOLEAN are also enumerated types. The fact that BOOLEAN is a built-in enumerated type means that in each Modula-2 program, it is as if we had typed

```
TYPE BOOLEAN = (FALSE, TRUE)   (* Actually, illegal Modula-2, *)
                               (* BOOLEAN is already since *)
                               (* defined by the system. *)
```

Many beginners have difficulty distinguishing Jan, a value available for variables of type Months, from 'Jan', the three-character string. To further illustrate the distinction, suppose that St is a String variable and Maybe is a BOOLEAN variable declared by

```
VAR    St     : ARRAY[0..79] OF CHAR;
       Maybe  : BOOLEAN;
```

Then, each of the following are legal:

```
St := 'TRUE';
Maybe := TRUE;
```

while these are illegal:

```
St := TRUE;          (* Illegal type mixing—String and BOOLEAN *)
Maybe := 'TRUE'      (* Illegal type mixing—BOOLEAN and String *)
```

Many beginners also write illegal statements like

```
Months := Feb;
```

Why is this illegal? Because Months is not the name of a variable! It is the name of a type! Feb can only be assigned to a variable of type Months. How do we obtain such variables? We declare them, just like we do variables of any other type. Thus, the following is legal:

```
VAR    Month : Months;
....
BEGIN
  Month := Feb;
```

The convention of using the singular to describe variables and the plural to define a type is a common one in programming. While there should be no difficulty if one is consistent, a safer convention is to use the suffix Type in type definitions. That is, we could write

```
TYPE
  MonthType = (Jan, Feb, Mar, Apr, May, Jun, Jul, Aug, Sep,
                                            Oct, Nov, Dec);
VAR
  Month : MonthType;
```

In this regard, Type is a reserved word of the system, but MonthType is a legal user-chosen identifier. We think the suffix Type is a good one to use when defining a new type.

As another example of the problems that beginners sometimes have, suppose we were writing a program that processed some information on a girl named Jan. Then we might want to have a variable called Jan. The reader should realize that it is impossible to have a variable called Jan and the type definition for Months in the same program. A constant value of a type cannot also be used as a variable. The situation described above with Jan is equivalent to trying to have a variable named 7. Like Jan, 7 already serves a purpose as an INTEGER value.

Another error to watch out for with enumerated types is attempting to use a constant value in more than one type. For instance, the following is illegal:

```
TYPE  StopLightColor = (Red, Yellow, Green);
      FlagColor      = (Red, White, Blue);          (* ILLEGAL *)
```

Of course, the problem is that Red is defined as a value for two different types, leading to possible ambiguities.

Types in programming languages serve two primary purposes:

1. Types determine the legal values that may be assigned to variables.
2. Types determine the legal operations that may be applied to variables.

With the built-in types, we are told by the system what values can be assigned to variables. For example, we are told what constitutes a legal real number—the legal values that can be assigned to a real variable. With an enumerated type, the values are explicitly listed for us in the type definition.

We have also seen that certain operations apply to certain types. For example, OR is a BOOLEAN operation, MOD is an INTEGER operation, / is a REAL operation, and * is, depending on its context, a REAL, INTEGER, or CARDINAL operation. Again, with the built-in types, the language definition of Modula-2 tells us what operations are legal. It turns out that there are certain operations that are also legal for all user-defined types. For example, the assignment operation is always available for any type: We can always assign values to variables of any type, so long as the type of the value and the variable are the same. The relational operators = and <> are also available to all types. As we should expect, we can always compare two values of the same type for equality or inequality.

There are some other operations that apply to enumerated types. First, the listing of the constant values of the enumerated type imposes an ordering on those values. Enumerated types are therefore **ordered** types and are sometimes referred to as **ordinal** types. Still another name for them is **discrete** types. So, in the `Months` example, `Jan` is the first month, `Dec` is the last month, and `Apr` comes immediately after `Mar` and immediately before `May`. Because of this ordering, any of the relational operators may be applied to enumerated types. So if `Month1` and `Month2` are variables of type `Months`, we can test whether `Month1 < Month2`. In the Months example, it may make sense to think that `Jan < Mar` (meaning that January comes before March). It certainly makes sense with the CHAR type to think that `'a' < 'z'`, meaning that `'a'` alphabetically precedes `'z'`. However, these comparisons may not always make sense. For example, while it is a fact that Modula-2 considers `FALSE` to be less than `TRUE`, it may not be a good idea to write programs using this fact, since it may not be known (nor obvious) to everyone who reads the program that this is how the BOOLEAN values are ordered. As a better example, if we defined a type

```
TYPE   ChemReactionColor = (Brown, Red, Orange, Yellow);
```

there may not be any significance to the fact that `Red < Orange`, and, in fact, it may not make any difference whether the type is defined as

```
TYPE   ChemReactionColor = (Red, Yellow, Orange, Brown);
```

If the type doesn't have any ordering significance, the program shouldn't contain any ordering comparisons.

Two more functions that apply to enumerated types are the procedures `INC` and `DEC`. We have already used these with the discrete numeric types (i.e., INTEGER and CARDINAL) and with CHAR. Since the values of user-defined types have unique predecessors and successors, it makes sense to increment and decrement those values as well. Of course, the first value doesn't have a predecessor and the last value doesn't have a successor, so in those special cases, `DEC` and `INC` do not apply. For example, if `Month` has the value `Jun`, then the statement `INC(Month)` assigns the value `Jul` to `Month`. If we had a program that wanted to assign `Month` the value of the next month (in real life, most people consider January to be the next month after December), we must be careful:

```
IF Month  = Dec THEN
   Month := Jan
ELSE
   INC(Month)
END;
```

It would be an error to execute `INC(Month)` if `Month` contained the value `Dec`. Thus, enumerated types in Modula-2 define a linear ordering, not a circular ordering. Another way to say this is that the values don't wrap-around—the last value doesn't wrap around to the first value. So it is usually necessary to employ defensive programming, as the above `IF...THEN...ELSE` demonstrates.

INC and DEC are actually more flexible than we have seen. It is possible to provide two inputs to these procedures to increment or decrement by more than one value. For example, if Count is a variable of type INTEGER currently equal to 5, INC(Count, 3) makes Count equal to 8. Likewise, if Month is currently May, then INC(Month, 2) assigns Month the value Jul. And of course, INC(Month, 8) would produce an overflow, or out-of-bounds error, since there isn't an eighth month beyond May.

ORD and VAL

Occasionally, we may want to know where, in the ordering of the type values, a certain value lies. To find this out, we can use the ORD function. The input to ORD is the value of an enumerated type (excluding the INTEGER type). Its output is the position of that value in the list of possible values. Unfortunately, for most people, the computer begins counting with 0. Therefore, if Month currently holds the value May, then ORD(Month) is 4, since ORD(Jan) is 0. ORD is often used with the character type. The ordinal value of 'A'—i.e., ORD('A')—is 65. Why isn't ORD('A') equal to 1? Isn't 'A' the first letter in the alphabet? Yes it is. But 'A' is not the first character in the Modula-2 character set, which is the ASCII character set described in Chapter 4. In fact, the first 32 characters in the ASCII set are control characters—characters that are typed with the CTRL key and that control various operations of the computer. The 33rd character (the character with ordinal value 32) is the blank. This character is then followed by several punctuation symbols, arithmetic symbols, and the numerals from 0 to 9. By this time, we are ready for the uppercase alphabet, but we have already gone through 65 characters. So the 66th character, the uppercase 'A', has ordinal value 65. We also say that 'A' has ASCII value 65.

ORD has an inverse function. That is, there is a function that performs the opposite function of ORD. Since ORD takes enumerated values and tells us their position, VAL takes a position and returns the value that occupies that position. Of course, for VAL to work, it needs to know what type is being considered. That is, does VAL(3) want the third character, the third month, or the third chemical-reaction color? So VAL needs an extra input; namely, the type involved. (Again, with VAL, we start counting at 0—so what is third to the computer is usually fourth to most people.) Hence, VAL(CHAR, 65) is 'A', while VAL(Months, 3) is Apr. Thus, we see that CHR, introduced in Chapter 4, is a special inverse of ORD. That is, for $0 \le k \le 127$, CHR(k) is the same as VAL(CHAR, k).

Subranges

There are many times when we don't need all the values that an enumerated type makes available to us. In these situations, Modula-2 allows us to make use of a convenient feature known as a **subrange**. A subrange is simply a contiguous set of values of an enumerated type. We first give some examples and then explain some of the finer details.

```
TYPE  Months = (Jan, Feb, Mar, Apr, May, Jun, Jul, Aug,
                                 Sep, Oct, Nov, Dec);
      Days   = (Sun, Mon, Tue, Wed, Thu, Fri, Sat);
```

```
SummerMonths  = [Jun .. Aug];
WeekDays      = [Mon .. Fri];
ExamScores    = [0 .. 100];
```

SummerMonths, WeekDays, and ExamScores all define subranges. Note that the constant values of a subrange must form a contiguous subset of the values of the parent type. Also notice that these values are enclosed in square brackets, [and], instead of in parentheses. SummerMonths defines a subrange of Months consisting of the values Jun, Jul, and Aug. This subrange definition, of course, would be illegal if not preceded by the definition of the Months type itself. Beginners often mistakenly think that SummerMonths is a set containing the values Jun, Jul, and Aug. Modula-2 does in fact have a set capability, and we cover it in a later chapter. But subranges are not sets. SummerMonths is a type just like Months is a type. So in light of the above type definitions, we could have the following variable declarations:

```
VAR    VacationMonth  : SummerMonths;
       WorkDay        : WeekDays;
       FinalGrade     : ExamScore;
```

Now, VacationMonth is a variable that may take on any of the three values Jun, Jul, or Aug. Although VacationMonth is of type SummerMonths, it is compatible with variables of type Months. The Months type is the parent type of SummerMonths, and in Modula-2 (unlike real life), parents are compatible with their children. So if BirthdayMonth is a variable of type Months, then the following assignment is syntactically legal:

```
VacationMonth := BirthdayMonth;
```

We say syntactically legal, because the above statement may turn out to be illegal during execution; i.e., it may produce a run-time error. Whether it does or not depends on whether the value of BirthdayMonth is out of range for VacationMonth or not.

Subranges may be declared **anonymously**. By this, we mean that a variable can have its values restricted to a subrange directly in a variable declaration, without giving the variable a type name. Such variables are said to be declared anonymously—they have no type name. In many ways, the following two schemes are equivalent:

```
TYPE   ExamScore = [0 .. 100];
VAR    Final : ExamScore;
```

and

```
VAR    Final : [0..100];
```

In each case, Final is a variable that can take on any of the CARDINAL values from 0 to 100. However, in the second case, Final is not of type CARDINAL, nor is it of type ExamScore (in the second example, the type ExamScore doesn't even exist). Moreover, if we declare two variables anonymously as follows:

```
VAR    Final        : [0..100];
       OralReport   : [0..100];
```

then these two variables are not considered to be of the same type. However, if we declare them in the same declaration, like this:

```
VAR    Final, OralReport : [0..100];
```

then they are assumed to be of the same type.

Which method should be used? Generally speaking, we prefer the named-type method. With type names, there is never any question of whether two variables have the same type. Also, there are times when Modula-2 requires variables to have a type name. If we needed to pass Final to a procedure as a parameter, Final must have a type name, so the anonymous method wouldn't work. The second method simply avoids naming a type and is acceptable if Final is a local variable of a given procedure or function.

Subranges serve two basic purposes. First, they tend to convey more information. Certainly, this example:

```
TYPE   ExamRange    = [0..100];
       QuizRange    = [0..40];
       PopQuizRange = [0..10];

VAR    Final      : ExamRange;
       MidTerm    : QuizRange;
       Surprise   : PopQuizRange;
```

is more informative than

```
VAR    Final      : CARDINAL;
       MidTerm    : CARDINAL;
       Surprise   : CARDINAL;
```

Second, subranges provide an extra check to make sure that variables are assigned only correct values. The assignment statement Surprise := 12 would not be allowed in the first case. Although such an assignment statement would probably not appear in a program with the above subranges, it is possible that such assignments could be entered from the keyboard. In this case, there is a real possibility for an incorrect data value to be entered. So, subranges provide another way for the system to protect us from our own mistakes.

Let us consider some more extensive examples. Suppose we are managing a resort hotel and we want to compute the room bill. Assume that we have several rates:

The basic rate, in March, April, May, September, and October
The summer rate, in June, July, and August
The Christmas rate, in December
The winter rate, in January, February, and November

Suppose the basic rate is $75 per person per night and that the other rates are as follows:

Summer   80% of Basic
Winter   115% of Basic
Christmas   125% of Basic

Suppose that the rate is determined by the date of the first night's lodging and that children under 12 stay for half price. The program of Listing 9.1 calculates the bill.

```
MODULE HotelCost;
(* This module computes a hotel bill where the rate is determined
by the time of year and the age of the guest.                    *)

FROM InOut IMPORT WriteLn, WriteString, ReadCard, WriteCard;
FROM RealInOut IMPORT WriteReal;

CONST  BasicRate      = 75.0;
       SummerRate     = 0.80;
       WinterRate     = 1.15;
       ChristmasRate  = 1.25;
       ChildRate      = 0.50;

TYPE   Months = (Jan, Feb, Mar, Apr, May, Jun, Jul, Aug,
                                          Sep, Oct, Nov, Dec);
       MonthNumberType = [1..12];

VAR    StartMonth       : Months;
       MonthNumber      : MonthNumberType;
       NumberOfDays     : CARDINAL;
       NumberOfAdults   : CARDINAL;
       NumberOfKids     : CARDINAL;
       Rate             : REAL;

PROCEDURE GetData(VAR NumberOfAdults, NumberOfKids,
                                      NumberofDays : CARDINAL;
                        VAR MonthNumber : MonthNumberType);
(* Pre:  None.
Post:   NumberOfAdults, NumberOfKids, NumberOfDays are assigned
CARDINAL values. MonthNumber is assigned a CARDINAL value in the
range from 1 to 12.                                              *)

  BEGIN
    WriteLn;
    WriteString('Enter the number of Adults: ');
    ReadCardinal(NumberOfAdults);
    WriteLn;
    WriteString('Enter the number of Children: ');
```

```
      ReadCardinal(NumberOfKids);
      WriteLn;
      WriteString('Enter the starting month of the stay.');
      WriteString('1 for January, 12 for December: ');
      ReadCardinal(MonthNumber);
      WriteLn;
      WriteString('Enter the number of days of the stay: ');
      ReadCardinal(NumberOfDays)
   END GetData;

BEGIN                         (* Body of main module HotelCost. *)
   GetData(NumberOfAdults, NumberOfKids, NumberOfDays,
                                        MonthNumber);

   (* Now compute the rate using a CASE statement. *)
   StartMonth := VAL(Months, MonthNumber - 1);    (* Convert to
                                                 month. *)
   CASE StartMonth OF
   Jan, Feb, Nov       : Rate := WinterRate * BasicRate      |
   Mar..May, Sep, Oct  : Rate := BasicRate                   |
   Jun..Aug            : Rate := SummerRate * BasicRate      |
   Dec                 : Rate := ChristmasRate * BasicRate
   END (* CASE *)

   (* Now correct for number of individuals. *)
   Rate := (FLOAT(NumberOf Adults) + ChildRate
           * FLOAT(NumberOfKids)) * Rate * FLOAT(NumberOfDays);
   WriteLn;
   WriteString('Thank you for staying with us.');
   WriteString('Your total is $');
   WriteReal(Rate)
END HotelCost.
```

Listing 9.1

As usual, there are some comments we need to make about the above example. First, notice that the variable StartMonth is used to control a CASE statement. In fact, the controlling expression of a CASE statement must be of some discrete type. That is, we can use an INTEGER, a CARDINAL, a BOOLEAN, a CHAR, or any enumerated type to control a CASE statement, but we can't use a REAL or a String.

Modula-2 has the same restriction on a FOR loop. That is, a FOR loop must have a discrete loop control variable. So, we could write a FOR loop like this:

```
FOR Month := Jan TO Dec DO
```

but not a FOR loop with a REAL or String control variable. It should seem reasonable why we need a discrete variable to control a FOR loop or a CASE statement. In a FOR loop, the control variable takes on the first value specified in the loop header and then takes on each subsequent value each time through the loop. The notion of a subsequent, or next value isn't well defined for nondiscrete types like the REALs. For example, what is the next REAL number after 1.0? Is it 1.00000001, or 1.01, or what? In CASE statements, we need to be able to list all possibilities. Again, with a nondiscrete type, an all-inclusive listing isn't possible. This restriction is what makes the FOR loop less flexible than the other kinds of loop structures.

The careful reader should wonder why we have used the variable MonthNumber in addition to the variable StartMonth of type Months. The reason is that, in Modula-2, values of a user-defined type are not permitted in the standard input and output statements. This is a major restriction—in fact, one that causes user-defined types to lose much of their effectiveness. Because of this restriction, user-defined types serve primarily to make the program clearer and easier to read from an internal standpoint. Nonetheless, this clarity is much desired, and we will continue to make heavy use of these enumerated types in the following chapters. The reason that Modula-2 has this restriction is that it greatly simplifies the writing of compilers. Nonetheless, some versions of modern languages with user-defined types do support input/output with these types.

What if one desires to do input/output? For example, suppose that we wanted sample output from the above program to look like this:

```
Thank you for staying with us.
The total for your stay of 12 nights, beginning in Dec,
with a party of 2 adults and 2 children is $3375.00
```

First of all, we remark that some Modula-2 systems only provide a routine that prints real numbers in scientific notation. So, to get the dollar amount pretty printed in decimal form, we need to write our own procedure. We did this in Chapter 7 and, by including the WriteRealPretty procedure in the HotelCost module, we could obtain the desired output. Aside from printing the dollar amount, it should be clear how we get everything else to print except the Dec. What do we do? The answer is that we need to write our own procedure. If StartMonth equals Dec, then we want to print the character string 'Dec'. Again, notice the important distinction between constants of type Months and constants of type String. Such a procedure follows:

```
PROCEDURE WriteMonths(Month : Months);
(* This procedure gives us an output capability for the type Months
by converting values of type Months to their corresponding string
equivalents.
Pre:  Month contains a value of type Months.
Post: The three-character string corresponding to the value of
Months is printed.                                              *)

TYPE   String3 = ARRAY[0..2] OF CHAR;

VAR    StMonth : String3;
```

```
BEGIN
  CASE Month OF
    Jan : StMonth := 'Jan'        |
    Feb : StMonth := 'Feb'        |
    Mar : StMonth := 'Mar'        |
    Apr : StMonth := 'Apr'        |
    May : StMonth := 'May'        |
    Jun : StMonth := 'Jun'        |
    Jul : StMonth := 'Jul'        |
    Aug : StMonth := 'Aug'        |
    Sep : StMonth := 'Sep'        |
    Oct : StMonth := 'Oct'        |
    Nov : StMonth := 'Nov'        |
    Dec : StMonth := 'Dec'
  END; (* CASE *)
  WriteString(StMonth)
END WriteMonths;
```

Listing 9.2

Given this function, the previous line of output with the month in it is printed with

```
WriteString('The total for your stay of ');
WriteCardinal(NumberOfDays : 0);
WriteString(' nights, beginning in ');
WriteMonth(StartMonth);
Write(",");
WriteLn;
```

All these writes, of course, would best be put into their own procedure called OutputSummary. That way, the main program would be much shorter, and a reader of the program, if needing the details, could then read the procedure. But if the details aren't important to a particular reader, they could be skipped.

Although this seems like a lot of work (and it is), this same approach works for input and output of all kinds of user-defined types. We can simulate input and output by writing input and output procedures that usually consist of single statements. We point out that we can't use a CASE statement for the input procedure, because our input will be of some string type and, as we mentioned a bit earlier, string types can't be used to control a CASE statement. We might use a nested IF...THEN...ELSIF..., but in Chapter 9, we will see an alternative method using arrays.

With separately compiled modules (which we'll learn about in Chapter 14), it is possible to collect all our specialized printing routines (WriteMonth or WriteRealPretty) into an external module. Then, we can import this module just as we import from the standard libraries of Modula-2. That way, we can use these procedures without being required to physically include them as part of the current module.

TWO EXAMPLES USING THE CHAR TYPE

Since the CHAR type is a built-in discrete type, let us look at two examples using the character type. In particular, we'll show the interaction between character values and numeric values.

In the first example, suppose we want to compute a numeric grade point average knowing the number of As, Bs, Cs, Ds and Fs, where an A counts 4 points, a B 3 points, ..., F 0 points. The question that we want to consider, without writing a complete program, is: How do we convert the character values into numeric values? The following CASE statement would work:

```
CASE Grade OF
  'A' : Points := 4      |
  'B' : Points := 3      |
  'C' : Points := 2      |
  'D' : Points := 1      |
  'F' : Points := 0
END;
```

Let's see if we can find a shorter way to do this. The ASCII value of 'A' is 65, of 'B' is 66, etc. Is there a way that we can use the ASCII values—that is, the ORD function—to convert properly for us? Moreover, what if we don't remember the ASCII value of the uppercase letters? The following IF... THEN... ELSE should do the trick for us:

```
IF Grade = 'F' THEN
  Points := 0
ELSE
  Points := ORD('A') + 4 - ORD(Grade)
END;
```

The reader should carefully trace the above statement to see that it gives us the correct values. Note that we don't need the magic number 65. The only reason we need an IF...THEN...ELSE is that the 'F' grade doesn't occur in sequence with the others. If the failing grade were denoted by an 'E' instead of an 'F', we could get by without an IF statement. Whenever we need to convert from a character value to a numeric value, we should remember the ORD function and carefully examine whether we need a possible correction factor.

In the next example, we'll perform an operation that many computers perform over and over, though usually undetected by the typical computer user. We are going to convert a number from the octal number base (base 8) to the decimal number base (base 10). Why would a computer ever do such a thing? As we learned in Chapter 1, computers store information as strings of 0s and 1s; that is, in the binary (base 2) number system. So when we input numbers to the computer, we input them as decimal numbers and the computer converts and stores them in binary. When the computer prints a number for us, it converts it from binary to decimal before printing. Thus, base conversion occurs many times.

It turns out that two other bases commonly used by computers are base 8 and base 16.

These are convenient compromises between binary and decimal. With that bit of motivation, let us see how to read in a number from the keyboard in octal (let's pretend that this is the number stored in the computer) and then print out its equivalent value in decimal. What does a number in base 8 look like? First of all, it consists only of the numerals 0, 1, 2, 3, 4, 5, 6, 7. Second, the columns of the number represent powers of 8—that is, the rightmost column is the 1s column, the next column is the 8s column, the next is the 64s column, etc. So, for example:

$$2145_8 = 2 * 8^3 + 1 * 8^2 + 4 * 8 + 5 = 2 * 512 + 1 * 64 + 4 * 8 + 5$$
$$= 1024 + 64 + 32 + 5 = 1125_{10}$$

where the subscript denotes the base in which the number is expressed.

Now, how should we read in this octal number? If we try to read it in as a CARDINAL (let's suppose we're dealing only with positive quantities), we end up reading it in as a decimal number. Then we would need to use DIV and MOD operations to split the number up into its individual digits and process these digits. Since we need the individual digits, let's just read in the number as a sequence of characters, converting each character to its numeric equivalent. Since the numeric characters occur in the ASCII set in order, even if we don't remember the ordinal value of a specific numeral, we can convert a numeral to its equivalent numeric value with the following:

```
NumericValue := ORD(Numeral)    ORD('0');
```

Again, we don't need a magic number—we simply observe that the ordinal value of a constant like the character ' 5 ' is five more than the ordinal value of the character ' 0 '.

Finally, how does the conversion to decimal take place? When we see the first digit, we assume that it occupies the 1s position. This is correct if we don't see any other digits. If we see a second digit, then the first digit actually occupies the 8s position and the second digit occupies the 1s position. Likewise, if we see a third digit, then the original digit is in the 64s position, the second one is in the 8s position, and the third one is in the 1s position. We hope the pattern is becoming clear. Each current digit that we read is considered to be the unit's digit (it will be if we see no subsequent digit), and each previous digit becomes worth eight times as much every time we read a new digit. Thus, we obtain the program in Listing 9.3. This program assumes that the number is positive and that it is entered correctly. We leave it to the exercises to incorporate the ability to handle negative numbers and an error-checking capability.

```
MODULE OctalToDecimal;
(* This module converts a base 8 number, entered from the keyboard,
to its decimal equivalent.                                        *)

FROM InOut IMPORT WriteLn, WriteString, WriteCard, Write, Read;

VAR    Decimal       : CARDINAL;
       OctalDigit    : CHAR;
```

```
BEGIN
  Decimal := 0;
  WriteLn;
  WriteString('Enter a positive octal integer.');
  WriteString('Use only the digits 0 through 7.');
  WriteString('Terminate entry with a carriage return: ');
  Read(OctalDigit);
  Write(OctalDigit);
  WHILE ('0' <= OctalDigit) AND (OctalDigit <= '7') DO
    Decimal := 8 * Decimal + (ORD(OctalDigit) - ORD('0'));
                        (* New value is 8 times the old one,
                                plus value of new digit. *)
    Read(OctalDigit); Write(OctalDigit)
  END; (* WHILE *)
  WriteString('The decimal equivalent is ');
  WriteCardinal(Decimal, 0)
END OctalToDecimal.
```

Listing 9.3

EXERCISES

9.1 Modify the OctalToDecimal conversion program so that it handles negative numbers and also prints an appropriate error message if the input is not a legal octal integer.

9.2 Write a program that converts an integer from base 16 to base 10. The base 16 system (hexadecimal) uses 16 different digits, 0 through 9, and A through F, where A stands for 10, B for 11, ..., F for 15. Of course, the columns of a hexadecimal number represent powers of 16. So, the number

$$1AB_{16} = 1 * 16^2 + A * 16 + B = 1 * 256 + 10 * 16 + 11$$
$$= 256 + 160 + 11 = 427_{10}$$

9.3 Write a program that prints out a base conversion table of the numbers from 1 to 31 as shown below:

Base Conversion Table

Decimal	Binary	Octal	Hexadecimal
1	00001	01	01
2	00002	02	02
...	...	...	...
...	...	...	...
31	11111	37	1F

Write three separate procedures `ConvertToBinary`, `ConvertToOctal`, and `ConvertToHexadecimal`. These procedures should write out the converted numbers character by character. For simplicity in aligning the columns of the table, print leading zeros as shown above. Note that we can convert 27 to octal, for example, by computing 27 `DIV` 8 and 27 `MOD` 8.

9.4 Write a program that defines a type for the days of the week and then interactively computes a weekly payroll. Include a procedure called `WriteDay` for a prompt message like

`Enter the number of hours worked on Monday:`

Then request seven hourly figures for Monday through Sunday. Pay on Monday through Friday is at the basic rate of $6.25 per hour, while Saturday is time and a half, and Sunday is double time. Use a `FOR` loop to control the entry of the five numbers for Monday through Friday. Finally, print out the total pay.

9.5 Write a program that picks a card at random from a standard, 52-card bridge deck. Define a type `Suit` with values `Clubs`, `Diamonds`, `Hearts`, and `Spades`, and a type `Rank` with values `Ace`, `Two`, `Three`, ..., `Jack`, `Queen`, `King`. Generate two random CARDINAL numbers, the first one to represent the suit and the second one to represent the rank. See the discussion of the `Bagels` program in Chapter 7 for some guidance in writing a random-number generator.

Chapter 10

ARRAYS, SEARCHING, AND SORTING

The INTEGER, REAL, CHAR, BOOLEAN, and CARDINAL types are known as **simple** types, because an identifier of any of those types can hold only one value at a time. In arrays, we are introduced to our first **compound** type—an identifier that can hold an aggregate of values rather than just one single value.

An **array** is simply a list. A grocery list can be viewed as an array of the items that you need at the grocery. You may not be familiar with the term array as used in computer science, but you are certainly comfortable with lists. Do not let the new terminology make you think that arrays are difficult or mysterious. As you can imagine, lists (of names, of scores, of grades, of salaries, etc.) arise frequently in real-world problems. Thus, arrays are an important data-structuring tool, and it will be worth your while to learn to use them effectively.

ARRAY DECLARATIONS AND ARRAY ACCESS

Every identifier in Modula-2 must be declared before it is used. If you need a list of 50 salaries, then you can declare an array, Salaries, with

```
VAR Salaries : ARRAY[1..50] OF REAL;
```

Salaries is the aggregate data structure consisting of 50 REAL memory locations. The individual elements of the list can be accessed by a method known as **indexing** or **subscripting**. Indices, as we shall call them, are enclosed within square brackets. Thus, to initialize the first location in Salaries to zero, we would write

```
Salaries[1] := 0.0;
```

The power of arrays comes from the fact that the index to an array can be a variable, rather than some specific constant. This means that the expression Salaries[Index] will run through all the values of the array if we simply let Index take on successively the values 1 through 50. For example, supposing that the array Salaries has values stored in it, the following segment will print out these values five per line:

```
FOR Index := 1 TO 50 DO
  WriteReal(Salaries[Index], 15);
  IF (Index MOD 5) = 0 THEN WriteLn  END (* IF *)
END;  (* FOR *)
```

This also illustrates the power of the FOR loop in conjunction with arrays. Note that

```
WriteReal(Salaries, 15);                              (* ERROR *)
```

will be flagged by the compiler as an error, since Salaries is not a REAL variable. Salaries is an ARRAY OF REALs, and it must be indexed before it represents a single REAL value.

An array declaration is of the form

```
VAR ArrayName[LoIndex..HiIndex] OF ComponentType;
```

where ArrayName is any legal identifier, LoIndex and HiIndex are constants of any ordinal type, and ComponentType is any type. Note the distinction between the component type and the index type. The component type can be anything and is the type of the objects stored in the array. The index type must be an ordinal type, so that there is always a next and a previous index, except for the first and last indices. The index type tells us *how many* things can be stored in the array and how we can access those things. The component type tells us *what kind* of thing can be stored in the array. In particular, note that the index need not be CARDINAL and need not begin at 1, as the following examples show:

```
(* Array Declaration Examples *)
TYPE   DayType       = (Mon, Tues, Wed, Thurs, Fri, Sat, Sun);
       GradeType     = (A, B, C, D, F, Inc, WP, WF);
       String30      = ARRAY[0 .. 29] OF CHAR;

VAR    HoursWorked   : ARRAY[Mon..Sun] OF REAL;
       FinalGrades   : ARRAY[1 .. 30] OF GradeType;
       Names         : ARRAY[1 .. 30] OF String30;
       FeesPaid      : ARRAY[1 .. 30] OF BOOLEAN;
       Sex           : ARRAY[1 .. 30] OF CHAR;
       CalifWines    : ARRAY[1980 .. 1989] OF REAL;
       DayOff        : ARRAY[1 .. 10] OF DayType;
       FuncValue     : ARRAY[-10 .. 10] OF REAL;
```

HoursWorked obviously is designed to keep track of the number of hours that someone works for each day of the week. `HoursWorked` is a very simple example, but worth keeping in mind because the distinction between the index and component type is so clear. The index type tells us that there are seven cells in the array that we can reference with expressions like `HoursWorked[Wed]`. The component type tells us that objects like 7.5 can be stored in the array. For example, to indicate that Wednesday is this person's day off, we can write:

```
HoursWorked[Wed] := 0.0;
```

`FinalGrades`, `Names`, `FeesPaid`, and `Sex` apparently keep information on 30 students. For example, assuming that these arrays have values, we could invite the females who have paid their fees and have a grade of B or better to a party with the segment

```
FOR Index := 1 TO 30 DO
   IF (Sex[Index] = "F") AND FeesPaid[Index] AND
                                    (FinalGrade[Index] <= B) THEN
      Invite(Names[Index])
   END (* IF *)
END; (* FOR *)
```

where we have assumed that `Invite` is a procedure that prints the invitations and that `Index` is a CARDINAL. The language "a grade of B or better" seems to suggest the `>=` relation. Note, however, that in the user-defined type `GradeType`, an A is less than a B, so we used `FinalGrade[Index] <= B` to collect the As and Bs. Also note that `Invite` is invoked with the argument `Names[Index]`, which is just a `String30`. There is no need to call Invite with

```
Invite(Names, Index);
```

which forces the `Invite` procedure to accept the entire array of names and then use just one of them. The point is that an array component, such as `Names[Index]`, can be used anywhere that a value of that type is expected.

Note in passing that `Names` is an array whose component type, `String30`, is also an array. `Names` is an example of a multidimensional array. For now, we will stay with one-dimensional arrays (or two-dimensional arrays like `Names`, where we only actively use one of the dimensions), but later in this chapter, we will introduce and use arrays of many dimensions.

`CalifWines` illustrates that indices, sometimes even CARDINAL indices, need not start at 1. Apparently, `CalifWines` is to keep track of wine production (in gallons) in California during the 1980s. It is very convenient to have the index 1988 for wine production in the year 1988.

`DayOff` apparently keeps track of the day of the week that each of 10 people have off from work. Contrast `DayOff` with `HoursWorked` to see how the index type of one has become the component type of the other.

`FuncValues` is probably being used to store the values of some function on the INTEGERS from -10 to 10. Note that the function values are REAL, but that the index is INTEGER. FuncValues might be used in a graphing procedure to graph the given function on the interval from -10 to 10. As an example, FuncValues simply points out that the indices can be negative.

Please keep in mind that the index type cannot be string or REAL. To see why, consider

```
VAR   X : ARRAY[0.0 .. 1.0] OF CARDINAL;          (* ERROR *)
      Y : ARRAY["Amelia" .. "Zeth"] OF CHAR;      (* ERROR *)
```

The problem is that the system cannot determine how many elements are in these arrays. How many REALs are there between 0.0 and 1.0? There are an infinite number in the real world and an indeterminate number in any computer implementation. There is no logical next REAL number after 0.0. Likewise, there is no next logical string after "Amelia" and no well-determined progression from "Amelia" to "Zeth".

Both of the arrays X and Y can be modified, however, and made legal. For example, if you want to step from 0.0 to 1.0 in steps of 0.01, then define an array with a CARDINAL index from 0 to 100. Note that as Index runs from 0 to 100, FLOAT(Index)/ 100.0 runs from 0.0 to 1.0. Likewise, if you are thinking of 17 students from Amelia to Zeth, then define an enumerated type with these 17 values and use it as the index. Remember that, as an enumerated type, Amelia to Zeth will appear without the quotation marks that delimit strings.

Types and a Word about Arrays as Parameters

The arrays we have declared are said to be declared **anonymously**, because there is no type name associated with the array type. As we know, anonymous declarations cannot be used to declare parameters in procedures and functions. Hence, it is better to declare a type name for each array type. This often adds to program readability and is required to pass arrays to procedures and functions. Thus, our examples would be better written as

```
                     (* Array Declaration Examples *)
TYPE   DayType      = (Mon, Tues, Wed, Thurs, Fri, Sat, Sun);
       GradeType    = (A, B, C, D, F, Inc, WP, WF);
       String30     = ARRAY[0 .. 29] OF CHAR;
       DailyList    = ARRAY[Mon .. Sun] OF REAL;
       GradeList    = ARRAY[1 .. 30] OF GradeType;
       NameList     = ARRAY[1 .. 30] OF String30;
       FeeList      = ARRAY[1 .. 30] OF BOOLEAN;
       SexList      = ARRAY[1 .. 30] OF CHAR;
       WineList     = ARRAY[1980 .. 1989] OF REAL;
       FreeList     = ARRAY[1 .. 10] OF DayType;
       FuncList     = ARRAY[-10 .. 10] OF REAL;
```

```
VAR    HoursWorked   :  DailyList;
       FinalGrades   :  GradeList;
       Names         :  NameList;
       FeesPaid      :  FeeList;
       Sex           :  SexList;
       CalifWines    :  WineList;
       DayOff        :  FreeList;
       FuncValues    :  FuncList;
```

Here we have used the suffix List to indicate each of the array types. Note that this is not a Modula-2 keyword and is not required. One will, however, run out of good identifiers if one does not use them with care. We believe that the suffix List is a good one to use, since it helps to remind us that an array type has been declared.

Let us return to our class example. Suppose that there are really only 26 students in the class. The 30 of the declarations is an upper bound on the number of students that will be in the class. We will waste some space by reserving memory for 30 components and then only using 26 of them, but we also gain a lot of flexibility. We can add up to four students to the class without having to change the declaration. Often, with arrays one must declare them by choosing a reasonable upper bound. If this upper bound is orders of magnitude too large, memory will be wasted. On the other hand, if the upper bound is too small, the program will fail with an index-out-of-bounds error after the array fills. The person supplying the data is often a good source for the programmer, who must pick the upper bounds for the arrays needed in a particular problem. Choosing appropriate array sizes is a part of good program design.

A procedure to print the students' names and their grades might well have the following heading:

```
PROCEDURE PrintGrades(Names : NameList;
            FinalGrades : GradeList; NumStudents : CARDINAL);
```

We omit the body of this simple procedure, which uses a FOR to loop NumStudents times, printing the names and grades. To print the grades, the procedure may invoke another procedure to convert the user-defined enumerated type, GradeType, to a printable string type. (A procedure to print user-defined types was discussed in Chapter 9. Using an array of strings, it is easy to write a procedure to read user-defined types. The details are left to the exercises.)

Arrays as Variable Parameters

We have shown the parameters to PrintGrades as value parameters. This should be no surprise, since it is the procedure's job to print this information and not to change it. In Chapter 7, we indicated that with one exception, to be discussed later, such parameters should be value parameters. It is time to discuss that exception. Remember that copies are made of arguments that correspond to value parameters. Therefore, if the arrays are value parameters, the system takes the time and the memory to make copies of the given arrays. Therefore, it is acceptable and, with very large arrays, even wise to pass an array parameter as a variable parameter, even if no changes to the array are planned by the procedure or function. Since the variable parameter is an alias for the actual argument, no time or memory is wasted in making copies of the array arguments. Therefore, a preferable heading for PrintGrades would be

```
PROCEDURE PrintGrades(VAR Names : NameList;
            VAR FinalGrades : GradeList; NumStudents : CARDINAL);
```

There is no reason to make the simple parameter NumStudents a variable parameter. It does not take much memory or much time to copy a simple variable, so Num-Students is best left as a value parameter.

THE NEED FOR ARRAYS

Consider the following two problems:

Snidely Whiplash, sales manager at The Widget Works, has at most a 100-member sales staff. The name and dollar amount of sales for each person is kept in a text file. Snidely wants a program to read the text file and print the names of all the salespersons who have sales of less than $5000 worth of widgets.

Snidely Whiplash, sales manager at The Widget Works, has at most a 100-member sales staff. The name and dollar amount of sales for each person is kept in a text file. Snidely wants a program to read the text file and print the names of all the salespersons who have sales of less than the average sales of all salespersons.

These two problems seem very similar. However, the second problem is considerably more complex than the first. In the first problem, there is no need for arrays. We simply loop through the text file reading names and sales figures. If the sales figure is less than $5000, we print the name. Then we go on to the next name. Even though there may be 100 names and sales figures, we have no need for arrays in which to store all these values. Simple Name and SalesFigure identifiers that are used over and over will suffice to solve the problem. In this case the data for one salesperson are *independent* of the data for the other salespersons. Since we have no need to compare one person's data with another person's, there is no need to store the data in arrays. The beginner needs to understand this example and not be misled by the fact that there are 100 names and sales figures into automatically assuming that an array will be needed. Using arrays when they are not needed simply makes your solution unnecessarily complex.

The second problem is more difficult, since the data for each individual are not independent from the data for the other salespersons. Suppose, for example, that the first line of the text file reads

```
Otto Mobile 7629.29
```

Is Otto in trouble with Snidely? We can't tell until we know the average sales, and we can't determine the average sales until we have seen all the sales figures. Once we have seen all the sales figures, we can compute the average, and then we can go back through the data deciding each salesperson's fate. Therefore, we have the following pseudo-code for our solution to the problem:

Read the data into arrays
Sum the sales figures
Compute the average
Look at the arrays and find those people in trouble with Snidely

Actually, this outline is still fairly vague. To compute the average, we will need a count of the data. This can be done while we are reading the data in. Upon reflection, we see that we can also sum the sales figures as we read them in, so let's combine the first two steps of our solution. Adding some details about the last two steps gives us a more thorough and efficient pseudo-code:

Declare FName, LName, and SalesFigures as arrays of size 100
Read the data into the arrays. Count and Sum the data as we go
Compute and print the average
Loop through the arrays and find those with less than average sales

The first line of pseudo-code will become declarations in the main module. The last three lines will become procedures. Here is an outline for reading, counting, and summing the data:

Initialize Count and Sum to zero
While reading the text file succeeds
    Increment Count
    Read FName[Count], LName[Count] and SalesFigures[Count]
    Add SalesFigures[Count] to the Sum

Of course, finding the average is easy, but for completeness, its pseudo-code is

Compute the Average as Sum/Count
Output the Average

Finally, to identify those in trouble, we can use a FOR loop to look through the array SaleFigures for those with poor sales. The outline is

For Index from 1 to Count
    If SalesFigures[Index] < Average then
        Print FName[Index], LName[Index], and SalesFigures[Index]

There are several important remarks to make about these pieces of pseudo-code. Note that the loop in the reading procedure will be implemented as a WHILE, since we have no idea how many salespersons Snidely actually has. However, the second loop, in the last procedure, can be implemented as a FOR, since we have counted the salespersons in the first loop. Observe that Count is the index of the first loop, but that Count is the limit of the second loop. Notice that the Average is computed between the two loops.

There is only one Average and, therefore, its calculation should not be within any loop. The most important thing to understand is that the second loop does *not* read the data from the text file again. The first loop reads the text file and stores the data in arrays in memory. The second loop need only access these values. That is the power of the array: It only needs to have values read into it once. Then, via the magic of indexing, any or all of those values are available as many times as needed in the program. Listing 10.1 shows the module Snidely that solves our second problem. Snidely assumes a text file, WidgetSales.Txt, of at most 100 lines of the form shown above.

```
MODULE Snidely;

(* This module solves the second of the Snidely Whiplash problems
and illustrates the use of arrays. It uses a text file,
WIDGETSALES.TXT, that is of the form:

    Firstname Lastname SalesAmount

where there is such a line for each salesperson. Note that when a
ReadString of a first name succeeds, then termCH will be a blank.
Since we don't know how many lines there are in the text file, we
use a

    WHILE termCH = Space DO ...

to process the text file (read, count, and sum the data).    *)

FROM InOut IMPORT ReadString, Write, WriteString, WriteLn,
                                        OpenInput, termCH;
FROM RealInOut IMPORT ReadReal, WriteReal;

CONST NumSalesPersons   = 100;
      Space             = " ";

TYPE  String30   = ARRAY[0..29] OF CHAR;
      NameList   = ARRAY[1..NumSalesPersons] OF String30;
      SalesList  = ARRAY[1..NumSalesPersons] OF REAL;

VAR   FNames        : NameList;  (* Arrays of *)
      LNames        : NameList;  (* Names and *)
      SalesFigures  : SalesList; (* Sales Figures. *)
      Count         : CARDINAL;
      Sum           : REAL;
      Average       : REAL;

PROCEDURE ReadAndCount(VAR FNames, LNames : NameList;
VAR SalesFigures : SalesList; VAR Sum : REAL; VAR Count : CARDINAL);
```

(* This procedure opens the text file and reads and counts the data. It also sums the sales figures. Note the use of VAR parameters for the arrays, too. This procedure loops, while the read of the first name "succeeds" by putting a space in termCH.

Pre: A text file of valid data with at most 100 items already exists.

Post: Count is assigned the number of data lines in the file (1 ≤ Count ≤ 100). Sum is assigned the total of the Count SalesFigures, while Fnames, LNames, and SalesFigures are assigned values for all indices between 1 and Count.   *)

```
  BEGIN
    WriteString("Please enter the name of the text file.");
    WriteLn;
    WriteString('"WIDGETSALES" is the sample file. ');
    WriteLn;
    OpenInput; (* Redirect input to come from the text file. *)
    Sum := 0.0;
    Count := 1;
    ReadString(FNames[Count]);  (* Read FName of 1st person. *)
    While termCH = Space DO      (* While read is successful. *)
      ReadString(LNames[Count]);(* Read rest of data on person. *)
      ReadReal(SalesFigures[Count]);
      Sum := Sum + SalesFigures[Count];
      INC(Count);
      ReadString(FNames[Count])            (* Read next FName. *)
    END;  (* WHILE *)
    DEC(Count) (* Count has been incremented once too often. *)
  END ReadAndCount;

PROCEDURE FindAverage(Sum : REAL; Count : CARDINAL) : REAL;
```

(* Pre: Sum and Count have values.

Post: The function FindAverage returns the REAL value of sum divided by Count.   *)

```
    BEGIN
      RETURN( Sum / FLOAT(Count))
    END FindAverage;

PROCEDURE IdentifyTrouble(VAR FNames, LNames : NameList;
                VAR SalesFigures : SalesList; Count : CARDINAL;
                                            Average : REAL);
```

```
(* This procedure identifies those salespersons in trouble for not
selling widgets at a level of at least the average of all
salespersons. Note that the arrays are VAR parameters to save space
and time.
Pre:   All five parameters already have values.
Post: SalesFigures from 1 to Count are compared with the Average
and whenever an entry of SalesFigures is less than the Average, the
corresponding entries of FNames and LNames are printed.        *)

    VAR Index : CARDINAL; (* Index of FOR loop. *)

   BEGIN
     WriteString("These have sales figures below average:");
     WriteLn; WriteLn;
     FOR Index := 1 TO Count DO
       IF SalesFigures[Index] < Average THEN
       WriteString(FNames[Index]); Write(Space);
       WriteString(LNames[Index]); Write(Space);
       WriteReal(SalesFigures[Index], 0); WriteLn
     END  (* IF *)
   END  (* FOR *)
 END IdentifyTrouble;

BEGIN                           (* Body of main module Snidely. *)
  ReadAndCount(FNames, LNames, SalesFigures, Sum, Count);
  Average := FindAverage(Sum, Count);
  WriteLn; WriteLn;
  WriteString("The average of the sales figures is ");
  WriteReal(Average, 0); WriteLn; WriteLn;
  IdentifyTrouble(FNames, LNames, SalesFigures, Count, Average)
END Snidely.
```

Listing 10.1

MORE SNIDELY WHIPLASH EXAMPLES

Let us continue the Widget Works example by solving some more problems for
Snidely. Suppose Snidely would like to know the maximum sales by any of the
salespersons. Let us write a procedure that could be added to Snidely to find and print
the maximum of the sales. But first, let's think about how we find the maximum from
a list. One obvious way, depicted in progress in Figure 10.1, is to look down the list and
remember the biggest number seen so far. Obviously, when you get to the end of the
list, you have found the maximum element of the list.

84
49
63
93
12
88
96
72

Figure 10.1

Lets try to implement this same algorithm on the computer. Note that the first number is the biggest seen when you are starting, so that suggests how to initialize Biggest. This gives the following pseudo-code for finding the maximum in an array:

Initialize Biggest to the first array element
Loop through the rest of the array
    Compare each element with the Biggest
        If any element is bigger than the Biggest then
            Remember that element as the new Biggest

Listing 10.2 shows a function, MaxSales, that implements our pseudo-code and returns through its name the biggest element found. Note that MaxSales uses generic parameters to make it clear that the concept is general, not specific just to widgets.

```
PROCEDURE MaxSales(VAR Arr : SalesList; Last : CARDINAL) : REAL;

(* This function finds the maximum element of the array, Arr. It
returns a REAL type, since the component type of SalesList is REAL.

Pre:  The array Arr has values stored in it between the indices
of 1 and Last.
Post: The function MaxSales returns the largest entry of Arr
between the indices of 1 and Last.                            *)

   VAR  Index   : CARDINAL;
        Biggest : REAL;

   BEGIN
      Biggest := Arr[1];(* Initialize Biggest to First Element. *)
        FOR Index := 2 TO Last DO    (* Look through the rest. *)
          IF Arr[Index] > Biggest THEN
          Biggest := Arr[Index]
        END  (* IF *)
      END;  (* FOR *)
      RETURN(Biggest)
   END MaxSales;
```

Listing 10.2

If we add the function `MaxSales` to the module `Snidely` of Listing 10.1, then we can invoke `MaxSales` by adding the following to the body of Snidely:

```
WriteString("Maximum sales of widgets were $ ");
WriteRealPretty(MaxSales(SalesFigures, Count), 6, 2);
```

This will produce output of the form

```
Maximum sales of widgets were $ 13584.79
```

Although the procedure `MaxSales` answers Snidely's question, he isn't very happy. "Who has sales of $13584.79?" he demands. To answer that question, we need to remember the index of the maximum value, as well as the maximum value itself. This is illustrated by our human in Figure 10.2. Please observe the distinction between the largest array element, which is of component type, and the position of that element, which is of index type.

Figure 10.2

Realize that both `Biggest` and `Position` will have to be initialized and both will have to be modified when a bigger element is found in the array. Listing 10.3, `MaxPlace`, shows the changes made to implement this version. `MaxPlace` is a procedure, because it returns two results: the maximum value and its place in the array.

```
PROCEDURE MaxPlace(VAR Arr : SalesList; Last : CARDINAL;
                   VAR Biggest : REAL; VAR Position : CARDINAL);

(* The array Arr is a VAR parameter to save space and time.
Pre:  The array Arr has values stored in it between the indices
of 1 and Last.
Post: Biggest is assigned the largest entry of Arr between the
indices of 1 and Last, and Position is assigned the index of that
Biggest value.                                                  *)

  VAR Index : CARDINAL;
```

```
BEGIN
  Biggest := Arr[1]; (* Initialize Biggest to 1st Element. *)
  Position := 1;                        (* ADDED STATEMENT. *)

  FOR Index := 2 TO Last DO      (* Look through the rest. *)
    IF Arr[Index] > Biggest THEN
      Biggest := Arr[Index];
      Position := Index                 (* ADDED STATEMENT. *)
    END  (* IF *)
  END  (* FOR *)
END PosMaxSales;
```

Listing 10.3

If we declare Position and Biggest in the main module, too, then we can invoke
MaxPlace with

```
MaxPlace(SalesFigures, Count, Biggest, Position);
WriteString("Salesperson # ");
WriteCard(Position, 0);
WriteString(" sold the most with sales of $");
WriteRealPretty(Biggest, 6, 2);
```

and this will produce output of the form

```
Salesperson # 18 sold the most with sales of $ 13584.79
```

Snidely still isn't very happy, because he doesn't know who salesperson #18 is. "Why can't computers speak English?" Snidely sneers. Well, as a matter of fact, it is easy to have the computer print the name of this most successful salesperson. Observe that there is a very strong relationship between the arrays FNames, LNames, and SalesFigures. Namely, for any Index in range, FNames[Index], LNames[Index], and SalesFigures[Index] are all pieces of information about the same person. Figure 10.3 depicts this situation and helps to explain why such arrays are called **parallel** arrays.

	FNames	LNames	SalesFigures
1	Otto	Mobile	7629.29
	...	...	...
18	Wally	Widget	13584.79
	...	...	...

Figure 10.3

Our method of finding the name of the most successful salesperson can be summarized as follows:

Find the maximum entry—and the index of this entry—in the array SalesFigures. Take the index and run to the parallel arrays where the first and last names of the winner will be found.

Thus, we can find and identify our salesperson to Snidely's satisfaction with

```
MaxPlace(SalesFigures, Count, Biggest, Position);
WriteString(FNames[Position]); Write(" ");
WriteString((LNames[Position]);
WriteString(" is the winner with sales of $");
WriteRealPretty(SalesFigures[Position], 6, 2);
```

and the output will be of the form

Wally Widget is the winner with sales of $ 13584.79

The alert reader will want to know what happens if there are ties in the sales figures. Since we change Position only when a larger Biggest is found, the answer is that our procedure will find the first individual with the maximum sales. Often, the official response to the question of ties is that this is a first course and, therefore, we assume that there are no ties. The proper handling of ties is not difficult, however, so we'll outline a simple method and leave the details for the reader. Our approach will use two passes through the array. On the first pass, we use the approach of MaxSales to find the Biggest element of the array and do not worry about the index or indices of this element. We know that this biggest element appears in the array at least once, so we make a second pass through the array, finding all occurrences of Biggest in the array. For each such occurrence, we count it and print the corresponding names from the parallel arrays. At the end, we know that our count, CountWinners, is at least one. If it is one, then we print a singular message such as " is the winner ...", but if CountWinners is larger than one, we use a plural message such as " are tied for first place ...". This is another example of the power of arrays—they allow us to access the data in memory as often as necessary.

SORTING

Another reasonable request from Snidely would be to print the list of salespersons in some order; i.e., to sort the data before printing it. Snidely might ask for the salespersons to be listed alphabetically, or he might ask for the salespersons to be listed in decreasing order by sales figures. Or, knowing Snidely, he might ask for both lists, since each has its uses. The alphabetical listing is handy if you want to know how so-and-so is doing, and the list ranked by sales figures is handy if you quickly want to see who your 10 most successful salespersons are. We will develop sorting algorithms that can be modified easily to sort either the names alphabetically or the sales figures in decreasing order.

Many different methods have been developed to sort an array. In this chapter, we will introduce three common, simple sorting algorithms: **selection** sort, **bubble** sort, and **insertion** sort. Selection sort is so named because it repeatedly selects an element (such as the largest not yet selected) and puts it into its proper place in the array. Bubble sort is so named because one can "see" the smallest elements bubbling to the top, as in a glass of soda. Insertion sort receives its name from the fact that the elements of the array are inserted one after another in their proper order with respect to the previous elements.

Selection Sort

First, we need to discuss how our sort will work in general. Again, this sort repeatedly selects an element and puts it into its proper position in the array. Let us illustrate the idea of selection sort with the unsorted list of names of Figure 10.4a.

Tyler	Pierce	Pierce
Polk	Polk	Polk
Taylor	Taylor	Fillmore
Fillmore	Fillmore	Taylor
Pierce	Tyler	Tyler
a)	b)	c)

Pierce	Fillmore
Fillmore	Pierce
Polk	Polk
Taylor	Taylor
Tyler	Tyler
d)	e)

Figure 10.4

First, we find the biggest name, Tyler, and its position, 1. We know that Tyler should be on the bottom of the list. So we swap whatever is in the last place, which happens to be Pierce, with Tyler. This gives us the array of Figure 10.4b, and we know that Tyler is in his correct position. Therefore, we continue the same process with the *first four names* of Figure 10.4b. The biggest is Taylor in position 3, so we swap the third and fourth names to get the array of Figure 10.4c. Notice that at this point both Taylor and Tyler are correctly placed. Now we look at the *first three names* of Figure 10.4c and swap the biggest of these, Polk, in position 2, with the third name. This gives us the array of Figure 10.4d. One more comparison of the *first two names* (and one more swap) gives us the sorted array of Figure 10.4e.

Observe that we needed to make only four passes through the sorting algorithm to sort the five names. That is because on each pass, another name was placed in its correct place, and when four of them are in their correct positions, the fifth must also be in its correct position. Also notice that on each pass, we swapped the biggest name left with the bottom name, where bottom successively took on the values 5, 4, 3, and 2. Therefore, we have the following pseudo-code for the selection sort:

For Bottom from ArraySize to 2 by -1 do
    Find the Position of the biggest element of the array between the indices
      1 and Bottom
    Swap the elements with indices Position and Bottom

We have already discussed the elements of this selection sort: Finding the position of the biggest element in an array was discussed in the previous section, and swapping was discussed in Chapter 7. Hence, without further ado, please examine and study the procedure Selection of Listing 10.4. To show the generality of selection sort, we have used generic parameters and generic parameter types in Selection. For simplicity, we have shown procedure Swap and function PosBiggest as internal to Selection. Either of these could be pulled out of Selection if they were needed by other procedures or functions of the module. Swap, for example, might be used in other sorting methods. We have chosen to implement PosBiggest as a function, since its job is to find the *position* of the biggest element. Since it does not also need to return the biggest element, PosBiggest returns only one result.

```
PROCEDURE Selection(VAR Arr : List; ArrSize : CARDINAL);

(* This procedure sorts the array Arr using selection sort. List
is assumed to be some array type such as NameList or SalesList and
CompType is assumed to be the component type of the array, such as
String30 or REAL.
Pre:   ArrSize has a value less than or equal to the upper bound
on the index of Arr. The array Arr already has values stored in it
between the indices of 1 and ArrSize.
Post: Arr is sorted into increasing order.                        *)

  VAR Bottom   : CARDINAL;
      Position : CARDINAL;

  PROCEDURE Swap(VAR X, Y : CompType);
  (* Pre:  X and Y have values.
  Post:    The values of X and Y have been interchanged.          *)

    VAR Temp : CompType;
    BEGIN
      Temp := X;
      X := Y;
      Y := Temp
    END Swap;
```

```
PROCEDURE PosBiggest(VAR Arr:List; Bottom:CARDINAL) : CARDINAL;
(* The array Arr is a VAR parameter to save space and memory.
Pre:   Arr and Bottom already have values and Bottom is less
       than or equal to Arr's upper index bound.
Post:  This function returns the index of the biggest
       element in Arr between the indices of 1 and Bottom.  *)


VAR Biggest    : CompType;
    Index      : CARDINAL;
    Position   : CARDINAL;

BEGIN
   Position := 1;          (* First element is biggest so far. *)
   Biggest := Arr[1];
   FOR Index := 2 TO Bottom DO
     IF Arr[Index] > Biggest THEN       (* Bigger one found? *)
        Biggest := Arr[Index];    (* If so, keep new Biggest *)
        Position := Index         (* and remember its index. *)
     END  (* IF *)
   END;  (* FOR *)
   RETURN(Position)
END PosBiggest;

BEGIN                              (* Body of procedure Selection. *)
  FOR Bottom := ArrSize TO 2 BY -1 DO
    Position := PosBiggest(Arr, Bottom);
    Swap(Arr[Position], Arr[Bottom])
  END  (* FOR *)
END Selection;
```

Listing 10.4

Sorting Parallel Arrays

We must be careful with parallel arrays when we sort one of them. For example consider the two parallel, unsorted arrays shown in Figure 10.5a. If we simply sort the array LName, we arrive at the jumbled data shown in Figure 10.5b.

FNames	LNames		FNames	LNames
John	Tyler		John	Fillmore
James	Polk		James	Pierce
Zachary	Taylor		Zachary	Polk
Millard	Fillmore		Millard	Taylor
Franklin	Pierce		Franklin	Tyler

a)   **b)**

FNames	LNames	FNames	LNames
Franklin	Fillmore	Millard	Fillmore
James	Pierce	Franklin	Pierce
John	Polk	James	Polk
Millard	Taylor	Zachary	Taylor
Zachary	Tyler	John	Tyler

c)   d)

Figure 10.5

It does no good to sort the first names into order, since that gives us the two ordered, but nonsensical, arrays of Figure 10.5c. What we need is Figure 10.5d, where the first names have been moved to keep them parallel to the last names. We can do this by performing swaps in all the parallel arrays every time a swap is made in the array that is being sorted. Thus, the body of Selection to sort Arr and keep two parallel arrays Brr and Crr arranged properly becomes

```
FOR Bottom := ArrSize TO 2 BY -1 DO
  Position := PosBiggest(Arr, Bottom);
  Swap(Arr[Position], Arr[Bottom]);
                                  (* Swap in Arr to sort it. *)
  Swap(Brr[Position], Brr[Bottom]);
                                  (* Swap in Brr and Crr to *)
  Swap(Crr[Position], Crr[Bottom])
                                  (* keep them parallel to Arr. *)
END  (* FOR *)
```

Strictly speaking, Brr and Crr will also need to be parameters to procedure Selection. However, if there are many parallel arrays for addresses, cities, states, zip codes, telephone numbers, social-security numbers, etc., then it may make sense, appropriately so noted in comments, to pass all the parallel arrays globally. Also, if the component types of Arr, Brr, and Crr are not all the same, then different swap procedures will be needed for each type. That is, if Arr's component type is REAL and Brr's component type is String30, then we will need a SwapReal procedure to swap components of Arr and a SwapString procedure to swap components of Brr. The necessity for these various swapping procedures is caused by Modula-2's strong typing. Modula-2 provides ways to break these strong typing rules, but such methods are not elementary.

If, in procedure Selection, we change the type List to NameList and CompType to String30 and use SwapString on the first two arrays and SwapReal on the third array, then we can invoke the selection sort in our module Snidely to alphabetize the last names and print the sorted data with

```
Selection(LNames, Count, FNames, SalesFigures);
                                  (* Sort on LNames. *)
PrintLists(FNames, LNames, SalesFigures, Count);
```

where `PrintLists` is a very simple procedure left to the reader to design.

Note that the computer already knows the alphabetical ordering of strings and that `StringA < StringB` is true if `StringA` comes before `StringB` in the dictionary. Thus:

`"John" < "Marsha"`

and

`"John" < "Jon"`

and

`"Jon" < "Jonathon"`

are all `TRUE`. The ordering of strings is determined by the ASCII values of their characters. Therefore, all uppercase letters precede all lowercase letters. This leads to the unusual result that

`"Zebra" < "ant"`

is also `TRUE`, since `"Z" < "a"` and, therefore, the comparison stops.

If, on the other hand, we change the type `List` to `SalesList` and `CompType` to REAL and use `SwapReal` for the first array and `SwapString` for the other two arrays, then we can sort and print the data in *increasing* order by sales figures with

```
Selection(SalesFigures, Count, FNames, LNames);
                                        (* Sort on Sales. *)
PrintLists(FNames, Lnames, SalesFigures, Count);
```

Finally, if we simply change the comparison in the body of the function `PosBiggest` from a > to a <, then the sort will be in decreasing order on sales figures, as desired by Snidely. However, since our selection sort is now finding the smallest and putting it to the bottom of the array, to preserve the sanity of anyone reading the procedure, we should change the name of the function `PosBiggest` to `PosSmallest` and its local variable from `Biggest` to `Smallest`. We leave the details to the reader.

The alert reader will again have noticed that our sort may not work if there are ties in the array being sorted. For example, suppose that the data include John Smith, Abagail Smith, and Millard Smith in some order. Since our first sort was on last names, only blind luck can be depended on to have arranged these Smiths in the correct order. Often, the official party-line answer is that in this first course, we assume that ties will not occur. Indeed, if one is sorting on social-security numbers or other identification numbers that are supposed to be unique, then ties are not supposed to occur. We indicate one method of resolving ties and leave the details to the reader in the exercises.

The data item on which we order the data is referred to as the **key** of the sort. Our sorts have had only one key, which we now call the **primary key**. In our first example, the last name is the primary key. Obviously, the first name will be a **secondary key**. By this, we mean that we first look at the primary key and then at the secondary key only if a tie results in the primary keys. Thus, our pseudo-code for the body of PosBiggest becomes

Set Position to 1
Set Biggest to Arr[1]
For Index from 2 to Bottom do
    If Arr[Index] equals Biggest then
        CheckSecondKeys(Brr[Index], Brr[Position], Biggest, Position)
    Else if Arr[Index] > Biggest then
        Keep Arr[Index] as new Biggest
        Keep Index as new Position

where, of course, CheckSecondKeys is a procedure that looks at the secondary keys in the array Brr and modifies Biggest and Position if Index's secondary key is bigger than the secondary key, Brr[Position], of the current biggest element. Note that CheckSecondKeys is called only when there is a tie in the primary key. Obviously, this method can be extended to tertiary keys (middle names or initials) if there is another tie in the secondary key. We leave the details to the reader.

Bubble Sort and Insertion Sort

Selection sort is not the only sort known to humankind. We chose to discuss it first because we believe it to be the easiest to understand, since the notion of finding a maximum or a minimum is so natural. Selection sort is also relatively efficient—at least, as compared to the two new sorts about to be introduced. This section, therefore, can be omitted on a first reading.

Our objective is to make the methods of the bubble and insertion sorts clear and then to leave the details of the implementations to the reader. We believe that these sorts provide good exercises, since the best way to understand a sort is to consider it for yourself in enough detail to be able to implement it as a Modula-2 procedure.

Consider the unordered array of Figure 10.6a. Bubble sort begins by considering the final pair of elements, in this case 11 and 7. Since they are out of order, the bubble sort swaps them to obtain the data of Figure 10.6b.

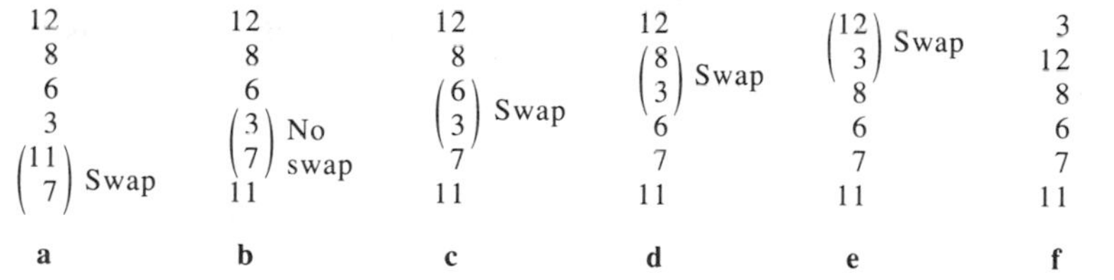

Figure 10.6

Bubble sort now considers the next-to-last pair, 3 and 7, of the array of Figure 10.6b. Note that this pair overlaps the previous pair. This time, since the elements are in order, no swap is made. Now the next pair, the 6 and 3, as shown in Figure 10.6c, are compared. This time, we swap to get the array of Figure 10.6d. Here, we compare the next pair, 8 and 3, and swap again to get Figure 10.6e. Finally, we compare the first pair, 12 and 3, and again swap to get the array of Figure 10.6f. The array is not yet sorted, but the smallest element, the 3, has "bubbled up" to the top (this explains the name of this sort). We see that each such pass of the bubble sort will bring the next lightest element to its proper position. Also note that the second pass does not need to compare the first two elements, since the smallest is already at the top. Likewise, the third pass can stop when it has considered the pair consisting of the third and fourth elements. We urge the reader to take scrap paper and check that our results of the next four passes of the bubble sort are as shown in Figure 10.7. Note that each part of this figure shows the result of one complete pass, which results in the next element bubbling to the top. They are not the atomic steps of the sort shown in Figure 10.6.

3	3	3	3
6	6	6	6
12	7	7	7
8	12	8	8
7	8	12	11
11	11	11	12
a	b	c	d
2nd pass	3rd pass	4th pass	5th pass

Figure 10.7

As we expected, on each pass, at least one more element is in its proper place. Again, after five passes, all six elements must be in their correct places, since when all but one are correct, the last must be correct, too. As promised, we leave the details of the implementation to the reader, with the following hints and admonitions: Write a procedure `BubblePass` that performs one pass of the bubble sort. Make sure that `BubblePass` does not bubble all the way to the top each time, but uses parameters so that the bubbling goes from the bottom up to some limit point passed to the procedure. Develop a procedure `Bubble` that uses `BubblePass` to perform the sort. Make sure that `Bubble` does not call `BubblePass` more times than necessary to guarantee that the data are sorted.

Our next sort is familiar to card players who sort their cards as they are dealt them. That is, as they receive a new card, they insert it into their hand to keep the cards that they presently have in proper order. This explains why this sort is known as the insertion sort. We will illustrate the insertion sort with the same array, now shown in Figure 10.8a.

12	8	6	3	3	3
8	12	8	6	6	6
6	6	12	8	8	7
3	3	3	12	11	8
11	11	11	11	12	11
7	7	7	7	7	12
a	b	c	d	e	f

Figure 10.8

The secret of understanding insertion sort is to ignore the end of the array (which represents cards that haven't been dealt yet). The first card we were dealt was a 12. There is never a problem ordering one object so we do nothing but await our second card, an 8. The 8 is smaller than the 12 so it is inserted before the 12. In other words, the 12 slides down and the 8 is inserted in its place. This gives us the array of Figure 10.8b. Note that neither the 8 nor the 12 is in its final resting place, but that they are in the correct order relative to each other. Now consider the third card, a 6, and its proper position relative to the first two. Obviously, both 8 and 12 must slide down, allowing the 6 to be inserted at the top. This gives us the array of Figure 10.8c. Again, the reader should take scrap paper in hand and check that the results of the insertion of the fourth, fifth, and sixth cards are as shown in Figures 10.8d-f. Of course, after the last card has been inserted, the array is sorted. Note that since we began inserting with the second card, again only five passes were needed to sort the six objects.

Before we leave the details to the reader, we'll suggest an efficient way to implement the sliding of objects during an insertion. Consider, for example, the array of Figure 10.9a (which is also Figure 10.8e), where the 7 is to be inserted into the array. First, store the 7 in a temporary location, so that it will be safe. We know that the use of a temporary is common in swapping values, so we should not be surprised by its use here. The fact that the 7 is safely stored somewhere else is indicated in Figure 10.9a by showing the 7 in shadowed form. This means that the place occupied by the 7 in the array is really free. Hence, we begin checking at the previous value, 12 in this case, to see whether that value should slide. Since 12 is larger than the 7 (of Temp) we put the 12 in 7's old place, as shown in Figure 10.9b. This leaves a free spot where the 12 was. Backing up, we see in Figures 10.9c and 10.9d how the 11 and 8 also slide down. Since the 6 is not larger than the 7 of Temp, the sliding stops and the 7 is inserted in the free spot, giving us the final array of Figure 10.9e.

Temp					
	3	3	3	3	3
7	6	6	6	6	6
	8	8	8	**8**	7
	11	11	**11**	8	8
	12	**12**	11	11	11
	7	12	12	12	12
	a	b	c	d	e

Figure 10.9

This method of sliding is fairly efficient because we performed the slides without using any swaps. We leave it to the reader to verify that swapping the 7 all over the array involves a lot more work! To implement the insertion sort, we suggest that you design, implement, and test a OneInsertion procedure that inserts a given element into a given segment of an array. Be very careful to make sure that your OneInsertion procedure works properly when inserting a new smallest element. Then write an Insertion procedure that calls your subprocedure appropriately to sort the array.

SEARCHING

Another reasonable question that Snidely might ask is, "How is Millard Fillmore doing these days?" Snidely means, of course, for us to look up and report the sales figures for Millard Fillmore. We can do this by looking through the names arrays until we find him, and then, remembering the index where he was found, run over to the array of sales figures and look up the amount for that index. Or Snidely might remember that there were several salespersons with sales figures under $2000 and ask us to look them up and give him their names. In this case, we search through the array of sales figures, and every time we find an amount smaller than $2000, we use the index of that amount to print the names (first and last) of the individual in question. From these simple examples, we see that searching is a common and useful application in programs.

A search has a target. This target can be compound, as in our first example where we were looking for an individual with a certain first name and a certain second name, or the target can be simple, consisting of a single, indivisible value. In our development, for simplicity, we will assume a simple target and leave the modifications for more complex examples to the reader. The target can appear in the array zero, one, or many times. Because zero is an important case, we shall consider it, but we will, again for simplicity, assume that the target appears at most once in the array. The reader should be able to make the modifications necessary to our code to find all occurrences of the target. Therefore, we restrict our considerations to a search for a single match of the target. The reader can modify the ideas to search for all items smaller or greater than the target.

In our search, we are given an array, `Arr`; a target, `Target`, that appears in the array at most once; and the array size, `Size`. For simplicity, we assume that the array is indexed from 1 to `Size`, but this is not a restrictive assumption, since our technique will work as well if the index varies from `Jan` to `Dec` or from `"A"` to `"Z"`.

Now that we know what we are given, what is it that the search does? Obviously, it searches for the target in the array. What result does it report? Usually, the user wants more than a BOOLEAN `TRUE` for "I found it" or `FALSE` for "It's not here." Beginners sometimes think that the `Target` is the result of the search. But wait a minute—the `Target` was input to the search! Reporting "Fillmore" back to me is pretty meaningless if I asked you to search for "Fillmore." From Snidely's examples above, we see that it is the *index* of the `Target` in the array that is useful, for with this index we can print all the parallel information from the other arrays. For example, if the search reports that "Fillmore" is the 18th name in `LNames`, then we can look in `FNames[18]` and `SalesFigures[18]` and report all the information that we have about this individual. Therefore, our searches will report the *index* of the target in the array. What do we report if our search fails to find the target in the array? Because of the strong typing of Modula-2, we will have to return some index value, since we are returning index values to report sucessful searches. Therefore, it is common practice to return the index zero to indicate that the search did not find the target in the array. Note that the choice of zero is arbitrary, but common. If zero is a legal index of the array, then our search should return some other silly value such as 32767 when failure is to be reported. Since we are assuming indices for the array range from 1 to `Size`, we will use zero for this purpose.

We will study two common search methods: Linear search and binary search. Linear search is very simple: It begins at one end of the array and searches consecutive elements until it either finds the target or reaches the other end of the array. Binary search, on the other hand, is an ordered search. By this we mean that the array must be in order before we can use binary search on an array. Binary search looks in the middle of the array and, if this element is not the target, then depending on the relative values of the target and the array's middle value, binary search continues in either the smaller or the larger half of the array. Thus, binary search is much more efficient than linear search, and we'll discuss the efficiency question after we carefully describe the two searching algorithms.

Linear Search

The method known as linear search is very simple. We simply begin at one end of the array and search element by element until we find our target or until we come to the end of the array. This method of search is called linear because we search in a straight line from one end of the array to the other. We can, of course, stop the search when we find the target, and this suggests the use of a BOOLEAN, Found, to help control the loop. Pseudo-code for such a linear search is

```
Set Found to False                              --Target hasn't been found yet
Set Index to 1
While Index ≤ Size and Not Found do
    If Arr[Index] = Target then
        Set Found to True                       --Eureka! Get out of loop with success
    Else
        Increment Index                         --Try the next element
If Found then
    Return(Index)
Else
    Return(0)                                   --Target never found, report failure
```

While the above pseudo-code is easy to implement, we will make some simplifications to it before implementing it. Our first observation is that since we have no idea where the target is in the array, it is just as efficient to search from the bottom of the array upward as it is to search from the top of the array downward. It doesn't seem to make any difference which way we search, but, as we shall see, searching backward will, with our second observation, make the reporting of failure much easier. The second observation is that the search is made more complicated by the fact that we don't know whether the search will succeed or not. If we knew that the target were present in the array, then we could eliminate the need for the compound test in the WHILE to see if we have come to the end of the array, and we could eliminate the need for the IF after the WHILE. But, alas, it would be very dangerous to assume that the target always will be present. After all, the human might misspell the Target, "Filmoore," and then the search would fail. But if we put the Target into the array at a special zeroth location, then we would know that it would be found. What's more, if we search from the bottom (high index) and if the Target really is in the array, then we find and report this index. But if the Target isn't in the array, then we find it at index 0, and this reports the failure to the user. Note that this trick assumes that the array is declared from 0 to Size instead of 1 to Size and, further, that no real data are stored in the 0th cell. That cell is reserved exclusively for our use in the linear search. Notice how much simpler our pseudo-code has become, and that, in particular, the complex WHILE has become a simple LOOP:

```
Set Arr[0] to Target                        --Search will eventually succeed!
Set Index to Size
Loop
    If Arr[Index] = Target then
        Exit loop                           --Eureka! Get out of loop with success
    Else
        Decrement Index                     --Try the previous element
Return(Index)
```

We urge the reader to trace this code and see that it would return 18 if "Fillmore" is the 18th name in a list of 100 names, and that it would return 0 if "Filmoore" is not in the array at all. Listing 10.5 shows the complete function Linear that implements the linear search.

```
PROCEDURE Linear(VAR Arr : List; Size : CARDINAL; Target :
                                        CompType) : CARDINAL;

(* This function implements linear search.
Pre:  The value of Target appears at most once in the array Arr.
Arr is indexed starting at 0, but no data are stored in Arr[0]. Size
is less than or equal to Arr's upper index bound.
Post: This function returns the index of Target in Arr if found
and zero otherwise.                                               *)

VAR Index : CARDINAL;

BEGIN
  Arr[0] := Target;        (* Make sure that search succeeds. *)
  Index := Size;           (* Start search at high end of array. *)
  LOOP
    IF Arr[Index] = Target THEN
      EXIT                                 (*  EXIT Loop with index. *)
    ELSE
      DEC(Index)
    END (* IF *)
  END;  (* LOOP *)
  RETURN(Index)
END Linear;
```

Listing 10.5

To use Linear in Snidely, we make the types List and CompType the appropriate types and add the following segment (with declarations of the new variables) to the module Snidely:

```
REPEAT
  WriteString("Please enter last name of salesperson: ");
  ReadString(LastName); WriteLn;
  Place := Linear(LNames, Count, LastName);
  IF Place = 0 THEN
    WriteString("Sorry, not found. Please check spelling.");
    WriteLn
  ELSE
    WriteReport(FName[Place], LastName, SalesFigures[Place])
END (* IF *)
UNTIL UserQuits();
```

where WriteReport is a simple procedure that prints out a readable message containing the three bits of information about the given individual. Notice that the second argument can be written either as LastName or as LName[Place], since these are equal. UserQuits is a simple BOOLEAN function that asks the user whether another search is wanted. Again, trace the execution of this segment using the targets "Fillmore" and "Fillmore."

Binary Search

It might seem that linear search is the best we can do. But wait, we don't use a linear method when we look up a name in a telephone directory. Think how long it would take to find James Madison's telephone number if we began at one end of the directory and looked name by name! On the other hand, if we had a telephone number, 234-3100, wanted to know who it belonged to, and didn't have a reverse directory, then we would have no choice but to proceed number by number. What is it about a normal telephone book that makes one search so easy and the other so difficult? Obviously, it is that the telephone book is ordered, alphabetically by name. In a linear search of unordered data, a probe that isn't our target gives us no other information. In an ordered search, a probe that is not our target still gives us information—it tells us on which side of the target to continue the search. That is, if we are looking for James Madison and we open the book to Abraham Lincoln, then we know that our target comes after our current place in the book.

Our method is illustrated in Figure 10.10. Before the probe finds Abraham Lincoln, we are searching the entire list, as illustrated by the low and high limit markers. When Abraham Lincoln fails to match our target, James Madison, all is not lost! Rather, we know that the target, if in the array at all, is in the array below the position of the probe. This is indicated by moving the low limit to the element after the current probe. The search can then continue in the lower half of the array.

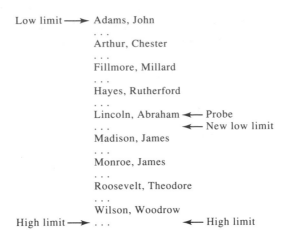

Figure 10.10

A reasonable choice for our probe is the middle of the array. This guarantees that unless we get very lucky and find our target, we can throw away one half of the array with each probe. Because of this halving of the array, this search is called binary search (**Bi** for two). Its method is set forth in the following pseudo-code, which assumes (temporarily) that the target will be found in the array. The pseudo-code also supposes that the array is in increasing order:

Set Found to False since we haven't found the target yet
Set Low and High to the low and high bounds of the search
While Not Found do
    Set Mid to the midpoint of Low and High   --Try in the middle
    If Arr[Mid] = Target then
        Set Found to True   --Get out with success
    Else if Arr[Mid] < Target then   --Probe at Mid was too small
        Set Low to Mid + 1   --Move Low to element below Mid
    Else   --Probe at Mid was too big
        Set High to Mid - 1   --Move High to element above Mid
Return(Mid)

The reader should take the time to trace this pseudo-code on the array of Figure 10.11 and make sure that the search for 37 proceeds as indicated in that figure. The midpoint of 1 and 10 could be 5 or 6, since $(1 + 10) \div 2 = 5.5$. We have used 5, since we we want Mid to be a CARDINAL and 5 is what we get with DIV.

	Arr	Target	Low	High	Mid	Found
1	8	37	1	10		FALSE
2	11				5	
3	14		6			
4	21				8	
5	23			7		
6	32				6	
7	37		7			
8	44				7	
9	49					TRUE
10	50					

Figure 10.11

Let us see what happens if we use our pseudo-code for the binary search on a target that is not present in the array. For example, suppose we search the array of Figure 10.11 for the target 35. The first part of the search proceeds as illustrated in that figure. Let us pick up the search at the point where Low is 6, High is 7, and Mid becomes 6. Since Arr[Mid] is 32, which is too small, Low becomes 7, as in the illustration. The point is that if 35 is in the array, it must be at the 7th place or below. Now, as in the figure, Low and High—and therefore Mid—are 7. Since Arr[Mid] is 37, which is too big, High becomes 6. The point is that if 35 is in the array, it must be at the 6th place or before! This, together with our earlier observation, is absurd. Notice that Low with the value 7 has passed High with the value 6. This is our signal that the search has failed. Therefore, pseudo-code for the binary search is

```
Set Found to False since we haven't found the target yet
Set Low and High to the low and high bounds of the search
While Not Found and Low ≤ High do
    Set Mid to the midpoint of Low and High          --Try in the middle
    If Arr[Mid] = Target then
        Set Found to True                                --Get out with success
    Else if Arr[Mid] < Target then             --Probe at Mid was too small
        Set Low to Mid + 1                 --Move Low to element below Mid
    Else                                          --Probe at Mid was too big
        Set High to Mid - 1                --Move High to element above Mid
If Found then
    Return(Mid)                                         --Search was successful
Else
    Return(some absurd value)                    --Search was not successful
```

Listing 10.6 shows the complete listing of the function Binary, which searches from 1 to Size for a given Target in a given array with CARDINAL indices. It returns the index of the Target if found and the value zero otherwise.

```
PROCEDURE Binary(VAR Arr : List; Size : CARDINAL; Target :
                                    CompType) : CARDINAL;


(* This function implements binary search.
Pre:  The value of Target appears at most once in the array Arr.
Arr is ordered in increasing order. Size is less than or equal to
the upper bound on the index for Arr.
Post: This function returns the index of Target if present in Arr
and zero otherwise.                                           *)

CONST  Absurd = 0;     (* Absurd index for reporting failure. *)

VAR    Low   : CARDINAL;
       High  : CARDINAL;
       Mid   : CARDINAL;
       Found : BOOLEAN:

BEGIN
  Found := FALSE;                        (* Target not found yet. *)
  Low := 1;
  High := Size;
  While (NOT Found) AND (Low <= High) DO
    Mid := (Low + High) DIV 2;
    IF Arr[Mid] = Target THEN
      Found := TRUE                      (* Exit with sucess. *)
    ELSIF Arr[Mid] < Target THEN
      Low := Mid + 1                     (* Move Low limit up. *)
    ELSE
      High := Mid - 1                    (* Move High limit down. *)
    END  (* IF *)
  END;  (* WHILE *)
  IF Found THEN
    RETURN(Mid)
  ELSE
    RETURN(Absurd)
  END  (* IF *)
END Binary;
```

Listing 10.6

If we have already used one of our sorts to order the array upon which the search is to be conducted, then we can invoke our binary search in our module Snidely by simply replacing the call to Linear with a call to Binary:

```
REPEAT
  WriteString("Please enter last name of salesperson: ");
  ReadString(LastName); WriteLn;
  Place := Binary(LNames, Count, LastName);
  IF Place = 0 THEN
    WriteString("Sorry, not found. Please check spelling.");
    WriteLn
  ELSE
    WriteReport(FName[Place], LastName, SalesFigures[Place])
END (* IF *)
UNTIL UserQuits();
```

This illustrates another advantage of procedures and functions. If they have the same interface with the module through their parameters, then one can be replaced by the other without any problems. As you would suspect, if the array LNames is large, the binary search method will be considerably more efficient than the linear search method. We now consider such efficiency questions.

"BIG OH" EFFICIENCY CONSIDERATIONS FOR SEARCHING

How much faster is a binary search than a linear search? To try to answer this question, let us construct some tables that will indicate the amount of work being done by each search on various arrays. For linear search, the situation is simple. We can get lucky and find the target quickly, or we can get unlucky and find the target at the end of the array. On the average, for a target in the array, we will have to search about half the array before we find the target. That is, for an array of 1000 items, we will need on the average about 500 probes before we find a target in the array. Of course, a search for a target that is not in the array will have to probe all 1000 cells before reporting failure. Such searches will increase the average, so we are being generous to linear search by not considering such cases. Table 10.1 shows the behavior of linear search for various array sizes.

Table 10.1: Linear Search Efficiency

ArrSize	10	100	1000	2000	1,000,000
Average No. of Probes	5	50	500	1000	500,000

We see that the amount of work done by linear search grows like the function

$$f(N) = \frac{N}{2}$$

where N is the array size. The reader should recognize this as a linear function (another reason for calling it linear search) whose graph is a straight line. All we are interested in is the shape of this graph. Realize that $g(N) = N$ is the simplest linear function, so we ignore the constant 2 in the denominator and summarize our conclusion by writing

Linear search is $O(N)$

which is read, "The order of the linear search is linear" or colloquially, "Linear search is Big Oh of N." "Big Oh," of course, stands for "the order of." The English translation of this formalism is simply: "The graph of the work done by linear search as the array size increases is a straight line."

To investigate the behavior of binary search, we first need to examine Table 10.2, which shows the first 10 powers of 2. The reader should quickly verify that the powers of 2 do increase as shown.

Table 10.2: Table of Powers of Two

2^1	2	2^6	64
2^2	4	2^7	128
2^3	8	2^8	256
2^4	16	2^9	512
2^5	32	2^{10}	1024

To see why Table 10.2 is relevant to binary search, consider an ordered array of 16 elements. After one probe in the middle, we are left with an array of at most 8 elements (we might have only 7 or we might have found the target on the first try). After another probe, we have an array of at most 4 elements. A third probe gives us 2 elements, and a fourth probe leaves us with 1 element. Since 4 is the exponent of 2, that gives us 16; at most 4 probes are needed for binary search to reduce an array of 16 elements to one element. Likewise, by using Table 10.2, you can verify that 10 probes will reduce an array of 1024 elements to one element. What do we do with an array size of 10 or 1000 that is not an exact power of 2? Well, obviously, an array of 10 elements is easier to search than an array of 16 elements; likewise, an array of 1000 elements is a little easier than an array of 1024 elements. Note that after we reduce the array to one element, we need one last probe to see if that element is the target or not. Hence, in the worst case when we don't find the target until the end, the number of probes is one more than the exponent of two. This is summarized in Table 10.3.

Table 10.3: Binary Search Efficiency

ArrSize	10	100	1000	2000	1,000,000
Largest No. of Probes	5	8	11	12	21

Again, for example, the entries under array sizes 10 and 1000 are 5 and 11, respectively, because

$$2^3 < 10 \leq 2^4 \quad \text{and} \quad 4 + 1 = 5$$

and

$$2^9 < 1000 \leq 2^{10} \quad \text{and} \quad 10 + 1 = 11$$

An easy way to verify the entry under the array size of 2000 is to observe that after the first probe in the middle of the array, we will be left with a subarray of at most 1000 elements. Hence, one probe has reduced the case of 2000 elements to the case of 1000 elements and, thus, the entry for 2000 is just one more than the entry for 1000. We leave it for the reader to verify the final entry in Table 10.3.

Note that while we were generous with our estimates on linear search, using as we did an average of only successful searches, we have been harsh on binary search by using an absolute maximum or worst-case analysis for it. This just makes binary search look that much better, because for large arrays, its worst-case behavior is fantastically better than linear search's average-case behavior. For example, for an array of 1 million elements, the linear search does almost 25,000 times as much work, on the average, as the binary search does in the worst case. Remember that for moderate and large arrays, binary search is far more efficient than linear search and that the difference in efficiency grows rapidly as the array size increases.

The behavior of binary search is clearly different from that of linear search. What is the nature of the binary search's growth? Graphs of the results of Tables 10.1 and 10.3 are sketched in Figure 10.12.

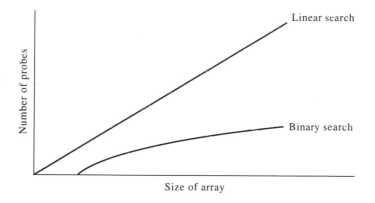

Figure 10.12

We have presented our discussion with exponents rather than logarithms, since the average reader is more comfortable with exponents. However, realize that

$$2^{10} = 1024$$

simply means that

$\log_2(1024) = 10$

Thus, we see that the behavior of binary search is given by the function

$f(N) \approx \log_2(N) + 1$

where N is the array size. The constant term 1 does not change the shape of the graph, so we summarize this by writing

Binary search is $O(\log(N))$

This is read as "The order of the binary search is logarithmic" or "Binary search is Big Oh of log N." In English, this simply expresses the fact that binary search grows as the logarithm of the array size.

We urge the reader to experimentally observe the vast difference for large arrays between the efficiency of binary and linear searches. To do this, we suggest developing a module that declares an array of, say, 10,000 elements, initializes this array to all zeroes, and then searches via a linear and binary search for a 1 in the array. The linear search will have to probe all 10,000 cells before reporting failure, while the binary search will look in only 15 cells (why?). Depending on the speed of your processor, you may have to increase the array size to see the difference in performance. The binary search should appear instantaneous, while the linear search produces a noticeable pause. Furthermore, if you now make the array size 20,000, then the time needed by the linear search can be seen to double, while the time needed for binary search does not measurably change. This experimental module can quickly make you a fan of binary search in large arrays.

"BIG OH" EFFICIENCY CONSIDERATIONS FOR SORTING

The alert reader will wonder if we can apply our "Big Oh" methods to our three sorts (selection, bubble, and insertion) to determine which is the best. The answer is "Yes and No!" That is, we can find the "Big Oh" of each sorting method, but it turns out that all three are $O(N^2)$, so this rough analysis does not indicate which is best.

To see where the N^2 comes from, first consider a specific case, say an array of 10 elements. Each of the sorts calls a subprocedure 9 times to sort the array. In each case, the amount of work done in the subprocedure varies. For example, the bubble sort does at most 9 swaps on the first pass, then at most 8 swaps, etc. Hence, to sort 10 elements, bubble sort performs at most

$9 + 8 + 7 + 6 + 5 + 4 + 3 + 2 + 1$ swaps

Likewise, insertion sort slides at most one element on the first pass. Then it slides at most two elements on pass two, etc. Thus, the number of slides done by insertion sort is at most

$1 + 2 + 3 + 4 + 5 + 6 + 7 + 8 + 9$ slides

Selection sort, on the other hand, compares the first element with 9 others to find the maximum on the first pass. On the second pass, the first element is compared with 8 others, etc. Hence, the amount of work done by selection sort is at most

$9 + 8 + 7 + 6 + 5 + 4 + 3 + 2 + 1$ comparisons

Thus, we see that for all three sorts, the worst case for each in sorting N elements is

$1 + 2 + 3 + ... + N - 2 + N - 1$ units of work

Figure 10.13 illustrates the ancient Greek demonstration that our sum is $O(N^2)$. Namely, the sum $1 + 2 + 3 + ...$ is represented as a triangular array of dots. Two of these triangles clearly give us a rectangle of size N by $N - 1$. Thus, there are $N(N - 1)$ or $N^2 - N$ dots in the rectangle and half that many in each triangle. Thus:

$$1 + 2 + 3 + ... + N - 2 + N - 1 = \frac{N^2 - N}{2} = \frac{N^2}{2} - \frac{N}{2}$$

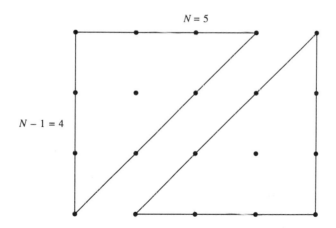

Figure 10.13

The shape of the graph of $N^2/2 - N/2$ is a parabola, as shown in Figure 10.14. The simplest parabola is given by N^2, so we summarize by writing

Selection sort is $O(N^2)$
Bubble sort is $O(N^2)$
Insertion sort is $O(N^2)$

Each of these is read "The order of ... sort is quadratic" or "The ... sort is Big Oh of N^2."
In English, this formalism is simply saying that the graph of each sort grows like a
parabola as the array size increases.

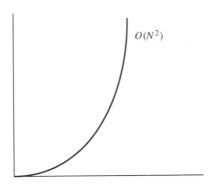

Figure 10.14

Are all three of our sorts equal, then? No, we didn't say that. We simply found with
our rough analysis that all belong to the same class, $O(N^2)$. That is, they all grow
quadratically with N. We urge the reader to write a module that compares the three sorts
on randomly generated data (see procedure `Generate` of module `Bagels` of Chapter
7 for one way to generate random data). Be sure to keep a copy of the original unsorted
array, so that each sort is given the same array to sort! By comparing the amount of
work done in a swap, a slide, and a comparison, can you justify the order of finish of
the three sorts in your experiment? Also, time each of the sorts on arrays of 100, 200,
and 400 elements. Depending on the speed of your processor, these sizes may need to
be modified. Also, see the section below on *open* arrays for help in passing different
sized arrays to the same sort procedure. Make a table of your results and check to see
that each sort of 200 elements takes about four times as long as the corresponding sort
of 100 elements. This is the $O(N^2)$ nature of these sorts: Twice as much work takes four
times as long. Verify for each sort that the times for the array of size 400 are about 4
times and 16 times as long as the times for the arrays of 200 and 100, respectively.
Estimate how long it would take on your processor to sort 4000 elements. (You may
not want to wait around to see if you are correct).

There are sorts that are better than $O(N^2)$, but none of them are as elementary as the
three discussed in this chapter. One of these faster sorts, whose class is $O(N\log(N))$, is
introduced in Chapter 13.

OPEN ARRAY PARAMETERS

Suppose, as suggested in the last section, that you have arrays of 100, 200, and 400
CARDINALs in your program. Suppose further that these are declared to be the types
`SmallList`, `MedList`, and `BigList`, respectively. By the methods we have described, we cannot sort these three arrays with one sort procedure, because that

procedure will have a parameter Arr with some specific type. If the parameter has the type SmallList, then the procedure will not accept arguments of type MedList or BigList, even if we pass the array size as an additional parameter. This is due to the strong typing of Modula-2, but is frustrating—since sorting 200 elements is essentially the same task as sorting 100 elements. Therefore, Modula-2 has a method of avoiding the problem through so-called **open array parameters**, which provide a means of declaring a parameter as an array without declaring the exact range of its indices. An open array parameter is declared as follows:

```
Arr : ARRAY OF CompType
```

This is the one instance where something other than a type name can be used as a parameter type. Of course, the procedure or function probably needs to know the range of the indices, and these can be found effectively by the built-in function HIGH. No matter how the actual array argument was declared, an open array parameter Arr is indexed from 0 to HIGH(Arr). That is, a SmallList that is really indexed from 1 .. 100, when passed as an open array parameter, is treated as if indexed from 0 .. 99. MedLists and BigLists are treated as if indexed from 0 .. 199 and 0 .. 399, respectively. Even a WeirdList that is indexed with the user-defined type from Jan to Dec would be treated, through an open array parameter, as if indexed from 0 .. 11. As an example, Listing 10.7 shows a function SumArray that sums the elements of any array of CARDINALS.

```
PROCEDURE SumArray(VAR Arr : ARRAY OF CARDINAL) : CARDINAL;

(* This function accepts any array of CARDINALs and illustrates the
use of HIGH to access the elements of the array.
Pre:  Arr has values in all of its cells.
Post: This function returns the sum of all the entries of Arr.
                                                                *)

VAR    Sum    : CARDINAL;
       Index  : CARDINAL;
       Size   : CARDINAL;

BEGIN
  Sum := 0;
  Size := HIGH(Arr);                      (* Find array size. *)
  FOR Index := 0 TO Size DO        (* Loop through array. *)
    Sum := Sum + Arr[Index]
  END;  (* FOR *)
  RETURN(Sum)
END SumArray;
```

Listing 10.7

Open array parameters, therefore, provide some flexibility to functions and procedures. However, open array parameters are only for several arrays of different sizes,
but of the same component type. If you have an array of CARDINALs, an array of
REALs, and an array of strings, then you cannot use open array parameters to write one
sort procedure that will sort all three arrays.

STRINGS

The string type was introduced in Chapter 2 in an ad hoc manner. Now that we
understand arrays, we see that a string is just an array of characters, and the mysterious
type definition

```
TYPE String30 = ARRAY[0 .. 29] OF CHAR;
```

now makes perfect sense. The reader familiar with other languages will probably be
accustomed to procedures and functions that find the length of strings, put strings
together, and take strings apart. These are not standard in Modula-2, but they can be
written easily by the user. We could write such procedures and functions at this point,
but we postpone this discussion until Chapter 14, where we can develop a full string
package as an example of a separately compiled module. Other modules can then
import our string procedures and functions just as we import from the standard library
modules.

MULTIDIMENSIONAL ARRAYS

Arrays, as we have discussed them, have been one-dimensional lists that are sequential
from a first element to a last element. Arrays can be multidimensional, and the most
common case of this is the two-dimensional array. This means that the array has two
different indices, or degrees of freedom. Such an array is usually called a **table**. For
example, the widget production table of Figure 10.15 is a two-dimensional array. That
figure tells the well-known story of the demise of widget production in the United
States. Beginning in the early 1980s we see that pressure from Japanese widgets drove
down U.S. production. Then, in the mid-1980s we see that the new Republic of
Madeinusa began making widgets so cheaply that both U.S. and Japanese manufacturers had virtually been wiped out by the late 1980s. Of course, most observers credit
Madeinusa's marketing strategy (they stamped their widgets MadeInUSA) for their
great success in the American market!

	USA	Japan	Madeinusa
1980	10.2	0.3	0.0
1981	11.4	0.5	0.0
1982	7.5	4.9	0.0
1983	7.2	5.5	0.1
1984	5.3	5.6	2.7
1985	1.7	3.5	6.4
1986	1.2	2.1	9.3
1987	0.7	1.3	11.6
1988	0.4	0.9	13.4

Figure 10.15

The point is that the table of Figure 10.15 is a very common way to structure data. It is two-dimensional, because it takes two indices to determine a particular REAL value of the table. For example, to assign the value 5.3 tons to the U.S. production in 1984, we would write

```
Widgets[1984, USA] := 5.3;
```

where the array Widgets would have been declared by

```
TYPE Country = (USA, Japan, Madeinusa);

VAR Widgets : ARRAY[1980 .. 1988], [USA .. Madeinusa] OF REAL;
```

Or, better, we could declare Widgets with a named type for use as arguments in procedures and functions with

```
TYPE   Country     = (USA, Japan, Madeinusa);
       WidgetTable = ARRAY[1980 .. 1988], [USA .. Madeinusa]
                                                          OF REAL;

VAR    Widgets : WidgetTable;
```

Arrays can have many dimensions. For example, an array to keep track of the amount of red, white, and rose wines produced during the 1980s in California, Italy, France, and Germany might be declared by

```
VAR Wines : ARRAY[Red .. Rose], [1980 .. 1989],
                                [California .. Germany] OF REAL;
```

where, for simplicity, we have not shown the declaration of the obvious user-defined types Color and Country. Three indices are needed to specify a specific value of this array. For example, Wines[White, 1985, Italy] is the REAL number representing the quantity (liters) of white wine produced in Italy in 1985. If Hue is an identifier of type Color, Year a CARDINAL, and Nation a Country, then the reference

`Wines[Hue, Year, Nation]` is the corresponding production for that `Nation` in that `Year` of wine of that `Hue`.

Be aware that multidimensional arrays can easily be great memory hogs. For a two-dimensional array, the number of cells involved is the product of the extensions of the indices. That is, if an array is declared with indices from 1980 .. 1989 and `Jan ..Dec`, then there are 10 possible values for the first index and 12 for the second. Therefore, this array will consist of 120 cells, as can be seen by viewing the array as a table of 10 rows of 12 items each. An array to keep track of sales for the last 12 months for each of 100 salespersons for each of 50 products sounds like it might be useful in a real example. However, this three-dimensional array uses 12 • 100 • 50 = 60,000 cells. If each cell is an 6-byte REAL, then this one array uses 360,000 bytes of memory! Here is an array that you certainly wouldn't want to pass to a function or procedure through a value parameter!

Arrays of three, four, five, and more dimensions are harder to draw pictures for, but their manipulation is very similar to that of the two-dimensional case. Hence, we will concentrate our examples on two-dimensional arrays. The reader who thoroughly understands arrays of two dimensions can easily make the extension to cases of more dimensions.

AN EXTENDED EXAMPLE: MORE WIDGETS

In a previous section, we discussed how to use a one-dimensional array to keep track of up to 100 salespersons selling widgets. Of course, the reader understood that the example was artificial. Who has ever heard of a manufacturer that has exactly one product? Since we are pressed into a corner, we now reveal the truth that The Widget Works has nearly 50 different products from widgets to wadgets and other gadgets. Therefore, to keep track of his sales force, Snidely Whiplash clearly needs a two-dimensional array. The declaration of an array that will store the *quantity* of each product sold by each person can be given by

```
CONST NumSP   = 100;      (* Maximum number of salespersons. *)
      NumProd = 50;          (* Maximum number of products. *)

TYPE  SalesTable = ARRAY[1..NumSP], [1..NumProd] OF CARDINAL;
(* A SalesTable will store the QUANTITY of each product (1 ..
NumProd) sold by each salesperson (1 .. NumSP).            *)

VAR Sales : SalesTable;
```

If we assume for a moment that the array has already been loaded with values, then Snidely can find out how salesperson 34 is doing with product 18 with

```
WriteCard(Sales[34, 18], 0);
```

Observe that `Sales[34, 18]` is *not* the same thing as `Sales[18, 34]`. When we have two or more indices, we must always be sure to use them in the correct order. In this case, Sales was declared with its first index running over the 100 salespersons and its second index running over the 50 products. Hence, Sales' first index always refers to the salesperson and its second index always refers to the product. But, of course, we cannot expect Snidely to know this. Indeed, we cannot expect Snidely to even know who salesperson 34 is or what product 18 is. Snidely will be likely to ask questions like "How is Wilson doing selling gidgets?" But we are getting ahead of our story. First, we need to see how values might be read into the table.

We will assume that somewhere in The Widget Works are the data we need for our tables. These data may have been prepared by someone in the business office for his or her purposes and may not be exactly in the form that you would have prepared the data. The point is that, unless you want the exciting job of reentering the data, you must accept the data in the format that you find it and learn to adjust your program so that it reads the data properly. For example, let us suppose that the data are in a text file that begins as follows:

```
Washington George
23 4 0 12 93 ... 32  0 21
Adams John
15 0 3 0 2 0 ... 0 0 11
...
```

Clearly, we have a line with the name of the salesperson and then a line with the quantity sold of each product by that individual. There are nearly 100 such pairs of lines, and each line of quantities contains about 50 items. There are nearly 5000 data items in all!

With the data as indicated, we cannot read in all the names and then read in all the sales figures. Since the data have these items intertwined, our read module will have to intertwine the reading of these items. For simplicity, the reader might have preferred to have the data in two separate text files of the form

```
Washington George
Adams John
  ...
```

and

```
23 4 0 12 93 ... 32  0 21
15 0 3 0 2 0 ... 0 0 11
...
```

but realize that the first form is more reasonable from a human point of view. The point is that the programmer must know the structure of the data and adjust his or her program to read the data correctly.

Let's write a procedure that will read the first set of data. To read these data, do we first need to count the number of names in the file as well as the number of sales figures on each line? This would be awkward and error-prone, since humans do not count beyond 10 with great reliability. Also, the procedure would be very specific. What if next month we have one less salesperson or a new product? In that case, the procedure would have to be modified. We want a more general solution, so we will let the procedure do the counting for us. Obviously, we need code to read the names and sales figures of each individual. We can have the computer count the salespersons until it finds the end of the text file. Also, the computer can watch for EOL as we read and count the quantities. Using CountSP to count and index the salespersons and CountProd to count and index the products, we have the following pseudo-code for a procedure to read the text file:

```
Initialize CountSP to 1
    Read Last[CountSP]                          --Read the first Last name
        While the read was successful
            Read First[SP]                      --Get the rest of the name
            Initialize CountProd to 1
            Read Sales[CountSP, CountProd]      --Read the first sales figure
            While not EOL
                Increment CountProd by 1
                Read Sales[SP, CountProd]       --Read the next sales figure
            Increment CountSP by 1
            Read Last[SP]                        --Get the next Last name
        Decrement CountSp by 1 since it has been incremented once too often
```

It would be wise for the reader to trace this pseudo-code with our first set of data to see how it reads and counts those data. We leave it to you to explain why the initializations of CountSP and CountProd are handled separately. What happens if both are placed outside, or both placed inside, the outer WHILE? In what follows, we will assume that each row of quantities contains the same number of values. That is, if The Widget Works has 42 products, then there are 42 quantities listed for each salesperson. In a real-world example, it would not be safe to assume that the data, prepared by humans, were valid. But, since we are beginners and we want to emphasize certain concepts, we will make this simplifying assumption. Hence, the final value of CountProd tells us how many products The Widget Works makes. Also, the final value of CountSP indicates the current number of salespersons. These values, along with the arrays, must be exported by this procedure. Since this procedure finds the number of salespersons and products, all other processing of the given arrays can use counted FOR loops.

Also note that the arrays Last and First for the names are only one-dimensional. There are at most 5000 quantities stored in the 100 by 50 array of sales, but there are at most 100 first and last names. Since these names are strings and not CARDINALS, they must also be stored in separate arrays. The array Sales has component type CAR-DINAL and cannot store strings. Since each person does have two names, we could use one two-dimensional array Names to store this information. Names would be 100 by 2, Names[CountSP, 1] would be the last name, and Names[CountSP, 2] would be the first name of the salesperson with index CountSP. Since our purpose is to illustrate the care and feeding of two-dimensional arrays, we make this change to our outline.

We also need a list of the names of the products. This list will contain at most 50 items (why?). In fact, we know that it should contain exactly CountProd items (why?). We leave it to the reader to develop the pseudo-code to read a second text file containing

the names of the products and place these data in an array, Products. Listing 10.8
shows the declaration of the arrays Sales, Names, and Products.

```
CONST  NumSP    = 100;        (* Maximum number of salespersons. *)
       NumProd  = 50;             (* Maximum number of products. *)

TYPE   SalesTable   = ARRAY[1..NumSP], [1..NumProd] OF CARDINAL;
       String30     = ARRAY[0 .. 29] OF CHAR;
       NameTable    = ARRAY[1 .. NumSP], [1 .. 2] OF String30;
       ProductList  = ARRAY[1 .. NumProd] OF String30;

VAR    Sales    : SalesTable;
       Names    : NameTable;
       Products : ProductList;

(* Sales keeps track of quantity sold by each salesperson of each
product. Names stores the last and first names of each salesperson.
Products lists the names of each of the products.              *)
```

Listing 10.8

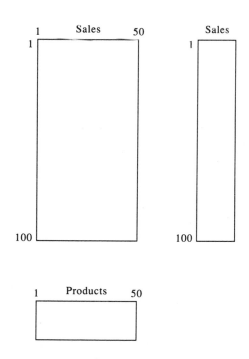

Figure 10.16

Notice how we have drawn Names vertically and Products horizontally in Figure 10.16. This was done to illustrate the parallel nature of these arrays. The reader should understand that if we have a particular item, Sales[SP, Prod], from the array Sales, then Names[SP, 1] is the last name of the salesperson and Products[Prod] is the name of the product sold. Note that Names[Prod, 1] will make sense to the computer, but is probably nonsense in that it is not what we intended. Likewise, Products[SP], if we don't get lucky and get an index-out-of-bounds error, will be accepted by the literal computer even though it is not likely to be logically correct. The moral of this example is to be very careful about using the correct indices in the correct order with multidimensional arrays and their associated parallel arrays. There is no rule to be memorized that will tell you what is the correct index. Rather, understanding the situation is the only way to pick the correct index. Since each salesperson has a name, and each product has a description, it should be obvious that SP and Prod are the proper indices, respectively, for Names and Products. This is also an excellent example of the usefulness of choosing meaningful identifiers. If we had indexed Sales with garbage indices like X and Y, or I and J, then it would be much more difficult to decide how Names and Products should be indexed. In complex situations, diagrams like Figure 10.16 and the use of meaningful identifiers are two good tools to use. When in doubt, draw a picture. Indeed, we invite the reader to declare arrays of social-security numbers of the salespersons and selling prices of the products and to add these two arrays to Figure 10.16. Which one is declared 1 .. NumSp and which one is declared 1 .. NumProd and why? Which is better drawn horizontally and which vertically?

Finally, Listing 10.9 contains the code for our procedure ReadData, which reads the names and sales data from one text file and then reads the product names from a second text file.

```
PROCEDURE ReadData(VAR Sales : SalesTable;
              VAR Names : NameTable; VAR Products : ProductList;
              VAR CountSP, CountProd : CARDINAL);

(* This procedure reads two text files. The first, Sales.Txt,
contains two lines for each individual. The first line has the last
and first names of the salesperson, and the second line has the sales
quantities for each product. The second file, Products.Txt, has the
name of each of the products produced by The Widget Works. This
procedure assumes that the necessary reads, file opens, EOL, and
termCH have been imported from InOut by the main module.
Pre:  The text files contain valid data concerning at most NumSP
people and NumProd products.
Post: CountSP and CountProd are assigned the number of people and
products, respectively, in the text files. The arrays Sales, Names,
and Products receive values.                                    *)

CONST Space = " ";

VAR Index : CARDINAL;
```

```
BEGIN
  WriteString("Please enter the name of the text file.");
  WriteLn;
  WriteString("SALES is the sample file of the text.");
  WriteLn;
  OpenInput;
  CountSP := 1;
  ReadString(Names[CountSP, 1]);(* Read the first Last name. *)
  WHILE termCH = Space DO   (* While the read was successful. *)
    ReadString(Names[CountSP, 2];(* Then get the first name. *)
    CountProd := 1;
    ReadCard(Sales[CountSp, CountProd]); (* Get first sales. *)
    WHILE termCH <> EOL DO
      INC(CountProd);
      ReadCard(Sales[CountSp, CountProd])
    END;   (* Inner WHILE *)
    INC(CountSP);
  ReadString(Names[CountSP, 1)      (* Get the next Last name. *)
  END; (* Outer WHILE *)
  CloseInput;

  DEC(CountSP);                    (* Decrement CountSP since we *)
                                   (* have counted an extra item. *)

  WriteString("Please enter the name of the second text file.");
  WriteLn;
  WriteString("PRODUCTS is the sample file of the text.");
  WriteLn;
  OpenInput;
  FOR Index := 1 TO CountProd DO
    ReadString(Products[Index])
  END;  (* FOR *)
  CloseInput
END ReadData;
```

Listing 10.9

Now that the arrays have data in them, we can begin to answer queries for Snidely. For example, remember his question, "How is Wilson doing these days selling gidgets?" Obviously, we need to search for "Wilson" among the last names and remember the index—say, PersonNo. We also need to search for "Gidget" among the list of products and remember its index—say, ItemNo. Then, using these two indices, in the right order, we can look up the answer for Snidely in the array Sales. Listing 10.10 shows a procedure, LookUp, that implements these ideas. Lookup calls search routines that are not shown, since search was discussed earlier. Of course, it would be better to accept both the first and last names of the salesperson, rather than just the last name, but we leave this minor modification to the reader.

```
PROCEDURE LookUp(VAR Sales : SalesTable; VAR Names : NameTable;
    VAR Products : ProductList; CountSP, CountProd : CARDINAL);

(* This procedure reports on the sales of a particular product by
a particular individual. The user enters the salesperson's last
name and the name of the product. A search for these targets is made
from 1 to CountSp and 1 to CountProd in the appropriate arrays. The
user is asked to repeat the data entry until the data are found.
At that point, the answer is looked up in the sales table.
Pre:  All five parameters have values stored in them.
Post: When the user enters a last name in the array Names and a
product in the array Products, then the corresponding item in the
indicated row and column of Sales is printed.               *)

VAR    PersonNo : CARDINAL;    (* Index of Salesperson search. *)
       ItemNo   : CARDINAL;      (* Index of product search. *)
       Person   : String30;   (* Target of salesperson search. *)
       Item     : String30;     (* Target of product search. *)


BEGIN
  REPEAT
    WriteString("Please enter last name of salesperson: ");
    ReadString(Person); WriteLn;
    PersonNo := NameSearch(Names, CountSP, Person)
  UNTIL PersonNo > 0;   (* Repeat until search is successful. *)
  REPEAT
    WriteString("Please enter name of product: ");
    ReadString(Item); WriteLn;
    ItemNo := ProductSearch(Products, CountProd, Item)
  UNTIL ItemNo > 0;   (* Repeat until search is successful. *)
  WriteString(Person);
  WriteString(" has sold ");
  WriteCard(Sales[PersonNo, ItemNo], 0);
  WriteString(Item);
  WriteString("s.")
END LookUp;
```

Listing 10.10

The output of LookUp is of the form

```
Wilson has sold 84 Gidgets.
```

ROW AND COLUMN OPERATIONS

LookUp answers one kind of question that Snidely can ask. This question deals with a particular item of the sales array. Other common questions deal with groups of items. For example, reasonable requests from Snidely would be "Show me all of Wilson's sales figures" or "Show me the sales by each person just for the gidgets." The first of these, sales by Wilson, is a simple **row operation** on the array, since what Snidely wants is just a particular row of the array. Likewise, the request for a list of sales figures for a particular product such as gidgets is an example of a **column operation** on the array. The procedure shown in Listing 10.11 does the row operation. We leave the minor changes for a column operation to the reader.

```
PROCEDURE RowOp(VAR Sales : SalesTable; VAR Names : NameTable;
                               CountSP, CountProd : CARDINAL);

(* This procedure reports on the sales figures for a specific
individual. It searches the Names table for the given name and then
prints the appropriate row of the array Sales.
Pre:  All four parameters have values stored in them.

Post: When the user enters a last name in the array Names, then
the row of Sales corresponding to that individual is printed.*)

VAR    TargetName  : String30;
       Row         : CARDINAL;
       Col         : CARDINAL;

BEGIN
  REPEAT
    WriteString("Please enter last name of salesperson: ");
    ReadString(TargetName); WriteLn;
    Row := NameSearch(Names, CountSP, TargetName)
  UNTIL Row > 0;        (* Repeat until search is successful. *)

  WriteString("Here are the sales for ");
  WriteString(TargetName); WriteLn;
  FOR Col := 1 TO CountProd DO
    WriteCard(Sales[Row, Col], 5);
    IF Col MOD 10 = 0 THEN  (* Write 10 sales figs per line. *)
      WriteLn
    END  (* IF *)
  END  (* FOR *)
END RowOp;
```

Listing 10.11

The beginner often finds it confusing that the column index, not the row index, varies in a row operation. This is because the row is fixed. For example, the elements of the seventh row of an array `Arr` are the elements `Arr[7,1]`, `Arr[7,2]`, `Arr[7,3]`, etc. A glance back at Figure 10.16 also, hopefully, will help convince you of this simple, but crucial, fact.

Sometimes, row and column operations are less obvious than our examples have shown. For instance, another reasonable request from Snidely would be, "Get me the total sales of gidgets for the last month!" (Here, we assume that the array `Sales` holds monthly totals.) Since Snidely is interested in gidgets, he is interested in a specific column of the sales array. But Snidely doesn't want nearly 50 numbers to try to interpret. Rather, he wants us to total the entries of that column and give him this last result. We leave the details of this simple modification to the reader.

Another row operation example might be to total the sales figures for a given individual. But since gidgets cost $10 and Gadgets cost $1000, simply totaling the entries in a given row has little meaning. (You can't add apples and oranges.) If we declare an array `SellPrices` appropriately (see the exercises) and assume that `SellPrices` has values already read into it, then we can determine the total dollar amount of sales for a given individual. The details are left to the reader with the hint that a statement such as

```
TotalSales := TotalSales + Sales[SP, Prod] * SellPrices[Prod];
```

will have to be nested appropriately in a loop. Notice how the total dollar amount is accumulated by adding in the value of the sales for the given person for each product.

Snidely can also make requests about the entire array `Sales`. For example, a simple request would be to sum all the entries of the array. This we can do in either of the following ways:

```
Sum := 0;                          Sum := 0;
FOR := 1 TO CountSP DO             FOR := 1 TO CountProd DO
  FOR := 1 TO CountProd DO           FOR := 1 TO CountSP DO
    Sum := Sum + Sales[R, C]           Sum := Sum + Sales[R, C]
  END  (* Inner FOR *)               END  (* Inner FOR *)
END;  (* Outer FOR *)              END;  (* Outer FOR *)
WriteCard(Sum, 0);                 WriteCard(Sum, 0);
```

The reader should trace each of the above to see how it works. The first processes the array in row order, while the second processes the array in column order. A careful trace of each segment will make this terminology obvious.

Clearly, if we are simply totaling all the items in the array, it doesn't matter whether we proceed in row order or in column order. However, there are many instances where it does matter. For example, Snidely might want summary information about each product. He might ask, "Get me a list of total sales of each product." Here he wants a list of column totals—he wants to know the total sales of product 1, the total sales of product 2, etc. Since there may be up to 50 such totals, we use an array, `ProdTotals`, to keep these results. Suppose `ProdTotals` has been declared by

```
TYPE ProdList : ARRAY[1..NumProd] OF CARDINAL;

VAR    ProdTotals : ProdList;
```

Carefully study FindProdTotals of Listing 10.12, which finds these product totals.

```
PROCEDURE FindProdTotals(VAR Sales : SalesTable; CountSP,
              CountProd : CARDINAL; VAR ProdTotals : ProdList);

(* This procedure fills the array ProdTotals. Each entry in
ProdTotals is the sum of elements in the corresponding column of
the array Sales.
Pre:  Sales, CountSP, and CountProd already have values.
Post: For each index, Col, from 1 to CountProd, ProdTotals[Col]
is assigned the sum of the entries of the Col-th column (from 1 to
CountSP) of Sales.                                          *)

VAR    Row : CARDINAL;
       Col : CARDINAL;

BEGIN
  FOR Col := 1 TO CountProd DO    (* Process in column order. *)
    ProdTotals[Col] := 0;
    FOR Row := 1 TO CountSP DO
      ProdTotals[Col] := ProdTotals[Col] + Sales[Row, Col]
    END  (* Inner FOR *)
  END  (* Outer FOR *)
END FindProdTotals;
```

Listing 10.12

Likewise, Snidely might want the total dollar amount of sales for each salesperson. This calculation, of course, will need the array SellPrices as well as Sales. Snidely might even want these dollar amounts by salespersons to be sorted into descending order. These and other requests by Snidely are left to the exercises.

AN ALTERNATIVE FORM OF ARRAY DECLARATIONS

There is an alternative way to declare multidimensional arrays that is sometimes advantageous. Let us consider an example. Suppose we need an array to keep track of scores of 50 students on 10 exams. We might declare such an array, Grades1, with

```
VAR Grades1 : ARRAY[1..50], [1..10] OF [0..100];
```

An almost equivalent declaration could be given by

```
VAR Grades2 : ARRAY[1..50] OF ARRAY[1..10] OF [0..100];
```

That is, since we can use any type as the component type, we can put an array type as the component type of another array. Grades2, as we will see, is slightly more flexible than Grades1.

We know how to use Grades1. It can be used with zero or two indices. With two indices, it names a particular element of the array. With no indices, Grades1 names the whole array. If we had declared another array, OldGrades, at the same time as Grades1, and if OldGrades had values, then the assignment

```
Grades1 := OldGrades;
```

would be legal and would copy all the values from OldGrades into Grades1.

Grades2 can be used in exactly the same ways, or with one index. With zero or two indices, the meaning is exactly as above. With one index, Grades2[Index] names another array, in this case an array of 10 scores. Thus, Grades2[Index] represents an entire row of the array Grades2. We can even do operations such as assigning the third row to the seventh row with

```
Grades2 [7] := Grades2 [3];
```

With the array Grades1, this row assignment would need a FOR loop. To assign the fifth student a zero on the third quiz, we can even write

```
Grades2 [5] [3] := 0;
```

for the more common

```
Grades2 [5, 3] := 0;
```

As a specific example where the alternative declaration can be useful, recall that we used two different search procedures, NameSearch and ProductSearch, in the example of Listing 10.10. Two search procedures were needed because different kinds of arrays were passed in each case. If we modified the array declarations, then we could call just one search procedure. For example, if we declared the name and product arrays with

```
TYPE   String30  = ARRAY[0..29] OF CHAR;
       ProdList  = ARRAY[1..NumProd]  OF String30;
       NameList  = ARRAY[1..NumSP] OF String30;
       NameTable = ARRAY[1..2] OF NameList;

VAR    Names      : NameTable;
       Products   : ProdList;
```

then Names[1] would be a NameList, which is itself an array of names. We think of Names[1] as the list of last names and Names[2] as the list of first names of the salespersons. The search for a given last name, Person, and the search for a given product, Item, can now be done with one Search procedure:

```
PersonNo := Search(Names[1], Person);
ItemNo := Search(Products, Item);
```

Search will need the first parameter to be an open array parameter of type ARRAY OF String30, since we are calling Search with arrays of different lengths. Its second parameter is just the target of the search and is of type String30 in each case. We leave the actual implementation of these changes to the interested reader. Note that the order of the indices of the array Names has been reversed. This was necessary so that Names[1] would be the proper list of last names, but this change will necessitate other changes to the parent module.

Another application of the alternative array definition can be found in sorts where it is necessary to swap entire rows of an array based on one entry in the given rows. We leave the details to the exercises.

CONCLUSION

This lengthy chapter has introduced the array data structure. By data structure, we simply mean a way to structure data. Without arrays, we could not conveniently keep track of lists or tables of information. It should be clear that lists and tables occur very frequently in real-world problems. Hence, the mastery of arrays is critically important to the mastery of elementary computer science. With the array data structure and the divide-and-conquer strategy of procedures and functions that can manipulate these arrays, such as sorting or searching them, you are beginning to develop some real programming powers. (You might even know enough now to be dangerous!)

In many ways, this chapter marks the end of the second section of this book. The first section, Chapters 1 through 4 provided the introductory material. Chapters 5 through 10 have provided the heart of programming in Modula-2. No program will fail to use control structures, and no program should fail to use procedures and functions. An array or two will likely occur in the solution to most problems. The subsequent chapters of this book introduce some new data structures and refine your programming capabilities. These can be considered the advanced topics of the course and can be studied, with small exceptions, in almost any order.

EXERCISES

10.1   Using an array of strings, write a procedure ReadMonths(Month) that reads values of the user-defined type Months.

10.2   The Snidely Whiplash example of the text that found the winner of the sales contest assumed that there were no ties in the text file WidgetSales.Txt. Create a text file with ties for the maximum sales and modify the code of the text to handle such situations. See the text for hints.

10.3   Modify selection sort so that it will sort an arry of LNames and FNames properly even if there are several Smiths in the array of LNames. See the text for hints.

10.4   Modify the linear search algorithm so that it looks for a particular `TargetFName` and `TargetLName` in arrays of `FNames` and `LNames`. That is, implement a search for Millard Fillmore in our example from the text.

10.5   Modify linear search so that in the example from the text, it finds everyone with sales of $1000 or less.

10.6   Verify the final entry in Table 10.3. That is, verify that at most 21 probes will be needed in a binary search of 1,000,000 items in an ordered array. Hint: Extend Table 10.2.

10.7   Write a procedure `Bubble` that does a bubble sort of an array.

10.8   Write a procedure `Insertion` that does an insertion sort of an array.

10.9   Use random data to compare the three sorts discussed in this chapter. What is the order of finish of each sort on the same array of 200 elements?

10.10 Using the two-dimensional array example of the text, write a procedure to answer the following question for Snidely: "What are the total sales of gidgets for the last month?"

10.11 Declare the array `SellPrices` of the text and, assuming it has values stored in it, write a procedure to find the total sales of a given individual.

10.12 Declare an array `TotalSales` to hold the total dollar amount of each salesperson's sales. Assuming `SellPrices` has values stored in it, write a procedure to fill the entries of `TotalSales`.

10.13 Declare `Scores` to be a 30 by 10 array of CARDINALs. Modify one of the sort procedures so that the contents of `Scores` are sorted in decreasing order on the entries of the first column of `Scores`. Be sure to keep the rows of `Scores` together.

10.14 Modify `Snidely` so that it prints two lists. First, print a list of all the salespersons whose sales exceed the average sales, then print a list of all salespersons whose sales do not exceed the average. Be sure to include a title for each list.

10.15 Each bottle of Debug, the headache-relief medicine for programmers, contains a letter on the inside of the bottle cap. You win a free bottle of Debug if you collect letters to spell

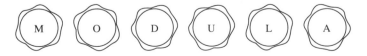

Out of every 100 bottles, there are

25 Ms
20 Os
20 Ds
15 Us
10 Ls
10 As

Write a procedure that simulates the collecting of bottle caps until you win the prize. Write a program that runs your simulation 20 times and computes an average number of bottles purchased to win a free bottle.

Chapter 11

RECORDS

The previous chapter introduced us to one of Modula-2's structured variable types—the array. Arrays are the most indispensable of the structured types. All programming languages have an array capability. In this chapter, we learn about another structured data type—the record. The record is almost as important as the array. Almost any significant real-world application uses both arrays and records, and all modern programming languages have a record capability.

The array is a homogeneous structure—that is, all components of an array must be of the same type. However, most data in the real world are stored in a nonhomogeneous fashion. For example, if you walk into the personnel office of any business and inspect the filing cabinet that contains all the employee information, you might expect to find a file folder for each individual who works for the company. Inside an individual's file folder, you would probably expect to see all the information pertaining to that person—name, address, salary, tax-withholding information, family information, history with the company, performance evaluations. This is nonhomogeneous information—it consists of strings (names and addresses), integers (number of dependents), and real numbers (salary). Of course, some of this information may also be stored homogeneously. For example, there might be a folder that has only income tax withholding information for every employee. But, for the most part, the most natural way to store the information is by the individual worker. We would probably not be too surprised to hear someone refer to an individual's personnel folder as a personnel record. In fact, that is precisely what a record is.

In programming languages, a **record** is all the data pertaining to a given item (e.g., an individual or a product). The individual items of information are called the **fields** of the record (corresponding to the components of an array). In Modula-2, we define a record type (or declare a record variable) by naming the fields that we want and specifying the types of each field. For example, we could define a type called EmployeeRec as follows:

```
TYPE EmployeeRec = RECORD
                  LastName    : String20;
                  FirstName   : String10;
                  MI          : CHAR;
                  Street      : String10;
                  City        : String10;
                  State       : String2;
                  Zip         : String5;
                  Dependents  : CARDINAL;
                  Salary      : REAL
                  END;
```

We assume that the various string types have been declared as usual. That is, we assume that we have

```
TYPE String5 = ARRAY[0..4] OF CHAR;
```

Note that a record definition begins with the keyword RECORD and ends with the keyword END. Between these keywords, we simply list the fields that we want included in the record and the types of these fields. The types are included so that the compiler can allocate the appropriate amount of memory for record variables and check the compatibility of the values that we try to assign to the various fields of the record.

We declare record variables just like any other kind of variable:

```
VAR Emp1, Emp2 : EmployeeRec;
```

Record variables can also be declared anonymously. That is, we can dispense with the type definition above and declare the identifiers directly with

```
VAR Emp1, Emp2 : RECORD
                  LastName    : String20;
                  FirstName   : String10;
                  MI          : CHAR;
                  Street      : String10;
                  City        : String10;
                  State       : String2;
                  Zip         : String5;
                  Dependents  : CARDINAL;
                  Salary      : REAL
                  END;
```

We prefer the method using the type definition, because it tends to be more readable. Also, recall that variables used as parameters to procedures and functions must have a type name—that is, such variables cannot be declared anonymously.

Just as it is possible to have arrays within arrays (e.g., multidimensional arrays), it is also possible—and, in fact, very desirable—to nest records inside other records. For example, in the type definition of EmployeeRec, we can consider the name of the employee as one unit of information and the address as another unit of information. Each of these pieces of information is composed of smaller pieces of information of differing types, so they, too, are candidates for records. To see the full generality of records, let's suppose that we want to keep salary information for the last five years on each employee. Then, the salary field becomes a structured variable of the record, but since it contains homogeneous information, we should make it an array. Thus, our definition of EmployeeRec becomes

```
TYPE EmployeeRec = RECORD
                Name        : RECORD
                                LastName   : String20;
                                FirstName  : String10;
                                MI         : CHAR
                             END;

                Address     : RECORD
                                Street : String10;
                                City   : String10;
                                State  : String2;
                                Zip    : String5
                             END;
                Dependents  : CARDINAL;
                Salary      : ARRAY[1984 .. 1988] OF REAL
             END;
```

It's not at all clear that nested records have helped us out any. In fact, they seem to have made things more cumbersome. When using nested records, it is generally best to define type names for all the records and then use these. So, a much better way to accomplish the above is:

```
TYPE   FullName    = RECORD
                LastName   : String20;
                FirstName  : String10;
                MI         : CHAR
             END;

       AddressType = RECORD
                Street : String10;
                City   : String10;
                State  : String2;
                Zip    : String5
             END;

       EmployeeRec = RECORD
                Name        : FullName;
                Address     : AddressType;
                Dependents  : CARDINAL;
                Salary      : ARRAY[1984 .. 1988] OF REAL
             END;
```

Observe that EmployeeRec now has only four fields. Of course, a variable of type EmployeeRec still takes as much memory as before, because two of these fields are in fact records with three fields each. After we see how to access the fields of a record, we will be able to see an advantage of this last way of defining EmployeeRec; that is, an advantage of using nested records.

ACCESSING FIELDS OF A RECORD

What do we mean when we talk about accessing the fields of a record? We simply mean: "How do we get at the individual fields of a record?" For example, suppose an employee just received a $1000.00 raise. If we have that individual's record available to us, how do we get to the salary field and increment it by $1000.00?

We access the individual components of an array by using subscripts. That is, if we want to access the first component of an array A, we say A[1]; if we want to enter the fifth component, we say A[5]. Records do not use subscripting as a method of access. The reason for this is a very good one. The fields of a record very likely involve different kinds of types and, in real-world applications, record definitions can become very long and complex. If we were to try to use subscripts to access record fields, it would be necessary to remember the order in which the fields were defined. In our very first example of a record definition for EmployeeRec, which field is Dependents? Which field was defined first, Dependents or Salary? The answers are: the eighth and Dependents. But we shouldn't have to worry about such details. In fact, Modula-2 doesn't care in what order we list the fields of a record. So the type EmployeeRec would be essentially the same if we listed the name after the address instead of before. Not needing to worry about order also means that we can't use subscripts with records.

Modula-2 references the individual fields of a record using a method called qualified access. This means that to access the field of a record variable, we simply use the name of the field (that's why we gave them names in the record definition!). This field name follows the variable name and is separated from the variable name by a period. For example, suppose that Emp1 contains the entire record for John Q. Public, who just received a raise of $1000.00. If we wanted to change his record to reflect that fact, we could write

```
Emp1.Salary := Emp1.Salary + 1000.0;
```

Suppose Jane Q. Doe's record is stored in Emp2 and that Jane and John perform exactly the same jobs with exactly the same qualifications and exactly the same longevity with the company. Then, we could compare Jane's and John's salaries with

```
IF Emp1.Salary > Emp2. Salary THEN
  WriteString('Sex Discrimination?')
ELSIF Emp2.Salary > Emp1.Salary THEN
  WriteString('Reverse Sex Discrimination?')
ELSE
  WriteString('Nonsexist Company')
END;
```

Now suppose we defined the type `EmployeeRec` using nested records. Furthermore, suppose that Jane M. Doe, whose information is stored in `Emp2`, and John Q. Public, whose information is stored in `Emp1`, get married, and that John decides to take Jane's last name. How do we change his last name? All of the following would be illegal:

```
Emp1.Name := 'Doe';            (* Illegal--Emp1.Name is a record.
                                     'Doe' is a character string.
                                   The types are not compatible. *)
Emp1.Last := 'Doe';              (* Illegal--Emp1 does not have
                                           a field called Last. *)
Name.Last := 'Doe';          (* Illegal--Name is not a variable,
                                     but is a field of a record.
                                     It should be used with its
                                          parent record's name.*)
```

The correct way to make the assignment is with a full name specification:

```
Emp1.Name.Last := 'Doe';           (* Find the Name field of Emp1,
                                        find the Last field of Name,
                                    and then assign 'Doe' to that. *)
```

We should point out that the reference to `Emp1.Name` above is not illegal. The statement as it appears is illegal simply because of the type incompatibility. For example, if `Person` is a variable of type `Names` with current values of `Person.First`, `Person.MI`, and `Person.Last` of `'John'`, `'Q'`, and `'Doe'`, respectively, then the statement

```
Emp1.Name := Person
```

would, in fact, be legal and would effect the desired change for us. This is one advantage to using nested records. If we need access to the entire name at once, we can do that with a reference to `Emp1.Name`. If we need just the first name, we reference `Emp1.Name.First`. When `EmployeeRec` is defined without using nested records, we are unable to reference an entire name or an entire address. We are forced to work with each individual component. The definition using nested records gives us more flexibility, and that is why we find it preferable.

THE WITH STATEMENT

Despite their great usefulness, records have one inherent drawback. Because of the need for qualified access to its components, one soon tires of repeating the name of the record. For example, suppose we have record types defined as follows:

```
TYPE   Tall        = RECORD
                       Feet    : CARDINAL;
                       Inches  : CARDINAL
                     END;
```

```
Description  =  RECORD
                Name    :  String30;
                Age     :  CARDINAL;
                Weight  :  CARDINAL;
                Height  :  Tall
              END;
```

Now, if we were printing a statistical table containing age, height, and weight information, we might find a statement sequence like this, assuming Person is a variable of type Description:

```
WriteCard(Person.Age,10);
WriteCard(Person.Height.Feet, 10);
Write("' ");                      (* Print a single quote for feet;
                                         i.e., 5 ' 10 ". *)
WriteCard(Person.Height.Inches, 2);
Write('"');                  (* Print a double quote for inches;
                                         i.e., 5 ' 10 ". *)
WriteCard(Person.Weight, 10);
```

One can imagine, in a long program, just how many times we might be typing the identifier Person. The WITH statement of Modula-2 provides a way to avoid the continual typing of the record name. We demonstrate how to use a WITH statement to handle the above example:

```
WITH Person DO
  WriteCard(Age,10);
  WriteCard(Height.Feet, 10);
  Write("' ");
  WriteCard(Height.Inches, 2);
  Write('"');
  WriteCard(Weight, 10)
END; (* WITH *)
```

The intent of the WITH statement should be pretty clear from this example. After the keyword WITH, we place a record name. In the statement sequence between DO and END, any reference to a field of the record listed after the WITH does not need to be fully qualified. The part of the record listed between the keywords WITH and DO may be omitted. To further illustrate the syntax, consider the following example using nested WITH statements:

```
WITH Person DO
  WriteCard(Age,10);
  WITH Height DO
    WriteCard(Feet, 10);
    Write("' ");
    WriteCard(Inches, 2);
```

```
    Write('"')
  END; (* Inner WITH *)
  WriteCard(Weight, 10)
END;  (* Outer WITH *)
```

Within the scope of the outer WITH, all references are assumed to have a prefix of
Person. Within the scope of the inner WITH, all references are assumed to have a prefix
of Person.Height. Continuing with this example, we show an illegal WITH statement:

```
WriteCard(Person.Age, 10);
WITH Person.Height DO
  WriteCard(Feet, 10);
  Write("' ");
  WriteCard(Inches, 2);
  Write('"');
  WriteCard(Weight, 10)                    (* Illegal reference. *)
END;
```

   The above segment is illegal because of the last statement in the body of the WITH.
The reference to Weight, since it is in the scope of the WITH, is preceded with the prefix
Person.Height. The subsequent reference is then to Person.Height.Weight, a
field name that doesn't exist.
   The reader may be wondering whether we can reference values other than record
fields inside a WITH statement. The answer is yes. If, in the above example, Count were
a simple variable labeling the entries in the table, we would be able to refer to Count:

```
WITH Person DO
  WriteCard(Count, 10);
  WriteCard(Age,10);
  WriteCard(Height.Feet, 10);
  Write("' ");
  WriteCard(Height.Inches, 2);
  Write('"');
  WriteCard(Weight, 10)
END;
```

Modula-2's behavior in the above example (in fact, in all WITH statements) is that it first
looks to see if the reference to a variable makes sense as part of the record identified
after the keyword WITH. If not, then the system considers that reference to be to a
variable that doesn't belong to the record in question. (Whether such a reference is legal
or not depends on Modula-2's scope rules, as discussed in Chapter 7, and has nothing
to do with WITH statements.) If Count existed as an independent variable and also if
Count were the name of a field in the record, then all references to Count inside the
WITH statement would mean Person.Count. It is impossible for the system to
recognize the independent variable Count inside the WITH. Again, the reason for this
is that the system looks *first* for a field of the record. Only if it doesn't find such a field
does the system then look for another variable.

VARIANT RECORDS

Suppose we are in charge of maintaining records of motorized vehicles for a given state. All records would likely have certain common fields--for example, name of owner, serial number, and year. However, certain fields may be common only to certain types of records. For example, if motorcycles are taxed based on engine size, cars based on number of cylinders, and trucks based on weight or number of axles, we can see how a motorcycle record might look different from an automobile or truck record. Modula-2 has a capability called **variant records** that allows precisely this kind of flexibility. A variant record contains a field called a **tag field**. The value of this field determines the structure of the record. Again, we'll give an example and then discuss the construct.

```
TYPE   VehicleType  = (Automobile, Truck, Motorcycle);
       VehicleReg   = RECORD
                     Owner              : NameType;
                     Address            : AddressType;
                     Year               : [1920..2000];
                     SerialNo           : String15;
                     Make               : String15;
                     Model              : String 15;
                     CASE VehType       : VehicleType OF
                      Automobile :
                        Cylinders        : [1..12]    |
                      Truck :
                        Axels            : [2..6];
                        Weight           : REAL       |
                      Motorcycle :
                        EngineSize       : [100 .. 1500]
                     END  (* CASE *)
                  END; (* RECORD *)
```

In the above example, we assume that the types NameType and AddressType have been defined as records and that String15 has been defined as an array of characters. The tag field in the above definition is VehType. Its value determines the structure of the remainder of the record. If Veh1 is a variable of type VehicleReg, and if Veh1.VehType currently contains the value Truck, then the form of Veh1 is

```
RECORD
   Owner       : NameType;
   Address     : AddressType;
   Year        : [1920..2000];
   SerialNo    : String15;
   Make        : String15;
   Model       : String 15;
   VehType     : VehicleType;
   Axels       : [2..6];
   Weight      : REAL
END; (* RECORD *)
```

Likewise, if `Veh1.VehType` is `Automobile,` then its structure is

```
RECORD
   Owner       : NameType;
   Address     : AddressType;
   Year        : [1920..2000];
   SerialNo    : String15;
   Make        : String15;
   Model       : String 15;
   VehType     : VehicleType;
   Cylinders   : [2 .. 12]
END; (* RECORD *)
```

and if `Veh1.VehType` is `Motorcycle,` then its structure is

```
RECORD
   Owner       : NameType;
   Address     : AddressType;
   Year        : [1920..2000];
   SerialNo    : String15;
   Make        : String15;
   Model       : String 15;
   VehType     : VehicleType;
   EngineSize  : [100 .. 1500]
END; (* RECORD *)
```

Variant records allow the compiler to use memory efficiently. Instead of requiring the compiler to reserve storage for all possible fields—`Weight, Axles, Cylinders,` and `EngineSize`—and then using only those fields that are applicable, with variant records the compiler can reserve enough space to handle any one of the three kinds of records. Note that the reserved storage for a motorcycle will be the same as that for a truck, even though a truck's record appears to be larger. That is because, during the course of execution, the value of the tag field might be changed from `Motorcycle` to `Truck`; in that case, the structure of the record would need to be able to reflect this change.

In fact, it is this changing of the tag field that makes variant records, in our opinion, more appropriate for advanced programmers than for beginning programmers. Suppose we have a variable `Veh1` with current values:

```
Veh1.Name--A.J. Foyt
Veh1.Address--Motor Speedway, Indianapolis, IN
Veh1.SerialNo--123456789A
Veh1.Year--1983
Veh1.Make--Ford
Veh1.Model--Escort
Veh1.VehType--Automobile
Veh1.Cylinders--4
```

Now, consider the effect of the following statement:

```
Veh1.VehType := Truck;
```

Such a statement is legal, but if this statement is not accompanied by statements that give values to `Veh1.Axles` and `Veh1.Weight`, then we have the following picture:

```
Veh1.Name--A.J. Foyt
Veh1.Address--Motor Speedway, Indianapolis, IN
Veh1.SerialNo--123456789A
Veh1.Year--1983
Veh1.Make--Ford
Veh1.Model--Escort
Veh1.VehType--Truck
Veh1.Cylinders--4
```

Of course, the above picture does not make sense. Trucks do not have a `Cylinders` field. They have `Weight` and `Axles` fields. The problem with variant records in Modula-2 is that it is the programmer's responsibility, not the compiler's, to make sure that things make sense. If the programmer doesn't carefully manage variant records, a Modula-2 compiler is likely to allow the above picture of a `Truck` with a `Cylinders` field. Furthermore, there is then much confusion about what the values of `Veh1.Weight` and `Veh1.Axles` are, and whether a reference to `Veh1.Cylinders` is illegal. We feel that the burden of managing the structure of a variant record should be on the compiler, not the beginning programmer. The compiler, for example, could allow a change to the tag field only if the entire record is being updated. Because the Modula-2 compiler doesn't worry about such details, we feel that variant records are best left to advanced programmers.

We close this discussion by mentioning that many computer scientists believe that variant records, as implemented in Modula-2, should be outlawed altogether. Because a compiler is likely to allow an incorrect structure of a variant record, advanced programmers often use variant records to trick the compiler into allowing them to do things that would otherwise be illegal. That is, variant records might help devious programmers work around many of the safety features that are incorporated into a language like Modula-2.

ARRAYS OF RECORDS AND FILES

In an application where a record type has been defined and records are being used, the chances are that there are many records involved. For example, a business keeps records on its employees and its customers, a school keeps records on its students and its faculty and staff, and government agencies keep records on everybody about everything. How do we write a program to access thousands of records? We saw in Chapter 10 how the array type gives us a naming capability that allows us to refer to many items easily. Of course, arrays are a homogeneous structure with all components of the same type. The value of records as a nonhomogeneous structure is the ability to store related information of varying types. How do we refer to many records in the same program? We simply use an array whose components are records! This gives us the advantage of both data structures. Consider the following example:

```
CONSTANT Size = 1000;

TYPE StudentRec = RECORD
                    Name          : NameType;
                    LocalAddress  : AddressType;
                    LocalPhone    : String7;
                    ParentGuard   : NameType;
                    HomeAddress   : AddressType;
                    HomePhone     : String10;
                    IDNum         : String9;
                    Class         : [1..4];
                    Major         : MajorType;
                    GPA           : REAL
                  END;

VAR StudentBody = ARRAY[1..Size] OF StudentRec;
```

Again, in the above definition, we assume that the missing types have been appropriately declared. For example, we assume that MajorType has been defined something like:

```
MajorType = (Art, Biology, Chemistry, ComputerScience, ... ,
                                                   Zoology);
```

Observe that we have defined only one variable, StudentBody. It is an array. Each component of the array is of type StudentRec. Therefore, StudentBody can hold information on 1000 students. Suppose that StudentBody has been declared as above, and further suppose that StudentBody does, in fact, contain information on 1000 students. An important issue that we are avoiding for now is: How do we get the 1000 student records assigned to the components of StudentBody in the first place? We'll take that up shortly. For now, we'll just assume the values are there.

Suppose we want to send a message to all senior computer-science majors with a grade point average of 3.5 or above. Assume we have a procedure, SendMessage, that takes as input a single student record and prepares the desired message for mailing to the student. Then, we could accomplish our task as follows:

```
FOR Index := 1 TO Size DO  (* Assume Index is of type CARDINAL *)
  IF StudentBody[Index].Major = ComputerScience THEN
    IF StudentBody[Index].Year = 4 THEN
      IF StudentBody[Index].GPA >= 3.5 THEN
        SendMessage(StudentBody[Index])
      END (* Inner IF *)
    END   (* Middle IF *)
  END     (* Outer IF *)
END;
```

First of all, the reader should understand why this works. Since `StudentBody` is an array, `StudentBody[Index]` is a specific component of that array. That is, `StudentBody[Index]` is of type StudentRec. Therefore, it has all the fields that any variable of type `StudentRec` has, so a reference to `StudentBody[Index]`.Major makes sense. There are a couple of things we might do to make the above segment a bit prettier. First, we could try to conduct all three tests in a single compound condition. This would avoid the nesting of three conditional statements. Second, with all the repetition of the (record) name `StudentBody[Index]`, the reader should suspect that we can use a `WITH` statement. Many beginners pass on this opportunity because they think that `WITH` statements are for records and not arrays. They're right, but in this segment, we are dealing with records. So we could rewrite the above as

```
FOR Index := 1 TO Size DO                    (* Assume Index is
                                                of type CARDINAL *)
  WITH StudentBody[Index] DO
    IF (Major = ComputerScience) AND (Year = 4) AND
                                             (GPA >= 3.5) THEN
      SendMessage(StudentBody[Index])
    END (* IF *)
  END (* WITH *)
END;
```

Obviously, we have cleaned up this segment a great deal. However, the very careful reader might ask, "Is there any difference in efficiency between the evaluation of the three conditions as a part of three nested `IF` statements and as part of a compound condition?" This is an excellent question and in many cases, the answer is: "Yes. The nested `IF` statements are much more efficient." However, in Modula-2, the answer is no. Both versions are equivalent, so we prefer the second because of its syntactic simplicity. Why might the answer be yes in one language and no in another? The explanation is found in a notion called **short-circuiting** of Boolean expressions.

Suppose we have a compound Boolean condition `IF A AND B THEN . . . . .` Now, if the computer evaluates the condition A and finds it `TRUE`, it should then evaluate B to determine whether to take the action of the `THEN` clause. However, if the computer evaluates the condition A and finds it `FALSE`, then there is absolutely no reason for the computer to waste its time evaluating B. B's value is irrelevant. The `THEN` clause will not be executed regardless of B's value, because there is no way the compound condition can be `TRUE` once A's value is `FALSE`. Compilers that avoid evaluating subsequent conditions of a compound `AND` clause are said to short-circuit. Clearly, such compilers are more efficient than those that don't short-circuit, since they do not evaluate any unnecessary conditions. There is also a short-circuiting opportunity for compound `OR` clauses. If we have `IF A OR B THEN . . .` and A evaluates to `TRUE`, then again there is no reason to test B.

We hope the reader can see why short-circuiting compilers treat the nested `IF`s and the compound `AND` the same. Maybe it is easier to see why non-short-circuiting compilers behave differently on the above two constructs. For example, suppose there are 1000 students, 25 of them computer-science majors. Of the 25, suppose 5 of them are seniors. With the nested if construct, the first condition is tested 1000 times. Only

25 times does flow of control even get to the second condition. Of these 25 times, flow of control reaches the third condition 5 times. However, with a compound AND construct, a non-short-circuiting compiler would evaluate each of the three conditions 1000 times. In this case, it is clear that the nested IF construct is more efficient. Although all Modula-2 compilers short-circuit Boolean expressions, many compilers for other languages do not. It is important when programming on different systems to determine whether the compiler short-circuits, so that efficient constructs can be used. One simple way to test whether a compiler short-circuits is to execute a segment like

```
X := 0;
IF (2 > 3) AND (5 / X > 0) THEN .....
```

A short-circuiting compiler will not attempt to evaluate the second condition (since the first is FALSE), while a non-short-circuiting compiler should produce a run-time error (division by zero) when it attempts to evaluate the condition $5/X > 0$.

FILES

Readers familiar with other high-level languages (especially Pascal) might expect to see a discussion of files at this point. In many real-world applications using a large number of records, an array of records stored internally in the computer's memory is not practical. A business with millions of customers may not be able to fit all its customer information into the memory of its computer. And since this information is of a permanent nature, the business would need some way to store it on a secondary storage device, like a disk. In many programming language environments, files are arrays of records stored on a disk. Modula-2, unfortunately, doesn't support such a general file structure. Files in Modula-2 are of two types, text files (discussed in Chapter 6) and binary files. The discussion of binary files is not particularly appropriate for a beginning course, since it deals with bytes and requires a fairly low-level point of view (low-level referring to the representation of information in a computer).

Each implementation of Modula-2 contains a FileSystem library. The following list includes some typical routines that one could expect in such a library:

```
PROCEDURE Create
PROCEDURE Delete
PROCEDURE Rename
PROCEDURE Open
PROCEDURE Close
PROCEDURE Reset
PROCEDURE SetPos
PROCEDURE ReadWord
PROCEDURE WriteWord
```

The effects of Create, Delete, and Rename should be obvious, so we'll describe typical behavior for the other procedures. Once a file exists, it must be opened before we can process information in the file. Once we are finished working with a file, we should close it—this protects the integrity of the information on the file. Closing a file might prevent the accidental loss of some information (which could occur in transferring information from the computer to the disk in the disk drive).

The next two procedures are concerned with the type of access we are allowed with files. All file systems support a sequential access capability. With sequential access, we must look at the information as it is stored on the disk, byte after byte. A Reset procedure positions us at the beginning of the file so that we can begin processing. Some file systems provide for a random access (also called direct access) to information. In such a system, if we know that we are interested in the 10th piece of information, we can set the position of the file marker to that position and process that information (without examining the first nine pieces of information, which is what a sequential system would do). Finally, the two basic operations that one does with files is to read from a file (extract information from the file) or write to a file (put information into a file).

In a general setting, a FileSystem library equips us with the capability to have files of records. We could have a file StudentBody that contains, on disk, information of the type we have been working with in this chapter. After creating such a file (with, of course, Create), we could Open the file, Reset it (if necessary—some Open procedures perform a Reset for us), and then get in a processing loop where we enter all the information on each student from the keyboard. As we enter it, we store it in the fields of a record variable. Once this variable has all its fields filled with information, we would Write that information to the disk (as opposed to writing it to the screen, for example). Once we have finished entering all the data, we Close the file.

Now, suppose we wanted to send our message to the senior computer-science majors with grade point averages of at least 3.5. We would Open the file (we don't need to create it), Reset (if necessary), and Read from the file the complete information on a single student. This information would be stored in a normal record variable. We would then examine the appropriate fields of the record (i.e., the Class, GPA, and Major fields) to decide whether that student gets a message or not. We would continue doing this until we reached the end of the file (the FileSystem library would provide a system variable for detecting this, as it does with Done in the context of text files). This is an example of sequential file processing.

As an example of random-access files, suppose we wanted to examine the grade point average of the student who is the 20th student in the list of all students. With sequential processing, we would need to get in a processing loop and execute 20 times the reading of a complete student record from the file into the memory of the computer. After this loop stopped, we would have the record of the 20th student, so we could examine the GPA. However, with a random-access capability, we could set the position (SetPos) of the file marker directly at the 20th record, read only that record into the computer, and examine the GPA. Random access is important because the transfer of information from a disk into the memory of a computer is generally thousands of times slower than transferring information internally in the computer.

In principle, file manipulation is not difficult if one learns the basic manipulations, as we have outlined them. The algorithms that use file information need to get information from the disk inside the memory of the computer before it is examined and/or modified. So once we know how to transfer information from the computer to the disk or from the disk to the computer, the programs that we need to write don't require any special file handling routines.

EXERCISES

11.1 Write a program that initializes an array of 10 student records as outlined in the text. Enter the students in alphabetical order by last name. Print out a table of the students in alphabetical order.

11.2 Add a procedure to the program of Exercise 11.1 to print out all computer-science majors with a GPA of 3.5 or better.

11.3 Add a procedure to the program of Exercise 11.1 that prints all students, ordered by grade point average.

11.4 Add a procedure to the program of Exercise 11.1 that prints all students alphabetically, by class. That is, print all the freshmen (in alphabetical order), then the sophomores, the juniors, and the seniors.

11.5 Using the FileSystem library for your particular implementation of Modula-2, repeat the above exercises, but store all the student information in a file on disk.

11.6 If your system supports random-access files, selectively modify the grade point average of student number 2.

Chapter 12

PONTERS AND LINKED LISTS

In this chapter, we'll introduce another type that is available in Modula-2, the **pointer** type. As the chapter title implies, we are also going to discuss **linked lists**. Pointers are used to build linked lists. What are linked lists? For now, just think of them as an alternative to arrays. Why do we need another alternative to arrays? Well, arrays have several inherent weaknesses. In the context of this chapter, we consider two such weaknesses:

1. Arrays are static data structures.
2. It is difficult to insert a new item into an ordered array and maintain the ordering.

The first weakness we have mentioned before. It simply means that we must specify the size of the array before we ever use it. We must decide, as we are writing a program, how big an array should be. To be sure that we can handle all possible cases, we are forced into using a worst-case scenario. For example, if we want to write a program that will sort student names and grade point averages, the first question we should ask, if we intend to use arrays, is: "How many students must we be able to handle?" Suppose the answer is 1000. Then we should define types and declare variables of size 1000. Such variables will claim storage for 1000 data items, even if we execute our program on a set of data for 100 students. Such a waste of storage can become critical if we have too many such variables. We may run out of memory and be unable to execute our program, even though the amount of actual data may easily fit into memory. We will see later in the chapter how a linked list is a **dynamic** data structure, able to grow and shrink to the desired size. Such a dynamic data structure makes much more efficient use of available memory.

To understand the second problem with arrays, suppose we have the following list of numbers stored in increasing order in an array:

| 203 | 218 | 225 | 234 | 278 | 298 | 305 | | |

These values might represent the number of favorable outcomes of an experiment that was conducted 1000 times on each of seven days. Now suppose we conduct the experiment an eighth time, this time obtaining 229 favorable responses. We would like to place the 229 into the array, but in its correct position: between 225 and 234. Of course, there is no room between 225 and 234. What we need to do is similar to what we did in the case of the insertion sort. We first need to find the correct position for 229 and then slide all those values larger than 229 one position to the right. Recall that the efficient way to do this is to start by comparing the largest values in the array to the target that we are trying to insert. Whenever we find a value that is less than or equal to our target, we can stop sliding and insert the new value. For example, if $Size$ represents the current size of the array (in the above case, $Size$ is 7), $Target$ represents the new item to be inserted, and $Outcome$ is the name of the array, the following segment will insert the target value properly:

```
Outcome[0] := Target;                (* Place the target in the *)
                                     (* bottom of the array. *)
Index := Size;              (* Start at the top and work down. *)
WHILE Outcome[Index] > Target DO
  Outcome[Index + 1] := Outcome[Index]        (* Slide up, *)
                                              (* if necessary. *)
END;
Outcome[Index + 1] := Target;   (* Insert Target one position *)
                (* above the value that stopped the sliding. *)
```

We put the $Target$ in the zeroth component of the array to be sure that there is something there that will stop the downward search. The actual data values are stored in the array beginning at the first component. We do this to avoid a subscript-out-of-bounds error if we try to insert a value that is smaller than all the values already present in the array. While this is an efficient way to insert values into an ordered array while maintaining the order, in some sense the whole idea is somewhat inefficient. For example, if we are using the computer to simulate experiments, it might be possible to generate thousands and thousands of outcomes. As the array gets very large, the amount of work we do to find the correct place to insert the new value also gets very large. Each time we get a new outcome, we need to slide, on the average, about half of the values to get the new value correctly inserted. Then, the next insertion might require us to slide most of those same values another position to the right.

So, although the array is a very useful data structure, it does have some weaknesses that linked lists can overcome. The purpose of this chapter is to show how linked lists can be used as an alternative to arrays. Simply stated, there are times when arrays are better than linked lists, times when linked lists are better than arrays, and times when a combination of the two structures is most appropriate. A programmer who knows about many different kinds of data structures can choose the right structure for the right application. Linked lists will be introduced after we discuss the syntax of pointers.

THE POINTER TYPE

As its name implies, the purpose of a pointer variable is to point to something. In fact, pointers point to other memory locations. You may wonder why we might need to do this. We ask for patience here, because, frankly, it doesn't make much sense to use pointers unless we are creating linked lists or some other more advanced data structure. But it is a bit early in the chapter to deal with linked lists, so we are going to discuss pointers independently of linked lists so that we can introduce the syntax and manipulation of pointers. That is, we are now going to see how pointers work. Once we get to the linked-lists section, we'll be able to see why pointers are useful.

Let us declare some pointer variables. Consider the following type definition:

```
TYPE Student = RECORD
                 Name  : String30;
                 Class : CARDINAL;
                 GPA   : REAL
               END;
```

Now consider the following variable declarations:

```
VAR Ptr1, Ptr2 : POINTER TO CARDINAL;
        Ptr3   : POINTER TO REAL;
        Ptr4   : POINTER TO Student;
```

Each of `Ptr1`, `Ptr2`, `Ptr3`, and `Ptr4` are pointer variables. Although they are all pointers, they are not all of the same type. As might be guessed, `Ptr1` and `Ptr2` are of the same type, but `Ptr3` is of a different type, and `Ptr4` is of yet another type. When such variable declarations are encountered, the compiler sets aside storage for each of these pointers. So, in the above situation, the compiler sets aside storage for four pointers. The compiler *does not* set aside storage for two CARDINAL values, one REAL value, and one `Student` record. We have not declared any CARDINAL, REAL, or `Student` variables—we have declared pointers to such variables.

What kind of storage does the compiler set aside for pointers? Actually, the compiler reserves enough storage so that a pointer variable can contain an **address**. That is how pointers work: **Pointers really are addresses**. For example, if `Ptr1` contains the value 1000, then we should find a CARDINAL value stored at memory location 1000. If `Ptr4` contains the value 2000, then we should find a student record (containing a student name, class designation, and a grade point average) stored at memory location 2000. Actually at memory location 2000, we would find the beginning of a student record—storing all the information would require many more locations than just the memory cell with address 2000. Although the pointers declared above are not all of the same type, they essentially all look alike: They all hold addresses. What makes them different is how the computer interprets the information found at those addresses.

Manipulating Pointers

The key to understanding pointers lies in making the distinction between two pieces of information—the value of the pointer itself and the value of the memory location referenced by the pointer. In Modula-2, the pointer's value is referenced just like the value of any other variable—we simply use the name of the pointer. To reference the value that is stored in the address indicated by the pointer, we use the caret symbol, ^, following the name of the pointer. Thus, `Ptr1^` is the CARDINAL that `Ptr1` points to.

For example, suppose that `Ptr1` contains the value 1000 and that memory location 1000 contains the value 7. Moreover, suppose that `Ptr2` contains the value 2000 and that memory location 2000 contains the value 10. Then, we have the following picture:

```
     Ptr1          Ptr2            1000          2000
   ┌──────┐      ┌──────┐        ┌──────┐      ┌──────┐
   │ 1000 │      │ 2000 │        │  7   │      │  10  │
   └──────┘      └──────┘        └──────┘      └──────┘
```

This is more commonly depicted as

```
   Ptr1 ------> ┌──────┐
                │  7   │
                └──────┘
   Ptr2 ------> ┌──────┐
                │  10  │
                └──────┘
```

Notice that in the second picture, we have no indication of what addresses are actually involved. In general, when we program in a high-level language, we don't need to know what specific locations the computer is using to execute our programs. Again, this is the beauty of high-level languages—we give names to the quantities that we want to deal with, and it is the compiler's responsibility to keep track of what is actually happening inside the computer's memory.

Now consider the following statements:

```
WriteCard(Ptr1, 0);   (* Illegal !!! *)
WriteCard(Ptr1^, 0);
```

As indicated, the first statement is illegal, because `Ptr1` is not a CARDINAL variable. It is a pointer to a CARDINAL variable. The second statement is legal and, upon execution, would cause a 7 to be printed. The second statement does not ask that the value of `Ptr1` be printed, but that the value of the memory location referenced by `Ptr1` be printed. Since `Ptr1` references memory location 1000, the contents of that memory location are printed.

To really understand pointers, you must understand the difference between the following two examples. In each example, we begin with this picture:

```
   Ptr1 ------> ┌──────┐
                │  7   │
                └──────┘
   Ptr2 ------> ┌──────┐
                │  10  │
                └──────┘
```

Example 1:

```
Ptr2 := Ptr1;
WriteCard(Ptr2^, 0);
```

Example 2:

```
Ptr2^ := Ptr1^;
WriteCard(Ptr2^, 0);
```

While both examples produce the same output—the value 7—their effects are very different. The first example results in the following picture, since it changes pointer values:

The effect of the second example, since it deals with contents, is

```
Ptr1 ------>  7
Ptr2 ------>  7
```

It is extremely important to understand why the examples produce the pictures indicated. In example 1, the statement

```
Ptr2 := Ptr1
```

is an *assignment involving pointers*. The value of Ptr2 is being changed. That is, we are making it point to something else—namely, whatever Ptr1 is pointing to. In English, the statement could be translated as: "Make Ptr2 point to the same thing that Ptr1 does." On the other hand, the assignment statement

```
Ptr2^ := Ptr1^
```

does not change pointers at all, but rather *CARDINAL values*. It changes the value Ptr2^; that is, it changes the value in the cell referenced by Ptr2. In English, it reads: "Give the value in the cell pointed to by Ptr2 the same value that is in the cell pointed to by Ptr1." If you understand the distinction between the two examples, mastering pointers should be easy. In the first example, there is still a 10 in memory, but neither pointer points to it. Rather, they both point to the same 7. In the second case, the pointers point to different locations, but both locations have the value 7.

The next question is: How do we get a picture like this in the first place?

```
Ptr1 ------>  |   7   |
Ptr2 ------>  |  10   |
```

Again, when we declare pointer variables, the compiler reserves storage for the pointers themselves. That is,

```
VAR    Ptr1, Ptr2 : POINTER TO CARDINAL;
```

reserves storage for `Ptr1` to hold an address and for `Ptr2` to hold an address. The compiler does not reserve any memory for holding CARDINAL values. The targets of pointers are created *dynamically*: The computer gives us locations for CARDINAL values when we need them. This dynamic creation of memory is the result of the built-in operation `NEW`, which can be used with any pointer type. So, we can have the following sequence:

```
NEW(Ptr1);
NEW(Ptr2);
NEW(Ptr3);
NEW(Ptr4);
```

The effect of `NEW(P)`, where `P` is a pointer, is as follows: Storage of the type pointed to by `P` is set aside in the computer's memory, and the value of the pointer `P` is set to the address of this storage. In other words, the compiler sets aside storage of the correct type and makes `P` point to this storage area. So, in the first statement above, a memory location for storing a CARDINAL value is set aside, and `Ptr1` is made to point to this location. Similarly, the fourth statement above causes memory to be allocated for the storing of a complete student record (e.g., name, class, GPA), and `Ptr4` then points to this. So, a picture of the effect of the above might be

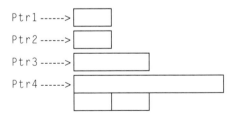

We drew the first two boxes alike, since both represent storage for a CARDINAL. The picture for `Ptr3`'s target is different (and larger), since computers typically require more memory to store REAL numbers than to store CARDINALs. The picture for `Ptr4`'s target attempts to show the structure of the student record—a string of 30 characters, a CARDINAL value, and a real GPA.

   Notice that all the boxes above are empty. We have not given any values to the targets
of the pointers. We have only allocated the storage. However, the following statements
would fill the boxes as indicated:

```
Ptr1^ := 7;
Ptr2^ := 10;
Ptr3^ := 3.5;
Ptr4^.Name := 'Joe College';
Ptr4^.Class := 2;
Ptr4^.GPA := 3.2;
```

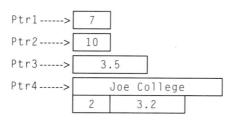

   Again, notice that assignments are made to the targets of the pointers—e.g., `Ptr1^`—
and not to the pointers themselves. That is because we wanted to change the values in
the boxes, and we weren't trying to change any of the arrows pointing to the boxes. Also
notice that `Ptr4^` is a record, so we use it just like any other record—we assign values
to its fields by using the dot notation.
   Given the previous picture, suppose we execute the assignment statement

```
Ptr2 := Ptr1;
```

This is a change to the pointers (i.e., this changes the arrows), and the picture now looks
like this:

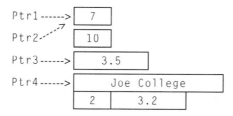

Notice that the box containing the value 10 is dangling there, without any arrows
pointing to it. Such a memory cell is now worthless—we can't get to it because it has
no arrows pointing to it and also because it doesn't have a name. Unlike the memory
locations allocated through the declaration of normal variables (i.e., nonpointer
variables), storage allocated with the NEW operation doesn't have a name attached to
it. We can get to such storage only through the name of the pointer. Once the pointer

connection is broken, that storage is inaccessible and, in fact, is referred to as **garbage**. How can the computer reclaim that storage for something useful? Well, the computer can perform an operation called **garbage collection**. However, garbage-collection algorithms tend to be complicated and costly. Responsible programmers can alleviate the garbage-collection problem by using the DISPOSE operation. DISPOSE is something like the opposite of NEW. If P is a pointer variable, DISPOSE(P) has the effect of breaking the connection between the pointer P and its target and returning the target memory to the computer for other use. If, as in the above example, we really wanted Ptr2 to point to the same memory cell as Ptr1, the following sequence would accomplish this without leaving the garbage cell containing the value 10:

```
DISPOSE(Ptr2);
Ptr2 := Ptr1;
```

Note that any reference to Ptr2^ after the first statement above and before the second statement would be meaningless. After the first statement, Ptr2 isn't pointing to anything, so Ptr2^, the target of Ptr2, has no meaning until the second statement establishes the connecting arrow between Ptr2 and the cell containing the value 7.

Before we look at linked lists, we'll mention a special value that can be assigned to any pointer variable. This value is the NIL value and indicates that a pointer is, in fact, not pointing to anything. Assigning a pointer the value NIL is similar to initializing a counter variable to 0. We will see how the NIL value is used in the next section.

LINKED LISTS

The use of pointers as described in the preceding section is not very common or very practical. In this section, however, we are ready to see how the pointer type is really used—as a method for building linked lists. As mentioned at the beginning of the chapter, arrays have two weaknesses—their static nature and the difficulty encountered when inserting a value into an array that is already ordered. The previous section has hinted at how pointers, with the NEW and DISPOSE operations, give us some dynamic memory-allocation capabilities. When we use pointers with linked lists, we get a data structure that also overcomes the insertion problem.

An advantage of arrays is that they are a direct-access structure. We can access any component of any array at any time simply by referencing the subscript. One of the things that makes arrays direct-access structures is that consecutive components of an array are stored in consecutive memory locations. If we could look into the memory of the computer, we would see that the fourth component of an array is stored right after the third component. The careful reader should realize that this feature of storing consecutive components in consecutive memory locations—i.e., the feature that makes an array a direct-access data structure—is also what forces an array to be a static structure. We must know ahead of time how much space to reserve for an array, so that we can put all the components next to each other. We wouldn't be able, for example, to reserve memory for the first 50 components of an array, only to realize later that we need another 50 components. If we tried to allocate storage as we needed it, it might be difficult to get component 51 adjacent to component 50 (if, for example, we have already allocated the memory right after component 50 for some other purpose, since originally we thought we only needed 50 components). However, if we drop the requirement that we have a direct-access structure—i.e., we don't necessarily require adjacent elements of a list to occupy adjacent locations in the computer's memory— then we can build a dynamically allocated data structure. This is how a linked list works.

A linked list may hold structured information, just as an array does. However, there is no requirement that consecutive pieces of information must occupy consecutive memory locations. For example, suppose we want to print out a list of senior students in descending order of grade point average. Further, suppose that the information regarding these students is stored in a file, where the information on each student is maintained as a record defined earlier in this chapter. Assume we know that there are 1000 student records in the file. Now, suppose we attempted to print the list using an array. How big does the array need to be? It only needs to be as big as the senior class. But how big is that? 250? 300? 500? If we have no way of knowing, we have to guess and hope we guess big enough. Five hundred would probably be a safe guess, but likely much too high. Anyway, we could read the records, one after the other, and each time we encounter a senior, we could place his or her record into the array of seniors, inserting it into the proper array position as we go. We would do this as outlined in the beginning of the chapter, by sliding those records already in the array with lower grade point averages further into the array. Again, the reason for all this work is that we are insisting that, upon completion, the student with the highest grade point average should occupy the first component of the array, the second highest student should occupy the next component, and so on.

It doesn't really matter how the information is stored in the computer, as long as we can accomplish our assigned task, i.e., print out a list of seniors in the proper order. It turns out that we can in fact accomplish our task, even if the data are stored in the computer in an apparently helter-skelter fashion. All we need is some information that tells us how to find the next student in the list. For example, if we have just printed out the name and GPA of the 25th best student, all we need to know is the location of the information of the 26th best student. It is not necessary that the information on the 26th best student be adjacent to the information on the 25th best student in the computer. All we need is a bit of extra information (a pointer!) stored with the 25th best student that tells us how to find the information on the 26th best student.

A linked list is simply a collection of information, most generally records, where each record contains an extra field, a link field, that points to the next record in the list. The records in a linked list are usually referred to as **nodes**. A node of a linked list is usually broken into two parts—the information field and the link field. The information field consists of the information that we wanted to store in the first place. In our example, that is the name and GPA of the student. The link field is the extra information, the pointer, that we need to locate the next node in the list. Consider the following two pictures of the GPA list:

The assumption here is that the individual records are on a file in alphabetical order. How might we arrive at the array picture? With lots of sliding! First, Ruthane Bopp's record comes in and occupies the first array position. Then, her record slides to position

Array:

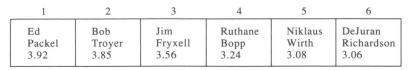

Linked list:

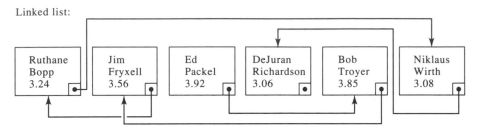

2 to make room for Jim Fryxell. Then, Ruthane's slides to position 3, Jim's to position 2, and Ed's to position 1. DeJuran's record is inserted without any work, but Bob Troyer's causes lots of sliding again. Finally, DeJuran's slides out of the way to make room for Niklaus.

Now let's consider the work involved in building the linked list. First, Ruthane's record comes in. Then Jim's is placed after Ruthane's, but we also keep a pointer with Jim's record that points to Ruthane's record to indicate that it follows Jim's. Then Ed's record is placed into memory, with a pointer to Jim's record. When DeJuran's record is entered, Ruthane's pointer is set to his. When Bob's record is processed, his pointer points to Jim's record, and Ed's pointer is changed from Jim's to Bob's. Finally, Ruthane's pointer is made to point to Niklaus's record, while Niklaus's pointer points at DeJuran's record.

The above paragraph may sound confusing, but it isn't, really. We encourage the reader to draw the evolution of both lists, the array and the linked list. With the array, each time a new student is encountered, place that information in the zeroth box, then slide necessary information to the right until the new information is placed appropriately. With the linked-list approach, each time a new student is encountered, place that information into the next box, and update the appropriate arrows. What you should see for yourself is that the second approach involves a lot less work—the only things that change are the arrows. We never need to move names and GPAs around.

We have omitted two important details from the linked-list picture. If we just look at the picture, how do we know who is first? It would be nice if there were a special pointer, let's call it First, that pointed to Ed Packel's record. Second, if all the information that we store in the list is uniform—that is, each node looks, in form, exactly like every other node—then to whom does DeJuran's pointer point? If DeJuran is last, his pointer shouldn't point to anyone. So the link field of DeJuran's node should be NIL. In the next section, we'll get much more precise as we look at a careful Modula-2 implementation of these ideas. We hope this narrative discussion has given you the idea of what we try to do with linked lists.

LINKED LISTS IN MODULA-2

In this section, we develop Modula-2 segments that enable us to build and print an ordered linked list. Variations on the ordered linked list are explored in the exercises at the end of the chapter. For simplicity, we continue with the example of the previous section, where we have six simple records containing a name and a grade point average. We will enter the names and averages in alphabetical order, store the information in a linked list ordered by grade point average, and then print the contents of the list.

The basic information that we want to store can be defined as a record:

```
TYPE Student = RECORD
              Name : RECORD
                     First : String15;    (* Assume String15 *)
                     Last  : String15   (* type definitions. *)
                     END;
              GPA  : REAL
              END;
```

Now, if we were proposing an array solution, an array of these records would be sufficient for our purposes: Each component of the array would store one student record. However, since we intend to use linked lists, each node in the list needs an extra field, the link field, that points to the next item in the list. So, the nodes of our list will contain more than the student record above. What should the type of the link field be? Obviously, it should be a pointer. But when we define pointers, we must tell what type of object they point to. The link field will *not* be a POINTER TO Student. The link field should point to the next node in the linked list —and we just remarked that the nodes of the list are not Student records, but Student records with a link field. So what we really need to do is define a type corresponding to the nodes of our list. **The following attempt is close, but incorrect**:

```
TYPE Node =  RECORD
             Info : Student;
             Link : POINTER TO Node           (* Illegal forward
                                                   reference *)
             END;
```

Again, the idea above is the right one—we want our link fields to point to nodes in our list, and these nodes all have link fields. The reason this definition is illegal is that while we are trying to define the Node type, we define a field called Link, which is a pointer to something of type Node. But the compiler doesn't know what a Node is, because it hasn't been defined yet. One way to avoid the reference to Node in its definition is to try to give Link a type name first. So consider the following attempt:

```
TYPE   NodePointer = POINTER TO Node;         (* This forward *)
       Node        = RECORD                 (* reference is OK! *)
                     Info: Student;
                     Link: NodePointer
                     END;
```

We have now removed the reference to Node that appeared inside the definition of Node. Unfortunately, we are now referring to Node even earlier. Although there appears to be the same problem of referring to the type Node before it is ever defined, Modula-2 allows this forward reference. The *definition of pointers to types* is the one place that Modula-2 allows reference to a type that has not yet been defined. It is necessary for the language to make an exception somewhere, because—as the two examples above show—something has to come first. Also, it knows how much memory to allocate for a *pointer*, since that is only an address, even if it doesn't yet know what a node is.

Now that we have defined our node type, what variables do we need? If this were an array solution, we would need to declare an array capable of holding all the student records involved. However, with the dynamic capability of linked lists with pointers, all we need to do is inform the compiler that we want to create one list. We do that by declaring a variable of type NodePointer. We call this variable List, since it will mark the beginning of the list. Each node in the list will point to the subsequent node in the list. The nodes that occur in the list will be created dynamically by the NEW operation. Recall that NEW takes a pointer as input, creates a node of the appropriate type, and then makes its input pointer point to that new node. Since List should always point to the first node, we don't want List to be used with NEW. So, we need another auxiliary pointer, called P, that will be useful for creating new nodes.

Building the list consists of two basic steps. First, we need to create a new node and fill it with the appropriate information. Then, we need to insert the node into its proper place in the list. The first step is easy. Assuming that P is of type NodePointer, the following statements create a node and fill its information field:

```
NEW(P);
WriteString('Enter First Name: ');
ReadString(P^.Info.Name.First);
WriteLn;
WriteString('Enter Last Name: ');
ReadString(P^.Info.Name.Last);
WriteLn;
WriteString('Enter GPA: ');
ReadReal(P^.Info.GPA);
```

After execution of the above statements, P would be pointing to a newly created node containing a name and a GPA. Of course, the node that P is pointing to has one other field, the link field, which also needs to be set appropriately. This is really more of step 2, where the node gets correctly inserted into the list. Specifically, the link field of this new node needs to point to the node that should follow it. We somehow must determine which node that is. Also, the node that precedes this new node must have its link field adjusted to point to this new node. Again, we must find out which node that is.

There are two special cases that we mention now and emphasize again, once we write the Modula-2 statements. What if this new node is last? Then, its link field should be set to NIL—it points to nothing because there is nothing following the node. What if the new node is first in the list? Then, there is no node ahead of it whose link field should point to it. Still, there is a pointer that should point to this new node, namely List.

Next, we discuss how to traverse a list. We again compare this situation to the array situation. Suppose we had an array A of student records and we wanted to count the number of students who had perfect 4.0 GPAs. Then, we could write

```
Count := 0;
Index := 1;
WHILE Index <= Size DO
   IF A[Index].GPA = 4.0 THEN
     Count := Count + 1
   END; (* IF *)
   Index := Index + 1
END; (* WHILE *)
```

We could have used a FOR loop, but a WHILE loop gives a better analogy to list processing. With a linked list, we need to do essentially the same things: Start at the beginning of the list, march through the list looking at the GPA in each node, and stop when we get to the end of the list. But linked lists are not direct-access structures, and we can't use a subscript. The way a list is processed is by using a pointer that points to the nodes in the list one after the other. Suppose this pointer is P. Then, how do we make it point to the first node in the list (analogous to the statement Index := 1)? With the statement

```
P := List;
```

This is an assignment between pointer variables—it says, "Make P point to the same thing that List points to."

The most important statement in this sequence to understand is the one analogous to Index := Index + 1. That is, how do we get P to move through the list? Well, suppose P is pointing to a node, and we wish to make it point to the next one:

Clearly, we must make an assignment to P, because in the pictures above, the only thing that changes is P's value; i.e., what P points to. We want P to point to the node on the right. But nodes in linked lists don't have names—we can refer to them only through pointers. And what pointer is pointing to the target node in the first picture? The link field of the node being pointed to by P. So, the linked-list analogy to Index := Index + 1 is the statement (crucial for the reader to understand):

```
P := P^.Link
```

The above statement says, "P should point to the same thing that the link field, in the node pointed to by P, points to."

To count perfect GPAs using linked lists, we now need to know how to stop our list traversal. In the array solution, we stop when Index exceeds Size. But linked lists are dynamic, so how do we know when we are at the end? Well, P takes on the values, in turn, of each of the link fields in the nodes of the list. As we remarked earlier, the link field of the last node is NIL. When P takes on this value, it means that P was just pointing to the last node, and so the processing should stop. Thus, a linked-list version that counts perfect GPAs is

```
Count := 0;
P := List;
WHILE P <> NIL DO
  IF P^.Info.GPA = 4.0 THEN
    INC(Count)
  END; (* IF *)
  P := P^.Link
END; (* WHILE *)
```

We can also use the above technique to look at the grade point averages in the list to determine where new nodes should go in the list. So, we are almost ready to implement a Modula-2 solution to the ordered linked-list problem. We have one final detail to consider: Once we know where the new node should go, how do we adjust all the necessary pointers to effect a correct insertion into the list? And there is a subtle difficulty with this. Suppose the current node we are creating has an associated GPA of 3.5. How do we determine its correct location? As suggested above, we have a pointer P march through the list, and we examine the GPA field of each node that P points to. Notice that we will determine the proper position for the new node as soon as we find a GPA that is smaller than (or equal to) 3.5. In other words, P will move one node beyond the correct position for the new node—we should insert the new node before the node P is pointing to. See the diagram below (where we display only the GPA field of the Student record):

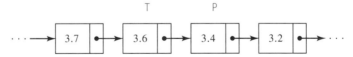

Now, the new node's link field should point to the same node that P is pointing to. That is easy enough to accomplish. But the link field of the node before P's node should be made to point to the new node. How do we do that, since we can't use names, only pointers? The solution is that we need another pointer, called T, that trails behind P. Then, when we find the appropriate insertion point, we'll have pointers to both the node that is to be before and the node that is to follow the new node. Again, there are some special cases that we need to consider for an insertion at the very front or the very rear of the list. We'll discuss these cases in the Modula-2 segments themselves.

Listing 12.1 contains a complete program that builds an ordered linked list from data entered from the keyboard. The list is then printed. The program OrderedList is an important example of linked-list processing and you should study it carefully.

```
MODULE OrderedList;

  FROM InOut IMPORT WriteLn, WriteString, Write, Read, ReadString;
  FROM RealInOut IMPORT WriteReal, ReadReal;

  TYPE      String10 = ARRAY[0..9] OF CHAR;
            Student  = RECORD
                          Name : RECORD
                                    First : String10;
                                    Last  : String10
                                 END;
                          GPA  : REAL
                       END;
         NodePointer = POINTER TO Node;
         Node        = RECORD
                          Info : Student;
                          Link : NodePointer
                       END;

  VAR List : NodePointer;          (* Pointer to the beginning *)
                                              (* of the list. *)
       P    : NodePointer;         (* Auxiliary pointer for *)
                                       (* creation of nodes. *)
       Resp : CHAR;

  PROCEDURE PrintList(P : NodePointer);
  (* This procedure prints out the information stored in the list
  Pre:   P points to the first node in the list of Student records.
  Post: The contents of the list are printed.               *)

  BEGIN
    WriteString('List by Grade Point Average');
    WriteLn;
    WHILE P <> NIL DO
      WriteString(P^.Info.Name.First);
      Write(' ');
      WriteString(P^.Info.Name.Last);
      WriteString('  ');
      WriteReal(P^.Info.GPA);    (* Could use WriteRealPretty *)
                                          (* from Ch 7. *)
      WriteLn;
      P := P^.Link                        (* Advance P. *)
    END (* WHILE *)
  END PrintList;
```

```
PROCEDURE Insert(VAR List : NodePointer; P : NodePointer);
(* Pre:List points to a list ordered by GPA, and P points to a
node to be inserted.
Post:  The node pointed to by P is inserted into the list in its
proper position.                                                *)

VAR  S : NodePointer;               (* S is the pointer that *)
                                    (* searches the list. *)
     T : NodePointer;              (* T is the pointer *)
                                    (* that trails behind S. *)


BEGIN
  S := List;                       (* S starts at the beginning. *)
  WHILE (S <> NIL) AND (S^.Info.GPA > P^.Info.GPA) DO
    T := S;                         (* Move T to where S is. *)
    S := S^.Link        (* Move S to next node in the list. *)
  END; (* WHILE *)
```

(* When the WHILE loop terminates, T and S mark the nodes that should
be before and after the new node. If the new node is first in the
list, S will still be equal to List. This case is handled differently
from all other cases, since the value of List needs to be updated.
That is why List is a VAR parameter to the procedure.   *)

```
    IF S = List THEN                    (* Insertion at front. *)
      P^.Link := List;            (* The new node's link should *)
                                        (* point to the old *)
      List := P                   (* front, while List points *)
                                        (* to the new front. *)

    ELSE
      P^.Link := S;                     (* Set new node's link *)
                                        (* to its successor *)
      T^.Link := P                (* and set its predecessor's *)
                                        (* link to it. *)

    END (* IF *)
  END Insert;

BEGIN
  List := NIL;                     (* The list starts out empty. *)
  REPEAT
    NEW(P);                               (* Create new node. *)
    WriteString('Enter first name: ');(* Fill its infomation *)
                                          (* fields. *)
    ReadString(P^.Info.Name.First);    (* Link field will be *)
                                          (* adjusted *)
    WriteLn;                        (* in the Insert procedure. *)
    WriteString('Enter last name: ');
```

```
      ReadString(P^.Info.Name.Last);
      WriteLn;
      WriteString('Enter GPA: ');
      ReadReal(P^.Info.GPA);
      WriteLn;
      Insert(List, P);                        (* Insert new node into
                                          (* its proper position. *)
      WriteString('Are there more names to process? (Y/N) ');
      Read(Resp); Write(Resp);
      UpCase(Resp)
    UNTIL Resp = 'N';
    PrintList(List)
END OrderedList.
```

Listing 12.1

CONCLUSION

Some concluding remarks are in order. The reader should carefully trace the program on the entire set of data found earlier in the chapter. Note particularly how the correctness of the very first insertion depends upon the statement that initializes List to NIL in the main program. Also note how insertions at the beginning of the list and at the end are also taken care of, and note that insertions at the end do not require a special case in the code. Finally, consider the disaster that occurs if we reverse the order of the two assignment statements in either the THEN clause or the ELSE clause of the Insert procedure.

EXERCISES

12.1 Write a function CountNodes that accepts a pointer to a list and returns a count of the number of nodes in the list.

12.2 Write a procedure Delete(List, LastName) that deletes the node from the linked list List containing a given LastName. Use the DISPOSE operation to return the deleted node to the system.

12.3 Write an insertion procedure that always inserts at the beginning of a list. Print the contents of the list. Of course, the information will be printed in the reverse order of its insertion. Such a list is referred to as a **stack**, and the insert operation is called a **push**. Stacks are extremely important in many computer applications.

12.4 Write an insert procedure that always inserts at the end of a list. Such a list is called a **queue**. Like stacks, queues are very important data structures.

Chapter 13

RECURSION

Rather than presenting a new data type or data structure, this chapter introduces a new and powerful programming technique. To the beginner, recursion is not so much difficult as it is mysterious. Well-written recursive programs appear to do a great deal of work with very little effort. We urge the reader to trace carefully each of the programs in this chapter to understand where all the work is being done.

Recursion is a problem-solving technique in which a big problem is solved by breaking it down into smaller problems. Other problem-solving techniques use the same approach. What distinguishes recursion from these other techniques is that the smaller problem is, in fact, the same problem as the original problem! If we couldn't solve the original problem, how do we expect to solve smaller versions of the same problem? Well, we break them into smaller problems, too (but again, the same problem). The hope is that, eventually, the problems become so small that a solution is immediately obvious. The other hope is that we can piece the small solutions together in such a way as to obtain a solution to the big problem.

For example, consider the problem of sorting a large list of numbers. If we don't have any idea how to sort a list of numbers, one thing we could do is split the list in half. Let's give half the list to a friend. Now if we could sort the smaller list, and if our friend could also sort the other half, maybe we could see a way to put the two sorted halves together to form a complete sorted list. So, how do we sort our smaller list? Maybe we could split it in half and find another friend. Hopefully, our original friend could do the same thing. Still, we eventually have to face the problem of doing a sort. We can't avoid the problem forever by just making it smaller. But what if we made it so small that the list we finally tried to sort had only one number in it? Surely we could handle such a problem, and probably all our friends involved could, too.

This is the idea behind a well-known, very efficient sorting algorithm called the **merge sort**. It is much faster than any of the sorts discussed earlier in the book. The implementation of merge sort in Modula-2 is probably best left for a second programming course. Still, we hope that the idea behind recursion makes a bit more sense. And, at the end of the chapter, we'll discuss a different recursive sort that is also much faster than any of the earlier sorts we discussed (and is, in fact, faster than merge sort).

The first recursive example that we examine in detail is the **factorial** function. The factorial problem is easily (and more efficiently) solved without using recursion, and because of this, many teachers feel it shouldn't be presented as a recursion problem. However, the factorial is naturally defined in a recursive manner, and its recursive solution is simple enough that we feel it is an excellent first example of recursion.

Recall that the factorial of a positive integer n, written n!, is simply the product of all the positive integers from 1 up to n. So:

$$5! = 1 * 2 * 3 * 4 * 5 = 120$$

Often the definition n! = n * (n-1) * (n-2) * ... * 3 * 2 * 1 is used. While the meaning of this definition is pretty clear, it's certainly not a precise one from a rigorous point of view. After all, what does "..." mean? One way to define the factorial function rigorously is to use recursion. Just as solving a problem recursively means trying to solve smaller versions of the same problem, defining a notion recursively involves trying to define a concept in terms of itself. This certainly sounds like circular logic and, in fact, care must be taken with recursive definitions to make sure that they don't depend on circular logic. Likewise, when we write recursive programs, we'll need to take extra care to make sure the programs themselves aren't based on circular logic. If they are, they will work themselves into infinite loops.

So, how might a recursive definition of the factorial function be stated? Well, how can we define factorials in terms of smaller factorials? Let's take a specific example. If someone asked you to compute 10! and you were allowed to consult with other people who knew factorial values for numbers smaller than 10, with whom would you like to consult? How about the person who knows what 9! is? If you were told that 9! = 362,880, it would be pretty simple to answer that 10! = 3,628,800. That's because

$$9! = 1 * 2 * 3 * 4 * 5 * 6 * 7 * 8 * 9$$

and

$$10! = 1 * 2 * 3 * 4 * 5 * 6 * 7 * 8 * 9 * 10$$

Or, more succinctly, 10! = 10 * 9!. In fact, this last equation is pretty general:

$$n! = n * (n-1)! \text{ for any } n \geq 1$$

However, we can't quite take that as a complete definition of the factorial function. Suppose we told someone who had never heard of the factorial function the above definition and asked him or her to compute 3!. Then, the person could conclude that

$$3! = 3 * 2! = 3 * 2 * 1! = 3 * 2 * 1 * 0! = 3 * 2 * 1 * 0 * (-1!)$$
$$= 3 * 2 * 1 * 0 * (-1) * (-2!) = ...$$

and would never arrive at an answer. You might argue that the person should just stop with the realization that 1! = 1. But that wasn't part of the definition. Working only from the definition, the only logical conclusion is the one shown above. However, if we make 1! = 1 part of the definition, then we could get the correct answer, that 3! = 6. That is how we might define factorial. But, as a concession to mathematicians, we will use 0! = 1 as part of the definition. It happens that, in many formulas, it is convenient to have a value for 0!, and this convenient value is 1. So, a complete recursive definition of the factorial function follows.

Let n be a nonnegative integer. Then, the factorial of n, written n!, is defined by

$$n! = \begin{cases} 1 \text{ if } n = 0 \\ n * (n-1)! \text{ if } n > 0 \end{cases}$$

We saw in an earlier chapter how simple it is to compute the factorial of a number using an **iterative** approach; that is, an approach that repeatedly loops, performing the same operation—in this case, multiplication. The basic statements are

```
Fact := 1;                      (* Initialize running product to 1. *)
FOR Index := 2 TO N DO
  Fact := Fact * Index
END;
```

As we mentioned earlier, the recursive version is not as efficient as the iterative version above, but it is still simple enough that we present it as our first recursive program.

What makes a program recursive? It's really the procedures within a program that might be recursive, so a better question is: What makes a procedure recursive? A procedure is recursive if it calls itself. Actually, this is a definition of direct recursion. There is also the possibility of indirect recursion—procedure A calls procedure B, procedure B calls procedure C, and procedure C calls procedure A, for example. We deal only with direct recursion in this chapter. Recursive definitions define concepts in terms of themselves, and recursive procedures try to solve problems by calling themselves. Recursive definitions need a nonrecursive portion (e.g., 0! = 1), and recursive procedures also need a nonrecursive option. In other words, if procedure P can execute only by making a call to procedure P, we will have an infinite loop on our hands, because each time we enter P, it will call itself again. There must be some way to execute a recursive procedure without it invoking itself again. This option is usually called the **trivial case**. In fact, the basic structure of a recursive procedure looks very much like the above recursive definition of the factorial function—there is a nonrecursive (trivial) case, and all other cases (the recursive part).

Listing 13.1 contains a program that calculates the factorial of a CARDINAL typed in from the keyboard. After the above discussion, the program itself should look very natural. Nonetheless, it is worthwhile to discuss how the program actually works.

```
MODULE RecFact;

  FROM InOut IMPORT WriteLn, WriteString, WriteCard, ReadCard;

  VAR N : CARDINAL;

  PROCEDURE Fact(N : CARDINAL) : CARDINAL;
  (* Pre:  N contains a value that will not result in factorial
           overflow.
   Post:    This function returns the value of N!              *)

    BEGIN
      IF N = 0 THEN
        RETURN 1
      ELSE
        RETURN N*Fact(N-1)
      END (* IF *)
    END Fact;

BEGIN                                      (* Main module. *)
  WriteLn;
  WriteString('Enter a nonnegative integer smaller than 9: ');
  ReadCard(N);
  WriteLn;
  WriteString('The factorial of ');
  WriteCard(N, 0);
  WriteString(' is ');
  WriteCard(Fact(N), 0);
  WriteString('.')
END RecFact.
```

Listing 13.1

The main body of RecFact is completely straightforward. The only interesting thing it does is invoke the recursive function procedure Fact. It is the operation of this procedure that is important. Let us trace this procedure with original input 3. When we enter the procedure, N is set equal to 3. We execute the IF-THEN-ELSE, taking the ELSE clause, since the condition is FALSE. The ELSE clause begins calculating a product where the first factor is 3. The second factor will be the result of the procedure call Fact(N-1). So, execution of the original call to Fact is suspended, and execution of the second call to Fact is initiated. In this case, the input is 2 (i.e., N-1 where N is 3), so N is initialized to 2. It is important to realize that this is a different N, one that is local to the inner call. With recursion, each time we enter a procedure, we usually want a new, local copy of all the variables. That way, we can manipulate them in inner procedure calls without disturbing values that belong to outer environments. So, a good rule of thumb for recursion is that parameters are usually value parameters.

This second invocation of Fact again takes the ELSE clause and calls Fact a third time with initial value 1. `Fact` is called a fourth time with initial value 0; so, finally, the `THEN` clause is executed and an invocation of `Fact` terminates. It is this fourth call that terminates, carrying back the value 1 (as specified by the `THEN` clause) to where it was called—namely, in the computation of the product in the third call. So now the third call can finish its multiplcation, terminate, and return a 1 (1 * 1) to the second call. This call can now also complete its multiplication (since it now knows what `Fact(1)` is) and terminate, returning a 2 to the original call. This original call can now finally complete the computation that it started long ago, obtaining a value of 6. This is returned to the main program, and printed, and then execution terminates. The sequence of calls is demonstrated in Figure 13.1.

```
MAIN N = 3

    Fact(3) =
           3 * Fact(2)

        Fact(2) =
               2 * Fact(1)

            Fact(1) =
                   1 * Fact(0)

                Fact(0) = 1
                        ┐
        Fact(1) =       ↓
                1 * 1 = 1
    Fact(2) =   ↓
           2 * 1 = 2
Fact(3) =   ↓
       3 * 2 = 6

MAIN--Output is a 6
```

Figure 13.1

Why so much discussion for such a simple process (which is more easily accomplished using iteration)? First of all, this example shows all the features of recursion: the recursive case, the necessary trivial case to prevent an infinite loop, the importance of scope rules that provide us with local copies of important variables. But, also, this example points out one of the weaknesses of recursion. There is an awful lot of work that goes on behind the scenes. Although the `Fact` procedure is very short, the computer is pretty busy keeping track of all the local variables and the locations of all the subroutine calls. So, in most cases, when there is a choice between a recursive solution and an iterative solution, the iterative solution tends to be much more efficient. And, in fact, if there is a recursive solution to a problem, there will be an iterative one as well. So why even bother with recursion? Well, there are many problems for which the recursive solution is extremely natural and very elegant, while an iterative solution is much more difficult and elusive. In fact, many important computer applications are of this variety. Although our next example is not a real-world computer application, it is one of our favorites, because it demonstrates so well a problem whose recursive solution is almost too simple and whose iterative solution is very complex.

THE TOWERS OF HANOI

The Towers of Hanoi is a puzzle dating back to ancient times. Figure 13.2 illustrates the puzzle, in which one must move the tower of disks from peg A to peg C subject to the following two restrictions:

1. Only one disk can be moved at a time.
2. A disk can never be placed on top of a smaller disk.

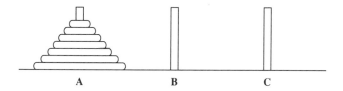

Figure 13.2

We will write a recursive procedure that solves the Towers of Hanoi puzzle. Specifically, we will write a procedure Hanoi that has four inputs: the number of disks involved, the starting peg, the finish peg, and the auxiliary peg. The output for the procedure will be the move-by-move sequence that solves the given problem. For example, if we have three disks on peg A that we want to end up on peg C, where peg B is used as a temporary storage area, the call would look like this:

```
Hanoi(3, 'A', 'C', 'B')
```

and the output would look like this:

```
Move Disk 1 from peg A to peg C.
Move Disk 2 from peg A to peg B.
Move Disk 1 from peg C to peg B.
Move Disk 3 from peg A to peg C.
Move Disk 1 from peg C to peg A.
Move Disk 2 from peg B to peg C.
Move Disk 1 from peg A to peg C.
```

It is not obvious how to write the Hanoi procedure. However, if we try to think recursively, we may be led to a surprisingly simple solution. And what is amazing is that we can write the Hanoi procedure that solves the problem for us even though we still might not be able to solve a Towers of Hanoi problem ourselves! (However, at the end of this section, we'll tell how it's done.)

Thinking recursively means trying to see how to solve the problem by tackling smaller versions of the problem. So let's think about a problem with seven disks, a somewhat standard number of disks on most commercially sold puzzles. (See Figure 13.2.) Let's not even worry about what moves we need to make to solve such a puzzle.

Let's just picture various phases during the solution. In particular, if we need to move the original tower from peg A to peg C, at some point we must move disk 7, the largest disk, from A to C. Of course, since that disk cannot sit on top of any other (restriction 2), then all the other disks must be on peg B. In what configuration will they be on peg B? Obviously, restriction 2 again tells us that they are in the same configuration (largest on bottom, smallest on top, etc.) as they were originally on peg A. See Figure 13.3.

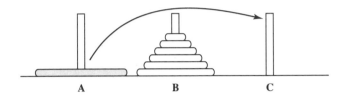

Figure 13.3

Now, before moving disk 7 from A to C, imagine that disk 7 doesn't even exist. Then, arriving at the configuration just described is equivalent to having solved the puzzle with six disks, except that the finishing peg is peg B, instead of peg C. Now, let's suppose we have moved the large disk 7 from A to C. (See Figure 13.4.) What must we now accomplish to complete our solution? All we need do (pretend the seventh disk is invisible again if that helps) is solve the six-disk problem, only this time our starting peg is B and our finishing peg is C. What we have shown is that to solve the seven-disk puzzle, we essentially need to solve the six-disk puzzle twice (moving disk 7 between those two solutions). Looking at things from a positive perspective, we can also say that *if* we can solve the six-disk puzzle, then we can solve the seven-disk puzzle.

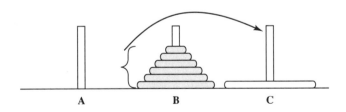

Figure 13.4

So, we've made our problem smaller. How do we solve the six-disk puzzle? Using the same reasoning, if we can solve the five-disk puzzle a couple of times, then we can solve the six-disk puzzle. We do need to be a little careful about starting pegs and finishing pegs. For example, to solve the six-disk puzzle from A to B (the first half of solving the seven-disk puzzle), we should

1. First solve the five-disk puzzle from A to C
2. Move disk 6 from A to B
3. Solve the five-disk puzzle from C to B

We hope the reader is catching on now. We still need to figure out how to solve the five-disk puzzle. But that is easy if we can solve the four-disk puzzle. How long can we keep going on? Let's look for a trivial case. Although the three-disk puzzle is pretty easy (we just indicated a solution a few paragraphs back), and the two-disk puzzle even easier, surely most people would find a one-disk Towers of Hanoi problem pretty simple. Hand them a puzzle and say, "Move the disk from peg A to peg C," and most people would probably solve this problem by moving the disk from peg A directly to peg C (without violating either of the two restrictions)! Thus, the one-disk puzzle becomes our trivial case, and, taking care with starting and finishing pegs, we have the recursive procedure of Listing 13.2.

```
PROCEDURE Hanoi(N : CARDINAL; Start, Finish, Aux : CHAR);
(* This procedure is a recursive solution to the Towers of Hanoi
Puzzle.
Pre:   All the parameters have values.
Post: A move-by-move solution of the Tower of Hanoi puzzle is
printed when the tower of disks begin on peg Start and end on peg
Finish.                                                      *)

   BEGIN
     IF N = 1 THEN                    (* For the trivial case, *)
                                      (* just move the disk! *)
       WriteLn;
       WriteString('Move Disk 1 from peg ');
       Write(Start);
       WriteString(' to peg ');
       Write(Finish);
       Write('.')
     ELSE
       Hanoi(N-1, Start, Aux, Finish);       (* The Aux peg for the
                                      (* original problem is the Finish *)
                                      (* peg for the smaller problem. *)
       WriteLn;
       WriteString('Move Disk '); (* Now move the largest disk. *)
       WriteCard(N, 0);
       WriteString('from peg ');
       Write(Start);
       WriteString(' to peg ');
       Write(Finish);
       Write('.');
       Hanoi(N-1, Aux, Finish, Start) (* Solve the smaller problem
                                  (* again. Now the disks start out *)
                          (* on the original problem's Auxiliary peg. *)
   END (* IF *)
END Hanoi;
```

Listing 13.2

We strongly urge the reader to trace carefully the above procedure with three disks and see how the output described earlier is produced. It is also very instructive to trace the procedure with three disks, when the starting peg is still A, but the finishing peg is B instead of C. One convenient way to trace the program is to draw a tree (lying sideways) indicating the procedure calls. Such a tree is shown in Figure 13.5 (with abbreviated output).

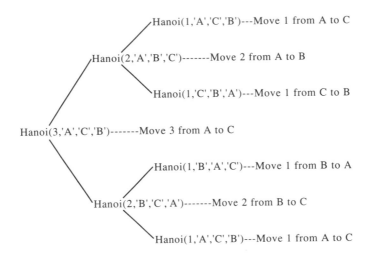

Figure 13.5

Now that you know how to solve the Towers of Hanoi puzzle, what would you do if someone handed you a seven-disk puzzle and asked you to show your stuff? You could try the recursive version, but most humans, unlike computers, don't have a good enough memory to actually attack the problem that way. To do that, you would need to solve the six-disk puzzle, move the seventh disk, then remember your moves for the six-disk puzzle and repeat them again, of course adjusting for the different designations of starting, finishing, and auxiliary pegs. A truly recursive version would solve the six-disk puzzle the same way—i.e., solve the five-disk puzzle, and then remember and repeat those moves after moving the sixth disk. To do it the human way, run the recursive program to get the answer for the seven-disk puzzle, stare at the solution, and see if you can detect a pattern. Then, follow this pattern without thinking. In case you don't see the pattern, we'll tell you what it is:

Move the smallest disk on every other move. Always move the smallest disk in a circular fashion. That is, when it is on peg A, move it to peg B. When it is on peg B, move it to peg C. When it is on peg C, move it to peg A. What about the moves involving disks other than the smallest one? On each such turn, there will only be one legal move. Make that move, then go back to moving the smallest disk.

Some ancient religions used the Towers of Hanoi to predict the end of the world. According to legend, there is a palace where monks work day and night solving a puzzle that consists of 64 golden disks. When the puzzle is completely solved, the world will end. Without giving a mathematical derivation, we state that an n-disk puzzle requires $2^n - 1$ moves. So, for $n = 3$ we need 7 moves, and for n = 64 we would need $2^{64} - 1$ moves. How big is this number? Well, if the monks could move a disk each second, it would still take them more than 250 billion years to complete the puzzle. That's pretty reassuring (as long as they didn't start too long ago).

To appreciate the power of recursion and the naturalness of recursion for this problem, we encourage the reader to consider a nonrecursive solution to the Towers of Hanoi problem.

PRINTING A LINKED LIST IN REVERSE ORDER

Now we give an example of recursion involving linked lists. We consider the problem of printing the information in a linked list in reverse order. That is, we print the information in the last node of the list first, the information in the next-to-last node second, ..., the information in the first node last. Although we are doing this example for practice, there are times when programmers actually need to do this. Lists of numbers stored in numeric order often need to be processed both in ascending and descending order.

How might we solve this problem recursively? Again, we need to figure out how to relate this problem to a smaller problem. If we had a list with 10 nodes in it, think of what it looks like printed in reverse. What we have is the information in the last node printed, followed by the reversal of the list just consisting of the first nine nodes. Although this approach can lead to a recursive algorithm for solving the problem, it's not the simplest. Following this approach, we would have a strategy like this:

1. Print information in the Last node.
2. Print information in reverse of first part of the list (all but the last node).

The second part above is the recursive feature. But the complications lie with the first part. With linked lists, we don't have easy access to the last node. We would need to traverse through the list until we get to the end. Let's try the same approach, except that we'll try to make use of the fact that we can access the first node of a list easily.

So, instead of picturing the reverse printing of the list as "the last node followed by the reverse of the first nine," let's look at it as "the reverse of the list consisting of nodes two through ten, followed by the first node." Then our strategy becomes

1. Print information, in reverse, of the list that starts with the second node.
2. Print information in the first node.

Since the first part involves the recursive idea, we see that we can accomplish it recursively as well:

1. Print information, in reverse, of the list that starts with the third node.
2. Print information in the second node.

What is the trivial case for this algorithm? A first guess might be a list with only one node, since printing that list in normal fashion is equivalent to printing it in reverse. However, we can't tell, without doing a little work, whether a list has only one node or more than one node. So we suggest a simpler trivial case—the empty list. That is, a list with no nodes is also easy to print in reverse order—don't print anything! We prefer this case to the one-node case since we can tell, by looking at the pointer to the beginning of the list, whether or not the list is empty (the list pointer will be NIL in this case). So, the procedure of Listing 13.3 accomplishes what we want. We assume that variables of type NodePointer are pointers to generic nodes, which contain an information field and a link field. We also assume the existence of a PrintInfo routine that performs the obvious task.

```
PROCEDURE RevPrint(List : NodePointer);
(* This procedure uses recursion to print a linked list in reverse
order.
Pre:   List points to the head of the list.
Post: The information field of the nodes are printed in reverse
order.                                                         *)

  BEGIN
    IF List <> NIL THEN
      RevPrint(List^.Link);
      PrintInfo(List^.Info)
    END (* IF *)
  END RevPrint;
```

Listing 13.3

Some remarks are in order. First, notice how simple the procedure appears. It is essentially the Modula-2 translation of our English strategy: If the list is nonempty, print its tail in reverse order, then print its head. Where is the trivial case in this procedure? It doesn't appear explicitly, because we don't need to do anything in the trivial case. That is, if the list is empty, the conditional test fails and the procedure terminates without doing anything.

The last remark we'll make concerns a common error in these types of situations. Many programmers, particularly beginners to recursion, mistakenly use a WHILE loop instead of an IF-THEN construct. The urge to do this is understandable—programmers feel the need to do something several times instead of just once, so they want a repetitive construct like the WHILE. The reader should execute the above procedure on a short list with a WHILE loop to see that an infinite loop results. Certainly, if List is not NIL upon initial entry to the procedure, it never will be (nowhere is the value of List changed), so the procedure will just keep executing. The repetition in the correct version doesn't come from the IF-THEN, but comes from the sequence of procedure calls—that is, RevPrint calling itself within the THEN clause.

QUICK SORT

We close the chapter by providing a sort routine that uses recursion and executes much more quickly than any of the sort routines we have considered. The sort is called quick sort (developed by Anthony Hoare), and, on random data, it is generally the fastest of all known sorts. To see how much faster quick sort is, the reader should race it against a sort like insertion sort on an array of size 1000.

The basic idea behind quick sort is a **pivot**. To perform a pivot, we select a pivot element and then adjust the data so that the following conditions are satisfied:

1. The pivot element is in its proper place in the array.
2. All items smaller than the pivot element occur in the array before the pivot element. All items larger than the pivot element occur in the array after the pivot element.

In other words, the pivot element is in its correct position and all other items are correct *relative* to the pivot element. For example, suppose we have an array with values:

33 57 48 37 12 92 86 25

If we choose 33 as the pivot element and perform a pivot, the array might look like this:

25 12 **33** 37 48 92 86 57

We say *might* look like this, because there is no requirement as to how the elements larger (or smaller) than 33 must be arranged. We must only ensure that the elements larger (or smaller) come after (or before) 33. So, another legal picture of the array is

12 25 **33** 57 92 37 48 86

Where does recursion fit in? Well, now that 33 is in its proper place, it naturally divides the array (let's use our second picture) into two halves, the subarray 12 25 and the subarray 57 92 37 48 86. Since these are correct relative to 33, if we could sort these individually, the entire array would be sorted. How do we sort these small arrays? Let's try the same approach. Let's choose the first element in each of those as pivot elements, perform a pivot, and obtain

12 25 **33** 48 37 **57** 92 86

Now, 33 originally divided the array into two pieces, a left half and a right half. Likewise, we can think of 12 as dividing the left half into two pieces. The first fourth of the array is empty and the second fourth contains 25. Similarly, 57 has divided the right half of the orginal array into two pieces, 48 37 and 92 86. Both the first fourth and the second fourth of the array are now easy to sort—they contain zero and one element, respectively. Hence, we have arrived at the trivial case for those pieces. We could next perform a pivot on 48 37, using 48 as the pivot element, and on 92 86, using 92 as the pivot element. After these pivots, which conceptually divide each fourth of the array into two pieces (eighths), all the pieces are so small that sorting becomes trivial (in fact, the array would now be sorted). This is the idea behind quick sort.

To repeat the basic approach, we perform a pivot. With each pivot, we get an element in its correct position with everything else positioned correctly relative to the pivot element. Thus, the pivot element splits the array into two smaller pieces, and we attack those pieces with the same strategy. If we really wanted to fine-tune our quick sort approach, we could get sophisticated about how we choose the pivot element. However, for our purposes, quick sort works just fine if we choose the first element of the array for the pivot element.

Our first task is to write a `Pivot` procedure. This procedure needs to move the pivot element to its correct position and also move the other elements of the array, if necessary, to the correct side of the pivot element. Consider the following array:

35 27 88 13 65 72 54 19 6 95

Our pivot element is 35. Where should 35 go? We can see that it belongs in the fifth position. We could scan the array to determine that and swap the 35 and the 65. Then we would need to pass back through the array adjusting anything that is out of place relative to 35. The first item we would see would be 65 (since it traded places with 35). It needs to move to the right of 35, but where? Actually, anywhere to the right is fine. But we need to make a place for it. Obviously we don't want to trade 65 with something else bigger than 35, or we won't have made much progress. So, it seems as if we should find something to the right of 35 that is smaller, and trade that with 65. This is the essential idea behind a pivot, but one of the tricks of quick sort is to do all of this data movement efficiently. So, we improve on the idea and give the following strategy:

1. Move 35 to a temporary location. (Note that this effectively frees the first position in the array.)
2. Since the first position should hold a small element (relative to 35), let's scan downward from the top of the array until we find something smaller than 35 (in our example, the 6). Let's move that element to the position 35 held, and remember with an arrow where we stopped.

$$\longleftarrow \quad \text{Temp}$$

6 27 88 13 65 72 54 19 **6** 95   35

3. Now the ninth position is effectively free and is ready to hold something larger than 35. So let's scan from the bottom this time, until we find something (88) bigger than 35, and move it to position nine. Again, we remember where we stopped.

$$\longrightarrow \qquad\qquad \text{Temp}$$

6 27 **88** 13 65 72 54 19 88 95   35

4. Now position three is free (even though the 88 is still there), so let's do what we did in step 2, but starting from where we last stopped. We find the 19, which is less than 35, and move it left.

<pre>
                                          ←———— Temp
         6 27 19 13 65 72 54 **19** 88 95   35
</pre>

5. Now we repeat step 3, working our way up through the array (again, from where we stopped), looking for an element larger than 35 to place where the 19 (upper 19) used to be.

<pre>
         ————————————→   Temp
         6 27 19 13 **65** 72 54 65 88 95   35
</pre>

6. Now we try to repeat step 2, but as we work down, we get to where we stopped on our upward swings before we ever find anything smaller than 35. This place happens to mark where 35 should be placed. So we store the value of Temp there.

<pre>
                      ←———————————— Temp
         6 27 19 13 35 72 54 56 88 95   **35**
</pre>

Our pivot is complete, since 35 is in the fifth place with everything smaller to the left and everything larger to the right. If we wish to attack the smaller arrays with the same Pivot procedure, the procedure essentially needs to know where the two smaller pieces of the array are. In our example, the left half of the array ranges from position 1 to position 4, while the right half ranges from position 6 to position 10. Observe that these bounds can be determined if we know the position of the pivot element (in this case, position 5). Thus, the Pivot procedure, in addition to doing the data movement, will also return the final resting place of the pivot element. With that lengthy explanation, we present in Listing 13.4 the procedure Pivot.

```
PROCEDURE Pivot( VAR A : ArrayType; Low, High : CARDINAL;
                VAR Pos : CARDINAL);
(* This procedure performs a pivot on the portion of the array A
beginning at position Low and ending at position High. The pivot
element is the first element of the array; i.e., the element at
position Low.
Pre:  A, Low, and High all have values.
Post: The pivot element, originally at position Low, is moved to
its correct position in the array, and all other elements in the
subarray from position Low to High are placed correctly relative
to the pivot element. Pos is given the value corresponding to the
new position of the pivot element.                              *)

VAR Temp : CARDINAL;
```

```
BEGIN
  Temp := A[Low];                       (* Store the pivot element, *)
                                        (* freeing its position. *)


  WHILE Low < High DO          (* Low works up, High works down.*)
                         (* When they meet, the pivot is complete. *)
    WHILE (Temp <= A[High]) AND (Low < High) DO
      High := High - 1                  (* Move High down until *)
                                        (* we find a small *)
    END; (* WHILE *)                    (* element or until *)
                                        (* High meets Low. *)


    IF Low < High THEN                  (* Did we find a small *)
                                        (* element? If so, *)
      A[Low] := A[High];                (* move it down and *)
                              (* start an upward scan. *)

      Low := Low + 1;

      WHILE (Temp >= A[Low]) AND (Low < High) DO
        Low := Low + 1                  (* Move Low up until *)
                                        (* we find a big *)
      END; (* WHILE *)                  (* element or until *)
                                        (* Low meets High. *)


      IF Low < High THEN                    (* Did we find a *)
                                   (* big element? If so, *)
        A[High] := A[Low];                (* move it up and *)
                               (* start another downward *)
        High := High - 1            (* scan, from the point *)
                                            (* where the *)
          END (* Inner IF *)     (* previous one stopped. *)
    END (* Outer IF *)

  END; (* Outer WHILE *)

  A[Low] := Temp;                       (* Low and High have met *)
                              (* where the pivot element *)
  Pos := Low                      (* belongs. Pos carries that *)
                                       (* value back to the *)
                                    (* module for subsequent *)
                                        (* calls to Pivot. *)
END Pivot;
```

Listing 13.4

The above procedure is probably the most complex one, logically speaking, of this
entire text. The nested structure of "WHILE inside IF inside WHILE" is necessary,

because we alternate downward swings and upward swings, but we don't know which kind of scan will be our last one. So we can't simply have one WHILE loop (say, the upward scan) follow the other (the downward scan). This procedure does perform the pivot rather efficiently, and the reader who can trace through this procedure can certainly lay claim to understanding the control structures of Modula-2.

We still aren't finished with quick sort. We need a recursive procedure that invokes the Pivot procedure. In our example, after the pivot, the array looks like this:

6 27 19 13 **35** 72 54 65 88 95

So, next, we should perform a pivot on the subarray 6 27 19 13 and the subarray 72 54 65 88 95. In general, knowing where the pivot element ended up (this is the purpose of Pos in the Pivot procedure) tells us where the next two pieces of the array can be found. Listing 13.5 demonstrates this idea with the recursive procedure QuickSort.

```
PROCEDURE QuickSort(VAR A : ArrayType; Low, High : CARDINAL);
(* This procedure calls Pivot, then uses the position of the pivot
element to recursively sort the array A.
Pre:   All the parameters have values.
Post:  The array A is sorted in increasing order.              *)

VAR Position : CARDINAL;

BEGIN              (* Trivial case--Low ≥ High--means we have an *)
   IF Low < High THEN(* array of size 0 or 1, so we do nothing. *)
      Pivot(A, Low, High, Position);     (* Perform the pivot. *)
      QuickSort(A, Low, Position - 1);   (* Left half goes up to
                                            Position - 1. *)
      QuickSort(A, Position + 1, High)   (* Right half begins at
                                            Position + 1. *)
   END (* IF *)
END QuickSort;
```

Listing 13.5

A main module containing QuickSort and Pivot would make an initial call of

```
QuickSort(A, 1, MaxSize);
```

where MaxSize is the upper bound on the size of the array A. Note that in our example, the QuickSort procedure, after performing the first pivot, would call QuickSort(A, 1, 4) and QuickSort(A, 6, 10). Let's consider the second of these calls to QuickSort. It would perform a pivot on positions 6 through 10 of A:

Before Pivot: 72 54 65 88 95

After Pivot : 65 54 72 88 95, Pos is 8

After this pivot is complete, it would call `QuickSort(A,6,7)` and `QuickSort(A,9,10)`, using *its values* for `Low` (`6`), `High` (`10`) and `Pos` (`8`).

By tracing a small, but complete, example, the reader should be able to see the magic of recursion taking over, sorting the entire array.

CONCLUSION

We conclude the chapter with some comments on the efficiency of quick sort. Note that if our pivot element ends up about in the middle of the array, then when we split the array into two pieces, each of those pieces is about half the size of the original. If we continue to get lucky (where the pivot element does end up near the middle), the entire sort process is controlled by how many times we can split an array in half. For example, an array with 1,000,000 elements can be split in half only 20 times before each piece is of size 1. So we see that quick sort can work very quickly on large arrays if the data are random—because with random data, we should expect to get reasonably lucky (i.e., the pivot element is likely to be about in the middle of the data). In fact, quick sort belongs to the class of algorithms denoted by O(NlogN) (see Chapter 10). For large N, NlogN is much smaller than N^2, which explains why quick sort outperforms the sorts discussed in Chapter 10. However, there is a drawback to quick sort if the data that we are trying to sort are nearly sorted. Then our pivots split the array into two unbalanced pieces, a very small piece and a very large one. The subsequent pivot on the large piece is likely to produce the same kind of splitting, so that for an array of 1,000,000 elements, we might need to perform nearly 1,000,000 pivots. In this situation, quick sort becomes one of the slowest sorts. But, as mentioned before, when sorting random data, quick sort tends to outperform all other known sorting algorithms.

EXERCISES

13.1 The greatest common divisor (GCD) of two positive integers X and Y is defined to be the largest positive integer that divides evenly into both X and Y. For example, GCD(21,15) = 3, GCD(22,15) = 1, and GCD(30,15) = 15. The Euclidean algorithm is a standard way of finding the GCD of two integers. The Euclidean algorithm essentially says: Divide Y into X where Y is the second of the two numbers. (Usually, Y is the smaller of the two numbers, but this is not necessary.) If Y divides evenly into X, then GCD(X,Y) = Y. If Y does not divide evenly into X, take the remainder and divide it into Y. If that division is not even, divide the second remainder into the first remainder. Continue this process until a division operation has a remainder of 0. The divisor for the last division is GCD(X,Y).

The following two statements give a nice recursive formulation of the Euclidean algorithm. Use these to write a recursive function to compute the GCD of two integers. Test your function on several pairs of cardinals by writing a main program that asks for two cardinals from the keyboard and computes their GCD.

1. GCD(X,Y) = Y if X MOD Y = 0
2. GCD(X,Y) = GCD(Y, X MOD Y) if X MOD Y ≠ 0

13.2 Multiplication can be defined recursively. That is, x * y = x if y = 1, and x * y = x * (y - 1) + x if y > 1. Write a procedure that multiplies recursively. Note: This is not an appropriate use of recursion from an efficiency standpoint. The ability to define multiplication recursively is important in areas related to logic and the foundations of mathematics. So, while meaningful from a theoretical point of view, such a formulation is of little practical value (unless the multiplication operation is broken on your computer).

13.3 The Fibonacci sequence is defined as follows:

1, 1, 2, 3, 5, 8, 13, 21, 34, 55, ...

The sequence begins with two 1s, and then each successive term is obtained by adding the previous two terms. Write both recursive and iterative procedures to produce a table of the first 25 Fibonacci numbers. Contrast the execution efficiency of the two algorithms. Why is one so much better than the other?

13.4 Wallalumps breed according to the following strange rules: One- and two-year old Wallalumps produce one child each. Three-year old Wallalumps produce two children each. Older Wallalumps do not bear children. Assuming that you begin with 10 one-year old Wallalumps and 10 two-year old Wallalumps and that no Wallalumps die, write recursive and nonrecursive versions of a program to count the Wallalump population for each of the next 10 years.

13.5 Write a main module that initializes an array of 1000 random CARDINALs. (See the discussion in the Bagels example of Chapter 7 for suggestions on generating random numbers.) Have this main module invoke both an insertion-sort routine and a quick-sort routine. Compare the time required for each to sort the array. Now try both sorts on an array that is already in order.

Chapter 14

SEPARATELY COMPILED MODULES

The separate compilation of modules is one of the most important aspects of Modula-2, athough the idea is not original with Modula-2. Indeed, FORTRAN has supported separate compilation since the 1950s, and this is often cited as one of the reasons for FORTRAN's longevity. Separate compilation is markedly different in Modula-2, however, from what it is in FORTRAN. FORTRAN does no parameter checking across compilation units, so you can declare a function Foo with three real parameters in one unit and invoke Foo in another unit with five integer parameters, and the FORTRAN compiler will not object—but your program will probably produce garbage. Modula-2 institutes ways for the compiler to continue its strong type checking across modules, even if they are separately compiled. Modula-2 does this by insisting that the definition module for Foo be compiled first; then, any module that implements Foo can (and will!) have its invocations of Foo checked to see that they have the correct number and type of parameters.

Separate compilation simply means that a large project can be broken into as many modules as you wish, and then each of these modules can be compiled by itself. As hinted above, certain modules that contain definitions will have to be compiled before other modules, but otherwise there are many orders in which the modules can be compiled. The advantages of separate compilation should be obvious. First, modules are like superprocedures and provide one more way to implement our divide-and-conquer problem-solving strategy. Second, suppose you have a 100,000-line payroll program with the social-security withholding rate at 7.15 percent, and you need to change this to 7.35 percent. If the program is one gigantic module, then you must find the correct location (hopefully, this is one line, a constant), change it, and recompile the entire program. Doesn't it seem unneccesary that all the procedures and functions, even those that have nothing to do with the social-security withholding rate, must be recompiled? If you have the program in several modules, then only the module that contains the constant must be changed and recompiled. In fact, in a large program, it might be wise to have a module that contains only such constants. This module would be easy to locate, modify, and recompile as necessary. Modules also provide an easy way for different people or teams of people to work on the same problem. We will discuss the details below, but if we agree that you will provide a procedure `Foo` with three real parameters that does so and so, then I can go off and use `Foo` just as if it were built in. Indeed, we will see that I import `Foo` exactly as I import `WriteCard`, except that I import it from your module instead of from `InOut`. Thus, separate modules also provide a means of **data abstraction** or **data hiding**. If I am not specifically concerned with the details of your `Foo`, I may never need to see them. As long as your `Foo` works as you promised, I need not be bothered with the details of your implementation. In fact, if you announce that you have a better (more efficient) implementation of `Foo`, then as long as you don't change the **public interface** to `Foo`, you can modify your module and recompile it. Except for enhanced performance, I will not know that you have changed `Foo`. By the public interface, we mean the way that `Foo` is invoked. If you change `Foo` so that it no longer takes three real parameters, then, of course, I will have to change my module and recompile it too. Hence, separate compilation of modules allows us to build our own libraries of useful functions and procedures. There is nothing to keep us from importing `Foo` into any module that we write—we can extend the system libraries in any way that we like. We can customize the language to our needs. As we begin a new project, we can import our favorite procedures and functions as easily as we now import `WriteCard` from `InOut`.

Thus, separate compilation is an invaluable tool for big programs. As we have admitted many times, there are no 100,000-line programs in this text. However, our objective is to illustrate the concept of separate compilation and to show you how the details of separate compilation are accomplished in Modula-2. While our examples are necessarily fairly small, we believe that the reader who stops to think about it will realize the power of the ideas expressed here. In fact, several of our short examples could be extended into useful modules, and we leave several such projects to the exercises.

KINDS OF MODULES

All the modules that we have seen in previous chapters have been **main** or **program modules**. Every executable collection of modules must have exactly one main or program module. Modules can be nested within one another. Such nested modules are called **internal**, **local**, or **nested modules**. This kind of module is discussed in Chapter 17. Here, we discuss **definition** and **implementation modules** used in separately compiled modules. Each separately compiled module, other than the main module, must have definition and implementation parts. The definition module is where the public information about the module is given. The definition module is really a promise about the objects defined in it. The implementation module contains the details and the actual implementations of these objects. This splitting of each separate module into two parts has two advantages. First, it makes the public part—the definitions—small and easy to understand, while keeping the messy details of the implementation in a separate, but easily found, location. Second, it allows the definition module and any modules that use it to be compiled before the implementation module is written! Of course, the main module won't run until all the implementation modules are written and compiled, but writing and compiling for error-testing can proceed on all other modules without waiting for the implementation module to be finished.

MODULES AND SOFTWARE ENGINEERING

To illustrate the power of these simple ideas, consider how a large, modern software project might be organized. First, the project manager and all the team leaders meet and design, in top-down form, the main module in pseudo-code. This is followed by the design of many definition modules that will be needed by the main module. The manager and the team leaders do not, however, need to worry at this time about the implementation details of the project. When there is agreement on the design, and it is stable, then the definition modules can be written and compiled. At this point, the main module can be written, importing what it needs from the system modules and the new modules. The main module can even be compiled! Now the design is complete and the teams can go their separate ways to write their implementation modules. As long as no changes are made to any of the definition modules, neither they nor the main module need ever be compiled again. This demonstrates what we have been preaching: "Time spent in planning is time well spent." If the manager rushes into some half-thought-out design, then later it is likely that many of the definition modules will have to be changed, causing changes and recompilation in other modules. But if a stable design is found, then any amount of modification at the implementation levels is no problem. Only the one implementation module in question will need to be modified and recompiled. Software engineering, simplified greatly here, studies methods for sucessfully implementing large programs and is a subject of great interest in computer science today. It is this modular approach to programming that both gives Modula-2 its name and makes it one of the most attractive languages available today.

THE ORDER OF COMPILATION

There are usually many orders in which the separate modules—main, definition, and implementation—that make up a large program can be compiled. Basically, the rule is simple: "Anything that uses anything else can be compiled when the *definition* module for that other thing has been compiled." Please note that only the definition module, not the implementation module, must be compiled before a module using that object is compiled. Also note that modules can import things from other modules. In that case, the definition module of the module that exports must be compiled before the implementation module of the module that imports. We can summarize this discussion as follows:

The order of compilation for separate modules is:

1. Definition modules are compiled first.
2. The main module can be compiled now or at any time later.
3. Any implementation module can be compiled when both of the following are true:

a. Its own definition module has been compiled.

b. The definition modules for anything it imports have already been compiled.

These rules should not be considered as arbitrary and need not be memorized by the reader. They simply state that the definitions must be compiled before the implementations. This is reasonable, if you realize that the definitions are needed to do the necessary type and parameter checking. After all, how can I check that your use of Foo is legal if you haven't compiled the definition of Foo yet?

MYINOUT: AN EXAMPLE OF SEPARATE COMPILATION

We begin with a very simple, but potentially very useful, example of a separately compiled module. Many programmers who are used to free-form I/O from other languages find the primitive I/O operations supplied in the library module InOut to be very restrictive. We will show how to develop a module MyInOut that contains extensions of the system's library routines. As such, MyInOut would be a good home for our WriteRealPretty of Chapter 7. As a simpler example, there are situations where it would certainly be useful to have a procedure PromptCard(S1, K) that would print the prompting message S1 and then read from the user a cardinal value and assign it to K. Or it would often be nice to have a WriteSCSLn(S1, K, S2) procedure that would write the string S1, the cardinal K, the string S2, and finally a new line. For example, assuming that NumSold is a cardinal, the statement

```
WriteSCSln("You sold ", NumSold, " widgets last week.");
```

produces one complete line of output, such as:

```
You sold 843 widgets last week.
```

Listing 14.1 shows the definition module for MyInOut. Notice that it is easy to recognize what it is because it begins with the keywords DEFINITION MODULE. Ignoring for a moment the EXPORT QUALIFIED comment, we see that the module simply consists of a list of procedure headings. Later we will see that a definition module can export types and constants as well as procedures and functions, but it is this very simple module's job to export the four indicated procedures. The EXPORT QUALIFIED statement is shown as a comment. In Wirth's original definition of Modula-2, this statement was required. Its job, obviously, was to list the objects that the module exported—and that could be imported by any other module. In Wirth's later definition of Modula-2, the need for an explicit EXPORT QUALIFIED was deleted from the language, and it was simply understood that all the objects defined in the module were available for export. Therefore, some Modula-2 compilers may still require the statement and others may not even permit it. You will have to check your manuals, ask your instructor, or try it out on your system to see how it works in your version of Modula-2.

```
DEFINITION MODULE MyInOut;

(* This module contains the definitions of several
new I/O procedures.                                                *)

(* EXPORT QUALIFIED PromptCardLn, WriteSCSLn, WriteStringLn,
                                        WriteFiveCards; *)
(* Some older Modula-2 compilers require the EXPORT QUALIFIED
statement. See the text for an explanation.                        *)

PROCEDURE PromptCard(S1 : ARRAY OF CHAR; VAR K : CARDINAL);
(* This procedure prints S1 as a prompt and gets K from the user.
Pre:   S1 has a string value.
Post: S1 is printed as a prompt and the CARDINAL value entered by
the user is stored in K.                                           *)

PROCEDURE WriteSCSLn(S1 : ARRAY OF CHAR; K : CARDINAL;
                     S2 : ARRAY OF CHAR);
(* Pre:  All three parameters have values.
Post:    The values of S1, K, and S2 are printed followed by a new
line.                                                              *)

PROCEDURE WriteStringLn(S1 : ARRAY OF CHAR);
(* Pre:  S1 has a string value.
Post:    The value of S1 and a new line are printed.               *)

PROCEDURE WriteFiveCards(K1, K2, K3, K4, K5, Width : CARDINAL);
(* Pre:  All six parameters have values.
Post:    Each of the five CARDINALs is written in a field of the
given width.                                                       *)

END MyInOut.
```

Listing 14.1

Again we point out that the definition module is the public portion of the separately compiled units. Anyone who has access to the above definition module can see that WriteFiveCards has six parameters and can see what their order is. A program that was producing a table might find such a procedure very useful.

MyInOut is very brief, but it will serve to illustrate our purpose. We admit that WriteFiveCards is pretty specific (and useless if you want to write four or six cardinals, or even five integers), but in the exercises you can add other objects to MyInOut.

The definition module, MyInOut, can now be compiled. Again, the details of compilation are system dependent, but this should be exactly like the compilation of a main program module, except that when you use the editor to create the definition module, you probably have to give it a different file extension. A common file extension for definition modules is **.def**, while for main and implementation modules, it is often **.mod**. We urge the reader to create the file My InOut . def, or whatever, and compile it now.

Listing 14.2 shows the outline of a program module, Main, that imports some of the objects of MyInOut, as well as objects from InOut.

```
MODULE Main;

(* This main module shows how to import from MyInOut.          *)

FROM InOut IMPORT WriteLn, WriteString;
FROM MyInOut IMPORT PromptCard, WriteFiveCards, WriteSCSLn;

VAR  ....

BEGIN
  ...
  PromptCard("How many widgets did you sell last week? ", NumSold);
  ...
  WriteSCSLn("You sold ", NumSold, " widgets last week.");
  ...
  WriteFiveCards(10, 20, 40, 80, 160, 8);    (* Use eight column
                                                fields. *)
  ...
END Main.
```

Listing 14.2

We have only outlined the module Main because it looks exactly like all the modules we have written in this book. The only difference is that it imports from MyInOut as well as from the system library. Main can now be compiled, and we urge the reader to complete the details of a file Main . mod, or whatever, and to compile that module. Of course, Main cannot be run because we have not yet defined the procedures promised in the definition module. The reader should begin to appreciate the work of the compiler and the linker. The compiler is translating our modules into computer form, and the linker is finding all the separate parts and binding them together, so that the whole assembly can execute as planned. The linker may need to find WriteLn from InOut and it may need to find WriteSCSLn from MyInOut. It might be instructive to see what error message you get if you try to link Main at this point. The system should bitterly complain about the absence of implementations for the objects desired from MyInOut.

Listing 14.3 shows the implementation module for MyInOut. Again, it is obvious from the keywords that begin the module that we are dealing with an implementation module. Note that this implementation module has the same name as the corresponding definition module. This tells the system that these are the two matching parts of one separate module. Also observe that an implementation module, like a main module, can import from other modules. In this case, the implementation module imports the primitive I/O operations from InOut that it will need to build up the I/O operations that have been promised. Indeed, except for the empty body of the implementation module and the keyword IMPLEMENTATION, the module of Listing 14.3 is identical to a program module. Implementation modules often do have empty bodies, but they need not be empty. An example later in this chapter will show the usefulness of bodies in implementation modules.

```modula2
IMPLEMENTATION MODULE MyInOut;

(* This module contains the implementation of the procedures
promised in the definition module of the same name.          *)

FROM InOut IMPORT WriteString, WriteCard, WriteLn, ReadCard;

PROCEDURE PromptCard(S1 : ARRAY OF CHAR; VAR K : CARDINAL);
(* This procedure prints S1 as a prompt and gets K from the user.

Pre:   S1 has a string value.
Post:  S1 is printed as a prompt and the CARDINAL value entered by
the user is stored in K.                                      *)

  BEGIN
    WriteString(S1);
    ReadCard(K)
  END PromptCard;

PROCEDURE WriteSCSLn(S1 : ARRAY OF CHAR; K : CARDINAL;
                     S2 : ARRAY OF CHAR);
(* Pre:  All three parameters have values.
Post:    The values of S1, K, and S2 are printed, followed by a new
line.                                                         *)

  BEGIN
    WriteString(S1);
    WriteCard(K, 0);
    WriteString(S2);
    WriteLn
  END WriteSCSLn;

PROCEDURE WriteStringLn(S1 : ARRAY OF CHAR);
(* Pre:  S1 has a string value.
Post:    The value of S1, then a new line, is printed.        *)

  BEGIN
    WriteString(S1);
    WriteLn
  END WriteStringLn;
```

```
PROCEDURE WriteFiveCards(K1, K2, K3, K4, K5, Width : CARDINAL);
(* Pre: All six parameters have values.
Post:   Each of the five CARDINALs is written in a field of the
given width.                                                    *)

  BEGIN
    WriteCard(K1, Width);
    WriteCard(K2, Width);
    WriteCard(K3, Width);
    WriteCard(K4, Width);
    WriteCard(K5, Width)
  END WriteFiveCards;

BEGIN                         (* Body of implementation module. *)
  (* Empty body. *)
END MyInOut.
```

Listing 14.3

We urge the reader to create a file My InOut . mod, or whatever, and to compile it. Then you can link the Main module with MyInOut (again, you will have to learn the particular details of how to modify your link command so that you link Main and MyInout). Now you can execute the main module in the normal manner. Except for some embellishments discussed below, that's all there is to separate modules! We can change the Main module by adding a line, and only it will need to be recompiled before we relink and run the new program. Likewise, if we discover a better way to implement one of the procedures, we would need to change only the implementation module and recompile it (relink on some systems, too) before running the updated program. However, if we make a change to the definition module, then we will also have to modify and recompile the implementation module, as well as recompilng the main module. This shows how critical it is to get the definition modules correct the first time.

A STRING PACKAGE

We have noted several times that the string type is not a first-class type in Modula–2. The interested reader is now in a position to do something about that by defining his or her own **string package**, by which we mean a separate module from which we could import a string type as well as various procedures and functions for manipulating strings. We suggest the definition module and leave most of the details of the implementation to the reader.

There are several ways to implement strings. We have chosen a representation that we think is quite easy to understand and manipulate. We emphasize, however, that our strings will not be compatible with an ARRAY OF CHAR and, thus, we cannot use the ReadString and WriteString of InOut with our strings. We shall, therefore, include I/O for our strings in our string package.

What is a string? Predominantly, it is an array of characters, but a string also has a length. Therefore, we shall use a record to define a string:

```
CONST SMax   = 80;                        (* String Maximum length. *)
TYPE STRING  = RECORD
                 Arr : ARRAY[1..SMax] OF CHAR;
                 Len : [0..SMax]
               END;
```

Our STRINGs will be arrays of 80 characters, as well as having a Len field that will tell us how many of the 80 characters are actually in use. We have chosen to set SMax to the arbitrary value 80, since that is the standard screen width on terminals today. Listing 14.4 contains the definition module for our string package, Strings. Note that the length of that listing is due mainly to the extensive comments. Since this is the public interface to our string package, it is important that the user be able to understand how each procedure or function is to work. Note that the comments Type, Func, and Proc let the reader easily see what kind of object is being defined. Even in Modula-2s that do not require an EXPORT QUALIFIED, it is certainly a good idea to list in a comment the objects available from this module for exportation.

```
DEFINITION MODULE Strings;
(* This module defines the public interface for a string package.
                                                                *)

EXPORT QUALIFIED    STRING,                          (* Type *)
                    Assign,                          (* Proc *)
                    PutString, GetString,            (* Proc *)
                    Length,                          (* Func *)
                    Concat,                          (* Proc *)
                    CR,                              (* Proc *)
                    Left, Right, Mid,                (* Proc *)
                    Pos,                             (* Func *)
                    UpCase, DownCase;                (* Proc *)

(* Above EXPORT statement needed by some Modula-2 compilers. *)

CONST SMax = 80;

TYPE  STRING = RECORD
                 Arr : ARRAY[1..SMax] OF CHAR;
                 Len : CARDINAL
               END;

PROCEDURE Assign(Lit : ARRAY OF CHAR; VAR S : STRING);
(* This procedure permits the assignment of a system string to one
of our STRING variables. For example, Assign("Hello world!", S)
assigns the character array "Hello world!" to S.Arr and the value
13 to S.Len.                                                    *)
```

```
PROCEDURE PutString(S : STRING);
(* This procedure writes out the value of the STRING S. It is called
PutString to avoid confusion with the WriteString procedure in
InOut.                                                            *)

PROCEDURE GetString(VAR S : STRING);
(* This procedure reads a string from the keyboard.              *)

PROCEDURE Length(S : STRING) : CARDINAL;
(* This function returns the length of the STRING S.             *)

PROCEDURE Concat(S1, S2 : STRING; VAR S3 : STRING);
(* This procedure concatenates STRING S1 and S2 together into STRING
S3. For example, "dog" concatenated with "house" is "doghouse." If
the length of the result is more than SMax characters, then the
result is truncated.                                             *)

PROCEDURE CR;                              (* Carriage Return *)
(* This parameterless procedure writes out a carraige return and
line feed. That is, it is the equivalent of WriteLn, but simpler
to type.                                                         *)

PROCEDURE Left(S1:STRING; LenSlice:CARDINAL; VAR S2:STRING);
(* This procedure puts the leftmost LenSlice characters of S1 into
S2. For example, if S1 is the string "doghouse" with length 8, then
Left(S1, 3, S2) assigns the string "dog" with length 3 to S2. If
LenSlice is greater than the length of S1, then Left assigns all
of S1 to S2.                                                     *)

Procedure Right(S1:STRING; LenSlice:CARDINAL;  VAR S2 : STRING);
(* This procedure puts the rightmost LenSlice characters of S1 into
S2. For example, if S1 is the string "doghouse" with length 8, then
Right(S1, 5, S2) assigns the string "house" with length 5 to S2.
If LenSlice is greater than the length of S1, then Right assigns
all of S1 to S2.                                                 *)

PROCEDURE Mid(S1 : STRING; StartPos  : CARDINAL;
                           LenSlice  : CARDINAL; VAR S2 : STRING);

(* This procedure puts the middle LenSlice characters of S1,
starting at the StartPos position, into S2. For example, if S1 is
the string "doghouse" with length 8, then Mid(S1, 2, 6, S2) assigns
the string "oghous" with length 6 to S2. If StartPos + LenSlice is
greater than the length of S1, then Mid is equivalent to a call to
Right.                                                           *)
```

```
PROCEDURE Pos(Pattern, Target : STRING) : CARDINAL;
(* This function searches the target string for the given pattern
and returns the index of the first occurrence of the Pattern in the
Target. It returns 0 if the Pattern is not found in the Target. For
example, if the Pattern is "is" and the target is "Mississippi",
then Pos would return 2. If the Pattern were "miss," then, with the
same Target, Pos would return 0.                                    *)

PROCEDURE UpCase(VAR S : STRING);
(* This procedure makes all the letters in S uppercase. It leaves
other characters (such as '3', '+', and '?' ) unchanged.         *)

PROCEDURE DownCase(VAR S : STRING);
(* This procedure makes all the letters in S lowercase. It leaves
other characters unchanged.                                        *)

END Strings.
```

Listing 14.4

Observe that the module Strings exports a new type, STRING (which we have arbitrarily chosen to capitalize), as well as various procedures and functions. Listing 14.5 outlines a main module that uses some of the objects from our string package. We leave it to the reader to determine what the segment does.

```
MODULE TryStrings;

FROM Strings IMPORT STRING, GetString, PutString, Concat, Assign;

VAR    FirstName : STRING;
       LastName  : STRING;
       FullName  : STRING;
       Title     : STRING;

BEGIN
   ...
   GetString(LastName);
   ...
   GetString(FirstName);
   ...
   Assign("Professor", Title);
   ...
   Concat(Title, FirstName, FullName);
   Concat(FullName, LastName, FullName);
   PutString(FullName);
      ...
END TryStrings.
```

Listing 14.5

Of course, the implementation module for Strings must still be written. We will set it up and do two of the procedures and functions, but leave the rest of the details to the reader in the exercises. The exercises also suggest other procedures and functions that could be added to the package.

Listing 14.6 contains the outline of the implementation module and the details of the Concat procedure and the Length function. Since its body is only one line long, let us first consider the Length function. The astute reader will observe that the user does not even need the Length function, since the expression S.Len can be used wherever the length of S is needed. While this is true, and it points out that the fields of a record are exported along with the record, it misses the main point: We are trying to produce a string package that will be easy and natural to use. Anyone with a little knowledge of Modula-2 will understand how to use the Length function. That person does not need to understand or even realize that we have implemented our strings as records. The user can import our STRING type and our Length function and use them without worrying about the details of the implementation. Again, this is the power of *data abstraction*. If the user had to know all the details about everything before beginning, very few programs would be completed. Furthermore, if we decide to change our STRING representation, then as long as we present the user with a STRING type and a Length function, the expression Length(S) will still make sense even if S.Len no longer does. Hence, Length is an execellent example of a useful one-line function. It hides the details of the implementation and gives the user a natural interface to the string package.

```
IMPLEMENTATION MODULE Strings;
(* This module contains the details of our string package.   *)

FROM InOut IMPORT Read, Write, WriteLn;            (* Needed in *)
                                                (* the exercises. *)

PROCEDURE Length(S : STRING) : CARDINAL;
(* Pre:  S has a STRING value.
Post:    This function returns S.Len.                       *)
   BEGIN
     RETURN(S.Len)
   END Length;

PROCEDURE Concat(S1, S2 : STRING; VAR S3 : STRING);
(* This procedure concatenates STRING S1 and S2 together into STRING
S3. For example "dog" concatenated with "house" is "doghouse." If
the length of the result is more than SMax characters, then the
result is truncated.
Pre:   S1 and S2 have STRING values.
Post:  S3 is assigned the result of concatenating S1 and S2. If the
result is more than SMax characters long, then the result is
truncated to SMax characters.                               *)
```

```
VAR  More  : CARDINAL;
     Index : CARDINAL;

BEGIN
  S3 := S1;              (* Copy all of S1 into the result, S3. *)


  (* Next, decide how much More of S2 will fit into S3. *)
  IF S1.Len + S2.Len <= SMax THEN        (* All of S2 fits. *)
    More := S2.Len;
    S3.Len := S1.Len + S2.Len
  ELSE                      (* The tail of S2 will be truncated. *)
    More := SMax - S1.Len;
    S3.Len := SMax
  END;  (* IF *)


  (* Now copy More characters from S2 to the tail of S3.   *)
    FOR Index := 1 TO More DO
      S3.Arr[S1.Len + Index] := S2.Arr[Index]
    END  (* FOR *)
END Concat;


(* * * * * * * * * * * * * * * * * * * * * * * * * * * * * *
   Details of other procedures and functions are left
   to the reader.
 * * * * * * * * * * * * * * * * * * * * * * * * * * * * * *)

BEGIN
  (*  Empty body of implementation module. *)
END Strings.
```

Listing 14.6

The procedure Concat is a little more complex, but is easy if taken in three stages. First, we copy all of S1 into S3. Then, we decide whether all of S2 will fit or whether truncation will have to occur to make the result fit into S3. For example, if we try to concatenate a STRING of length 50 with a STRING of length 40, we will only get the first 80 (SMax) characters of the result. Finally, we copy the appropriate characters from S2 into S3.

Note carefully that a procedure that defines a STRING S must place appropriate values in S.Arr and also in S.Len. For some reason, the beginner is apt to forget to assign an appropriate value to S.Len (even though that value is usually obvious). Please watch for and avoid this error!

Note that the CONSTants and TYPES defined in the definition module are available without further ado in the implementation module. That is, an implementation module does not need an explicit importation statement from its own definition module.

Wait a minute. A couple of paragraphs ago, we made a big deal out of using

Length(S) instead of S.Len, and then the body of procedure Concat is littered with expressions like S.Len. Is that not inconsistent? Well, actually not! Our point was that the user of our package would want to use Length(S) and not worry about how the STRING type was actually implemented. Concat, on the other hand, is a part of the implementation of the string package and, therefore, will not be seen by the casual user. It should be pointed out, however, that if Concat used Length(S) instead of S.Len, it would be more general, because it wouldn't need to be modified if we decided to modify our STRING type.

An implementation procedure can have its own variables or can define its own procedures and functions, in addition to those listed in the definition module. We will see a use for variables in an implementation module momentarily. As an example of a local procedure, we might write a Slice procedure within the implementation module for Strings. The statement

Slice(S1, StartPos, StopPos, S2)

would put the characters from S1 from the StartPos position to the StopPos position into S2 and give S2 the appropriate length. Using Slice, it would then be a piece of cake to implement Left, Right, and Mid. The point is that Slice is considered too specialized to be of use outside the implementation package, so it is not exported. We recommend that you implement Slice as a local procedure when asked in the exercises to implement and export Left, Right, and Mid. Slice is a detail hidden from the user by the concept of separate modules. Again, this shows the *data hiding* powers of separate modules.

A MONTE CARLO PACKAGE

There is a famous gambling casino at Monte Carlo where many dice and card games are played. From the early days of the computer, the simulation of such games has been a popular pastime. These techniques have also been directed to more serious applications, such as simulating tellers and customers at a bank to decide if more tellers are needed, simulating aircraft arriving and departing from a busy airport to determine the maximum safe load on the airport, or simulating the landing of a lunar module. However, the name **Monte Carlo techniques** has stuck to all these simulations. We therefore propose a Monte Carlo package as our final example of a separately compiled module. This example is especially nice in that it adds a useful package to the Modula-2 language and gives us an example of an implementation module with a variable declared in it and of an implementation module with a nonempty body.

First, however, we need to talk about the scope of a variable declared in an implementation module. Such a variable is created when the main module imports from the other module and exists for the life of the main program. However, the main program cannot see or use the variable! Such variables are often called **static** variables, in contrast to the **dynamic** variables of procedures and functions. But what is the good of a static variable if it can't be seen by the main module? Such a variable is a place where the implementation module can squirrel things away between calls. That is, since the static variable preserves its values between calls to the implementation module, values can be left by one procedure or function of the implementation module to be used by other procedures or functions on later calls.

But how do these static variables get initialized? (You ask such good questions.) That is exactly the purpose of the implementation body. These static variables provide any necessary initialization code and are executed in the order of importation in the main module *before* the execution of the main module's body. Please note that this is just the opposite of the bodies of procedures and functions, which are executed only when called. The implementation bodies, on the other hand, are all executed before the main module begins execution.

As a very simple example of these concepts, consider the definition module outline of Listing 14.7 and the implementation module outline of Listing 14.8. The implementation module uses a static variable, Count, to count the number of times that any of its objects were used.

```
DEFINITION MODULE Scope;
(* This module illustrates the scope of static variables.     *)

EXPORT QUALIFIED A, B, ..., PrintUsage;

PROCEDURE A(...);

PROCEDURE B(...);

...

PROCEDURE PrintUsage;

END Scope.
```

Listing 14.7

```
IMPLEMENTATION MODULE Scope;
(* This module illustrates the scope of static variables.     *)

FROM InOut IMPORT WriteCard, WriteString, WriteLn;

VAR Count : CARDINAL;                          (*Static variable. *)

PROCEDURE A(...);
  BEGIN
    ...
    INC(Count);
    ...
  END A;
```

```
PROCEDURE B(...);
  BEGIN
    ...
    INC(Count);
    ...
    END B;

...

PROCEDURE PrintUsage;
  BEGIN
    INC(Count);
    WriteString("You used objects from the module Scope ");
    WriteCard(Count, 0);
    WriteString(" times."); WriteLn
  END PrintUsage;

BEGIN                    (* Body of implementation module Scope. *)
  Count := 0
END Scope.
```

Listing 14.8

Note that `Count` is not exported by the module. `Count` cannot be seen or changed from any other module. However, a main module that imports A, B, ..., and `PrintUsage` from `Scope` can invoke `PrintUsage` at the bottom of its body to see a report such as

```
You used objects from the module Scope 87 times.
```

Note that `Count` was initialized to zero by the initialization code in the body of `Scope` before the main module began execution. This is exactly what was needed to make the static variable work properly!

Now back to our Monte Carlo package. Why does it need a static variable? The basis of a Monte Carlo package is a random-number generator. A random-number generator usually begins with some `Seed` value and then uses some arithmetic process to generate the next value from the previous one. Hence, it is important that the previous value of the `Seed` be kept between calls to the random-number generator. Also, the `Seed` needs to be initialized, and this will be done in the implementation body. If the `Seed` is initialized to some constant value, then the random-number generator will always generate the same sequence of values, so we shall discuss ways to randomly pick a `Seed`.

The `Seed` of the random-number generator is an excellent example of the need for *data hiding*. If we didn't have static variables, we would have to try to use a local variable or pass the `Seed` from the main module as a parameter to the random-number generator. A local variable in the random-number generator would not work for the `Seed`, because that variable would not have its value preserved between calls. It would be a dynamic variable and could not even be guaranteed to occupy the same location in memory each time the procedure was called. On the other hand, passing the Seed as a parameter from the calling module would work, but it is awkward and dangerous. First of all, the user might accidently clobber the value of the Seed and make the random-number generator work very poorly. But, more importantly, the user has no need to even know about the Seed. The user has enough other details to worry about without needing to keep track of some Seed that is not completely understood. The static variable and the initialization of the implementation module are exactly what is needed to hide this detail from the user.

There are several methods for generating random numbers, and the interested reader is referred to *The Art of Programming*, Vol. 2, by Donald Knuth (Addison Wesley, 1969), for a complete discussion of random-number generation. Here we use a simple method known as the **linear congruential method**. This simply says that the new value of the Seed is obtained from the old value of the Seed by

```
Seed <- (A * Seed + B) MOD C
```

where A, B, and C are carefully chosen CARDINALS. In this text, we pick three moderate primes for A, B, and C. In Modula-2, we must avoid CARDINAL overflow, which can easily happen in the expression A * Seed + B, so we will make all the arithmetic REAL. We will also divide the SEED by C to make the result between 0.0 and 1.0. We will then see how to convert this back to the CARDINAL values 1 to 6 to simulate a die (singular of dice) or to any other range that we want.

To save space, we will present a minimal Monte Carlo package and let the reader extend it in the exercises. Listing 14.9 contains the definition module for a package that exports the function Random( ) as well as the Die( ) function. Note that these are both parameterless functions.

```
DEFINITION MODULE Monte;
(* This module begins a Monte Carlo package. See the exercises for
additional functions and procedures that can be added to the
package.                                                        *)

EXPORT QUALIFIED    Random,                       (* Func *)
                    Die;                          (* Func *)

PROCEDURE Random() : REAL;
(* Pre:  None.
Post:    This parameterless function returns a REAL between 0.0 and
1.0.                                                            *)

PROCEDURE Die() : CARDINAL;
(* Pre:  None.
Post:    This parameterless function returns a CARDINAL in the
range 1 to 6.                                                   *)

END Monte.
```

Listing 14.9

Listing 14.10 contains the implementation module for the package. Note the static variables, Seed and Now, and their initialization in the body of the module. We have shown a body that is specific to Logitech Modula-2, in that it uses the type Time and makes a call to the procedure GetTime, from the module TimeDate supplied by Logitech. If you are using another Modula-2 compiler, you may find that it has the equivalent types and procedures in it. If not, you can always use some ASCII trick to prompt the user for an input from the keyboard and convert that input to the initial Seed value. (This is essentially what we did in Chapter 7.) Of course, the module will work if we simply initialize Seed to 12345.6789, or some other random value, but then our random-number generator will always produce the same sequence. It is certainly nicer to read the clock or do some ASCII trick to produce a random initial Seed value.

```
IMPLEMENTATION MODULE Monte;
(* This module contains the details of the Monte Carlo package.
WARNING: This module contains some specific Logitech Modula-2 im-
plementation details, such as the module TimeDate.          *)

FROM TimeDate IMPORT Time,               (* A record type. *)
            GetTime;        (* A procedure to read the clock. *)

CONST  A = 8191;              (* Three prime constants for the *)
       B = 4051;               (* linear congruential Method *)
       C = 61681;           (* of generating random numbers. *)

VAR    Now  : Time;                      (* Static variable. *)
       Seed : REAL;                      (* Static variable. *)

PROCEDURE RealMOD(X, Y : REAL) : REAL;
(* This function does the REAL equivalent of  X MOD Y.       *)
(* Note that X MOD Y is just  X - (X DIV Y) * Y.
Pre:   X and Y have REAL values and Y is not zero.
Post: This function returns the REAL equivalent of X MOD Y.  *)

   VAR Quotient : CARDINAL;

   BEGIN
     Quotient := TRUNC(X/Y);         (* Equivalent of X DIV Y. *)
     RETURN(X - FLOAT(QUOTIENT)*Y)  (* Equivalent of X MOD Y. *)
   END RealMod;

PROCEDURE Random() : REAL;
(* This parameterless function uses the additive congruence method
to return a random number in the interval 0.0 to 1.0. It uses the
old value of Seed to generate the new value of Seed, and so Seed
must be static.
```

```
Pre:   The static variable Seed already has a value.
Post: The static variable Seed is assigned a new value, and the
function returns a REAL in the range 0.0 to 1.0.              *)

   BEGIN
     Seed := RealMod(A*Seed + B, C);         (*Additive Congruence
                                                        formula. *)

      RETURN(Seed/C)                  (* Crunch to range 0.0 to 0.1. *)
   END Random;

PROCEDURE DIE() : CARDINAL;
(* This parameterless function simulates the rolling of a die
(singular of dice).
Pre:   None.
Post: This function returns a CARDINAL between 1 and 6.          *)

   BEGIN
     RETURN(TRUNC(6.0*Random() + 1.0))
   END Die;

BEGIN                               (* Body of implementation module:
                                          Initialization code. *)
   GetTime(Now);                        (* Read the clock. *)
   Seed := Now.millisec    (* Time has 3 fields: day, minute, *)
                           (* millisec. We use the millisec field, *)
                           (* since it is the most unpredictable. *)
END Monte.
```

Listing 14.10

Note that the procedure RealMOD is not exported from the module. It is needed to make the arithmetic REAL, but it is probably not of interest to the user of the package. It is best hidden from the casual user of random-number generation and is another good example of *data abstraction* through separately compiled modules. The reader should also study the one-line definition of the function Die() to see how it computes a CARDINAL in the required range from the REAL random number. Namely, Random() produces a value between 0.0 and 1.0, but never equal to 1.0. Thus, the expression

```
6.0 * Random() + 1.0
```

produces a value between 1.0 and 7.0, but never equal to 7.0. Truncating this gives us the range that we want. We leave the simulation of many other events—such as two dice, coins, and cards—to the reader in the exercises as extensions of the Monte Carlo package. Note that even though Die() is a one-line function, it is a messy definition. The *data-hiding* capabilities of separate modules let the casual user see the public interface in the definition module, but not worry about the details in the implementation module. Of course, you are going to be extending this example in the exercises, so you will have to understand the details.

Just to emphasize, one last time, how easy it is to import and use the function Die(), here is a fragment of a main module that simulates the rolling of a die 100 times:

```
FROM Monte IMPORT Die;

...

  FOR Roll := 1 TO 100 DO
    WriteCard(Die(), 0)
  END;  (* FOR *)
```

CONCLUSION

Our examples have been very simple and involved only one separate module (in its two parts), but hopefully the general picture is clear. We create and compile the definition modules. These form the public interface between modules. Any module can import from another, so it is possible for modules to use the products of other modules. Next, we create and compile the main program module. Finally, we must write and compile each of the implementation modules. Then the whole bundle can be linked and executed.

The advantages of separate compilation for large programs are manifold. Separate compilation speeds program development, since it allows one part of the program to be updated without recompiling the entire program. More importantly, separate compilation allows us to create our own libraries of utilities. If we create MyInOut, Strings, and Monte, then we can import from them at will in any program that we write. Further, separately compiled modules give us an excellent way to divide and conquer a large, complex problem. That problem can then be attacked a piece at a time, or all at once, by a team of programmers who are assured that their individual modules will fit together properly to solve the given problem. Finally, separately compiled modules provide a means of data hiding so that the casual user need see only those details about an object that are necessary to use that object. The implementation details are kept in a separate location and can be provided if needed.

EXERCISES

14.1 Extend MyInOut by adding procedures to read and write variables of user-defined types such as Days and Months.

14.2 Extend the Strings module by implementing the Assign, PutString, GetString, CR, Left, Right, Mid, Pos, UpCase, and DownCase procedures and functions described in the text.

14.3 A palindrome is a phrase that reads the same backward as forward. For example,

ABLE WAS I ERE I SAW ELBA

and

Able was I ere I saw Elba

are both considered to be palindromes (thus, case is not significant). The notion of a palindrome is also extended to include phrases that read the same except for punctuation and blanks. Thus,

A man, a plan, a canal, Panama

is a palindrome.
   Using the module `Strings`, write a main module to test a given string to see if it is a palindrome.

14.4 a) Extend the Monte Carlo package to include a function `Dice` that simulates the rolling of two dice.

b) Extend the Monte Carlo package to include a procedure `Cards(Rank, Suit)` that simulates the drawing of a card from a standard 52-card deck.

14.5 a) Use your Monte Carlo package to simulate the children's game of COOTIE, if you are familiar with it.

b) Use your Monte Carlo package to simulate the dealing of a five-card poker hand.

14.6 Develop a Complex Numbers package and implement it as Definition and Implementation modules.

Chapter 15

SETS

This chapter introduces another structured data type available in Modula-2: the SET type. Sets provide a good framework to appreciate the tradeoffs that must occur in deciding what features we would like to have in a programming language and what features can be efficiently implemented. We believe sets are an important feature of languages, although most languages don't have a set capability. We like sets because they are easy to understand and because sets provide a nice alternative to arrays in solving many problems. It is important for a beginning programmer to see that *how* data are structured and stored (i.e., do we use arrays, sets, or something else) is often just as important as figuring out the algorithm to solve the problem at hand. In fact, choosing the correct data structure may make the coding of the algorithm simpler.

Unfortunately, implementing sets—that is, making a compiler able to understand and execute programs using sets—tends to become very inefficient unless some restrictions are placed on how sets can be used. Modula-2 places two serious restrictions on sets to enable an efficient implementation. Of course, these restrictions decrease the attractiveness of using sets—at times, the use of sets may become more trouble than it is worth. Nevertheless, we feel that it is important for the beginner to see how sets can be used to simplify algorithms. Moreover, this chapter gives us the opportunity to use our programming skills to overcome some of Modula-2's restrictions. We begin by looking at the general idea of sets before considering the specifics of Modula-2.

A **set** is just a collection of objects, called **elements**. In mathematics, a set is referred to as an unordered collection. That just means that we attach no importance to the order of the elements in a set. Moreover, an element either belongs or doesn't belong to a set. There is no notion of an element belonging to a set more than once. For example, {2, 3, 5, 7, 11} is the set of the first five prime numbers. This set is equal to {5, 11, 3, 2, 7} and to {2, 3, 2, 5, 11, 2, 3, 7}.

RELATIONS AND OPERATIONS WITH SETS

There are several Boolean-valued relations involving sets. We can test whether two sets are **equal** or not. Obviously, two sets are equal if they have exactly the same elements. Set A is said to be a **subset** of set B if every element of A is also an element of B. In this case, B is called a **superset** of A. We can also describe this situation by saying that "A is contained in B" or "B contains A." If A and B are not equal, then such a containment is said to be **proper**. For example, if A = {1, 2, 3, 4}, B = {2, 3, 4, 5}, C = {1, 2, 3, 4, 6}, and D = {5, 4, 3, 2}, then

> A is a proper subset of C
> D contains B
> C properly contains A
> B is a subset (but not a proper subset) of D

Another Boolean relation is that of set membership. This relation compares an element and a set (as opposed to the previous relations, which compare two sets). Again, if A = {1, 2, 3, 4}, then we say that "3 is an element of A," or "3 is a member of A," or "3 is in A." Beginners often confuse the two notions of "element membership" and "subset containment". To illustrate the difference, we remark that the first two statements below are correct, while the second two are incorrect:

> {3} is a subset of A   (Both true)
> 3 is an element of A

> 3 is a subset of A   (Both false)
> {3} is an element of A

Just as there are arithmetic operations that we can perform on numbers that result in new numbers, there are set operations that we can perform on sets to produce new sets. We'll consider four such operations: union, intersection, difference, and symmetric difference.

Union: The union of two sets is the set that contains the elements that are in *either* of the two sets. For example, if A = {1, 2, 3, 4, 5} and B = {2, 4, 6, 8}, then the union of A and B is {1, 2, 3, 4, 5, 6, 8}. In Modula-2, union is denoted with a plus (+) sign.

Intersection: The intersection of two sets is the set that contains the elements that are in *both* of the two sets. For example, if A = {1, 2, 3, 4, 5} and B = {2, 4, 6, 8}, then the intersection of A and B is {2, 4}. In Modula-2, intersection is denoted with an asterisk (*). If C = {1, 3, 5}, then the intersection of B and C is a set with no elements in it. This set is called the **empty set** and is written in Modula-2 as { }.

Difference: This is denoted in Modula-2 with a minus (-) sign. A - B denotes the set that contains elements of A that are not also elements of B. So again, if A = {1, 2, 3, 4, 5} and B = {2, 4, 6, 8}, then A - B is {1, 3, 5}. Observe that B - A is {6, 8} and, in general, A - B ≠ B - A.

Symmetric Difference: The symmetric difference of two sets is the set that contains the elements that are found in exactly one of the sets. So if A = { 1, 2, 3, 4, 5 } and B = {2, 4, 6, 8}, then the symmetric difference of A and B is { 1, 3, 5, 6, 8 }. Symmetric difference in Modula-2 is denoted with a slash (/).

MODULA-2'S RESTRICTIONS ON SETS

Before we investigate how to use sets in Modula-2, let us state the two major restrictions that Modula-2 places on sets. The first is that the elements of a set must all be of the same discrete type. That is, we cannot have a set that contains more than one kind of element. So, a set containing integers and characters is not possible. Moreover, a set containing just real numbers is also not permitted in Modula-2. That is because the real numbers are not a discrete type. Recall that the discrete types in Modula-2 are INTEGER, CARDINAL, BOOLEAN, CHAR, and user-defined enumerated types dicussed in Chapter 9. So, in addition to real numbers, character strings are not permitted in sets.

The other restriction on sets in Modula-2 concerns their maximum allowable size. The size of a set—that is, the number of elements belonging to a set—is called its **cardinality**. The maximum cardinality of a set in Modula-2 is the **word size** of the computer that is running the Modula-2 compiler. For most microcomputers, this size is either 16 or 32. It is up to the programmer to determine what the specific upper limit on the size of sets is. Recall from Chapter 1 that computers eventually store information as strings of bits—that is, 0s and 1s. For reasons of efficiency, computers don't deal with information a bit at a time. Rather, bits are packaged into groups of size 8, called **bytes**, for more efficient processing. These bytes are then further packaged into **words**. A 32-bit machine has a word size of 32 bits, or 4 bytes. When computers move information around, they tend to do it in word-sized chunks. Regardless of the specific word size, from the standpoint of algorithms, a typical word-size limit is a severe one in using sets. For example, on a 16-bit machine, we can't even have a set that contains all the letters in the alphabet. As promised, later in this chapter we'll show a way around this size limitation.

We think it is worthwhile to point out how computers implement sets. Then we can at least see why programming languages with sets impose the restrictions that they do. We will also be able to understand better the one built-in set type provided by Modula-2. Suppose we wanted to have a set A that could contain any of the integers from 0 to 99. How should A be represented in the computer? Should we block out space (like an array) for 100 integer values? What if A currently contained only the values 2, 37, and 55? Should the first three locations of A contain these values, while the rest of A is blank? While such a technique is possible, this method is far too wasteful of memory resources. On a typical implementation, each integer in the range from 0 to 99 would be stored using at least 16 bits, so we would need at least 1600 bits to represent A.

Instead, computers represent A simply as a string of 100 bits. Each bit corresponds to a possible element of the set. The first bit corresponds to the smallest element possible in the set, while the last bit corresponds to the largest element in the set. If an element is present in the set, its bit is set to 1. If the element does not belong to the set, its bit is a 0. So, if A currently equals {2, 37, 55}, then the bit pattern for A would be

00100000000000000000000000000000000001000......etc

Note that the bit pattern for a set of characters is indistinguishable from the bit pattern for a set of integers or for a set containing elements from a user-defined enumerated type. All that is needed is an ordering of the potential elements of the set. That is why languages restrict us to discrete types—that is, types with a first and last value, where the successor and predecessor operations make sense. Think of the difficulty in trying to represent a set of real numbers in the range from 1.0 to 10.0. Also, once we see that computers like to store sets as a bit pattern, it also makes sense to tie the size of sets into the size of words, since those are the packages of 0s and 1s that are moved around in a computer. However, it would be nice if the size of sets were based on a multiple of the word size instead of the word size itself. That is what we do later. So, our set of 100 elements would use the smallest set of words that contains at least 100 bits. On a 16-bit machine, this would be 7 words (7 words * 16 bits per word = 112 bits), while on a 32-bit machine, it would be 4 words (4 * 32 = 128).

SETS IN MODULA-2

Now it is time to see how sets are managed in Modula-2. As with other types of variables, we may define set types and then declare variables of that type, or we may declare set variables anonymously (i.e., without giving them type names). We'll demonstrate several methods of obtaining sets in Modula-2 and then discuss the differences.

```
TYPE
   Ratings   = 0..10;
   Months    = (Jan, Feb, Mar, Apr, May, Jun, Jul, Aug, Sep, Oct,
                                                       Nov, Dec);
   RatingSet = SET OF Ratings;
   MonthSet  = SET OF Months;
   UpLetters = SET OF ['A' .. 'Z'];              (* Size problem on
                                                    16-bit machine. *)

CONST
   SummerMonths        = MonthSet { Jun .. Aug };
   ExceptionalRatings  = RatingSet { 8..10 };
   Vowels              = UpLetters {'A', 'E', 'I', 'O', 'U'};
   UpperCase           = UpLetters {'A' .. 'Z'};

VAR
   Gallup       : RatingSet;
   VacationPoss : MonthSet;
   DiceRoll     : SET OF [2..12];
```

When we define a set type, we essentially tell the computer what kind of elements sets of that type may contain. We can specify this type either by listing the type name of a user-defined enumeration type or by giving a subrange of a user-defined type or one of the built-in discrete types. Notice that in type definitions/variable declarations, we use square brackets, [and], to enclose the subranges. However, in using sets in module bodies and in assigning values to set constants, we use the braces of standard mathematics, { and }.

Note that in the constant assignments, it is necessary to include the name of the type of set. This is because computers store sets as bit patterns. All these bit patterns look basically alike, so we must explicitly tell the computer what kinds of sets we are dealing with. That is, the bit patterns for the four constant sets shown above are

```
0 0 0 0 0 1 1 1 0 0 0 0
0 0 0 0 0 0 0 0 1 1 1
1 0 0 0 1 0 0 0 1 0 0 0 0 0 1 0 0 0 0 0 1 0 0 0 0 0
1 1 1 1 1 1 1 1 1 1 1 1 1 1 1 1 1 1 1 1 1 1 1 1 1 1 1
```

A very common mistake is to assume that there is some initialization going on when set types are defined or when set variables are declared. For example, many beginners think that MonthSet is a set containing the values Jan through Dec. MonthSet is simply the name of a type, just like INTEGER and Months are names of types. We use MonthSet just like any other type name—we can declare variables of type MonthSet. Such variables are sets whose possible elements come from the type Months.

Moreover, declaring set variables does not provide initial values. Specifically, the declaration of the variable DiceRoll does not initialize DiceRoll to {2, 3, 4, 5, 6, 7, 8, 9, 10, 11, 12}. Nor does it initialize DiceRoll to { }, the empty set. The declaration doesn't initialize the variable at all. It simply says that DiceRoll is a set, and, during the course of its existence, it will be allowed to contain any set of the values from 2 to 12.

THE BUILT-IN BITSET TYPE

There is a built-in set type called BITSET. If a computer's word size is 32 bits, then sets of this type can have as elements any of the values from 0 to 31. In general, if W represents a computer's word size, then BITSET sets can have as elements any of the values from 0 to W-1. We'll see later in the chapter how to make use of the BITSET type to help us get around the size restriction imposed on the cardinality of Modula-2 sets. We also point out here that if we omit a set type name in assigning a value to a set constant, and if the element type for that set is in the range from 0 to W-1, then that set is assumed to be of type BITSET. That is, if we had written the assignment to ExceptionalRatings as

ExceptionalRatings = {8..10};

then ExceptionalRatings would be of type BITSET, not of type RatingsSet.

Relations and Operations

We have mentioned some of Modula-2's syntax for sets. Let us summarize here. The tests for set equality and inequality naturally use = and <>. The subset test uses <=, while the superset test uses >=. For example, the assignment statement

```
AContainsB := (A >= B)
```

sets the BOOLEAN variable `AContainsB` to `TRUE` if A is a superset of B. Some implementations of Modula-2 permit the testing of proper subsets and proper containment using < and >, respectively, although this is not standard.

The operations of union, intersection, difference, and symmetric difference are denoted by +, *, -, and /, respectively. The precedence of the set operators is inherited from the precedence established for the operators as normal arithmetic operators. This may not be natural, and we urge programmers to use parentheses to make the precedence as explicit as possible. For example:

```
AorBandC := A + B * C
```

is equivalent to

```
AorBandC := A + (B * C)
```

but we prefer the second statement, because the precedence of intersection over union is not quite as universally accepted as the precedence of multiplication over addition. Either statement, of course, assigns to the set `AorBandC` those elements that are either in A, or that are in both B and C.

Set membership is tested using the `IN` operator. That is, if A is a set containing CARDINALS and if J is a CARDINAL variable, we can test to see if the value assigned to J is a member of A with

```
IF J IN A THEN .....
```

We take the opportunity to point out a common mistake among beginners in making a negative test for membership. Suppose we wanted to take some action if A did not contain the value assigned to J. Many beginners write

```
IF J NOT IN A THEN  (* Syntax Error ! ! *)
```

The reason this is incorrect is due to the high precedence of the `NOT` operator. The compiler tries to apply the `NOT` operator to the expression `IN A`, which is nonsense. Beginners try to fix the above mistake with

```
IF NOT J IN A THEN  (*  Still a Syntax Error ! !  *)
```

Again, the high precedence of `NOT` causes the compiler to try to evaluate `NOT J`. But, of course, this is still nonsense, because J is a CARDINAL and `NOT` can only be applied to something of type BOOLEAN. Thus, the correct negative-membership test must be written like this:

```
IF NOT (J IN A) THEN
```

This time the parentheses cause the membership test to be applied first, yielding a BOOLEAN value of TRUE or FALSE, which may then have NOT applied to it.

The Built-in Procedures INCL and EXCL

Two common operations in programs involving sets are inserting a single element into a set or removing a single element from a set. Modula-2 provides built-in procedures for these operations, INCL and EXCL, respectively. Both procedures require two arguments. The first argument is the set involved and the second argument is the element that we want inserted or removed from the set. For example, if VacationPoss currently equals {May, Jul, Sep, Oct} and we must remove Sep from the set, we could write

```
EXCL(VacationPoss, Sep);
```

We point out that an EXCL operation does nothing if the element in question is not already in the set. That is, EXCL(VacationPoss, Feb) has no effect.

If Gallup equals {3, 5, 7, 9}, we could add 8 to the set with

```
INCL(Gallup, 8);
```

As with the EXCL operation, INCL has no effect if the element in question is already in the set. So INCL(Gallup, 7) does nothing.

Observe that the above operations could be accomplished with

```
VacationPoss := VacationPoss - {Sep}
```

and

```
Gallup := Gallup + {8}
```

However, the use of INCL and EXCL is syntactically simpler to write. More importantly, INCL and EXCL are more general than using the difference and union operators. Elements enclosed within set braces are required to be constants—they may not be variables or expressions. So, if we read in a NewRating from the keyboard, and wanted to add that to our set Gallup, we could write INCL(Gallup, NewRating), whereas Gallup := Gallup + {NewRating} would be illegal. (We remark that allowing nonconstants within braces is a change proposed by Wirth, and we urge the reader to check the specific implementation of the language to see if this change has been incorporated.)

Now it is time to see some simple examples of the use of sets in Modula-2.

SETS AS FILTERS

One of the simplest, but most useful, aspects of sets is in filtering out bad data. For example, suppose we are writing a program that constantly asks the user at the keyboard to type in a letter corrresponding to one of several responses displayed on the video screen. Such menu-driven software is very common and is typical of software used by people who have little understanding of how computers and software function. The user can read the questions on the screen and type the desired responses. Suppose the labels to the responses of our questions are letters. What should we do if the user types something that isn't a letter? What should we do if the user types an uppercase M when we were expecting a lowercase m? In the first instance, we should prompt the user to respond again, until an understandable response is given. In the second case, if we want to make the program as user-friendly as possible (some computer users may not know how to obtain the case that we are expecting), we should probably treat M and m as the same reponse, assuming that there aren't two different responses on the screen, one labeled M and one labeled m. A typical segment to obtain the response, while filtering out the meaningless responses, would be

```
REPEAT
  WriteString('Enter your response: ');
  WriteLn;
  Read(Response);              (* Response is of type CHAR. *)
  Write(Response)                     (* Echo the input. *)
UNTIL (('a' <= Response) AND (Response <= 'z')) OR
                (('A' <= Response) AND (Response <= 'Z'));
```

First, observe that we can't use just the two tests ('A' <= Response) AND (Response <= 'z'), because there are several characters in the enumerated type CHAR that occur between the uppercase and the lowercase alphabets. Although the above segment is correct, we prefer, for convenience and readability, the following segment:

```
REPEAT
  WriteString('Enter your response: ');
  WriteLn;
  Read(Response);              (* Response is of type CHAR. *)
  Write(Response)                     (* Echo the input. *)
UNTIL Response IN Letters;
```

Here, we assume that Letters is a set containing only the uppercase and lowercase letters. How could we get such a set?

```
TYPE CharSet = SET OF ['A' .. 'z'];        (* Possible Modula-2
                                              size problem. *)


CONST Letters = CharSet{'A' .. 'Z', 'a' .. 'z'};
```

Observe that if we are restricted to sets of size 32 or smaller, the above segment would not work. To be able to filter out data based on character values, we really need sets of size 128 (the number of different characters in the ASCII set). However, despite Modula-2's size limitations, sets can be used as filters in many situations—for example, entering A, B, C, D, or F as grades to be used in the computation of a grade point average. Also, this example points out how useful it will be when, through our own programming skills, we effectively increase the size of sets.

SOGGIES, THE BREAKFAST OF PROGRAMMERS

The Soggies company has placed into each of its boxes of cereal one of a collection of 10 trading cards depicting a pioneer of computer science. Assuming that there is always a one-in-ten chance of getting a particular card, how many boxes of Soggies should we expect to buy before we obtain all 10 cards? We invite the reader to guess what the answer is. A very lucky person might need to buy only 10 boxes of cereal, getting a new card in each box. However, after we have gotten a good start on our collection of cards, we probably shouldn't be too surprised if we open a box and find that the card inside is one we already have. One can do some statistical analysis on this problem to determine the answer. We have a better idea—let's just let the computer simulate the process of buying boxes of cereal for us and see how many it has to buy before obtaining all 10 cards. In fact, since computers can buy boxes of cereal very quickly, let's have the computer perform the experiment several times and compute an average of how long it takes. Then, without doing any serious statistical analysis, we should be able to come up with an answer in which we feel fairly confident.

Here is a pseudo-code solution to our problem:

```
Set GrandTotal equal to 0
For Experiment := 1 to 100 Do
    Buy Boxes of Cereal until all 10 cards are obtained
    Print total required for this experiment
    Add number of boxes required for this experiment to GrandTotal
Set Average equal to GrandTotal / 100
Print Average
```

All the above lines in the pseudo-code are directly translatable into Modula-2, with the exception of "Buy Boxes of Cereal until all 10 cards are obtained." We'll make this into a procedure. We make one simplifying assumption about this procedure: We assume that we have a random-number generator that generates random integers in the range from 1 to 10. (Some Modula-2 systems do not provide a random-number generator. We refer the reader to the examples in Chapters 7 and 14 for ideas on how to write a simple random-number generator.) Then, invoking this generator is how we simulate buying a box of cereal. Notice that we don't worry about how much the box of cereal costs or anything else about the cereal. We are interested only in what card is in the box. If we think of the cards as being numbered from 1 to 10, then generating the random number 4 simulates buying a box of cereal, opening it up, and finding card number 4 inside. In general, when the computer is used to simulate some process, focus only on the essential elements of that process, ignoring other nonessential details.

Where do sets come in? Well, we can think of the prizes that we currently have as a set of positive integers. And when our set is equal to the set { 1, 2, 3, 4, 5, 6, 7, 8, 9, 10}, we then have a complete set. So psuedo-code for our procedure becomes

Initialize our set of prizes to the empty set
Initialize total needed for this experiment to 0
Repeat
    Generate a random integer between 1 and 10
    Include this integer in our set of prizes
    Add one to the total number of boxes purchased on this experiment
Until our set is the complete set

Listing 15.1 contains the complete module for the solution to the Soggies problem.

```
MODULE Soggies;

(* This module determines how many boxes of Soggies Cereal we need
to buy to obtain all 10 different prizes available. We assume the
prizes are uniformly distributed.                              *)

FROM InOut IMPORT WriteLn, WriteString, WriteCard;
FROM MyInOut IMPORT WriteRealPretty;            (* See Chapters 7
                                                    and 14. *)

TYPE PrizeSet = SET OF [1 .. 10];

CONST MaxExperiments = 100;

VAR    Experiment  : CARDINAL;
       GrandTotal  : CARDINAL;
       SubTotal    : CARDINAL;
       Average     : REAL;

PROCEDURE ConductExperiment(VAR Number : CARDINAL);

(* This procedure simulates purchasing boxes of cereal until all
10 different prizes have been acquired. We assume the existence of
a random-number generator, called by Random(10), that returns a
random integer between 1 and 10, inclusive.
Pre:   None.
Post: Number is assigned the number of boxes required to obtain
all 10 different trading cards.                                *)

  CONST CompleteSet = PrizeSet { 1 .. 10 };

  VAR MySet : PrizeSet;
```

```
BEGIN
  Number := 0;
  MySet := { };                    (* Initialize set of prizes owned
                                        to the empty set. *)
  REPEAT
    INCL(MySet, Random(10));
    INC(Number)
  UNTIL MySet = CompleteSet;
  WriteString('This trial required ');
  WriteCard(Number, 0);
  WriteString(' purchases to obtain a complete
                set of prizes.');
  WriteLn
END ConductExperiment;

BEGIN                                           (* Main module. *)
  GrandTotal := 0;
  FOR Experiment := 1 TO MaxExperiments DO
    ConductExperiment(SubTotal);
    GrandTotal := GrandTotal + SubTotal
  END;
  Average := FLOAT(GrandTotal) / FLOAT(MaxExperiments);
  WriteString('The average number of purchases to get
              all prizes was ');
  WriteRealPretty(Average, 3, 2)          (* Write Average in the
                                              form XXX.XX. *)
END Soggies.
```

Listing 15.1

On our test run of the program in Listing 15.1, we got an average of 29.84, which is close to the theoretical average of about 29.5.

Notice that sets are an ideal structure for this problem because they reflect perfectly the fact that obtaining a given card after the first time gets us no closer to our goal of a complete set of cards. That is, including an integer in a set after it has already been placed in the set does not change the set at all. So we don't need any statements that worry about whether we have already won the prize or not. We encourage the reader to consider a solution using arrays.

INCREASING THE ALLOWABLE SIZE OF SETS

As we have mentioned several times, a severe restriction of sets in Modula-2 is that they cannot contain more elements than the word size of the host computer. In this section, we'll see how to get around this restriction. Not only does this example serve the useful purpose of making sets more flexible, it also points out how, in general, we can use our programming skills to do things we want to do, even if it looks at first as if the task may be impossible.

Suppose we have a computer with a word size of 32 bits and we would like to use a set that contains any character in the ASCII character set. That is, we would like to increase our set size to 128. Observe that to accomplish this, we really need a bit string of length 128 to represent a set, instead of a bit string of length 32. If we could put four 32-bit strings together, we would effectively have a 128-bit string. Since we have the built-in type BITSET, let us see how an array of BITSETS can increase our capability.

Let us think of any character with ASCII value from 0 to 31 as belonging to the first BITSET, a character with ASCII value from 32 to 63 as being in the second BITSET, a character with ASCII value from 64 to 95 as being in the third BITSET, and a character with ASCII value from 96 to 127 as being in the fourth BITSET. Suppose, for example, that we wanted to locate the bit that corresponds to 'X'. The ASCII for 'X' is 88. That should correspond to the 25th bit in the third BITSET. Now, if we number our BITSETS from 0 to 3 (instead of from 1 to 4), and if we number the bits within each of the sets from 0 to 31, instead of from 1 to 32, then 'X' actually corresponds to the 24th bit in BITSET number 2. If the reader doesn't see how to automatically translate 88 into (2,24), try another example. After some study, it should be clear that if we divide 88 by 32, the quotient tells us which BITSET we should investigate, and the remainder tells us which bit within the set is of interest to us. Similarly, on a 16-bit machine, we would need eight words for 128 bits, and since 88 = 5 * 16 + 8, 'X' would be the eighth bit in the fifth BITSET.

We now sketch how to write a software package that builds and manipulates sets of characters of maximum size 128. There are several procedures that need to be written. We demonstrate the procedures Include (a 128-bit version of the standard INCL), Join (a 128-bit version of set union), and Member (a 128-bit version of the standard IN). These procedures would make a nice external module from which they could be imported (see Chapter 14). To keep this chapter independent of Chapter 14, we leave the details to the reader.

We assume a 32-bit machine. The reader with a different word size can make appropriate adjustments.

```
CONST MachineWord = 32;              (* Fixed by the computer's
                                                architecture. *)

      MaxSize    = 128;             (* An arbitrary multiple
                                                of the above. *)

      NumBitSets = MaxSize Div MachineWord;

TYPE  ASCIISet = ARRAY [ 0 .. NumBitSets - 1] OF BITSET;

VAR   UpperCase : ASCIISet;
      LowerCase : ASCIISet;
      Letters   : ASCIISet;
```

Our goal is to build sets UpperCase—consisting of the uppercase letters from A to Z—and LowerCase—consisting of the lowercase letters from a to z—and then to form the union of these sets to obtain Letters—which, of course, contains all the letters. We could then use the Member operator (which is yet to be written) in conjunction with Letters and have a data filter, as suggested earlier in the chapter. We build the sets using Include, and we combine the two sets using Join. Listing 15.2 contains a listing of Include and Join.

```
PROCEDURE Include( VAR CharSet : ASCIISet; Ch : Char);
(* Pre:  Ch contains a CHAR value.
Post:    The bit position corresponding to the ASCII value of Ch
is set to 1 in CharSet.                                        *)

VAR    Value     : CARDINAL;
       Component : CARDINAL;
       Position  : CARDINAL;

BEGIN
  Value := ORD(Ch);
  Component := Value DIV MachineWord;

  Position := Value MOD MachineWord;
  INCL(Letters[Component], Position)(* Our Include procedure *)
                (* is based on the built-in INCL procedure. *)
END Include;



PROCEDURE Join(ChSet1, ChSet2 : ASCIISet; VAR ChSet3 : ASCIISet);
(* Pre:  ChSet1 and ChSet2 represent sets of Characters.
Post:    ChSet3 represents the union of ChSet1 and ChSet2.    *)

VAR Index : Cardinal;

BEGIN
  FOR Index := 0 TO NumBitSets - 1 DO
    ChSet3[Index] := ChSet1[Index] + ChSet2[Index](* The plus *)
    END (* FOR *)                      (* sign denotes the built-in *)
                                       (* set union, so again we are *)
END Join;                              (* using the built-in routines to *)
                                       (* create our customized routine. *)
```

Listing 15.2

Now let us write the membership test routine. As might be expected, we use the built-in operator IN. The procedure is given in Listing 15.3.

```
PROCEDURE Member(Ch : Char; CharSet : ASCIISet) : BOOLEAN;
(* Pre:  Ch contains a character value.
Post:    This function returns TRUE if the bit corresponding to Ch
in the set representation of CharSet is a 1, otherwise it returns
FALSE.                                                         *)
```

```
VAR Value : CARDINAL;

BEGIN
  Value := ORD(Ch);
  Component := Value DIV MachineWord;
  Position := Value MOD MachineWord;
  IF Position IN CharSet[Component] THEN
    RETURN(TRUE)
  ELSE
    RETURN(FALSE)
  END (* IF *)
END Member;
```

Listing 15.3

Next, let's see how a module with the above type definitions, variable declarations, and procedures could be used to simulate a filter for character input that is supposed to consist only of letters. We first build UpperCase and LowerCase and then union them together to obtain Letters. We assume that Ch and Response are of type **CHAR**.

```
FOR Ch := 'A' to 'Z' DO
  Include(UpperCase, Ch)
END; (* FOR *)
FOR Ch := 'a' to 'z' DO
  Include(LowerCase, Ch)
END; (* FOR *)
Join(UpperCase, LowerCase, Letters);
```

Now we can use Letters as a filter in the following way:

```
REPEAT
  WriteString('Enter your response: ');
  Read(Response);
  WriteLn
UNTIL Member(Response, Letters);
```

Several comments are in order. Probably the most important is that even though a variable of type ASCIISet is really an array, a user of a module with all these procedures can treat anything of type ASCIISet as if it were actually a set. That is, in any module that is subsequently written, all references to variables of type ASCIISet should occur without any subscripts. The user doesn't need to worry about the details of array subscripting. All this is handled in the procedures Include, Join, and Member. Of course, since Member is not a built-in function, we must use it as indicated above:

```
Member(Response, Letters)
```

instead of

```
Response IN letters
```

The ASCIISet package is another example of data abstraction, where we have created a new data type. In fact, the type we have created seems to be in direct conflict with the limitations of the language definition—namely, limiting the size of sets to the word size of the machine. But the notion of abstraction means that we really haven't created such a type at all. We have just created the concept of such a type. That is, we can convince a user of our package that ASCIISets are in fact sets that can contain up to 128 characters. We must also tell that user what operations can be performed on ASCIISets—i.e., Include instead of INCL and what the format of the operations are. But once we have specified these, the user can then write modules believing that ASCIISets are really sets instead of arrays.

Our procedures so far don't quite provide an example of true data abstraction. That is, a nosy user is able to see how we managed to create the illusion of ASCIISets. In fact, such a user would be able to use our ASCIISets as if they were arrays (this shouldn't be surprising, since that's what they are). True data abstraction not only allows a programmer to create and package an illusion, but then ensures that users of the package can use it only in the ways intended by its creator. The details of the illusion are hidden from the user. In complex programs involving complex algorithms on complex data structures, the ability of a language to provide a true data-abstraction capability is considered very important. We urge the reader to complete this suggested package as an external module that can be imported into any module where it is needed. In particular, this package can be very useful in solving the last example presented in this chapter.

We cannot stress strongly enough the importance of carefully tracing through the above procedures to see how they accomplish their tasks by making use of the built-in procedures for sets. For example, when we make use of INCL within Include, it is important that the first argument to INCL be a set and the second argument be of the same type as an element of the set. In our procedure, the first argument is CharSet[Component], which is, in fact, of type BITSET. Check the type definitions and the variable declarations, and review the ideas of arrays and subscripts to ensure that this is completely clear. Moreover, our second argument, Position, is an integer between 0 and 31 inclusive, which is what is allowed to be in a BITSET. So, in the above procedures, we sometimes deal with arrays and sometimes with sets. Be sure you understand the differences.

Finally, we comment on the use of the global constant MachineWord within the procedures Include and Member. Although the use of global variables is discouraged in procedure bodies, there are occasional instances where the use of global variables, and particularly global constants, can simplify the coding and calling of procedures. One of the dangers of using global variables in procedures is the unexpected side effects incurred by changing values while in the procedure. This, of course, cannot happen with global constants. Moreover, the insistence on making every value used in a procedure a parameter would, in this case, simply clutter up the heading and subsequent calls of the procedures. That is, a call to Member of

```
Member(Element, Set)
```

is certainly preferable to

```
Member(Element, Set, MachineWord)
```

since the value of MachineWord isn't really crucial to the membership test. Programmers should use judgment to determine when it is permissible to refer to global values inside procedures.

THE GAME OF TAXMAN

We conclude this chapter by introducing the reader to one of our favorite programming projects—the game of Taxman. In this section, we describe the game and indicate a strategy for its implementation.

Taxman is a one-player number game created by Diane Resek of San Francisco State University. The player chooses how many numbers (positive integers) are in the game, from 1 up to some upper limit. During the course of the game, the player and the computer each accumulate a total. The object of the game is for the player to accumulate a larger total than the computer, hereafter referred to as the Taxman.

The player's total accumulates simply by selecting one of the numbers left in the game. The Taxman then gets all the numbers left in the game that divide evenly into the player's chosen number. Once numbers are used (by either the player or the Taxman), they are removed from the game.

There is one major restriction on the numbers that the player may select. As in real life, the Taxman must always get something, so the player can never select a number unless at least one proper divisor of that number remains in the game. Once no numbers with divisors remain (at the end of the game), the Taxman gets all the numbers left and the game is over.

For example, suppose the game is played with the numbers 1, 2, 3, 4, 5, and 6. If the greedy player chooses 6, then the Taxman gets all the divisors of 6, namely 1, 2, and 3. But now the only numbers left in the game are 4 and 5. Neither has a divisor left in the game, so the Taxman gets those also and wins 15 to 6. However, if the player is a bit smarter and chooses 5 first, the player gets 5 and the Taxman gets 1. Now the numbers remaining are 2, 3, 4, and 6, and the smart player chooses the 4 (before the 6), giving the Taxman 2. Finally, the player chooses 6 and wins 15 to 6. When played with more than 50 numbers, the game can be quite challenging. Beginners are often surprised at the treasures they give the Taxman after a seemingly innocent choice (like 48).

Before we consider a solution using sets, let us think about a solution that uses arrays. Let us suppose we have an array of Boolean values, indexed from 1 to the upper limit of the game. A TRUE in the kth component means that the number k is still in the game, while a FALSE means k is no longer in the game. When the player chooses the next number, we should first check to make sure that the choice is still in the game and also check to make sure that the choice has a proper divisor that is still in the game. A complication that exists in playing the game is determining if the game should continue after a completed turn. For example, suppose that the game is played with the numbers 1, 2, 3, 4, 5, and 6 and that the player's first choice is 6. Then the Taxman gets 1, 2, and

3. 4 and 5 remain, but the game should actually be terminated at this point, since neither remaining number has a divisor left in the game. With a typical array solution, this involves a fair amount of looping through the array: We first loop through the array until we find a number left in the game and then we loop through the array again looking for divisors of this number that are also left in the game. This can become tedious. When that happens, it's time to look for a more elegant solution.

Sets provide an elegant solution. Suppose the upper limit of the game is k. Then we form a set NumberPool = {1, 2, 3, 4, 5, ... , k }. Let us also form a set of PossibleDivisors. What numbers can serve as possible divisors during the game? Each of the numbers from 1 to k DIV 2 is a divisor of its double. And clearly, no number larger than k DIV 2 is a divisor of anything in the game. So the set of PossibleDivisors is equal to {1, 2, 3, 4, ..., k DIV 2}. Now, each time the player selects a number, we can check to see if it is IN the NumberPool. If it isn't, then we know it's an illegal selection. If it is in the NumberPool, we can build the set of all its proper divisors (using the INCL procedure). If the intersection of this set with the PossibleDivisors set is nonempty, then we know that the player has made a legal selection. We then remove the player's selection from the NumberPool (using the EXCL procedure), and remove it and all its divisors from the set of PossibleDivisors (using the set difference operator). Of course, those numbers in the intersection of the PossibleDivisors set and the set of divisors of the player's choice are given to the Taxman. Finally, how do we determine when the game should end? We REPEAT UNTIL PossibleDivisors = { }. Note how simple the test for the end of the game has become. Also observe that to clean up, once the set of PossibleDivisors becomes empty, we give everything that remains in the NumberPool set to the Taxman.

We encourage the reader to work through a pseudo-code solution using arrays and a pseudo-code solution using sets to be sure that the difference between the two solutions is clear. We are confident that the set solution will seem simpler. This example shows that thinking about the most suitable way to store the data is as important as the statements that manipulate the data. Moreover, one can see how the array solution can be modified to mimic the set solution so that it becomes elegant as well. For example, let's not test for the end-of-game situation by looping through the array to see if a legal choice remains in the game (which was our strategy above). Now that we've seen the set solution, let's initialize a counter to k DIV 2, and each time we use a divisor, let's decrement the counter. Then, as in the set solution, we REPEAT UNTIL Counter = 0.

So, given that there is an array solution, parallel to the set solution, that is just as elegant, which data structure is more appropriate? We still say sets! Why? Because, in our experience of assigning this program to numerous students, the elegant solution was never thought of when the array solution was initially tried! It was only when students were thinking about sets that the elegant solution was discovered.

To make the play of Taxman interesting, it is nice to have a number pool between 50 and 100. Thus, it will be necessary to implement a set software package that increases the maximum cardinality of sets. The reader should refer to our ASCIISet procedures as a starting point for this. What procedures are needed? Obviously, the large set counterparts of INCL, EXCL, IN, and intersection. Another routine that might prove useful is an initialization routine that assigns the empty set to a set variable. This routine is missing from our ASCIISet package. We leave the writing of it as an exercise.

A student who completely implements Taxman for sets of size 100 will have the opportunity, at the beginning level, to see in one example three of the most important notions in computer programming:

1. A top-down structured approach to solving a problem
2. Data abstraction
3. The importance of the correct data structure in the solution of a problem

EXERCISES

15.1 Write a program that reads a sentence from the keyboard and provides three lists:

a) All the letters included in the sentence
b) All the letters excluded from the sentence
c) All the letters included exactly once in the sentence

15.2 (Primes revisited) If a whole number is not prime, then it must have a *prime* divisor less than or equal to its square root. Assume that the maximum cardinal value is 65,535. Since the square root of 65,536 is 256, any odd cardinal represented in Modula-2 must either be prime or divisible by some prime between 3 and the largest prime less than 256.

Write a procedure that generates the set of odd primes through 255. Note that since the square root of 256 is 16, you need only test as possible divisors the primes 3, 5, 7, 11, and 13.

Write a function that uses the set generated above to test any large odd integer entered by the user for primehood.

15.3 Write a program that compares the efficiency of the QWERTY and DVORAK typewriter keyboards. The QWERTY keyboard is the standard typewriter keyboard, so named because of the placement of the first six keys on the upper row of letters. This arrangement was chosen in the late 19th century because human typists were faster than the new typewriter technology and would cause keys to jam by typing too fast. The QWERTY keyboard intentionally placed the most common letters off the home row—the row on which the fingers rest—to force the fingers to do lots of jumping. Today, with microcomputer technology, most humans can't type too fast for electronic machines. Thus, the DVORAK keyboard has been proposed as a way to speed up typing. Its layout is shown in Figure 15.1. Note that the most common letters are now on the home row.

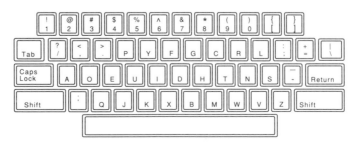

Figure 15.1

Write a program that reads a paragraph from the keyboard and computes the percentage of jumps from the home row required by each keyboard. Execute your program several times with random paragraphs from this book.

15.4 Write an `Initialization` procedure for the `ASCIISet` package. That is, write a procedure that takes a variable of type `ASCIISet` and initializes its value to the empty set.

15.5 Develop an external module, `CardSets`, patterned after the model described in the chapter, for sets of CARDINALs from 1 to 100.

15.6 Use your module `CardSets` to write a module to play Taxman.

Chapter 16

PROCEDURE TYPES

Procedures and functions are first-class citizens in Modula-2. By this, we mean that procedures and functions are objects that can be manipulated as are other objects in the language. In particular, they can be assigned to procedural variables and even passed as parameters to other functions or procedures. This chapter investigates these possibilities and indicates some of the flexibility and power provided by being able to pass procedures and functions as parameters to other procedures and functions.

A definition of a procedural type must indicate the number and type of each parameter of the procedure or function. In the case of functions, another type must be present to indicate the type returned by the function. Some examples will make the declaration of procedural types clear. For example, a procedure type for a function with one REAL input and one REAL output can be declared by

```
TYPE  RealFunc = PROCEDURE( REAL ) : REAL;
```

Or, we could declare a procedure type for a procedure with one CHAR and one CARDINAL parameter by

```
TYPE  SomeProc = PROCEDURE (CHAR, CARDINAL);
```

We can then declare identifiers of these new types:

```
VAR F : RealFunc;
    P : SomeProc
```

and then make assignments such as

```
F := sin;      (* This assumes sin has been imported already. *)
P := INC;
```

Hopefully, the reader begins to see the power of procedure types. For example, if we had a procedure, Update, with a parameter P of type SomeProc (among others), then we could write

```
Update(..., INC);                    (* Update by incrementing. *)
```

or

```
Update(..., DEC);                    (* Update by decrementing. *)
```

At some point in the definition of the procedure Update, it uses its parameter P, applying it to some other parameters. When called in the first manner, P becomes bound to INC and updates by incrementing. The second invocation binds P to DEC and decrements. This is a very simple example, but it shows how the exact behavior of Update can be controlled by the procedure passed to it.

EXAMPLE: A PROCEDURE TO GRAPH FUNCTIONS

As a complete example of procedure types, let us develop a procedure that will graph functions. Figures 16.1 and 16.2 show the output of the module that we want to discuss. To show the possibilities, Figure 16.1 depicts the graph of the built-in (in MathLib0) function sin(x), while Figure 16.2 graphs the (arbitrary) user-defined function $f(x) = 3x^2 - 8x - 31$.

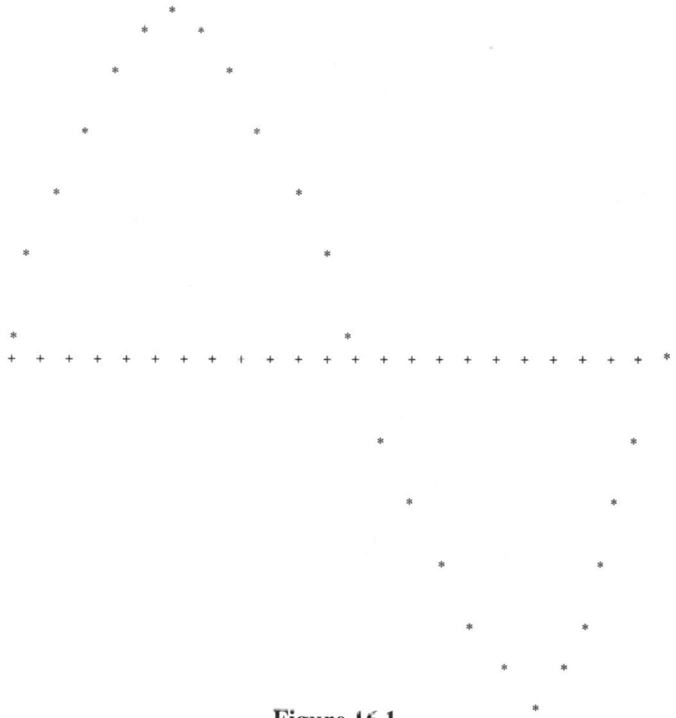

Figure 16.1

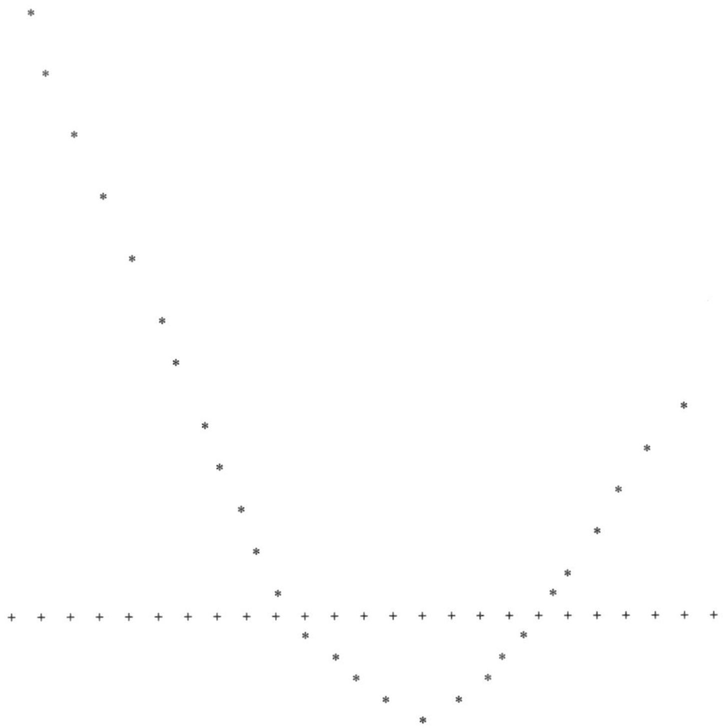

Figure 16.2

The reader should note that both Figures 16.1 and 16.2 were produced by the same procedure, Graph. In the first case, Graph was passed sin; in the second case, it was passed the user-defined function f. Hence, we see that Graph needs a parameter, F, of type RealFunc. What are the other parameters to Graph? Well, the procedure needs to know the starting and stopping *X*-axis values for the graph. These could be fixed at some predetermined values such as -3.0 to 3.0, but to give the procedure added flexibility, we will pass it XStart and XFinish, the limits for the *X*-axis. To make the procedure simple, we will also pass it a YMax, which is an upper bound for the absolute value of the function on the given interval. Graph needs YMax so that it can properly scale the graph of the function. Of course, it would be possible for Graph to examine F on the given interval and determine its own YMax. This would be preferable, since a range error will result if the user underestimates YMax. We suggest that the reader make this improvement to Graph in the exercises.

The graph of the function is produced assuming a normal screen of 80 columns. The graph is printed sideways so the actual *Y* values must be between 0 and 79. Actually, the values 0 to 38 represent negative values, 39 is the *X*-axis, and 40 to 79 are reserved for positive values. To get the function values, $F(X)$, in this range, they are first crushed by

$$Y \leftarrow \frac{F(X)}{YMax} * 39$$

We leave it to the reader to argue that for this y, we have

$$-39.0 \leq y \leq 39.0$$

and finally, if we add 39 to this y (and make y an integer), we have

$$0 \leq y + 39 \leq 78$$

which gets us in the range that we want.

The normal screen contains 24 lines, so if we make 24 samplings of the function values, we can just fill the screen with the graph. Therefore, we use a FOR loop to evaluate the function. We start at the given XStart value and increment x each time by Δx (delta x), where Δx is given by

$$\Delta x \leftarrow \frac{x\text{Finish} - x\text{Start}}{24}$$

The procedure Graph is shown in the complete module Graphics of Listing 16.1.

```
MODULE Graphics;

(* This module illustrates procedure types. It graphs any real
function of any real variable. As examples, it graphs sin(x) from
MathLib0, as well as a user-defined function.              *)

FROM InOut IMPORT WriteString, WriteLn, Read;
FROM MathLib0 IMPORT sin, entier;

CONST Pi = 3.14159;

TYPE RealFunc = PROCEDURE( REAL ) : REAL;

VAR Ch : CHAR;

PROCEDURE f(X : REAL) : REAL;
(* This function will be graphed by the procedure Graph.      *)
  BEGIN
    RETURN(3.0 * X * X - 8.0 * X - 31.0)        (* Any arbitrary
                                                 expression. *)
  END f;

PROCEDURE Graph(XStart, XFinish, YMax : REAL; F : RealFunc);
(* Pre:  This procedure graphs the function F between the X-axis
values of XStart and XFinish. To control the scaling, the procedure
has been promised that F will not exceed YMax in absolute value.
Post:   The graph is drawn using the 80-column by 24-line screen.
Note that the graph is sideways with the X-axis running up and down.
                                                            *)
```

```
CONST  XLimit = 24;                                    (* 24 rows. *)
       YLimit = 39;                    (* 80 cols, 39 negative, 1 zero,
                                                  39 positive. *)
                       (*  Actually, only 79 columns are used. *)
       Blank  = ' ';

TYPE   String = ARRAY[0..79] OF CHAR;

VAR  X       : REAL;
     DeltaX  : REAL:
     Y       : INTEGER;
     Line    : INTEGER;
     Col     : INTEGER
     Output  : String;

BEGIN
   DeltaX := (XFinish - XStart) / FLOAT(XLimit);        (* Find X
                                                  step size. *)
   X := XStart;    .
   FOR Line := 0 TO XLimit DO
     Y := entier(F(X) / YMax * FLOAT(YLimit));  (* Crush Y. *)
     FOR Col := 0 TO 79 DO
        Output[Col] := Blank;              (* Blank entire line. *)
     END;  (* Inner FOR *)
   Output[39] := "+";                    (* Add symbol for X-axis. *)
     Output[Y+39] := "*"; (* Add symbol for function value. *)
     WriteString(Output);   (* Print new line of the graph. *)
     X := X + DeltaX                 (* Get next X value. *)
     END  (* Outer FOR *)
   END Graph;

BEGIN  (* Body of main module Graphics. *)
  WriteString('Here is the graph of sin(x):'); WriteLn;
  Graph(0.0, 2.0 * Pi, 1.0, sin);
  WriteString('Hit RETURN key to continue:'); Read(Ch);
  WriteLn;
  WriteString('Here is the graph of f(x) = 3x*x - 8x -31: ');
  WriteLn;
  Graph(-10.0, 10.0, 350.0, f)
END Graphics.
```

Listing 16.1

The first call to Graph is

```
Graph(0.0, 2.0 * Pi, 1.0, sin);
```

This graphs the sin function from 0.0 to about 6.28 (two pi's). It is not important, but this happens to be the interval needed for the sin function to make one complete wave. To see two waves of the sin function, try graphing it from 0.0 to 4.0 * pi. The third argument in the above call to `Graph` is 1.0. This tells `Graph` that the given function will not exceed 1.0 in absolute value. (You may or may not recall that sin(*x*) never exceeds 1.0.)

The second call to `Graph` is

```
Graph(-10.0, 10.0, 350.0, f)
```

which graphs the user's f between -10.0 and 10.0. Here, we have had to estimate that the function does not exceed 350.0 on this interval. This estimate is important, since we will get a range-value error if we underestimate it. On the other hand, what will happen if we grossly overestimate it—say, by using 100,000.0 in all cases? (Try it.) This illustrates that it would be much better and safer if `Graph` would find its own `YMax`.

EXAMPLE: SORTING UP OR DOWN

Recall that we did a lot of sorting for Snidely Whiplash in Chapter 10. There we had many parallel arrays and we discussed several methods of sorting the arrays. Consider again two requests that Snidely might be interested in. Snidely could ask for the sales arrays to be printed out in *increasing* order by ID numbers (five-digit CARDINALs). It would also be reasonable for him to request that the sales information be printed out in *decreasing* order by quantities (CARDINALs) of widgets sold. Without procedure types, we would have to write two separate sorts (or one complex sort) to sort in ascending order at times and in descending order at other times.

We will indicate how to use a procedure type to let the sort know whether it should sort up or down, and then leave the details to the reader in the exercises. Realize that all our sorts have involved the basic comparison of two objects. That is, we either have

```
IF X < Y THEN ...
```

or

```
IF X > Y THEN ...
```

in the body of the sort. We suggest that you replace these comparisons in your favorite sort from Chapter 10 with a call to a `Compare` function that returns a Boolean:

```
IF Compare(X, Y) THEN ...
```

`Compare` will then be a parameter to the sort. Actual calls to the sort will be of the form

```
Sort(ID, ..., Up);          (* Sort on IDs in ascending order. *)
...
Sort(Widgets, ..., Down);            (* Sort on Widgets in
                                        descending order. *)
```

Of course, you will also have to define the very simple BOOLEAN functions Up(X, Y) and Down(X, Y) that return TRUE if their arguments are in ascending or descending order, respectively. The rest of the details are left as an exercise.

EXERCISES

16.1 Modify the procedure Graph so that it makes the parameter YMax a local variable of the procedure. This means that Graph will have to sample the function before it can begin the graphing. Do you need any other new local variables?

16.2 Write the BOOLEAN functions Up and Down of the text and rewrite one of the sorts of Chapter 10 so that your sort will accept Up or Down as a parameter and, therefore, do either ascending or descending sorts.

16.3 a) Can you describe in words what the following function returns?

```
TYPE  CardFunc  = PROCEDURE (CARDINAL) : CARDINAL;

PROCEDURE Mysterious(N : CARDINAL; F : CardFunc) : CARDINAL;

  VAR    Index :      CARDINAL;
  Sum    :       CARDINAL;

  BEGIN
    Sum := 0;
    FOR Index := 1 TO N DO
      Sum := Sum + F(Index)
    END;  (* FOR *)
    RETURN(Sum)
  END Mysterious;
```

b) In particular, if DoNothing is defined so that DoNothing(n) returns the value n, what is the value of Mysterious(10, DoNothing)?

c) In particular, if Square is defined so that Square(n) returns the value n^2, what is the value of Mysterious(6, Square)?

d) In particular, if Factorial is defined so that Factorial(n) returns the factorial of n, what is the value of Mysterious(5, Factorial)? Recall that 5 factorial, usually written 5!, is 5 * 4 * 3 * 2 * 1.

Chapter 17

NESTED MODULES: DATA HIDING

Modules can be nested in one another and, thus, can be in one compilation unit rather than in separate compilation units. In large programs, separate compilation is very useful and is the proper technique to use, but in small or moderately sized programs, many of the advantages of separate modules can be achieved by using nested modules. For example, nested modules can provide the means for hiding details that are not necessary in the main module, or they can provide static variables, as discussed in Chapter 14.

Although modules can be nested like procedures or functions, module walls are different from procedure and function walls, which were discussed in Chapter 7. Recall that procedure and function environments behaved as if they were surrounded by one-way glass walls. When an identifier was not found in a given procedure or function, the system looked outward for that identifier. In contrast, module walls are like brick walls that you cannot see through in either direction. This provides nested modules with their privacy or data-hiding capabilities. When nested modules want to share objects, they must explicitly import or export them, as is illustrated in the module, ModScope, of Listing 17.1.

```
MODULE ModScope;
(* This module illustrates nested modules and the scoping of
identifiers in nested modules.                               *)

FROM InOut IMPORT WriteLn, WriteCard;

VAR A : CARDINAL;
```

```
MODULE M1;(* This module is nested within the main module. *)
   IMPORT WriteLn, WriteCard;
   EXPORT B;

   VAR B, C : CARDINAL;        (* B is exported, C is hidden. *)


   BEGIN
          (* B and C are the only identifiers visible here. *)
      B := 5;
      C := 10;
      WriteCard(B, 4); WriteLn;
      WriteCard(C, 4); WriteLn
   END M1;

MODULE M2;(* This module is also nested in the main module. *)
   IMPORT A, B, WriteLn, WriteCard;
   EXPORT E;

   VAR D : CARDINAL;                  (* Another identifier hidden
                                            to the outside. *)

MODULE M3;        (* This module is nested inside module M2. *)
   IMPORT A, D, WriteLn, WriteCard;
   EXPORT E;

   VAR E : CARDINAL;
   BEGIN
      (* A, D, and E are the only identifiers visible here. *)
      A := 30;
      D := 40;
      E := 50;
      WriteCard(A, 4); WriteLn;
      WriteCard(D, 4); WriteLn;
      WriteCard(E, 4); WriteLn
   END M3;


   BEGIN                              (* Body of module M2. *)
      (* A, B, D, and E are the only identifiers visible here. *)
      WriteCard(A, 4); WriteLn;
      WriteCard(B, 4); WriteLn;
      WriteCard(D, 4); WriteLn;
      WriteCard(E, 4); WriteLn
   END M2;
```

```
BEGIN                          (* Body of main module ModScope. *)
        (* A, B, and E are the only identifiers visible here. *)
    WriteCard(A, 4); WriteLn;
    WriteCard(B, 4); WriteLn;
    WriteCard(E, 4); WriteLn
END ModScope.
```

Listing 17.1

Although the program of Listing 17.1 is nonsense, it is important to understand how it executes and to understand the variables that are visible to each of the modules. Figure 17.1 helps us understand this by graphically representing the declaration and the importation or exportation of identifiers. In that figure, an identifier in a large bold font (**A**) indicates the module in which the identifier was declared, while a regular, nonbold font (A) with an arrow represents an importation or exportation. An arrow into an environment shows, of course, an importation, while an arrow exiting an environment depicts an exportation. The reader should study Figure 17.1 to see that it correctly depicts the declarations and importations or exportations of A, B, C, D, and E of module ModScope.

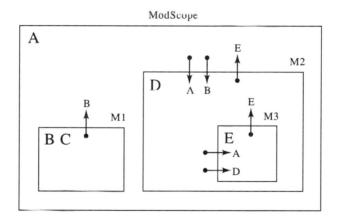

Figure 17.1

Figure 17.1 allows us to confirm the comments within Listing 17.1 concerning the visibility of the identifiers A, B, C, D, and E. The main module has access only to identifiers A, B and E. A is declared within the main module, B is made available to the main module by exportation from M1, and E is made available by double exportation from M3 and then M2. C and D are hidden from the main module, since they are not made available for exportation from their respective modules.

Since M1 does no importation of any of these identifiers, M1 has only its local identifiers B and C. This is in contrast to procedure environments, where a procedure M1 could look out and see the global A of the main module. The explanation is simply that module walls are more opaque than are procedure walls. Nested modules share identifiers only by the mechanism of import and export being explained by this example.

M2 can use A, B, D, and E. D is M2's own identifier, and A and B are imported into M2 from the surrounding environment. Notice that M2 can pick up the B that was exported into the surrounding environment by M1. M2 also has E available to its environment by exportation from M3. In this regard, it is important to note that E is not listed in M2's importation list! This is because E is exported by M3 into M2's environment, and such an identifier does not need to be imported. Likewise, we note that the main module did not import B and E, since these again were exported by nested modules into the main module's environment. That is, only when an identifier is imported from a surrounding or adjacent module is an explicit importation given.

M3 sees the identifiers A, D, and E. E is local to M3, and A and D are imported from the surrounding environment. M3 imports A from M2, which in turn imported it from the main module. M3 cannot import directly from the main module; importations can come only from the surrounding environment. Likewise, M3 makes E available by exportation to M2, and M2 makes it available by exportation to the main module. M3 cannot directly export E to the main module: An exportation makes an identifier available only to the nearest surrounding module. This explains why the FROM clause is not used in these importations. Since the object is available in the nesting module, it is not necessary to use the FROM clause in an import statement in these nested modules.

Notice how WriteLn and WriteCard are imported to each module. The main module uses

```
FROM Inout IMPORT WriteLn, WriteCard;
```

as usual. The FROM clause is, of course, required so that the system will know in which external module to find the required procedures. But each of the nested modules simply uses

```
IMPORT WriteLn, WriteCard;
```

since they are simply importing these objects from the surrounding environment.

Finally, we are almost ready to trace the execution of the module ModScope of Listing 17.1. First, we must indicate the order in which the module bodies are executed. The rule is that each body is executed in the order in which it is listed. Thus, the body of M1 executes first, then M3, then M2, and finally the body of the main module ModScope. In this regard, the bodies of the nested modules perform initialization code. Hence, the output of ModScope is

```
5
10
30
40
50
30
5
```

40
50
30
5
50

Suppose we had a main module with two nested modules N1 and N2 as depicted in Figure 17.2, and suppose that both N1 and N2 wanted to export an identifier X. How could the main module distinguish between N1's X and N2's X?

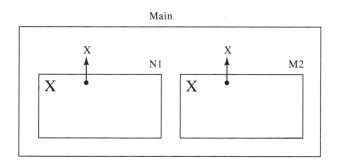

Main

N1

M2

Figure 17.2

The answer is that both N1 and N2 must use the phrase 'QUALIFIED' in their exportation of X. That is, both N1 and N2 must contain the statement

```
EXPORT QUALIFIED X;
```

and the main module can distinguish between the Xs by using N1.X and N2.X to refer to the two versions of X.

Recall that in Chapter 14 we mentioned that the old definition of Modula–2 required the EXPORT QUALIFIED statement in definition modules. It is easy to understand that when an EXPORT is required in a definition module, then it must be QUALIFIED. Otherwise, how can we guarantee that that the objects we are exporting from this module do not have the same names as objects being defined by someone else in some other external module? With the QUALIFIED option, the system will not complain. Further, if we import Something from YourModule and no other Somethings, then even though we have used the QUALIFIED option in exporting Something, we can use the unambiguous name Something instead of the more complete name YourModule.Something. However, if we import Something from MyModule as well, then, of course, we shall have to qualify our names by using MyModule.Something or YourModule.Something.

All these notions are illustrated in the program, XYZScope, of Listing 17.2. This module uses the three nonsense variables X, Y, and Z in five different ways and illustrates that modules can even be nested within procedures. The program does nothing useful, but if you understand how XYZScope executes, then you understand the scoping of identifiers with procedures and nested modules! This is very valuable to the serious Modula–2 programmer and, therefore, we urge the reader to study with care the example and our explanation that follows.

```
MODULE XYZScope;
(*This module illustrates the scoping of three garbage identifiers
through several nested procedures and modules.                    *)

  FROM InOut IMPORT WriteLn, WriteInt, WriteCard, Write, WriteString;
  FROM RealInOut IMPORT WriteReal;

  VAR X, Y, Z : CARDINAL;

  MODULE FirstNested;
  (* This module is nested in the main module XYZScope.        *)

    IMPORT WriteLn, WriteInt;
    EXPORT QUALIFIED X, Y;

    VAR X, Y, Z : INTEGER;

    BEGIN                          (* Body of module FirstNested. *)
      X := 5;  Y := 0;  Z := 5;
      WriteInt(X,4); WriteInt(Y,4); WriteInt(Z,4); WriteLn
    END FirstNested;

  PROCEDURE P1;
  (* This procedure is nested in the main module XYZScope.     *)

  VAR X, Y : REAL;                 (* Note the absence of Z. *)

  MODULE ProcNested;
  (* This module is nested inside the procedure P1!!!          *)

    IMPORT WriteLn, Write;
    EXPORT QUALIFIED X, Y;

    VAR X, Y, Z : CHAR;

    BEGIN                          (* Body of module ProcNested. *)
      X := 'E';  Y := 'T'; Z := 'H';
      Write(X); Write(Y); Write(Z); WriteLn
    END ProcNested;
```

```
    BEGIN                                    (* Body of procedure P1. *)
      X := 1.0;   Y := 6.0;
      WriteReal(X,10); WriteInt(FirstNested.X,4); WriteReal(Y,10);
      Write(ProcNested.Y); WriteCard(Z,4); WriteLn;
      IF LastNested.Y THEN
      WriteString('Niklaus Wirth'); WriteLn END (* IF *)
    END P1;

MODULE LastNested;
(* This module is also nested in the main module XYZScope.    *)

    EXPORT QUALIFIED X, Y;

    VAR X, Y, Z : BOOLEAN;

    BEGIN                              (* Body of module LastNested. *)
      X := FALSE;   Y := TRUE;   Z := FALSE
    END LastNested;

BEGIN                              (* Body of main module XYZScope. *)
    X := 10; Y := 20; Z := 30;
    WriteCard(X,4); WriteCard(Y,4); WriteCard(Z,4); WriteLn;
    P1;
    IF LastNested.X THEN
      WriteInt(FirstNested.X, 0)
    ELSE
      WriteInt(FirstNested.Y, 0)
    END;   (* IF *)
      WriteLn
END XYZScope.
```

Listing 17.2

Before attempting to trace the program XYZScope, it is a good idea to draw a picture showing the nesting of the modules, as in Figure 17.3. Note, however, that the figure depicts the trace during the execution of procedure P1. Before or after P1 executes, the diagram is simpler, since the environment for P1 is dynamically invoked and then recovered. This means that the module ProcNested, since it is contained within P1, also exists only during the lifespan of P1.

XYZ Scope

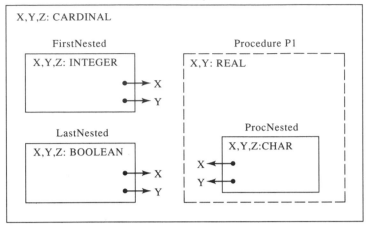

Figure 17.3

Let us now trace XYZScope. Execution begins with the initialization code of FirstNested. Hence, the first line of output is the integers

```
-5    0    5
```

As discussed above, execution skips the initialization body of ProcNested (since it doesn't exist yet) and continues with the initialization code for LastNested. This produces no output, but does initialize the Boolean versions of X, Y, and Z.

Execution now continues with the body of the main module. This first initializes the cardinal versions of X, Y, and Z and then produces the line of output:

```
10    20    30
```

The main module now calls the procedure P1. Dynamically, a new environment is created for P1. This environment contains a nested module, so that module's initialization body is executed before the body of the procedure. This causes the character versions of X, Y, and Z to be initialized and printed as

```
ETH
```

Finally, the body of procedure P1 begins to execute. This initializes the real versions of X and Y. Since P1 is a procedure, it can look out through its walls and see the global Z (the cardinal) of the main module. P1 can also look out and see the X or Y (the integers) left there by FirstNested, or the X and Y (the Booleans) of LastNested. However, because of all the ambiguity, it must qualify these to refer to them. That is, an unqualified X is the local X of P1, an unqualified Z is the global Z of the main module, and qualification must be used to access the X or Y of the other modules. Note that the Z of FirstNested and the Z of LastNested are not put up for export and, hence, are not available to P1 or the main module. By looking in all these various places, P1 produces the two lines of output:

```
1.0    -5    6.0    T    30
Niklaus Wirth
```

where, for simplicity, we have shown the reals in a simple, readable format.

   P1 has completed its call and its space is reclaimed. Execution continues with the main module that called P1. Here, an IF accesses the Boolean X of LastNested to test whether to print the integer X or the integer Y of FirstNested. This produces the final line of output:

```
0
```

CONCLUSION

Although none of the examples of this chapter have been used to solve real problems, the ideas expressed are important to a thorough understanding of the scope of identifiers in Modula-2. It is certainly true that you will probably use external modules more than internal modules, but internal modules may be the first step toward the creation of an external module.

   Also, any of the real examples of Chapter 14 can be written with internal modules. We leave a couple such programs for you to develop in the exercises that follow.

EXERCISES

17.1 Write a module that plays the game of craps. Include a nested module that contains the random-number generation and a function Dice.

17.2 Write a module that reads names of the form

   Wolfgang Amadaeus Mozart

and converts them to the form

   Mozart, W. A.

Include a nested module that contains any string-handling functions or procedures that your main module needs.

Appendix A

STANDARD MODULA-2 LIBRARIES

For reference purposes, the definition modules for `InOut`, `RealInOut`, and `MathLib0` are given below. These are as described by Niklaus Wirth's definition of Modula-2 in his book *Programming in Modula-2*, third edition, Springer Verlag, 1985.

INOUT

```
DEFINITION MODULE InOut; (*N. Wirth*)

CONST EOL = 36C;

VAR    Done    : BOOLEAN;
       TermCH  : CHAR;

PROCEDURE OpenInput(Ext : ARRAY OF CHAR);
(* This procedure requests a file name and then opens that file for
input. If the file name that is entered ends with a period, then
the value of the array Ext is appended (as the extension) to the
file name. If OpenInput succeeds in opening the file, then Done is
set to TRUE; otherwise, it is set to FALSE.                   *)

PROCEDURE OpenOutput(Ext : ARRAY OF CHAR);
(* This procedure requests a file name and then opens that file for
output. If the file name that is entered ends with a period, then
the value of the array Ext is appended (as the extension) to the
file name. If OpenOutput succeeds in opening the file, then Done
is set to TRUE; otherwise, it is set to FALSE.                *)
```

```
PROCEDURE CloseInput;
(* This procedure closes the current input file and restores input
to come from the user terminal.                              *)

PROCEDURE CloseOutput;
(* This procedure closes the current output file and restores output
to go to the user terminal.                                   *)

PROCEDURE Read(VAR Ch : CHAR);
(* This procedure reads the next character from the input file into
Ch. Done is set to TRUE unless the end of file is found.      *)


PROCEDURE ReadString(VAR Str: ARRAY OF CHAR);
(* This procedure ignores all leading blanks and stores in Str the
sequence of characters after any initial blanks, until another
blank or control character is found. In other words, ReadString
reads a "word" from the input file. TermCH is assigned the last
character read. Done is not set by ReadString.                *)

PROCEDURE ReadInt(VAR N : INTEGER);
(* This procedure ignores initial blanks and converts a string of
digits (with a possible leading sign) into an integer value that
is stored in N. Done is set to TRUE if ReadInt is successful.*)

PROCEDURE ReadCard(VAR K : CARDINAL);
(* This procedure ignores initial blanks and converts a string of
digits into a cardinal value that is stored in K. Done is set to
TRUE if ReadCard is successful.                               *)

PROCEDURE Write(Ch : CHAR);
(* This procedure writes the character Ch to the output file.*)

PROCEDURE WriteLn;
(* This procedure terminates the current line of output.       *)

PROCEDURE WriteString(Str : ARRAY OF CHAR);
(* This procedure writes out the sequence of characters in the array
Str.                                                          *)

PROCEDURE WriteInt(N : INTEGER; K : CARDINAL);
(* This procedure writes out the value of the integer N in a field
of at least K characters. If a field of more than K characters is
needed to express the value of N, then a field as wide as needed
is used. If fewer than K characters are needed, then the value is
padded with leading blanks.                                   *)
```

```
PROCEDURE WriteCard(J, K : CARDINAL);
(* This procedure writes out the value of the cardinal J in a field
of at least K characters. If a field of more than K characters is
needed to express the value of J, then a field as wide as needed
is used. If fewer than K characters are needed, then the value is
padded with leading blanks .                                       *)

PROCEDURE WriteOct(J, K : CARDINAL);
(*This procedure is like WriteCard, except the value of J is written
in a field of at least K characters using octal (base 8) instead
of decimal (base 10) notation.                                     *)

PROCEDURE WriteHex(J, K : CARDINAL);
(*This procedure is like WriteCard, except the value of J is written
in a field of at least K characters using hexadecimal (base 16)
instead of decimal (base 10) notation.                            *)

END InOut.
```

REALINOUT

```
DEFINITION MODULE RealInOut; (*N. Wirth*)

VAR Done : Boolean;

PROCEDURE ReadReal(VAR X : REAL);
(* This procedure ignores leading blanks and reads a real value into
X. Done is set to TRUE if ReadReal is successful.                 *)

PROCEDURE WriteReal(X : REAL; K : CARDINAL);
(* This procedure writes the value of X in scientific notation using
a field of at least K characters. Leading blanks are added if
necessary.                                                        *)

PROCEDURE WriteRealOct(X : REAL);
(* This procedure writes the value of X in scientific notation,
expressing the exponent and mantissa in octal.                   *)

END RealInOut.
```

MATHLIB0

DEFINITION MODULE MathLib0; (*N. Wirth*)

PROCEDURE sqrt(X : REAL) : REAL;
(* This function returns the square root of X. X must be nonnegative.
                                                                    *)

PROCEDURE exp(X : REAL) : REAL;
(* This function returns e to the power X.   *)

PROCEDURE ln(X : REAL) : REAL;
(* This function returns the natural logarithm of X. X must be
positive.   *)

PROCEDURE sin(X : REAL) : REAL;
(* This function returns the sine of X. X must be measured in radians.
*)

PROCEDURE cos(X : REAL) : REAL;
(* This function returns the cosine of X. X must be measured in
radians.   *)

PROCEDURE arctan(X : REAL) : REAL;
(* This function returns the arctangent of X in radians.   *)

PROCEDURE real(N : INTEGER) : REAL;
(* This function returns the real representation of its integer
input N.   *)

PROCEDURE entier(X : REAL) : INTEGER;
(* This function returns the integer part of its real input X.
                                                             *)

END MathLib0.

Appendix B

SYNTAX DIAGRAMS FOR MODULA-2

For purposes of quick reference, an alphabetical listing of the syntax diagrams for Modula-2 is given here. These are as specified by Niklaus Wirth in *Programming in Modula-2*, third edition, Springer Verlag, 1985.

Actual Parameters

AddOperator

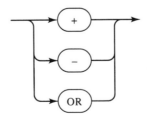

ArrayType

Assignment

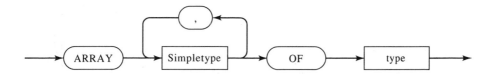

Block

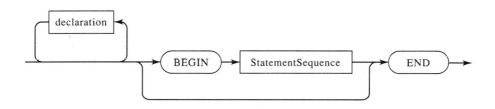

Case

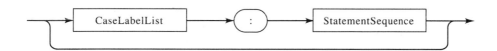

CaseLabels

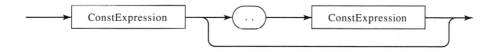

CaseLabelList

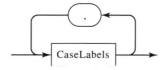

CaseStatement

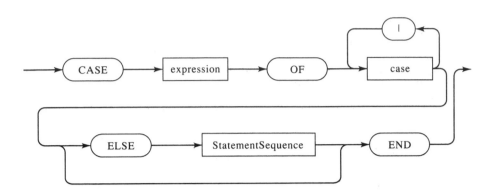

CompilationUnit

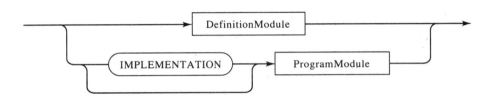

ConstExpression

Declaration

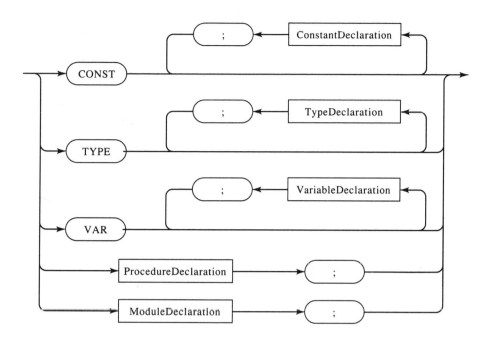

Definition

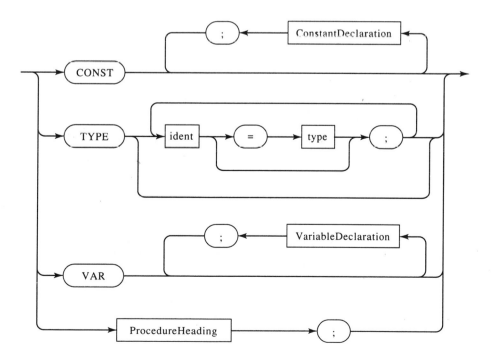

DefinitionModule

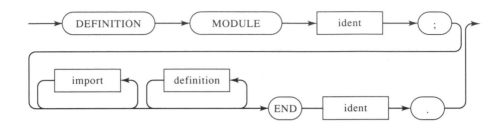

Designator

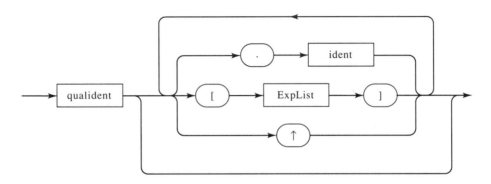

Digit

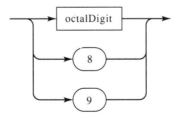

Element

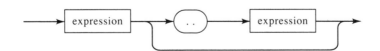

Enumeration

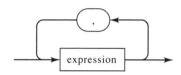

ExpList

Export

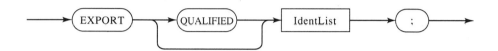

Expression

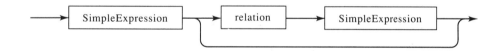

Factor

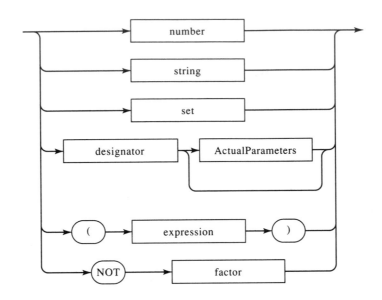

FieldList

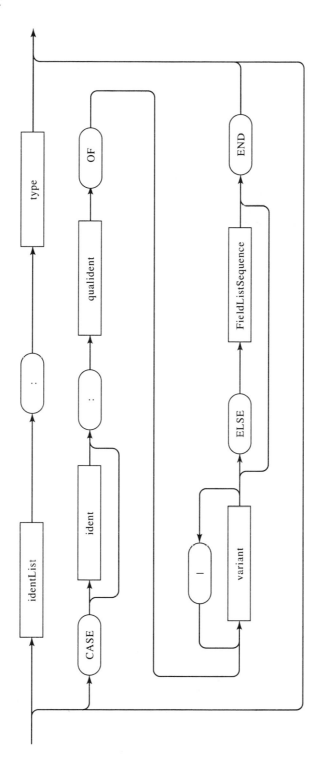

FieldListSequence

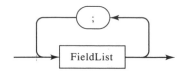

FormalParameters

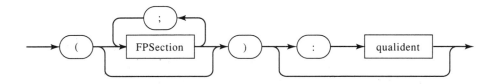

FormalTypeList

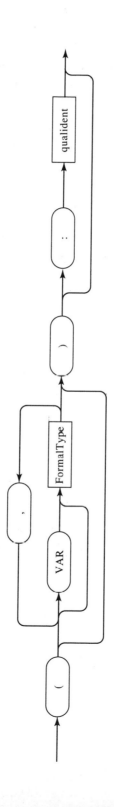

FormalType

ForStatement

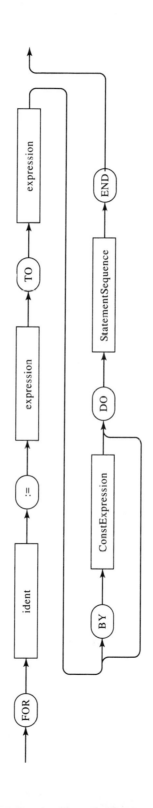

FPSection

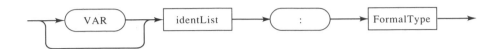

HexDigit

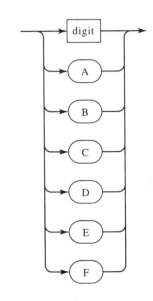

Ident

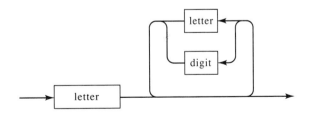

IdentList

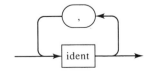

IfStatement

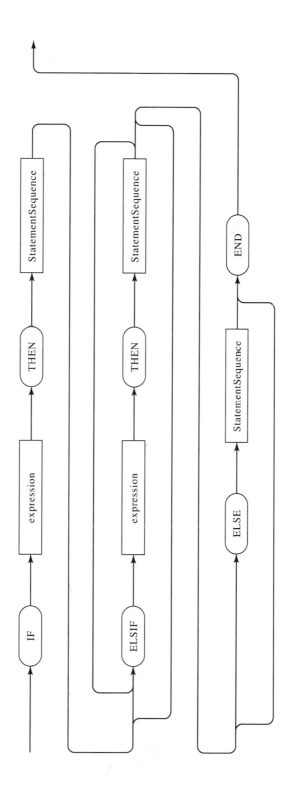

Import

Integer

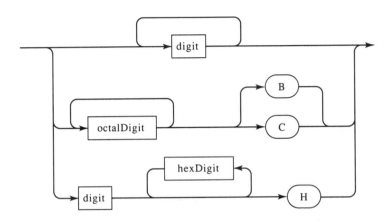

LoopStatement

ModuleDeclaration

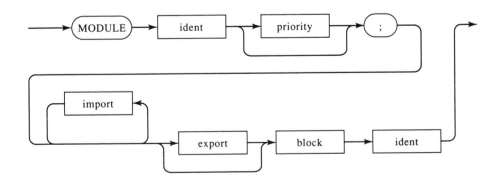

MulOperator

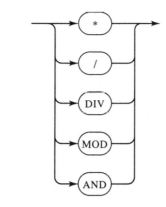

Number

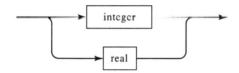

OctalDigit

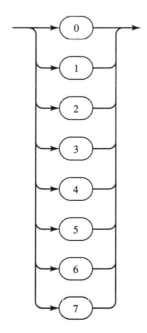

PointerType

Priority

ProcedureCall

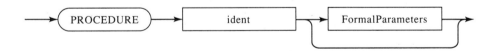

ProcedureDeclaration

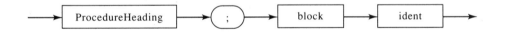

ProcedureHeading

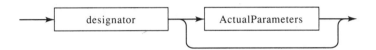

ProcedureType

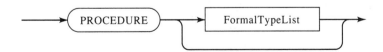

ProgramModule

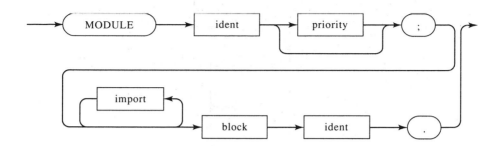

Qualident

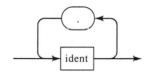

Real

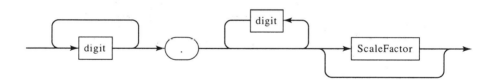

RecordType

Relation

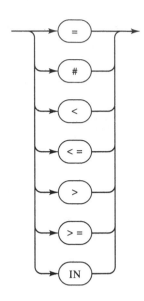

RepeatStatement

ScaleFactor

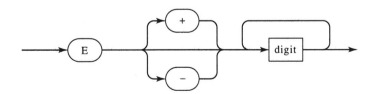

Set

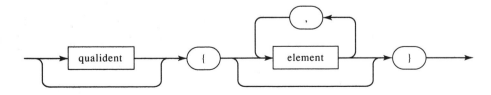

SetType

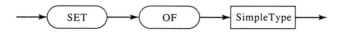

SimpleExpression

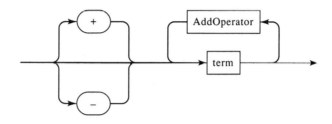

SimpleType

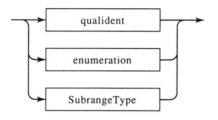

VariableDeclaration

Statement

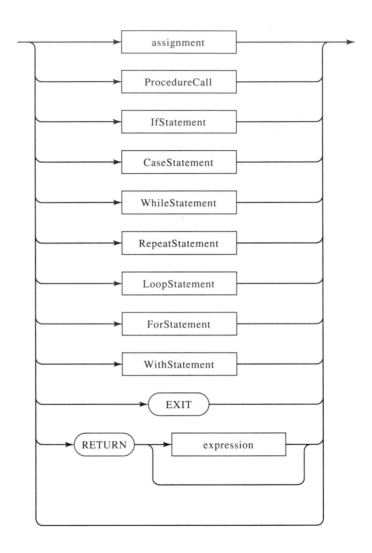

StatementSequence

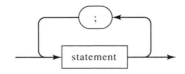

String

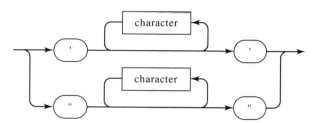

SubrangeType

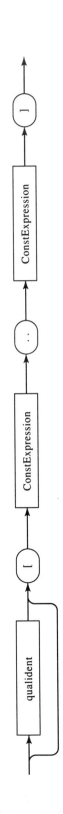

Term

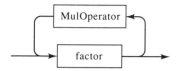

Type

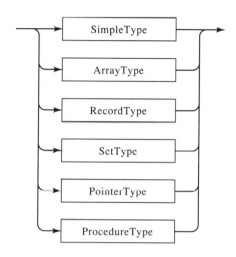

TypeDeclaration

VariableDeclaration

Variant

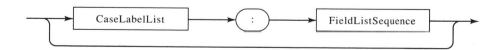

WhileStatement

WithStatement

Appendix C

STANDARD FUNCTIONS AND PROCEDURES FOR MODULA-2

The following procedures and functions are built into the language, according to Niklaus Wirth's definition of Modula-2 as described in his book *Programming in Modula-2*, third edition, published by Springer-Verlag, 1985.

Standard Functions	
ABS(X)	X any numeric type. The absolute value is returned with the result type equal to the argument type.
CAP(Ch)	If the value of Ch is a lowercase letter, then the corresponding uppercase letter is returned. If Ch is already uppercase, then that same letter is returned.
CHR(X)	X CARDINAL. The CHAR with ASCII value X is returned. CHR is a special case of the VAL function: CHR(X) = VAL(CHAR, X).
FLOAT(X)	X CARDINAL. A REAL value equivalent to the input is returned.
HIGH(Arr)	A CARDINAL value that is the high index bound of the array Arr is returned.
MAX(T)	The maximum value of the type T is returned.
MIN(T)	The minimum value of the type T is returned.

ODD(X)   X CARDINAL or INTEGER. This Boolean function returns
                  TRUE if X is odd and FALSE if X is even.

ORD(X)   X is of any enumerated type: CHAR, INTEGER, or CARDINAL.
                  The ordinal number of X in the set of values of its type is returned.

SIZE(T)   The number of bytes of storage required by a variable of type T is
                  returned.

TRUNC(X)   X REAL. The CARDINAL value of X truncated to a whole value
                  is returned.

VAL(T,X)   This function returns the value of the type T with ordinal number
                  X, where T is any enumerated type: CHAR, INTEGER, or
                  CARDINAL. VAL is related to ORD by: VAL(T, ORD(X)) = X
                  if X is of type T.

Standard Procedures

DEC(X)   X of any ordinal type. This procedure decrements X to the previ-
                  ous value of its type. DEC is not defined for the first value of the
                  type.

DEC(X,N)   This procedure decrements X by N values, where X is of any
                  ordinal type.

EXCL(S, E)   This procedure excludes the element E from the set S: (S := S -
                  {E}).

HALT   This procedure halts program execution.

INC(X)   X of any ordinal type. This procedure increments X to the next
                  value of its type. INC is not defined for the last value of the type.

INC(X,N)   This procedure increments X by N values, where X is of any
                  ordinal type.

INCL(S, E)   This procedure includes the element E in the set S: (S := S + {E}).

INDEX